STATUTORY SUPPLEMENT TO LEGAL PROTECTION FOR THE INDIVIDUAL EMPLOYEE

Seventh Edition

■ ■ ■

Kenneth G. Dau-Schmidt
Willard and Margaret Carr
Professor of Labor and Employment Law
Indiana University–Bloomington, School of Law

Matthew W. Finkin
Swanlund Chair and Center for Advanced Study
Professor of Law
University of Illinois, College of Law

Ruben J. Garcia
Ralph Denton Professor of Law
Director, Workplace Law Program
University of Nevada–Las Vegas, Boyd School of Law

Jason R. Bent
Professor of Law
Stetson University, College of Law

for

THE LABOR LAW GROUP

AMERICAN CASEBOOK SERIES®

WEST ACADEMIC

Published in the United States of America

ISBN: 979-8-88786-538-6

FOREWORD

Thanks to James Lincoln Baker V, Sarah Behrens, Summer Park, and John H. Bunck for their work on this supplement.

THE LABOR LAW GROUP

Editorial Policy Committee

Members

Steven D. Anderman
University of Essex

Sameer Ashar
University of California–Irvine

Brad Areheart
University of Tennessee

Rachel Arnow-Richman
University of Florida

Harry W. Arthurs
York University (Emeritus)

James B. Atleson
State University of New York–Buffalo (Emeritus)

Dianne Avery
State University of New York–Buffalo (Emerita)

Richard A. Bales
Ohio Northern University

Stephen Befort
University of Minnesota (Emeritus)

Jason R. Bent
Stetson University

Susan Bisom-Rapp
California Western School of Law

Adele Blackett
McGill University

Matthew Bodie
University of Minnesota

Christopher David Ruiz Cameron
Southwestern Law School

Lance Compa
Cornell University (Emeritus)

Laura Cooper
University of Minnesota (Emerita)

Roberto L. Corrada
University of Denver

Marion G. Crain
Washington University–St. Louis

Kenneth G. Dau-Schmidt
Indiana University–Bloomington

Cynthia Estlund
New York University

Matthew Finkin
University of Illinois

Catherine L. Fisk
University of California–Berkeley

Joel W. Friedman
Tulane University

Ruben J. Garcia
University of Nevada–Las Vegas

Charlotte Garden
University of Minnesota

Lise Gelernter
University of Buffalo (Emerita)

Rafael Gely
University of Missouri

Julius G. Getman
University of Texas (Emeritus)

Alvin L. Goldman
University of Kentucky (Emeritus)

Llezlie Green
Georgetown University

Michael Z. Green
Texas A&M University

Joseph R. Grodin
University of California–Hastings (Emeritus)

Hon. Melissa Hart
Colorado Supreme Court

Jeffrey M. Hirsch
University of North Carolina

Ann C. Hodges
University of Richmond (Emerita)

Alan Hyde
Rutgers University–Newark

Pauline T. Kim
Washington University–St. Louis

Thomas C. Kohler
Boston College

Brian A. Langille
University of Toronto

Stephen Lee
University of California–Irvine

Orly Lobel
University of San Diego

Anne Marie Lofasso
West Virginia University

Deborah Malamud
New York University

Martin H. Malin
Illinois Institute of Technology
Chicago–Kent College of Law (Emeritus)

Marcia L. McCormick
Saint Louis University

Mordehai Mironi
University of Haifa

Robert B. Moberly
University of Arkansas

Charles J. Morris
Southern Methodist University (Emeritus)

Cynthia Nance
University of Arkansas–Fayetteville

Dennis R. Nolan
University of South Carolina (Emeritus)

Maria L. Ontiveros
University of San Francisco

Angela Onwuachi-Willig
Boston University

Michael M. Oswalt
Wayne State University Law School

Sachin S. Pandya
University of Connecticut

Nicole Buonocore Porter
College of William & Mary

Robert J. Rabin
Syracuse University (Emeritus)

Kerry Rittich
University of Toronto

Brishen Rogers
Georgetown University

César F. Rosado Marzán
University of Iowa

Alvaro Santos
Georgetown University

George Schatzki
Arizona State University (Emeritus)

Michael Selmi
George Washington University

Calvin W. Sharpe
Case Western Reserve University (Emeritus)

Eileen Silverstein
University of Connecticut (Emerita)

Joseph E. Slater
University of Toledo

Sara Slinn
York University

Peggie R. Smith
Washington University–St. Louis

Susan J. Stabile
University of St. Thomas

Katherine V. W. Stone
University of California–Los Angeles

Lea S. VanderVelde
University of Iowa

Laura Weinrib
Harvard University

June Weisberger
University of Wisconsin–Madison (Emerita)

Marley Weiss
University of Maryland

Michael Wishnie
Yale University

Noah Zatz
University of California–Los Angeles

TABLE OF CONTENTS

FOREWORD III

THE LABOR LAW GROUP V

Genetic Information Nondiscrimination Act of 2008 1

Rhode Island Urine and Blood Tests as a Condition of Employment Act (Title 28 Gen. Laws of R.I.) 21

Employee Polygraph Protection Act (Title 29 U.S.C.) 25

Family and Medical Leave Act (Title 29 U.S.C.) 37

Model Employment Termination Act 61

New Jersey Employment Protection Act 73

Worker Adjustment and Retraining Notification Act (Title 29 U.S.C.) 81

Fair Labor Standards Act (Title 29 U.S.C.) 89

Portal-to-Portal Pay Act (Title 29 U.S.C.) 141

Consumer Credit Protection Act Restrictions on Garnishment (Title 15 U.S.C.) 147

Federal Employers' Liability Act (Title 45 U.S.C.) 151

Longshore and Harbor Workers' Compensation Act (Title 33 U.S.C.) 155

Maximum Workers' Compensation Benefit for Lost Wages by Scheduled Injury and Jurisdiction (2023) 209

Occupational Safety and Health Act (Title 29 U.S.C.) 211

Employee Retirement Income Security Act (Selected Sections) 253

STATUTORY SUPPLEMENT TO

LEGAL PROTECTION FOR THE INDIVIDUAL EMPLOYEE

Seventh Edition

GENETIC INFORMATION NONDISCRIMINATION ACT OF 2008

(Title 42 U.S.C.)

§ 2000ff. Definitions

In this title—

(1) **Commission.**

The term "Commission" means the Equal Employment Opportunity Commission as created by section 2000e–4 of this title.

(2) **Employee; Employer; Employment Agency; Labor Organization; Member—**

(A) **In General—**

The term "employee" means—

(i) an employee (including an applicant), as defined in section 2000e(f) of this title;

(ii) a State employee (including an applicant) described in section 2000e–16c(a) of this title;

(iii) a covered employee (including an applicant), as defined in section 1301 of Title 2;

(iv) a covered employee (including an applicant), as defined in section 411(c) of Title 3; or

(v) an employee or applicant to which section 2000e–16(a) of this title applies.

(B) **Employer—**

The term "employer" means—

(i) an employer (as defined in section 2000e(b) of this title);

(ii) an entity employing a State employee described in section 2000–16c(a) of this title;

(iii) an employing office, as defined in section 1301 of Title 2;

(iv) an employing office, as defined in section 411(c) of Title 3; or

(v) an entity to which section 2000e–16(a) of this title applies.

(C) **Employment Agency; Labor Organization—**

The terms "employment agency" and "labor organization" have the meanings given the terms in section 2000e of this title.

(D) **Member—**

The term "member", with respect to a labor organization, includes an applicant for membership in a labor organization.

(3) **Family Member—**

The term "family member" means, with respect to an individual—

(A) a dependent (as such term is used for purposes of section 1181(f)(2) of Title 29) of such individual, and

(B) any other individual who is a first-degree, second-degree, third-degree, or fourth-degree relative of such individual or of an individual described in subparagraph (A).

(4) **Genetic Information—**

(A) **In General—**

The term "genetic information" means, with respect to any individual, information about—

(i) such individual's genetic tests,

(ii) the genetic tests of family members of such individual, and

(iii) the manifestation of a disease or disorder in family members of such individual.

(B) **Inclusion of Genetic Services and Participation in Genetic Research—**

Such term includes, with respect to any individual, any request for, or receipt of, genetic services, or participation in clinical research which includes genetic services, by such individual or any family member of such individual.

(C) **Exclusions—**

The term "genetic information" shall not include information about the sex or age of any individual.

(5) **Genetic Monitoring—**

The term "genetic monitoring" means the periodic examination of employees to evaluate acquired modifications to their genetic material, such as chromosomal damage or evidence of increased occurrence of mutations, that may have developed in the course of employment due to exposure to toxic substances in the workplace, in order to identify, evaluate, and respond to the effects of or control adverse environmental exposures in the workplace.

(6) **Genetic Services—**

The term "genetic services" means—

(A) a genetic test;

(B) genetic counseling (including obtaining, interpreting, or assessing genetic information); or

(C) genetic education.

(7) **Genetic Test—**

(A) **In General—**

The term "genetic test" means an analysis of human DNA, RNA, chromosomes, proteins, or metabolites, that detects genotypes, mutations, or chromosomal changes.

(B) **Exceptions—**

The term "genetic test" does not mean an analysis of proteins or metabolites that does not detect genotypes, mutations, or chromosomal changes.

§ 2000ff–1. Employer practices

(a) Discrimination Based on Genetic Information—

It shall be an unlawful employment practice for an employer—

(1) to fail or refuse to hire, or to discharge, any employee, or otherwise to discriminate against any employee with respect to the compensation, terms, conditions, or privileges of employment of the employee, because of genetic information with respect to the employee; or

(2) to limit, segregate, or classify the employees of the employer in any way that would deprive or tend to deprive any employee of employment opportunities or otherwise adversely affect the status of the employee as an employee, because of genetic information with respect to the employee.

(b) Acquisition of Genetic Information—

It shall be an unlawful employment practice for an employer to request, require, or purchase genetic information with respect to an employee or a family member of the employee except—

(1) where an employer inadvertently requests or requires family medical history of the employee or family member of the employee;

(2) where—

(A) health or genetic services are offered by the employer, including such services offered as part of a wellness program;

(B) the employee provides prior, knowing, voluntary, and written authorization;

(C) only the employee (or family member if the family member is receiving genetic services) and the licensed health care professional or board certified genetic counselor involved in providing such services receive individually identifiable information concerning the results of such services; and

(D) any individually identifiable genetic information provided under subparagraph (C) in connection with the services provided under subparagraph (A) is only available for purposes of such services and shall not be disclosed to the employer except in aggregate terms that do not disclose the identity of specific employees;

(3) where an employer requests or requires family medical history from the employee to comply with the certification provisions of section 2613 of Title 29 or such requirements under State family and medical leave laws;

(4) where an employer purchases documents that are commercially and publicly available (including newspapers, magazines, periodicals, and books, but not including medical databases or court records) that include family medical history;

(5) where the information involved is to be used for genetic monitoring of the biological effects of toxic substances in the workplace, but only if—

(A) the employer provides written notice of the genetic monitoring to the employee;

(B)(i) the employee provides prior, knowing, voluntary, and written authorization; or

(ii) the genetic monitoring is required by Federal or State law;

(C) the employee is informed of individual monitoring results;

(D) the monitoring is in compliance with—

(i) any Federal genetic monitoring regulations, including any such regulations that may be promulgated by the Secretary of Labor pursuant to the Occupational Safety and Health Act of 1970 (29 U.S.C. 651 et seq.), the Federal Mine Safety and Health Act of 1977 (30 U.S.C. 801 et seq.), or the Atomic Energy Act of 1954 (42 U.S.C. 2011 et seq.); or

(ii) State genetic monitoring regulations, in the case of a State that is implementing genetic monitoring regulations under the authority of the Occupational Safety and Health Act of 1970 (29 U.S.C. 651 et seq.); and

(E) the employer, excluding any licensed health care professional or board certified genetic counselor that is involved in the genetic monitoring program, receives the results of the monitoring only in aggregate terms that do not disclose the identity of specific employees; or

(6) where the employer conducts DNA analysis for law enforcement purposes as a forensic laboratory or for purposes of human remains identification, and requests or requires genetic information of such employer's employees, but only to the extent that such genetic information is used for analysis of DNA identification markers for quality control to detect sample contamination.

(c) Preservation of Protections—

In the case of information to which any of paragraphs (1) through (6) of subsection (b) applies, such information may not be used in violation of paragraph (1) or (2) of subsection (a) or treated or disclosed in a manner that violates section 2000ff–5 of this title.

§ 2000ff–2. Employment agency practices

(a) Discrimination Based on Genetic Information—

It shall be an unlawful employment practice for an employment agency—

(1) to fail or refuse to refer for employment, or otherwise to discriminate against, any individual because of genetic information with respect to the individual;

(2) to limit, segregate, or classify individuals or fail or refuse to refer for employment any individual in any way that would deprive or tend to deprive any individual of employment opportunities, or otherwise adversely affect the status of the individual as an employee, because of genetic information with respect to the individual; or

(3) to cause or attempt to cause an employer to discriminate against an individual in violation of this title.

(b) Acquisition of Genetic Information—

It shall be an unlawful employment practice for an employment agency to request, require, or purchase genetic information with respect to an individual or a family member of the individual except—

(1) where an employment agency inadvertently requests or requires family medical history of the individual or family member of the individual;

(2) where—

(A) health or genetic services are offered by the employment agency, including such services offered as part of a wellness program;

(B) the individual provides prior, knowing, voluntary, and written authorization;

(C) only the individual (or family member if the family member is receiving genetic services) and the licensed health care professional or board certified genetic counselor involved in providing such services receive individually identifiable information concerning the results of such services; and

(D) any individually identifiable genetic information provided under subparagraph (C) in connection with the services provided under subparagraph (A) is only available for purposes of such services and shall not be disclosed to the employment agency except in aggregate terms that do not disclose the identity of specific individuals;

(3) where an employment agency requests or requires family medical history from the individual to comply with the certification provisions of section 2613 of Title 29 or such requirements under State family and medical leave laws;

(4) where an employment agency purchases documents that are commercially and publicly available (including newspapers, magazines, periodicals, and books, but not including medical databases or court records) that include family medical history; or

(5) where the information involved is to be used for genetic monitoring of the biological effects of toxic substances in the workplace, but only if—

(A) the employment agency provides written notice of the genetic monitoring to the individual;

(B)(i) the individual provides prior, knowing, voluntary, and written authorization; or

(ii) the genetic monitoring is required by Federal or State law;

(C) the individual is informed of individual monitoring results;

(D) the monitoring is in compliance with—

(i) any Federal genetic monitoring regulations, including any such regulations that may be promulgated by the Secretary of Labor pursuant to the Occupational Safety and

Health Act of 1970 (29 U.S.C. 651 et seq.), the Federal Mine Safety and Health Act of 1977 (30 U.S.C. 801 et seq.), or the Atomic Energy Act of 1954 (42 U.S.C. 2011 et seq.); or

(ii) State genetic monitoring regulations, in the case of a State that is implementing genetic monitoring regulations under the authority of the Occupational Safety and Health Act of 1970 (29 U.S.C. 651 et seq.); and

(E) the employment agency, excluding any licensed health care professional or board certified genetic counselor that is involved in the genetic monitoring program, receives the results of the monitoring only in aggregate terms that do not disclose the identity of specific individuals.

(c) Preservation of Protections—

In the case of information to which any of paragraphs (1) through (5) of subsection (b) applies, such information may not be used in violation of paragraph (1), (2), or (3) of subsection (a) or treated or disclosed in a manner that violates section 2000ff–5 of this title.

§ 2000ff–3. Labor organization practices

(a) Discrimination Based on Genetic Information—

It shall be an unlawful employment practice for a labor organization—

(1) to exclude or to expel from the membership of the organization, or otherwise to discriminate against, any member because of genetic information with respect to the member;

(2) to limit, segregate, or classify the members of the organization, or fail or refuse to refer for employment any member, in any way that would deprive or tend to deprive any member of employment opportunities, or otherwise adversely affect the status of the member as an employee, because of genetic information with respect to the member; or

(3) to cause or attempt to cause an employer to discriminate against a member in violation of this chapter.

(b) Acquisition of Genetic Information—

It shall be an unlawful employment practice for a labor organization to request, require, or purchase genetic information with respect to a member or a family member of the member except—

(1) where a labor organization inadvertently requests or requires family medical history of the member or family member of the member;

(2) where—

(A) health or genetic services are offered by the labor organization, including such services offered as part of a wellness program;

(B) the member provides prior, knowing, voluntary, and written authorization;

(C) only the member (or family member if the family member is receiving genetic services) and the licensed health care professional or board certified genetic counselor involved in providing such services receive individually identifiable information concerning the results of such services; and

(D) any individually identifiable genetic information provided under subparagraph (C) in connection with the services provided under subparagraph (A) is only available for purposes of such services and shall not be disclosed to the labor organization except in aggregate terms that do not disclose the identity of specific members;

(3) where a labor organization requests or requires family medical history from the members to comply with the certification provisions of section 2613 of Title 29 or such requirements under State family and medical leave laws;

(4) where a labor organization purchases documents that are commercially and publicly available (including newspapers, magazines, periodicals, and books, but not including medical databases or court records) that include family medical history; or

(5) where the information involved is to be used for genetic monitoring of the biological effects of toxic substances in the workplace, but only if—

(A) the labor organization provides written notice of the genetic monitoring to the member;

(B)(i) the member provides prior, knowing, voluntary, and written authorization; or

(ii) the genetic monitoring is required by Federal or State law;

(C) the member is informed of individual monitoring results;

(D) the monitoring is in compliance with—

(i) any Federal genetic monitoring regulations, including any such regulations that may be promulgated by the Secretary of Labor pursuant to the Occupational Safety and Health Act of 1970 (29 U.S.C. 651 et seq.), the Federal Mine

Safety and Health Act of 1977 (30 U.S.C. 801 et seq.), or the Atomic Energy Act of 1954 (42 U.S.C. 2011 et seq.); or

(ii) State genetic monitoring regulations, in the case of a State that is implementing genetic monitoring regulations under the authority of the Occupational Safety and Health Act of 1970 (29 U.S.C. 651 et seq.); and

(E) the labor organization, excluding any licensed health care professional or board certified genetic counselor that is involved in the genetic monitoring program, receives the results of the monitoring only in aggregate terms that do not disclose the identity of specific members.

(c) Preservation of Protections—

In the case of information to which any of paragraphs (1) through (5) of subsection (b) applies, such information may not be used in violation of paragraph (1), (2), or (3) of subsection (a) or treated or disclosed in a manner that violates section 2000ff–5 of this title.

§ 2000ff–4. Training program

(a) Discrimination Based on Genetic Information—

It shall be an unlawful employment practice for any employer, labor organization, or joint labor-management committee controlling apprenticeship or other training or retraining, including on-the-job training programs—

(1) to discriminate against any individual because of genetic information with respect to the individual in admission to, or employment in, any program established to provide apprenticeship or other training or retraining;

(2) to limit, segregate, or classify the applicants for or participants in such apprenticeship or other training or retraining, or fail or refuse to refer for employment any individual, in any way that would deprive or tend to deprive any individual of employment opportunities, or otherwise adversely affect the status of the individual as an employee, because of genetic information with respect to the individual; or

(3) to cause or attempt to cause an employer to discriminate against an applicant for or a participant in such apprenticeship or other training or retraining in violation of this chapter.

(b) Acquisition of Genetic Information—

It shall be an unlawful employment practice for an employer, labor organization, or joint labor-management committee described in subsection (a) to request, require, or purchase genetic information with respect to an individual or a family member of the individual except—

(1) where the employer, labor organization, or joint labor-management committee inadvertently requests or requires family medical history of the individual or family member of the individual;

(2) where—

(A) health or genetic services are offered by the employer, labor organization, or joint labor-management committee, including such services offered as part of a wellness program;

(B) the individual provides prior, knowing, voluntary, and written authorization;

(C) only the individual (or family member if the family member is receiving genetic services) and the licensed health care professional or board certified genetic counselor involved in providing such services receive individually identifiable information concerning the results of such services; and

(D) any individually identifiable genetic information provided under subparagraph (C) in connection with the services provided under subparagraph (A) is only available for purposes of such services and shall not be disclosed to the employer, labor organization, or joint labor-management committee except in aggregate terms that do not disclose the identity of specific individuals;

(3) where the employer, labor organization, or joint labor-management committee requests or requires family medical history from the individual to comply with the certification provisions of section 2613 of Title 29 or such requirements under State family and medical leave laws;

(4) where the employer, labor organization, or joint labor-management committee purchases documents that are commercially and publicly available (including newspapers, magazines, periodicals, and books, but not including medical databases or court records) that include family medical history;

(5) where the information involved is to be used for genetic monitoring of the biological effects of toxic substances in the workplace, but only if—

(A) the employer, labor organization, or joint labor-management committee provides written notice of the genetic monitoring to the individual;

(B)(i) the individual provides prior, knowing, voluntary, and written authorization; or

(ii) the genetic monitoring is required by Federal or State law;

(C) the individual is informed of individual monitoring results;

(D) the monitoring is in compliance with—

(i) any Federal genetic monitoring regulations, including any such regulations that may be promulgated by the Secretary of Labor pursuant to the Occupational Safety and Health Act of 1970 (29 U.S.C. 651 et seq.), the Federal Mine Safety and Health Act of 1977 (30 U.S.C. 801 et seq.), or the Atomic Energy Act of 1954 (42 U.S.C. 2011 et seq.); or

(ii) State genetic monitoring regulations, in the case of a State that is implementing genetic monitoring regulations under the authority of the Occupational Safety and Health Act of 1970 (29 U.S.C. 651 et seq.); and

(E) the employer, labor organization, or joint labor-management committee, excluding any licensed health care professional or board certified genetic counselor that is involved in the genetic monitoring program, receives the results of the monitoring only in aggregate terms that do not disclose the identity of specific individuals; or

(6) where the employer conducts DNA analysis for law enforcement purposes as a forensic laboratory or for purposes of human remains identification, and requests or requires genetic information of such employer's apprentices or trainees, but only to the extent that such genetic information is used for analysis of DNA identification markers for quality control to detect sample contamination.

(c) Preservation of Protections—

In the case of information to which any of paragraphs (1) through (6) of subsection (b) applies, such information may not be used in violation of paragraph (1), (2), or (3) of subsection (a) or treated or disclosed in a manner that violates section 2000ff–5 of this title.

§ 2000ff–5. Confidentiality of Genetic Information

(a) Treatment of Information as Part of Confidential Medical Record—

If an employer, employment agency, labor organization, or joint labor-management committee possesses genetic information about an employee or member, such information shall be maintained on separate forms and in separate medical files and be treated as a confidential medical record of the employee or member. An employer, employment agency, labor organization, or joint labor-management committee shall be considered to be in compliance with the maintenance of information requirements of this subsection with respect to genetic information subject to this subsection that is maintained with and treated as a confidential medical record under section 12112(d)(3)(B) of this title.

(b) Limitation on Disclosure—

An employer, employment agency, labor organization, or joint labor-management committee shall not disclose genetic information concerning an employee or member except—

(1) to the employee or member of a labor organization (or family member if the family member is receiving the genetic services) at the written request of the employee or member of such organization;

(2) to an occupational or other health researcher if the research is conducted in compliance with the regulations and protections provided for under part 46 of title 45, Code of Federal Regulations;

(3) in response to an order of a court, except that—

(A) the employer, employment agency, labor organization, or joint labor-management committee may disclose only the genetic information expressly authorized by such order; and

(B) if the court order was secured without the knowledge of the employee or member to whom the information refers, the employer, employment agency, labor organization, or joint labor-management committee shall inform the employee or member of the court order and any genetic information that was disclosed pursuant to such order;

(4) to government officials who are investigating compliance with this chapter if the information is relevant to the investigation;

(5) to the extent that such disclosure is made in connection with the employee's compliance with the certification provisions of section 2613 of Title 29 or such requirements under State family and medical leave laws; or

(6) to a Federal, State, or local public health agency only with regard to information that is described in section 2000ff(4)(A)(iii) of this title and that concerns a contagious disease that presents an imminent hazard of death or life-threatening illness, and that the employee whose family member or family members is or are the subject of a disclosure under this paragraph is notified of such disclosure.

(c) Relationship to HIPAA Regulations—

With respect to the regulations promulgated by the Secretary of Health and Human Services under part C of title XI of the Social Security Act (42 U.S.C. 1320d et seq.) and section 264 of the Health Insurance

Portability and Accountability Act of 1996 (42 U.S.C. 1320d–2 note), this chapter does not prohibit a covered entity under such regulations from any use or disclosure of health information that is authorized for the covered entity under such regulations. The previous sentence does not affect the authority of such Secretary to modify such regulations.

§ 2000ff–6. Remedies and Enforcement

(a) Employees Covered By Title VII of the Civil Rights Act of 1964—

(1) In General—

The powers, procedures, and remedies provided in sections 705, 706, 707, 709, 710, and 711 of the Civil Rights Act of 1964 (42 U.S.C. 2000e–4 to 2000e–6, 2000e–8 to 2000e–10) to the Commission, the Attorney General, or any person, alleging a violation of title VII of that Act (42 U.S.C. 2000e et seq.) shall be the powers, procedures, and remedies this chapter provides to the Commission, the Attorney General, or any person, respectively, alleging an unlawful employment practice in violation of this chapter against an employee described in section 2000ff(2)(A)(i) of this title, except as provided in paragraphs (2) and (3).

(2) Costs and Fees—

The powers, remedies, and procedures provided in subsections (b) and (c) of section 1988 of this title, shall be powers, remedies, and procedures this chapter provides to the Commission, the Attorney General, or any person, alleging such a practice.

(3) Damages—

The powers, remedies, and procedures provided in section 1981a of this title, including the limitations contained in subsection (b)(3) of such section 1981a, shall be powers, remedies, and procedures this chapter provides to the Commission, the Attorney General, or any person, alleging such a practice (not an employment practice specifically excluded from coverage under section 1981a(a)(1) of this title).

(b) Employees Covered By Government Employee Rights Act of 1991—

(1) In General—

The powers, remedies, and procedures provided in sections 302 and 304 of the Government Employee Rights Act of 1991 (42 U.S.C. 2000e–16b, 2000e–16c) to the Commission, or any person, alleging a violation of section 302(a)(1) of that Act (42 U.S.C. 2000e–16b(a)(1)) shall be the powers, remedies, and procedures this chapter provides to the Commission, or any person, respectively, alleging an unlawful employment practice in violation of this chapter against an employee described in section 2000ff(2)(A)(ii) of this title, except as provided in paragraphs (2) and (3).

(2) Costs and Fees—

The powers, remedies, and procedures provided in subsections (b) and (c) of section 1988 of this title, shall be powers, remedies, and procedures this chapter provides to the Commission, or any person, alleging such a practice.

(3) Damages—

The powers, remedies, and procedures provided in section 1981a of this title, including the limitations contained in subsection (b)(3) of such section 1981a, shall be powers, remedies, and procedures this chapter provides to the Commission, or any person, alleging such a practice (not an employment practice specifically excluded from coverage under section 1981a(a)(1) of this title).

(c) Employees Covered By Congressional Accountability Act of 1995—

(1) In General—

The powers, remedies, and procedures provided in the Congressional Accountability Act of 1995 (2 U.S.C. 1301 et seq.) to the Board (as defined in section 101 of that Act (2 U.S.C. 1301)), or any person, alleging a violation of section 201(a)(1) of that Act (2 U.S.C. 1311(a)(1)) shall be the powers, remedies, and procedures this chapter provides to that Board, or any person, alleging an unlawful employment practice in violation of this chapter against an employee described in section 2000ff(2)(A)(iii) of this title, except as provided in paragraphs (2) and (3).

(2) Costs and Fees—

The powers, remedies, and procedures provided in subsections (b) and (c) of section 1988 of this title, shall be powers, remedies, and procedures this chapter provides to that Board, or any person, alleging such a practice.

(3) Damages—

The powers, remedies, and procedures provided in section 1981a of this title, including the limitations contained in subsection (b)(3) of such section 1981a, shall be powers, remedies, and procedures this chapter provides to that Board, or any person, alleging such a practice (not an employment practice specifically excluded from coverage under section 1981a(a)(i) of this title).

(4) Other Applicable Provisions—

With respect to a claim alleging a practice described in paragraph (1), title III of the Congressional Accountability Act of 1995 (2 U.S.C. 1381 et seq.) shall apply in the same manner as such title applies with respect to a claim alleging a violation of section 201(a)(1) of such Act (2 U.S.C. 1311(a)(1)).

(d) Employees Covered By Chapter 5 of Title 3—

(1) In General—

The powers, remedies, and procedures provided in chapter 5 of title 3 to the President, the Commission, the Merit Systems Protection Board, or any person, alleging a violation of section 411(a)(1) of that title, shall be the powers, remedies, and procedures this chapter provides to the President, the Commission, such Board, or any person, respectively, alleging an unlawful employment practice in violation of this chapter against an employee described in section 2000ff(2)(A)(iv) of this title, except as provided in paragraphs (2) and (3).

(2) Costs and Fees—

The powers, remedies, and procedures provided in subsections (b) and (c) of section 1988 of this title, shall be powers, remedies, and procedures this chapter provides to the President, the Commission, such Board, or any person, alleging such a practice.

(3) Damages—

The powers, remedies, and procedures provided in section 1981a of this title, including the limitations contained in subsection (b)(3) of such section 1981a, shall be powers, remedies, and procedures this chapter provides to the President, the Commission, such Board, or any person, alleging such a practice (not an employment practice specifically excluded from coverage under section 1981a(a)(1) of this title).

(e) Employees Covered By Section 717 of the Civil Rights Act of 1964—

(1) In General—

The powers, remedies, and procedures provided in section 717 of the Civil Rights Act of 1964 (42 U.S.C. 2000e–16) to the Commission, the Attorney General, the Librarian of Congress, or any person, alleging a violation of that section shall be the powers, remedies, and procedures this chapter provides to the Commission, the Attorney General, the Librarian of Congress, or any person, respectively, alleging an unlawful employment practice in violation of this chapter against an employee or applicant described in section 2000ff(2)(A)(v) of this title, except as provided in paragraphs (2) and (3).

(2) Costs and Fees—

The powers, remedies, and procedures provided in subsections (b) and (c) of section 1988 of this title, shall be powers, remedies, and procedures this chapter provides to the Commission, the Attorney General, the Librarian of Congress, or any person, alleging such a practice.

(3) Damages—

The powers, remedies, and procedures provided in section 1981a of this title, including the limitations contained in subsection (b)(3) of such section 1981a, shall be powers, remedies, and procedures this chapter provides to the Commission, the Attorney General, the Librarian of Congress, or any person, alleging such a practice (not an employment practice specifically excluded from coverage under section 1981a(a)(1) of this title).

(f) Prohibition Against Retaliation—

No person shall discriminate against any individual because such individual has opposed any act or practice made unlawful by this chapter or because such individual made a charge, testified, assisted, or participated in any manner in an investigation, proceeding, or hearing under this chapter. The remedies and procedures otherwise provided for under this section shall be available to aggrieved individuals with respect to violations of this subsection.

(g) Definition—

In this section, the term "Commission" means the Equal Employment Opportunity Commission.

§ 2000ff–7. Disparate impact

(a) General Rule—

Notwithstanding any other provision of this Act, "disparate impact", as that term is used in section 2000e–2(k) of this title, on the basis of genetic information does not establish a cause of action under this Act.

(b) Commission—

On the date that is 6 years after May 21, 2008, there shall be established a commission, to be known as the Genetic Nondiscrimination Study Commission (referred to in this section as the "Commission") to review the developing science of genetics and to make recommendations to Congress regarding whether to provide a disparate impact cause of action under this Act.

(c) Membership—

(1) In General—

The Commission shall be composed of 8 members, of which—

(A) 1 member shall be appointed by the Majority Leader of the Senate;

(B) 1 member shall be appointed by the Minority Leader of the Senate;

(C) 1 member shall be appointed by the Chairman of the Committee on Health, Education, Labor, and Pensions of the Senate;

(D) 1 member shall be appointed by the ranking minority member of the Committee on Health, Education, Labor, and Pensions of the Senate;

(E) 1 member shall be appointed by the Speaker of the House of Representatives;

(F) 1 member shall be appointed by the Minority Leader of the House of Representatives;

(G) 1 member shall be appointed by the Chairman of the Committee on Education and Labor of the House of Representatives; and

(H) 1 member shall be appointed by the ranking minority member of the Committee on Education and Labor of the House of Representatives.

(2) Compensation and Expenses—

The members of the Commission shall not receive compensation for the performance of services for the Commission, but shall be allowed travel expenses, including per diem in lieu of subsistence, at rates authorized for employees of agencies under subchapter I of chapter 57 of title 5, while away from their homes or regular places of business in the performance of services for the Commission.

(d) Administrative Provisions—

(1) Location—

The Commission shall be located in a facility maintained by the Equal Employment Opportunity Commission.

(2) Detail of Government Employees—

Any Federal Government employee may be detailed to the Commission without reimbursement, and such detail shall be without interruption or loss of civil service status or privilege.

(3) Information From Federal Agencies—

The Commission may secure directly from any Federal department or agency such information as the Commission considers necessary to carry out the provisions of this section. Upon request of the Commission, the head of such department or agency shall furnish such information to the Commission.

(4) Hearings—

The Commission may hold such hearings, sit and act at such times and places, take such testimony, and receive such evidence as the Commission considers advisable to carry out the objectives of this section, except that, to the extent possible, the Commission shall use existing data and research.

(5) Postal Services—

The Commission may use the United States mails in the same manner and under the same conditions as other departments and agencies of the Federal Government.

(e) Report—

Not later than 1 year after all of the members are appointed to the Commission under subsection (c)(1), the Commission shall submit to Congress a report that summarizes the findings of the Commission and makes such recommendations for legislation as are consistent with this Act.

(f) Authorization of Appropriations—

There are authorized to be appropriated to the Equal Employment Opportunity Commission such sums as may be necessary to carry out this section.

§ 2000ff–8. Construction

(a) In General—

Nothing in this title shall be construed to—

(1) limit the rights or protections of an individual under any other Federal or State statute that provides equal or greater protection to an individual than the rights or protections provided for under this chapter, including the protections of an individual under the Americans with Disabilities Act of 1990 (42 U.S.C. 12101 et seq.) (including coverage afforded to individuals under section 102 of such Act (42 U.S.C. 12112)), or under the Rehabilitation Act of 1973 (29 U.S.C. 701 et seq.);

(2)(A) limit the rights or protections of an individual to bring an action under this chapter against an employer, employment agency, labor organization, or joint labor-management committee for a violation of this chapter; or

(B) provide for enforcement of, or penalties for violation of, any requirement or prohibition applicable to any employer, employment agency, labor organization, or joint labor-management committee subject to enforcement for a violation under—

(i) the amendments made by title I of this Act;

(ii)(I) subsection (a) of section 1181 of Title 29 as such section applies with respect to genetic information pursuant to subsection (b)(1)(B) of such section;

(II) section 1182(a)(1)(F) of Title 29; or

(III) section 1182(b)(1) of Title 29 as such section applies with respect to genetic information as a health status-related factor;

(iii)(I) subsection (a) of section 2701 of the Public Health Service Act as such section applies with respect to genetic information pursuant to subsection (b)(1)(B) of such section;

(II) section 2702(a)(1)(F) of such Act; or

(III) section 2702(b)(1) of such act as such section applies with respect to genetic information as a health status-related factor; or

(iv)(I) subsection (a) of section 9801 of Title 26 as such section applies with respect to genetic information pursuant to subsection (b)(1)(B) of such section;

(II) section 9802(a)(1)(F) of Title 26; or

(III) section 9802(b)(1) of Title 26 as such section applies with respect to genetic information as a health status-related factor;

(3) apply to the Armed Forces Repository of Specimen Samples for the Identification of Remains;

(4) limit or expand the protections, rights, or obligations of employees or employers under applicable workers' compensation laws;

(5) limit the authority of a Federal department or agency to conduct or sponsor occupational or other health research that is conducted in compliance with the regulations contained in part 46 of title 45, Code of Federal Regulations (or any corresponding or similar regulation or rule);

(6) limit the statutory or regulatory authority of the Occupational Safety and Health Administration or the Mine Safety and Health Administration to promulgate or enforce workplace safety and health laws and regulations; or

(7) require any specific benefit for an employee or member or a family member of an employee or member under any group health plan or health insurance issuer offering group health insurance coverage in connection with a group health plan.

(b) Genetic Information of a Fetus or Embryo—

Any reference in this chapter to genetic information concerning an individual or family member of an individual shall—

(1) with respect to such an individual or family member of an individual who is a pregnant woman, include genetic information of any fetus carried by such pregnant woman; and

(2) with respect to an individual or family member utilizing an assisted reproductive technology, include genetic information of any embryo legally held by the individual or family member.

(c) Relation to Authorities Under Title I—

With respect to a group health plan, or a health insurance issuer offering group health insurance coverage in connection with a group health plan, this chapter does not prohibit any activity of such plan or issuer that is authorized for the plan or issuer under any provision of law referred to in clauses (i) through (iv) of subsection (a)(2)(B).

§ 2000ff–9. Medical information that is not genetic information

An employer, employment agency, labor organization, or joint labor-management committee shall not be considered to be in violation of this chapter based on the use, acquisition, or disclosure of medical information that is not genetic information about a manifested disease, disorder, or pathological condition of an employee or member, including a manifested disease, disorder, or pathological condition that has or may have a genetic basis.

§ 2000ff–10. Regulation

Not later than 1 year after May 21, 2008, the Commission shall issue final regulations to carry out this Chapter.

§ 2000ff–11. Authorization of appropriations

There are authorized to be appropriated such sums as may be necessary to carry out this chapter (except for section 2000ff–7 of this title).

Rhode Island Urine and Blood Tests as a Condition of Employment Act (Title 28 Gen. Laws of R.I.)

28–6.5–1. Testing permitted only in accordance with this section

(a) No employer or agent of any employer shall, either orally or in writing, request, require, or subject any employee to submit a sample of his or her urine, blood, or other bodily fluid or tissue for testing as a condition of continued employment unless that test is administered in accordance with the provisions of this section. Employers may require that an employee submit to a drug test if:

(1) The employer has reasonable grounds to believe based on specific aspects of the employee's job performance and specific contemporaneous documented observations, concerning the employee's appearance, behavior or speech that the employee may be under the influence of a controlled substances, which may be impairing his or her ability to perform his or her job;

(2) The employee provides the test sample in private, outside the presence of any person;

(3) Employees testing positive are not terminated on that basis, but are instead referred to a substance abuse professional (a licensed physician with knowledge and clinical experience in the diagnosis and treatment of drug related disorders, a licensed or certified psychologist, social worker, or EAP professional with like knowledge, or a substance abuse counselor certified by the National Association of Alcohol and Drug Abuse Counselors (all of whom shall be licensed in Rhode Island)) for assistance; provided, that additional testing may be required by the employer in accordance with this referral, and an employee whose testing indicates any continued use of controlled substances despite treatment may be terminated;

(4) Positive tests of urine, blood or any other bodily fluid or tissue are confirmed by a federally certified laboratory by means of gas chromatography/mass spectrometry or technology recognized as being at least as scientifically accurate;

(5) The employer provides to the employee, at the employer's expense, the opportunity to have the sample tested or evaluated by an independent testing facility and so advises the employee;

(6) The employer provides the test to the employee with a reasonable opportunity to rebut or explain the results;

(7) The employer has promulgated a drug abuse prevention policy which complies with requirements of this chapter; and

(8) The employer keeps the results of any test confidential, except for disclosing the results of a "positive" test only to other employees with a job-related need to know, and to defend against any legal action brought by the employee against the employer.

(b) Any employer who subjects any person employed by him or her to this test, or causes, directly or indirectly, any employee to take the test, except as provided for by this chapter, shall be guilty of a misdemeanor punishable by a fine of not more than one thousand dollars ($1,000) or not more than one year in jail, or both.

(c) In any civil action alleging a violation of this section, the court may:

(1) Award punitive damages to a prevailing employee in addition to any award of actual damages;

(2) Award reasonable attorneys' fees and costs to a prevailing employee; and

(3) Afford injunctive relief against any employer who commits or proposes to commit a violation of this section.

(d) Nothing in this chapter shall be construed to impair or affect the rights of individuals under chapter 5 of this title.

(e) Nothing in this chapter shall be construed to:

(1) Prohibit or apply to the testing of drivers regulated under 49 CFR § 40.1 et seq. and 49 CFR part 382 if that testing is performed pursuant to a policy mandated by the federal government;

(2) Prohibit an employer in the public utility or mass transportation industry from requiring testing otherwise barred by this chapter if that testing is explicitly mandated by federal regulation or statute as a condition for the continued receipt of federal funds; or

(3) Prohibit an employer in the highway maintenance industry, which shall include the construction, upkeep, maintenance and repair of the state's highways, roads and bridges including the repaving or resurfacing of the same, from requiring testing otherwise barred by this chapter, provided the testing is performed as regulated under 49 C.F.R. part 40.

(f) Notwithstanding the foregoing, this chapter shall not apply to members of the International Association of Bridge, Structural, Ornamental and Reinforcing Iron Workers and its signatory contractors jointly participating in the IMPACT National Substance Abuse Program for purpose of pre-qualifying workers for employment on and ensuring the maintenance of designated drug free work sites; provided, however, that:

(1) Participation by each worker is voluntary; and

(2) Workers who refuse to participate shall not be subjected to any adverse employment action other than an inability to work on a designated drug free work site; and

(3) The penalty for a first "positive" test shall not exceed a thirty (30) day suspension from work on designated drug free work sites.

28–6.5–2. Testing of prospective employees

(a) Except as provided in subsections (b) and (c) of this section, an employer may require a job applicant to submit to testing of his or her blood, urine, or any other bodily fluid or tissue if:

(1) The job applicant has been given an offer of employment conditioned on the applicant's receiving a negative test result;

(2) The applicant provides the test sample in private, outside the presence of any person; and

(3) Positive tests of urine, blood, or any other bodily fluid or tissue are confirmed by a federal certified laboratory by means of gas chromatography/mass spectrometry or technology recognized as being at least as scientifically accurate.

(b) The pre-employment drug testing authorized by this section shall not extend to job applicants for positions with any agency or political subdivision of the state or municipalities, except for applicants seeking employment as a law enforcement or correctional officer, firefighter, or any other position where that testing is required by federal law or required for the continued receipt of federal funds.

(c) An employer shall not be required to comply with the conditions of testing under subsection (a) of this section to the extent they are inconsistent with federal law.

28–6.5–3. Severability

If any provision of this chapter or the application of it to any person or circumstances is held invalid, that invalidity shall not affect other provisions or applications of the chapter, which can be given effect without the invalid provision or application, and to this end the provisions of this chapter are declared to be severable.

Employee Polygraph Protection Act (Title 29 U.S.C.)

§ 2001. Definitions

As used in this chapter:

(1) Commerce

The term "commerce" has the meaning provided by section 203(b) of this title.

(2) Employer

The term "employer" includes any person acting directly or indirectly in the interest of an employer in relation to an employee or prospective employee.

(3) Lie detector

The term "lie detector" includes a polygraph, deceptograph, voice stress analyzer, psychological stress evaluator, or any other similar device (whether mechanical or electrical) that is used, or the results of which are used, for the purpose of rendering a diagnostic opinion regarding the honesty or dishonesty of an individual.

(4) Polygraph

The term "polygraph" means an instrument that—

(A) records continuously, visually, permanently, and simultaneously changes in cardiovascular, respiratory, and electrodermal patterns as minimum instrumentation standards; and

(B) is used, or the results of which are used, for the purpose of rendering a diagnostic opinion regarding the honesty or dishonesty of an individual.

(5) Secretary

The term "Secretary" means the Secretary of Labor.

§ 2002. Prohibitions on lie detector use

Except as provided in sections 2006 and 2007 of this title, it shall be unlawful for any employer engaged in or affecting commerce or in the production of goods for commerce—

(1) directly or indirectly, to require, request, suggest, or cause any employee or prospective employee to take or submit to any lie detector test;

(2) to use, accept, refer to, or inquire concerning the results of any lie detector test of any employee or prospective employee;

(3) to discharge, discipline, discriminate against in any manner, or deny employment or promotion to, or threaten to take any such action against—

(A) any employee or prospective employee who refuses, declines, or fails to take or submit to any lie detector test, or

(B) any employee or prospective employee on the basis of the results of any lie detector test; or

(4) to discharge, discipline, discriminate against in any manner, or deny employment or promotion to, or threaten to take any such action against, any employee or prospective employee because—

(A) such employee or prospective employee has filed any complaint or instituted or caused to be instituted any proceeding under or related to this chapter,

(B) such employee or prospective employee has testified or is about to testify in any such proceeding, or

(C) of the exercise by such employee or prospective employee, on behalf of such employee or another person, of any right afforded by this chapter.

§ 2003. Notice of protection

The Secretary shall prepare, have printed, and distribute a notice setting forth excerpts from, or summaries of, the pertinent provisions of this chapter. Each employer shall post and maintain such notice in conspicuous places on its premises where notices to employees and applicants to employment are customarily posted.

§ 2004. Authority of the Secretary

(a) In general

The Secretary shall—

(1) issue such rules and regulations as may be necessary or appropriate to carry out this chapter;

(2) cooperate with regional, State, local, and other agencies, and cooperate with and furnish technical assistance to employers, labor organizations, and employment agencies to aid in effectuating the purposes of this chapter; and

(3) make investigations and inspections and require the keeping of records necessary or appropriate for the administration of this chapter.

(b) Subpoena authority

For the purpose of any hearing or investigation under this chapter, the Secretary shall have the authority contained in sections 49 and 50 of Title 15.

§ 2005. Enforcement provisions

(a) Civil penalties

(1) In general

Subject to paragraph (2), any employer who violates any provision of this chapter may be assessed a civil penalty of not more than $10,000.

(2) Determination of amount

In determining the amount of any penalty under paragraph (1), the Secretary shall take into account the previous record of the person in terms of compliance with this chapter and the gravity of the violation.

(3) Collection

Any civil penalty assessed under this subsection shall be collected in the same manner as is required by subsections (b) through (e) of section 1853 of this title with respect to civil penalties assessed under subsection (a) of such section.

(b) Injunctive actions by the Secretary

The Secretary may bring an action under this section to restrain violations of this chapter. The Solicitor of Labor may appear for and represent the Secretary in any litigation brought under this chapter. In any action brought under this section, the district courts of the United States shall have jurisdiction, for cause shown, to issue temporary or permanent restraining orders and injunctions to require compliance with this chapter, including such legal or equitable relief incident thereto as may be appropriate, including, but not limited to, employment, reinstatement, promotion, and the payment of lost wages and benefits.

(c) Private civil actions

(1) Liability

An employer who violates this chapter shall be liable to the employee or prospective employee affected by such violation. Such employer shall be liable for such legal or equitable relief as may be appropriate, including, but not limited to, employment, reinstatement, promotion, and the payment of lost wages and benefits.

(2) Court

An action to recover the liability prescribed in paragraph (1) may be maintained against the employer in any Federal or State court of competent jurisdiction by an employee or prospective employee for or on behalf of such employee, prospective employee, and other employees or prospective employees similarly situated. No such action may be commenced more than 3 years after the date of the alleged violation.

(3) Costs

The court, in its discretion, may allow the prevailing party (other than the United States) reasonable costs, including attorney's fees.

(d) Waiver of rights prohibited

The rights and procedures provided by this chapter may not be waived by contract or otherwise, unless such waiver is part of a written settlement agreed to and signed by the parties to the pending action or complaint under this chapter.

§ 2006. Exemptions

(a) No application to Governmental employers

This chapter shall not apply with respect to the United States Government, any State or local government, or any political subdivision of a State or local government.

(b) National defense and security exemption

(1) National defense

Nothing in this chapter shall be construed to prohibit the administration, by the Federal Government, in the performance of any counterintelligence function, of any lie detector test to—

(A) any expert or consultant under contract to the Department of Defense or any employee of any contractor of such Department; or

(B) any expert or consultant under contract with the Department of Energy in connection with the atomic energy defense activities of such Department or any employee of any contractor of such Department in connection with such activities.

(2) Security

Nothing in this chapter shall be construed to prohibit the administration, by the Federal Government, in the performance of any intelligence or counterintelligence function, of any lie detector test to—

(A)(i) any individual employed by, assigned to, or detailed to, the National Security Agency, the Defense Intelligence Agency, the National Geospatial-Intelligence Agency, or the Central Intelligence Agency,

(ii) any expert or consultant under contract to any such agency,

(iii) any employee of a contractor to any such agency,

(iv) any individual applying for a position in any such agency, or

(v) any individual assigned to a space where sensitive cryptologic information is produced, processed, or stored for any such agency; or

(B) any expert, or consultant (or employee of such expert or consultant) under contract with any Federal Government department, agency, or program whose duties involve access to information that has been classified at the level of top secret or designated as being within a special access program under section 4.2(a) of Executive Order 12356 (or a successor Executive order).

(c) FBI contractors exemption

Nothing in this chapter shall be construed to prohibit the administration, by the Federal Government, in the performance of any counterintelligence function, of any lie detector test to an employee of a contractor of the Federal Bureau of Investigation of the Department of Justice who is engaged in the performance of any work under the contract with such Bureau.

(d) Limited exemption for ongoing investigations

Subject to sections 2007 and 2009 of this title, this chapter shall not prohibit an employer from requesting an employee to submit to a polygraph test if—

(1) the test is administered in connection with an ongoing investigation involving economic loss or injury to the employer's business, such as theft, embezzlement, misappropriation, or an act of unlawful industrial espionage or sabotage;

(2) the employee had access to the property that is the subject of the investigation;

(3) the employer has a reasonable suspicion that the employee was involved in the incident or activity under investigation; and

(4) the employer executes a statement, provided to the examinee before the test, that—

(A) sets forth with particularity the specific incident or activity being investigated and the basis for testing particular employees,

(B) is signed by a person (other than a polygraph examiner) authorized to legally bind the employer,

(C) is retained by the employer for at least 3 years, and

(D) contains at a minimum—

(i) an identification of the specific economic loss or injury to the business of the employer,

(ii) a statement indicating that the employee had access to the property that is the subject of the investigation, and

(iii) a statement describing the basis of the employer's reasonable suspicion that the employee was involved in the incident or activity under investigation.

(e) Exemption for security services

(1) In general

Subject to paragraph (2) and sections 2007 and 2009 of this title, this chapter shall not prohibit the use of polygraph tests on prospective employees by any private employer whose primary business purpose consists of providing armored car personnel, personnel engaged in the design, installation, and maintenance of security alarm systems, or other uniformed or plainclothes security personnel and whose function includes protection of—

(A) facilities, materials, or operations having a significant impact on the health or safety of any State or political subdivision thereof, or the national security of the United States, as determined under rules and regulations issued by the Secretary within 90 days after June 27, 1988, including—

(i) facilities engaged in the production, transmission, or distribution of electric or nuclear power,

(ii) public water supply facilities,

(iii) shipments or storage of radioactive or other toxic waste materials, and

(iv) public transportation, or

(B) currency, negotiable securities, precious commodities or instruments, or proprietary information.

(2) Access

The exemption provided under this subsection shall not apply if the test is administered to a prospective employee who would not be employed to protect facilities, materials, operations, or assets referred to in paragraph (1).

(f) Exemption for drug security, drug theft, or drug diversion investigations

(1) In general

Subject to paragraph (2) and sections 2007 and 2009 of this title, this chapter shall not prohibit the use of a polygraph test by any employer authorized to manufacture, distribute, or dispense a controlled substance listed in schedule I, II, III, or IV of section 812 of Title 21.

(2) Access

The exemption provided under this subsection shall apply—

(A) if the test is administered to a prospective employee who would have direct access to the manufacture, storage, distribution, or sale of any such controlled substance; or

(B) in the case of a test administered to a current employee, if—

(i) the test is administered in connection with an ongoing investigation of criminal or other misconduct involving, or potentially involving, loss or injury to the manufacture, distribution, or dispensing of any such controlled substance by such employer, and

(ii) the employee had access to the person or property that is the subject of the investigation.

§ 2007. Restrictions on use of exemptions

(a) Test as basis for adverse employment action

(1) Under ongoing investigations exemption

Except as provided in paragraph (2), the exemption under subsection (d) of section 2006 of this title shall not apply if an employee is discharged, disciplined, denied employment or promotion, or otherwise discriminated against in any manner on the basis of the analysis of a polygraph test chart or the refusal to take a polygraph test, without additional supporting evidence. The evidence required by such subsection may serve as additional supporting evidence.

(2) Under other exemptions

In the case of an exemption described in subsection (e) or (f) of such section, the exemption shall not apply if the results of an analysis of a polygraph test chart are used, or the refusal to take a polygraph test is used, as the sole basis upon which an adverse employment action described in paragraph (1) is taken against an employee or prospective employee.

(b) Rights of examinee

The exemptions provided under subsections (d), (e), and (f) of section 2006 of this title shall not apply unless the requirements described in the following paragraphs are met:

(1) All phases

Throughout all phases of the test—

(A) the examinee shall be permitted to terminate the test at any time;

(B) the examinee is not asked questions in a manner designed to degrade, or needlessly intrude on, such examinee;

(C) the examinee is not asked any question concerning:

(i) religious beliefs or affiliations,

(ii) beliefs or opinions regarding racial matters,

(iii) political beliefs or affiliations,

(iv) any matter relating to sexual behavior; and

(v) beliefs, affiliations, opinions, or lawful activities regarding unions or labor organizations; and

(D) the examiner does not conduct the test if there is sufficient written evidence by a physician that the examinee is suffering from a medical or psychological condition or undergoing treatment that might cause abnormal responses during the actual testing phase.

(2) Pretest phase

During the pretest phase, the prospective examinee—

(A) is provided with reasonable written notice of the date, time, and location of the test, and of such examinee's right to obtain and consult with legal counsel or an employee representative before each phase of the test;

(B) is informed in writing of the nature and characteristics of the tests and of the instruments involved;

(C) is informed, in writing—

(i) whether the testing area contains a two-way mirror, a camera, or any other device through which the test can be observed,

(ii) whether any other device, including any device for recording or monitoring the test, will be used, or

(iii) that the employer or the examinee may (with mutual knowledge) make a recording of the test;

(D) is read and signs a written notice informing such examinee—

(i) that the examinee cannot be required to take the test as a condition of employment,

(ii) that any statement made during the test may constitute additional supporting evidence for the purposes of an adverse employment action described in subsection (a),

(iii) of the limitations imposed under this section,

(iv) of the legal rights and remedies available to the examinee if the polygraph test is not conducted in accordance with this chapter, and

(v) of the legal rights and remedies of the employer under this chapter (including the rights of the employer under section 2008(c)(2) of this title); and

(E) is provided an opportunity to review all questions to be asked during the test and is informed of the right to terminate the test at any time.

(3) Actual testing phase

During the actual testing phase, the examiner does not ask such examinee any question relevant during the test that was not presented in writing for review to such examinee before the test.

(4) Post-test phase

Before any adverse employment action, the employer shall—

(A) further interview the examinee on the basis of the results of the test; and

(B) provide the examinee with—

(i) a written copy of any opinion or conclusion rendered as a result of the test, and

(ii) a copy of the questions asked during the test along with the corresponding charted responses.

(5) Maximum number and minimum duration of tests

The examiner shall not conduct and complete more than five polygraph tests on a calendar day on which the test is given, and shall not conduct any such test for less than a 90-minute duration.

(c) Qualifications and requirements of examiners

The exemptions provided under subsections (d), (e), and (f) of section 2006 of this title shall not apply unless the individual who conducts the polygraph test satisfies the requirements under the following paragraphs:

(1) Qualifications

The examiner:

(A) has a valid and current license granted by licensing and regulatory authorities in the State in which the test is to be conducted, if so required by the State; and

(B) maintains a minimum of a $50,000 bond or an equivalent amount of professional liability coverage.

(2) Requirements

The examiner:

(A) renders any opinion or conclusion regarding the test:

(i) in writing and solely on the basis of an analysis of polygraph test charts,

(ii) that does not contain information other than admissions, information, case facts, and interpretation of the charts relevant to the purpose and stated objectives of the test, and

(iii) that does not include any recommendation concerning the employment of the examinee; and

(B) maintains all opinions, reports, charts, written questions, lists, and other records relating to the test for a minimum period of 3 years after administration of the test.

§ 2008. Disclosure of information

(a) In general

A person, other than the examinee, may not disclose information obtained during a polygraph test, except as provided in this section.

(b) Permitted disclosures

A polygraph examiner may disclose information acquired from a polygraph test only to:

(1) the examinee or any other person specifically designated in writing by the examinee;

(2) the employer that requested the test; or

(3) any court, governmental agency, arbitrator, or mediator, in accordance with due process of law, pursuant to an order from a court of competent jurisdiction.

(c) Disclosure by employer

An employer (other than an employer described in subsection (a), (b), or (c) of section 2006 of this title) for whom a polygraph test is conducted may disclose information from the test only to:

(1) a person in accordance with subsection (b); or

(2) a governmental agency, but only insofar as the disclosed information is an admission of criminal conduct.

§ 2009. Effect on other laws and agreements

Except as provided in subsections (a), (b), and (c) of section 2006 of this title, this chapter shall not preempt any provision of any State or local law or of any negotiated collective bargaining agreement that prohibits lie detector tests or is more restrictive with respect to lie detector tests than any provision of this chapter.

FAMILY AND MEDICAL LEAVE ACT (TITLE 29 U.S.C.)

§ 2601. Findings and purposes

(a) Findings

Congress finds that—

(1) the number of single-parent households and two-parent households in which the single parent or both parents work is increasing significantly;

(2) it is important for the development of children and the family unit that fathers and mothers be able to participate in early childrearing and the care of family members who have serious health conditions;

(3) the lack of employment policies to accommodate working parents can force individuals to choose between job security and parenting;

(4) there is inadequate job security for employees who have serious health conditions that prevent them from working for temporary periods;

(5) due to the nature of the roles of men and women in our society, the primary responsibility for family caretaking often falls on women, and such responsibility affects the working lives of women more than it affects the working lives of men; and

(6) employment standards that apply to one gender only have serious potential for encouraging employers to discriminate against employees and applicants for employment who are of that gender.

(b) Purposes

It is the purpose of this Act—

(1) to balance the demands of the workplace with the needs of families, to promote the stability and economic security of families, and to promote national interests in preserving family integrity;

(2) to entitle employees to take reasonable leave for medical reasons, for the birth or adoption of a child, and for the care of a child, spouse, or parent who has a serious health condition;

(3) to accomplish the purposes described in paragraphs (1) and (2) in a manner that accommodates the legitimate interests of employers;

(4) to accomplish the purposes described in paragraphs (1) and (2) in a manner that, consistent with the Equal Protection Clause of the Fourteenth Amendment, minimizes the potential for employment discrimination on the basis of sex by ensuring generally that leave is available for eligible medical reasons (including maternity-related disability) and for compelling family reasons, on a gender-neutral basis; and

(5) to promote the goal of equal employment opportunity for women and men, pursuant to such clause.

§ 2611. Definitions

As used in this subchapter:

(1) Commerce

The terms "commerce" and "industry or activity affecting commerce" mean any activity, business, or industry in commerce or in which a labor dispute would hinder or obstruct commerce or the free flow of commerce, and include "commerce" and any "industry affecting commerce", as defined in paragraphs (1) and (3) of section 142 of this title.

(2) Eligible employee

(A) In general

The term "eligible employee" means an employee who has been employed—

(i) for at least 12 months by the employer with respect to whom leave is requested under section 2612 of this title; and

(ii) for at least 1,250 hours of service with such employer during the previous 12-month period.

(B) Exclusions

The term "eligible employee" does not include—

(i) any Federal officer or employee covered under subchapter V of chapter 63 of Title 5; or

(ii) any employee of an employer who is employed at a worksite at which such employer employs less than 50 employees if the total number of employees employed by that employer within 75 miles of that worksite is less than 50.

(C) Determination

For purposes of determining whether an employee meets the hours of service requirement specified in subparagraph (A)(ii), the legal standards established under section 207 of this title shall apply.

(D) Airline Flight Crews

(i) Determination

For purposes of determining whether an employee who is a flight attendant or flight crew member (as such terms are defined in regulations of the Federal Aviation Administration) meets the hours of service requirement specified in subparagraph (A)(ii), the employee will be considered to meet the requirement if—

(I) the employee has worked or been paid for not less than 60 percent of the applicable total monthly guarantee, or the equivalent, for the previous 12-month period, for or by the employer with respect to whom leave is requested under section 2616 of this title; and

(II) the employee has worked or been paid for not less than 504 hours (not counting personal commute time or time spent on vacation leave or medical or sick leave) during the previous 12-month period, for or by that employer

(ii) File

Each employer of an employee described in clause (i) shall maintain on file with the Secretary (in accordance with such regulations as the Secretary may prescribe) containing information specifying the applicable monthly guarantee with respect to each category of employee to which such guarantee applies.

(iii) Definition

In this subparagraph, the term "applicable monthly guarantee" means—

(I) for an employee described in clause (i) other than an employee on reserve status, the minimum number of hours for which an employer has agreed to schedule such employee for any given month; and

(II) for an employee described in clause (i) who is on reserve status, the number of hours for which an employer has agreed to pay such employee on reserve status for any given month, as established in the applicable collective bargaining agreement or, if none exists, in the employer's policies.

(E) GAO Employees

In the case of an employee of the Government Accountability Office, the requirement of subparagraph (A) shall not apply with respect to leave under section 2612(a)(1)(A) or (B) of this title.

(3) Employ; employee; State

The terms "employ", "employee", and "State" have the same meanings given such terms in subsections (c), (e), and (g) of section 203 of this title.

(4) Employer

(A) In general

The term "employer"—

(i) means any person engaged in commerce or in any industry or activity affecting commerce who employs 50 or more employees for each working day during each of 20 or more calendar workweeks in the current or preceding calendar year;

(ii) includes—

(I) any person who acts, directly or indirectly, in the interest of an employer to any of the employees of such employer; and

(II) any successor in interest of an employer;

(iii) includes any "public agency", as defined in section 203(x) of this title; and

(iv) includes the Government Accountability Office and the Library of Congress.

(B) Public agency

For purposes of subparagraph (A)(iii), a public agency shall be considered to be a person engaged in commerce or in an industry or activity affecting commerce.

(5) Employment benefits

The term "employment benefits" means all benefits provided or made available to employees by an employer, including group life insurance, health insurance, disability insurance, sick leave, annual leave, educational benefits, and pensions, regardless of whether such benefits are provided by a practice or written policy of an employer or through an "employee benefit plan", as defined in section 1002(3) of this title.

(6) Health care provider

The term "health care provider" means—

(A) a doctor of medicine or osteopathy who is authorized to practice medicine or surgery (as appropriate) by the State in which the doctor practices; or

(B) any other person determined by the Secretary to be capable of providing health care services.

(7) Parent

The term “parent” means the biological parent of an employee or an individual who stood in loco parentis to an employee when the employee was a son or daughter.

(8) Person

The term “person” has the same meaning given such term in section 203(a) of this title.

(9) Reduced leave schedule

The term “reduced leave schedule” means a leave schedule that reduces the usual number of hours per workweek, or hours per workday, of an employee.

(10) Secretary

The term “Secretary” means the Secretary of Labor.

(11) Serious health condition

The term “serious health condition” means an illness, injury, impairment, or physical or mental condition that involves—

(A) inpatient care in a hospital, hospice, or residential medical care facility; or

(B) continuing treatment by a health care provider.

(12) Son or daughter

The term “son or daughter” means a biological, adopted, or foster child, a stepchild, a legal ward, or a child of a person standing in loco parentis, who is—

(A) under 18 years of age; or

(B) 18 years of age or older and incapable of self-care because of a mental or physical disability.

(13) Spouse

The term “spouse” means a husband or wife, as the case may be.

(14) Covered active duty

The term “covered active duty” means—

(A) in the case of a member of a regular component of the Armed Forces, duty during the deployment of the member with the Armed Forces to a foreign country; and

(B) in the case of a member of a reserve component of the Armed Forces, duty during the deployment of the member with the Armed Forces to a foreign country under a call or order to active duty under a provision of law referred to in section 101(a)(13)(B) of Title 10.

(15) Covered servicemember

The term "covered servicemember" means—

(A) a member of the Armed Forces (including a member of the National Guard or Reserves) who is undergoing medical treatment, recuperation, or therapy, is otherwise in outpatient status, or is otherwise on the temporary disability retired list, for a serious injury or illness; or

(B) a veteran who is undergoing medical treatment, recuperation, or therapy, for a serious injury or illness and who was a member of the Armed Forces (including a member of the National Guard or Reserves) at any time during the period of 5 years preceding the date on which the veteran undergoes that medical treatment, recuperation, or therapy.

(16) Outpatient status

The term "outpatient status", with respect to a covered servicemember, means the status of a member of the Armed Forces assigned to—

(A) a military medical treatment facility as an outpatient; or

(B) a unit established for the purpose of providing command and control of members of the Armed Forces receiving medical care as outpatients.

(17) Next of kin

The term "next of kin", used with respect to an individual, means the nearest blood relative of that individual.

(18) Serious injury or illness

The term "serious injury or illness"—

(A) in the case of a member of the Armed Forces (including a member of the National Guard or Reserves), means an injury or illness that was incurred by the member in line of duty on active duty in the Armed Forces (or existed before the beginning of the member's active duty and was aggravated by service in line of duty on active duty in the Armed Forces) and that may render the member medically unfit to perform the duties of the member's office, grade, rank, or rating; and

(B) in the case of a veteran who was a member of the Armed Forces (including a member of the National Guard or Reserves) at any time during a period described in paragraph (15)(B), means a qualifying (as defined by the Secretary of Labor) injury or illness that was incurred by the member in line of duty on active duty in the Armed Forces (or existed before the beginning of the member's active duty and was aggravated by service in line of duty on active duty in the Armed

Forces) and that manifested itself before or after the member became a veteran.

(19) Veteran

The term "veteran" has the meaning given the term in section 101 of Title 38.

§ 2612. Leave requirement

(a) In General.

(1) Entitlement to Leave.

Subject to section 2613 of this title and subsection (d)(3), an eligible employee shall be entitled to a total of 12 workweeks of leave during any 12-month period for one or more of the following:

(A) Because of the birth of a son or daughter of the employee and in order to care for such son or daughter.

(B) Because of the placement of a son or daughter with the employee for adoption or foster care.

(C) In order to care for the spouse, or a son, daughter, or parent, of the employee, if such spouse, son, daughter, or parent has a serious health condition.

(D) Because of a serious health condition that makes the employee unable to perform the functions of the position of such employee.

(E) Because of any qualifying exigency (as the Secretary shall, by regulation, determine) arising out of the fact that the spouse, or a son, daughter, or parent of the employee is on covered active duty (or has been notified of an impending call or order to covered active duty) in the Armed Forces.

(F) During the period beginning on the date the Emergency Family and Medical Leave Expansion Act takes effect, and ending on December 31, 2020, because of a qualifying need related to a public health emergency in accordance with section 2620 of this title.

(2) Expiration of Entitlement.

The entitlement to leave under subparagraphs (A) and (B) of paragraph (1) for a birth or placement of a son or daughter shall expire at the end of the 12-month period beginning on the date of such birth or placement.

(3) Servicemember family leave

Subject to section 2613 of this title, an eligible employee who is the spouse, son, daughter, parent, or next of kin of a covered servicemember shall be entitled to a total of 26 workweeks of leave during a 12-month period to care for the servicemember. The leave described in this paragraph shall only be available during a single 12-month period.

(4) Combined leave total

Subject to subsection (d)(3), during the single 12-month period described in paragraph (3), an eligible employee shall be entitled to a combined total of 26 workweeks of leave under paragraphs (1) and (3). Nothing in this paragraph shall be construed to limit the availability of leave under paragraph (1) during any other 12-month period.

(5) Calculation of leave for airline flight crews

The Secretary may provide, by regulation, a method for calculating the leave described in paragraph (1) with respect to employees described in section 2611(2)(D) of this title.

(b) Leave Taken Intermittently or on Reduced Leave Schedule.

(1) In General.

Leave under subparagraph (A) or (B) of subsection (a)(1) shall not be taken by an employee intermittently or on a reduced leave schedule unless the employee and the employer of the employee agree otherwise. Subject to paragraph (2), subsection (e)(2), and subsection (b)(5) or (f) (as appropriate) of section 2613 of this title, leave under subparagraph (C) or (D) of subsection (a)(1) or under subsection (a)(3) may be taken intermittently or on a reduced leave schedule when medically necessary. Subject to subsection (e)(3) and section 2613(f) of this title, leave under subsection (a)(1)(E) may be taken intermittently or on a reduced leave schedule. The taking of leave intermittently or on a reduced leave schedule pursuant to this paragraph shall not result in a reduction in the total amount of leave to which the employee is entitled under subsection (a) beyond the amount of leave actually taken.

(2) Alternative Position.

If an employee requests intermittent leave, or leave on a reduced leave schedule, under subparagraph (C) or (D) of subsection (a)(1) or under subsection (a)(3), that is foreseeable based on planned medical treatment, the employer may require such employee to transfer temporarily to an available alternative position offered by the employer for which the employee is qualified and that—

(A) has equivalent pay and benefits; and

(B) better accommodates recurring periods of leave than the regular employment position of the employee.

(c) Unpaid Leave Permitted.

Except as provided in subsection (d), leave granted under subsection (a) (other than certain periods of leave under subsection (a)(1)(F)) may consist of unpaid leave. Where an employee is otherwise exempt under regulations issued by the Secretary pursuant to section 213(a)(1) of this title, the compliance of an employer with this subchapter by providing unpaid leave shall not affect the exempt status of the employee under such section.

(d) Relationship to Paid Leave.

(1) Unpaid Leave.

If an employer provides paid leave for fewer than 12 workweeks (or 26 workweeks in the case of leave provided under subsection (a)(3)), the additional weeks of leave necessary to attain the 12 workweeks (or 26 workweeks, as appropriate) of leave required under this subchapter may be provided without compensation.

(2) Substitution of Paid Leave.—

(A) In General.—An eligible employee may elect, or an employer may require the employee, to substitute any of the accrued paid vacation leave, personal leave, or family leave of the employee for leave provided under subparagraph (A), (B), (C), or (E) of subsection (a)(1) of this section for any part of the 12-week period of such leave under such subsection.

(B) Serious Health Condition.—An eligible employee may elect, or an employer may require the employee, to substitute any of the accrued paid vacation leave, personal leave, or medical or sick leave of the employee for leave provided under subparagraph (C) or (D) of subsection (a)(1) for any part of the 12-week period of such leave under such subsection, except that nothing in this subchapter shall require an employer to provide paid sick leave or paid medical leave in any situation in which such employer would not normally provide any such paid leave. An eligible employee may elect, or an employer may require the employee, to substitute any of the accrued paid vacation leave, personal leave, family leave, or medical or sick leave of the employee for leave provided under subsection (a)(3) for any part of the 26-week period of such leave under such subsection, except that nothing in this subchapter requires an employer to provide paid sick leave or paid medical leave in any situation in which the employer would not normally provide any such paid leave.

(3) Special Rule for GAO Employees

(A) Substitution of Paid Leave

An employee of the Government Accountability Office may elect to substitute for any leave without pay under subparagraph (A) or (B) of subsection (a)(1) any paid leave which is available to such employee for that purpose.

(B) Amount of Paid Leave

The paid leave that is available to an employee of the Government Accountability Office for purposes of subparagraph (A) is—

(i) the number of weeks of paid parental leave in connection with the birth or placement involved that corresponds to the number of administrative workweeks of paid parental leave available to employees under section 6382(d)(2)(B)(i) of Title 5; and

(ii) during the 12-month period referred to in subsection (a)(1) and in addition to the administrative workweeks described in clause (i), any additional paid vacation, personal, family, medical, or sick leave provided by such employer.

(C) Limitation

Nothing in this section shall be considered to require or permit an employer to require that an employee first use all or any portion of the leave described in subparagraph (B)(ii) before being allowed to use the paid parental leave described in clause (i) of subparagraph (B).

(D) Additional Rules

Paid parental leave under subparagraph (B)(i)—

(i) shall be payable from any appropriation or fund available for salaries or expenses for positions with the Government Accountability Office;

(ii) if not used by the employee of such employer before the end of the 12-month period (as referred to in subsection (a)(1)) to which it relates, shall not accumulate for any subsequent use; and

(iii) shall apply without regard to the limitations in subparagraph (E), (F), or (G) of section 6382(d)(2) of Title 5 or section 2614(c)(2) of this title.

(4) Special Rule for Library of Congress Employees

Consistent with section 1301(a)(3)(J) of Title 2, the rights and protections established by sections 2611 through 2615 of this title, including section 2612(d)(3), shall apply to employees of the Library of Congress under section 1312 of Title 2.

(e) Foreseeable Leave.

(1) Requirement of Notice.

In any case in which the necessity for leave under subparagraph (A) or (B) of subsection (a)(1) is foreseeable based on an expected birth or placement, the employee shall provide the employer with not less than 30 days' notice, before the date the leave is to begin, of the employee's intention to take leave under such subparagraph, except that if the date of the birth or placement requires leave to begin in less than 30 days, the employee shall provide such notice as is practicable.

(2) Duties of Employee.

In any case in which the necessity for leave under subparagraph (C) or (D) of subsection (a)(1) or under subsection (a)(3) is foreseeable based on planned medical treatment, the employee—

(A) shall make a reasonable effort to schedule the treatment so as not to disrupt unduly the operations of the employer, subject to the approval of the health care provider of the employee or the health care provider of the son, daughter, spouse, parent, or covered servicemember of the employee, as appropriate; and

(B) shall provide the employer with not less than 30 days' notice, before the date the leave is to begin, of the employee's intention to take leave under such subparagraph, except that if the date of the treatment requires leave to begin in less than 30 days, the employee shall provide such notice as is practicable.

(3) Notice for leave due to covered active duty of family member

In any case in which the necessity for leave under subsection (a)(1)(E) is foreseeable, whether because the spouse, or a son, daughter, or parent, of the employee is on covered active duty, or because of notification of an impending call or order to covered active duty, the employee shall provide such notice to the employer as is reasonable and practicable.

(f) Spouses Employed by the Same Employer.

(1) In General

In any case in which a husband and wife entitled to leave under subsection (a) of this section are employed by the same employer, the aggregate number of workweeks of leave to which both may be entitled may be limited to 12 workweeks during any 12-month period, if such leave is taken—

(A) under subparagraph (A) or (B) of subsection (a)(1); or

(B) to care for a sick parent under subparagraph (C) of such subsection.

(2) Servicemember family leave

(A) In General—the aggregate number of workweeks of leave to which both that husband and wife may be entitled under subsection (a) may be limited to 26 workweeks during the single 12-month period described in subsection (a)(3) if the leave is—

(i) leave under subsection (a)(3); or

(ii) a combination of leave under subsection (a)(3) and leave described in paragraph (1).

(B) Both limitations applicable—If the leave taken by the husband and wife includes leave described in paragraph (1), the limitation in paragraph (1) shall apply to the leave described in paragraph (1).

§ 2613. Certification

(a) In general

An employer may require that a request for leave under subparagraph (C) or (D) of paragraph (1) or paragraph (3) of section 2612(a) of this title be supported by a certification issued by the health care provider of the eligible employee or of the son, daughter, spouse, or parent of the employee, or of the next of kin of an individual in the case of leave taken under such paragraph (3), as appropriate. The employee shall provide, in a timely manner, a copy of such certification to the employer.

(b) Sufficient certification

Certification provided under subsection (a) shall be sufficient if it states—

(1) the date on which the serious health condition commenced;

(2) the probable duration of the condition;

(3) the appropriate medical facts within the knowledge of the health care provider regarding the condition;

(4)(A) for purposes of leave under section 2612(a)(1)(C) of this title, a statement that the eligible employee is needed to care for the son, daughter, spouse, or parent and an estimate of the amount of time that such employee is needed to care for the son, daughter, spouse, or parent; and

(B) for purposes of leave under section 2612(a)(1)(D) of this title, a statement that the employee is unable to perform the functions of the position of the employee;

(5) in the case of certification for intermittent leave, or leave on a reduced leave schedule, for planned medical treatment, the dates on which such treatment is expected to be given and the duration of such treatment;

(6) in the case of certification for intermittent leave, or leave on a reduced leave schedule, under section 2612(a)(1)(D) of this title, a statement of the medical necessity for the intermittent leave or leave on a reduced leave schedule, and the expected duration of the intermittent leave or reduced leave schedule; and

(7) in the case of certification for intermittent leave, or leave on a reduced leave schedule, under section 2612(a)(1)(C) of this title, a statement that the employee's intermittent leave or leave on a reduced leave schedule is necessary for the care of the son, daughter, parent, or spouse who has a serious health condition, or will assist in their recovery, and the expected duration and schedule of the intermittent leave or reduced leave schedule.

(c) Second opinion

(1) In general

In any case in which the employer has reason to doubt the validity of the certification provided under subsection (a) for leave under subparagraph (C) or (D) of section 2612(a)(1) of this title, the employer may require, at the expense of the employer, that the eligible employee obtain the opinion of a second health care provider designated or approved by the employer concerning any information certified under subsection (b) for such leave.

(2) Limitation

A health care provider designated or approved under paragraph (1) shall not be employed on a regular basis by the employer.

(d) Resolution of conflicting opinions

(1) In general

In any case in which the second opinion described in subsection (c) differs from the opinion in the original certification provided under subsection (a), the employer may require, at the expense of the employer, that the employee obtain the opinion of a third health care provider designated or approved jointly by the employer and the employee concerning the information certified under subsection (b).

(2) Finality

The opinion of the third health care provider concerning the information certified under subsection (b) shall be considered to be final and shall be binding on the employer and the employee.

(e) Subsequent recertification

The employer may require that the eligible employee obtain subsequent recertifications on a reasonable basis.

(f) Certification related to covered active duty or call to covered active duty—An employer may require that a request for leave under section 2612(a)(1)(E) of this title be supported by a certification issued at such time and in such manner as the Secretary may by regulation prescribe. If the Secretary issues a regulation requiring such certification, the employee shall provide, in a timely manner, a copy of such certification to the employer.

§ 2614. Employment and benefits protection

(a) Restoration to position

(1) In general

Except as provided in subsection (b), any eligible employee who takes leave under section 2612 of this title for the intended purpose of the leave shall be entitled, on return from such leave—

(A) to be restored by the employer to the position of employment held by the employee when the leave commenced; or

(B) to be restored to an equivalent position with equivalent employment benefits, pay, and other terms and conditions of employment.

(2) Loss of benefits

The taking of leave under section 2612 of this title shall not result in the loss of any employment benefit accrued prior to the date on which the leave commenced.

(3) Limitations

Nothing in this section shall be construed to entitle any restored employee to—

(A) the accrual of any seniority or employment benefits during any period of leave; or

(B) any right, benefit, or position of employment other than any right, benefit, or position to which the employee would have been entitled had the employee not taken the leave.

(4) Certification

As a condition of restoration under paragraph (1) for an employee who has taken leave under section 2612(a)(1)(D) of this title, the employer may have a uniformly applied practice or policy that requires each such employee to receive certification from the health care provider of the employee that the employee is able to resume work, except that nothing in this paragraph shall supersede a valid State or local law or a collective bargaining agreement that governs the return to work of such employees.

(5) Construction

Nothing in this subsection shall be construed to prohibit an employer from requiring an employee on leave under section 2612 of this title to report periodically to the employer on the status and intention of the employee to return to work.

(b) Exemption concerning certain highly compensated employees

(1) Denial of restoration

An employer may deny restoration under subsection (a) to any eligible employee described in paragraph (2) if—

(A) such denial is necessary to prevent substantial and grievous economic injury to the operations of the employer;

(B) the employer notifies the employee of the intent of the employer to deny restoration on such basis at the time the employer determines that such injury would occur; and

(C) in any case in which the leave has commenced, the employee elects not to return to employment after receiving such notice.

(2) Affected employees

An eligible employee described in paragraph (1) is a salaried eligible employee who is among the highest paid 10 percent of the employees employed by the employer within 75 miles of the facility at which the employee is employed.

(c) Maintenance of health benefits

(1) Coverage

Except as provided in paragraph (2), during any period that an eligible employee takes leave under section 2612 of this title, the employer shall maintain coverage under any "group health plan" (as defined in section 5000(b)(1) of Title 26) for the duration of such leave at the level and under the conditions coverage would have been provided if the employee had continued in employment continuously for the duration of such leave.

(2) Failure to return from leave

The employer may recover the premium that the employer paid for maintaining coverage for the employee under such group health plan during any period of unpaid leave under section 2612 of this title if—

(A) the employee fails to return from leave under section 2612 of this title after the period of leave to which the employee is entitled has expired; and

(B) the employee fails to return to work for a reason other than—

(i) the continuation, recurrence, or onset of a serious health condition that entitles the employee to leave under subparagraph (C) or (D) of section 2612(a)(1) of this title or under section 2612(a)(3) of this title; or

(ii) other circumstances beyond the control of the employee.

(3) Certification

(A) Issuance

An employer may require that a claim that an employee is unable to return to work because of the continuation, recurrence, or onset of the serious health condition described in paragraph (2)(B)(i) be supported by—

(i) a certification issued by the health care provider of the son, daughter, spouse, or parent of the employee, as appropriate, in the case of an employee unable to return to work because of a condition specified in section 2612(a)(1)(C) of this title;

(ii) a certification issued by the health care provider of the eligible employee, in the case of an employee unable to return to work because of a condition specified in section 2612(a)(1)(D) of this title; or

(iii) a certification issued by the health care provider of the servicemember being cared for by the employee, in the case of an employee unable to return to work because of a condition specified in section 2612(a)(3) of this title.

(B) Copy

The employee shall provide, in a timely manner, a copy of such certification to the employer.

(C) Sufficiency of certification

(i) Leave due to serious health condition of employee

The certification described in subparagraph (A)(ii) shall be sufficient if the certification states that a serious health condition prevented the employee from being able to perform the functions of the position of the employee on the date that the leave of the employee expired.

(ii) Leave due to serious health condition of family member

The certification described in subparagraph (A)(i) shall be sufficient if the certification states that the employee is needed to care for the son, daughter, spouse, or parent who has a serious health condition on the date that the leave of the employee expired.

§ 2615. Prohibited acts

(a) Interference with rights

(1) Exercise of rights

It shall be unlawful for any employer to interfere with, restrain, or deny the exercise of or the attempt to exercise, any right provided under this subchapter.

(2) Discrimination

It shall be unlawful for any employer to discharge or in any other manner discriminate against any individual for opposing any practice made unlawful by this subchapter.

(b) Interference with proceedings or inquiries

It shall be unlawful for any person to discharge or in any other manner discriminate against any individual because such individual—

(1) has filed any charge, or has instituted or caused to be instituted any proceeding, under or related to this subchapter;

(2) has given, or is about to give, any information in connection with any inquiry or proceeding relating to any right provided under this subchapter; or

(3) has testified, or is about to testify, in any inquiry or proceeding relating to any right provided under this subchapter.

§ 2616. Investigative authority

(a) In general

To ensure compliance with the provisions of this subchapter, or any regulation or order issued under this subchapter, the Secretary shall have, subject to subsection (c), the investigative authority provided under section 211(a) of this title.

(b) Obligation to keep and preserve records

Any employer shall make, keep, and preserve records pertaining to compliance with this subchapter in accordance with section 211(c) of this title and in accordance with regulations issued by the Secretary.

(c) Required submissions generally limited to an annual basis

The Secretary shall not under the authority of this section require any employer or any plan, fund, or program to submit to the Secretary any books or records more than once during any 12-month period, unless the Secretary has reasonable cause to believe there may exist a violation of this subchapter or any regulation or order issued pursuant to this subchapter, or is investigating a charge pursuant to section 2617(b) of this title.

(d) Subpoena powers

For the purposes of any investigation provided for in this section, the Secretary shall have the subpoena authority provided for under section 209 of this title.

§ 2617. Enforcement

(a) Civil action by employees

(1) Liability

Any employer who violates section 2615 of this title shall be liable to any eligible employee affected—

(A) for damages equal to

(i) the amount of—

(I) any wages, salary, employment benefits, or other compensation denied or lost to such employee by reason of the violation; or

(II) in a case in which wages, salary, employment benefits, or other compensation have not been denied or lost to the employee, any actual monetary losses sustained by the employee as a direct result of the violation, such as the cost of providing care, up to a sum equal to 12 weeks (or 26 weeks, in a case involving leave under section 2612(a)(3) of this title) of wages or salary for the employee;

(ii) the interest on the amount described in clause (i) calculated at the prevailing rate; and

(iii) an additional amount as liquidated damages equal to the sum of the amount described in clause (i) and the interest described in clause (ii), except that if an employer who has violated section 2615 of this title proves to the satisfaction of the court that the act or omission which violated section 2615 of this title was in good faith and that the employer had reasonable grounds for believing that the act or omission was not a violation of section 2615 of this title, such court may, in the discretion of the court, reduce the amount of the liability to the amount and interest determined under clauses (i) and (ii), respectively; and

(B) for such equitable relief as may be appropriate, including employment, reinstatement, and promotion.

(2) Right of action

An action to recover the damages or equitable relief prescribed in paragraph (1) may be maintained against any employer (including a public agency) in any Federal or State court of competent jurisdiction by any one or more employees for and in behalf of—

(A) the employees; or

(B) the employees and other employees similarly situated.

(3) Fees and costs

The court in such an action shall, in addition to any judgment awarded to the plaintiff, allow a reasonable attorney's fee, reasonable expert witness fees, and other costs of the action to be paid by the defendant.

(4) Limitations

The right provided by paragraph (2) to bring an action by or on behalf of any employee shall terminate

(A) on the filing of a complaint by the Secretary in an action under subsection (d) in which restraint is sought of any further delay in the payment of the amount described in paragraph (1)(A) to such employee by an employer responsible under paragraph (1) for the payment; or

(B) on the filing of a complaint by the Secretary in an action under subsection (b) in which a recovery is sought of the damages described in paragraph (1)(A) owing to an eligible employee by an employer liable under paragraph (1),

unless the action described in subparagraph (A) or (B) is dismissed without prejudice on motion of the Secretary.

(b) Action by the Secretary

(1) Administrative action

The Secretary shall receive, investigate, and attempt to resolve complaints of violations of section 2615 of this title in the same manner that the Secretary receives, investigates, and attempts to resolve complaints of violations of sections 206 and 207 of this title.

(2) Civil action

The Secretary may bring an action in any court of competent jurisdiction to recover the damages described in subsection (a)(1)(A).

(3) Sums recovered

Any sums recovered by the Secretary pursuant to paragraph (2) shall be held in a special deposit account and shall be paid, on order of the Secretary, directly to each employee affected. Any such sums not paid to an employee because of inability to do so within a period of 3 years shall be deposited into the Treasury of the United States as miscellaneous receipts.

(c) Limitation

(1) In general

Except as provided in paragraph (2), an action may be brought under this section not later than 2 years after the date of the last event constituting the alleged violation for which the action is brought.

(2) Willful violation

In the case of such action brought for a willful violation of section 2615 of this title, such action may be brought within 3 years of the date of the last event constituting the alleged violation for which such action is brought.

(3) Commencement

In determining when an action is commenced by the Secretary under this section for the purposes of this subsection, it shall be considered to be commenced on the date when the complaint is filed.

(d) Action for injunction by Secretary

The district courts of the United States shall have jurisdiction, for cause shown, in an action brought by the Secretary—

(1) to restrain violations of section 2615 of this title, including the restraint of any withholding of payment of wages, salary, employment benefits, or other compensation, plus interest, found by the court to be due to eligible employees; or

(2) to award such other equitable relief as may be appropriate, including employment, reinstatement, and promotion.

(e) Solicitor of Labor

The Solicitor of Labor may appear for and represent the Secretary on any litigation brought under this section.

(f) Government Accountability Office and Library of Congress

In the case of the Government Accountability Office and the Library of Congress, the authority of the Secretary of Labor under this subchapter shall be exercised respectively by the Comptroller General of the United States and the Librarian of Congress.

§ 2618. Special rules concerning employees of local educational agencies

(a) Application

(1) In general

Except as otherwise provided in this section, the rights (including the rights under section 2614 of this title, which shall extend throughout the period of leave of any employee under this section), remedies, and procedures under this subchapter shall apply to—

(A) any "local educational agency" (as defined in section 7801 of Title 20) and an eligible employee of the agency; and

(B) any private elementary or secondary school and an eligible employee of the school.

(2) Definitions

For purposes of the application described in paragraph (1):

(A) Eligible employee

The term "eligible employee" means an eligible employee of an agency or school described in paragraph (1).

(B) Employer

The term "employer" means an agency or school described in paragraph (1).

(b) Leave does not violate certain other Federal laws

A local educational agency and a private elementary or secondary school shall not be in violation of the Individuals with Disabilities Education Act (20 U.S.C. 1400 *et seq.*), section 794 of this title, or title VI of the Civil Rights Act of 1964 (42 U.S.C. 2000d *et seq.*), solely as a result of an eligible employee of such agency or school exercising the rights of such employee under this subchapter.

(c) Intermittent leave or leave on reduced schedule for instructional employees

(1) In general

Subject to paragraph (2), in any case in which an eligible employee employed principally in an instructional capacity by any such educational agency or school requests leave under subparagraph (C) or (D) of section 2612(a)(1) of this title or under section 2612(a)(3) of this title that is foreseeable based on planned medical treatment and the employee would be on leave for greater than 20 percent of the total number of working days in the period during which the leave would extend, the agency or school may require that such employee elect either—

(A) to take leave for periods of a particular duration, not to exceed the duration of the planned medical treatment; or

(B) to transfer temporarily to an available alternative position offered by the employer for which the employee is qualified, and that—

(i) has equivalent pay and benefits; and

(ii) better accommodates recurring periods of leave than the regular employment position of the employee.

(2) Application

The elections described in subparagraphs (A) and (B) of paragraph (1) shall apply only with respect to an eligible employee who complies with section 2612(e)(2) of this title.

(d) Rules applicable to periods near conclusion of academic term

The following rules shall apply with respect to periods of leave near the conclusion of an academic term in the case of any eligible employee employed principally in an instructional capacity by any such educational agency or school:

(1) Leave more than 5 weeks prior to end of term

If the eligible employee begins leave under section 2612 of this title more than 5 weeks prior to the end of the academic term, the agency or school may require the employee to continue taking leave until the end of such term, if—

(A) the leave is of at least 3 weeks duration; and

(B) the return to employment would occur during the 3-week period before the end of such term.

(2) Leave less than 5 weeks prior to end of term

If the eligible employee begins leave under subparagraph (A), (B), or (C) of section 2612(a)(1) of this title or under section 2612(a)(3) of this title during the period that commences 5 weeks prior to the end of the academic term, the agency or school may require the employee to continue taking leave until the end of such term, if—

(A) the leave is of greater than 2 weeks duration; and

(B) the return to employment would occur during the 2-week period before the end of such term.

(3) Leave less than 3 weeks prior to end of term

If the eligible employee begins leave under subparagraph (A), (B), or (C) of section 2612(a)(1) of this title or under section 2612(a)(3) of this title during the period that commences 3 weeks prior to the end of the academic term and the duration of the leave is greater than 5 working days, the agency or school may require the employee to continue to take leave until the end of such term.

(e) Restoration to equivalent employment position

For purposes of determinations under section 2614(a)(1)(B) of this title (relating to the restoration of an eligible employee to an equivalent position), in the case of a local educational agency or a private elementary or secondary school, such determination shall be made on the basis of established school board policies and practices, private school policies and practices, and collective bargaining agreements.

(f) Reduction of amount of liability

If a local educational agency or a private elementary or secondary school that has violated this subchapter proves to the satisfaction of the court that the agency, school, or department had reasonable grounds for believing that the underlying act or omission was not a violation of this subchapter, such court may, in the discretion of the court, reduce the amount of the liability provided for under section 2617(a)(1)(A) of this title to the amount and interest determined under clauses (i) and (ii), respectively, of such section.

§ 2619. Notice

(a) In general

Each employer shall post and keep posted, in conspicuous places on the premises of the employer where notices to employees and applicants for employment are customarily posted, a notice, to be prepared or approved by the Secretary, setting forth excerpts from, or summaries of, the pertinent provisions of this subchapter and information pertaining to the filing of a charge.

(b) Penalty

Any employer that willfully violates this section may be assessed a civil money penalty not to exceed $100 for each separate offense.

* * *

§ 2651. Effect on other laws

(a) Federal and State antidiscrimination laws

Nothing in this Act or any amendment made by this Act shall be construed to modify or affect any Federal or State law prohibiting discrimination on the basis of race, religion, color, national origin, sex, age, or disability.

(b) State and local laws

Nothing in this Act or any amendment made by this Act shall be construed to supersede any provision of any State or local law that provides greater family or medical leave rights than the rights established under this Act or any amendment made by this Act.

§ 2652. Effect on existing employment benefits

(a) More protective

Nothing in this Act or any amendment made by this Act shall be construed to diminish the obligation of an employer to comply with any collective bargaining agreement or any employment benefit program or plan that provides greater family or medical leave rights to employees than the rights established under this Act or any amendment made by this Act.

(b) Less protective

The rights established for employees under this Act or any amendment made by this Act shall not be diminished by any collective bargaining agreement or any employment benefit program or plan.

§ 2653. Encouragement of more generous leave policies

Nothing in this Act or any amendment made by this Act shall be construed to discourage employers from adopting or retaining leave policies more generous than any policies that comply with the requirements under this Act or any amendment made by this Act.

§ 2654. Regulations

The Secretary of Labor shall prescribe such regulations as are necessary to carry out subchapter I of this chapter and this subchapter not later than 120 days after February 5, 1993.

MODEL EMPLOYMENT TERMINATION ACT

(Recommended by the National Conference of Commissioners on Uniform State Laws—1991)

§ 1. Definitions.

In this [Act]:

(1) "Employee" means an individual who works for hire, including an individual employed in a supervisory, managerial, or confidential position, but not an independent contractor.

(2) "Employer" means a person[, excluding this State, a political subdivision, a municipal corporation, or any other governmental subdivision, agency, or instrumentality,] that has employed [five] or more employees for each working day in each of 20 or more calendar weeks in the two-year period next preceding a termination or an employer's filing of a complaint pursuant to Section 5(c), excluding a parent, spouse, child, or other member of the employer's immediate family or of the immediate family of an individual having a controlling interest in the employer.

(3) "Fringe benefit" means vacation leave, sick leave, medical insurance plan, disability insurance plan, life insurance plan, pension benefit plan, or other benefit of economic value, to the extent the leave, plan, or benefit is paid for by the employer.

(4) "Good cause" means (i) a reasonable basis related to an individual employee for termination of the employee's employment in view of relevant factors and circumstances, which may include the employee's duties, responsibilities, conduct on the job or otherwise, job performance, and employment record, or (ii) the exercise of business judgment in good faith by the employer, including setting its economic or institutional goals and determining methods to achieve those goals, organizing or reorganizing operations, discontinuing, consolidating, or divesting operations or positions or parts of operations or positions, determining the size of its work force and the nature of the positions filled by its work force, and determining and changing standards of performance for positions.

(5) "Good faith" means honesty in fact.

(6) "Pay," as a noun, means hourly wages or periodic salary, including tips, regularly paid and nondiscretionary commissions and bonuses, and regularly paid overtime, but not fringe benefits.

(7) "Person" means an individual, corporation, business trust, estate, trust, partnership, association, joint venture, or any other legal or

commercial entity[, excluding government or a governmental subdivision, agency, or instrumentality].

(8) "Termination" means:

(i) a dismissal, including that resulting from the elimination of a position, of an employee by an employer;

(ii) a layoff or suspension of an employee by an employer for more than two consecutive months; or

(iii) a quitting of employment or a retirement by an employee induced by an act or omission of the employer, after notice to the employer of the act or omission without appropriate relief by the employer, so intolerable that under the circumstances a reasonable individual would quit or retire.

§ 2. Scope.

(a) This [Act] applies only to a termination that occurs after the effective date of this [Act].

(b) This [Act] does not apply to a termination at the expiration of an express oral or written agreement of employment for a specified duration, which was valid, subsisting, and in effect on the [effective] date of this [Act].

(c) Except as provided in subsection (e), this [Act] displaces and extinguishes all common-law rights and claims of a terminated employee against the employer, its officers, directors, and employees, which are based on the termination or on acts taken or statements made that are reasonably necessary to initiate or effect the termination if the employee's termination requires good cause under Section 3(a), is subject to an agreement for severance pay under Section 4(c), or is permitted by the expiration of an agreement for a specified duration under Section 4(d).

(d) An employee whose termination is not subject to Section 3(a) or 4(d) and who is not a party to an agreement under Section 4(c) retains all common-law rights and claims.

(e) This [Act] does not displace or extinguish rights or claims of a terminated employee against an employer arising under state or federal statutes or administrative rules or regulations having the force of law [or local ordinances valid under state law], a collective-bargaining agreement between an employer and a labor organization, or an express oral or written agreement relating to employment which does not violate this [Act]. Those rights and claims may not be asserted under this [Act], except as otherwise provided in this [Act]. The existence or adjudication of those rights or claims does not limit the employee's rights or claims under this [Act], except as stated in Section 7(d).

§ 3. Prohibited Terminations.

(a) Unless otherwise provided in an agreement for severance pay under Section 4(c) or for a specified duration under Section 4(d), an employer may not terminate the employment of an employee without good cause.

(b) Subsection (a) applies only to an employee who has been employed by the same employer for a total period of one year or more and has worked for the employer for at least 520 hours during the 26 weeks next preceding the termination. A layoff or other break in service is not counted in determining whether an employee's period of employment totals one year, but the employee is considered to be employed during paid vacations and other authorized leaves. If an employee is rehired after a break in service exceeding one year, not counting absences due to labor disputes or authorized leaves, the employee is considered to be newly hired. The 26-week period for purposes of this subsection does not include any week during which the employee was absent because of layoffs of one year or less, paid vacations, authorized leaves, or labor disputes.

§ 4. Agreements between Employer and Employee.

(a) A right of an employee under this [Act] may not be waived by agreement except as provided in this section.

(b) By express written agreement, an employer and an employee may provide that the employee's failure to meet specified business-related standards of performance or the employee's commission or omission of specified business-related acts will constitute good cause for termination in proceedings under this [Act]. Those standards or prohibitions are effective only if they have been consistently enforced and they have not been applied to a particular employee in a disparate manner without justification. If the agreement authorizes changes by the employer in the standards or prohibitions, the changes must be clearly communicated to the employee.

(c) By express written agreement, an employer and an employee may mutually waive the requirement of good cause for termination, if the employer agrees that upon the termination of the employee for any reason other than willful misconduct of the employee, the employer will provide severance pay in an amount equal to at least one month's pay for each period of employment totaling one year, up to a maximum total payment equal to 30 months' pay at the employee's rate of pay in effect immediately before the termination. The employer shall make the payment in a lump sum or in a series of monthly installments, none of which may be less than one month's pay plus interest on the principal balance. The lump-sum payment must be made or payment of the monthly installments must begin within 30 days after the employee's termination. An agreement under this subsection constitutes a waiver by the employer and the employee of the right to civil trial, including jury trial, concerning disputes over the nature of the termination and the employee's entitlement to severance pay, and constitutes a stipulation by the parties that those disputes will be subject to the procedures and remedies of this [Act].

(d) The requirement of good cause for termination does not apply to the termination of an employee at the expiration of an express oral or written agreement of employment for a specified duration related to the completion of a specified task, project, undertaking, or assignment. If the employment continues after the expiration of the agreement, Section 3 applies to its termination unless the parties enter into a new express oral or written agreement under this subsection. The period of employment under an agreement described in this subsection counts toward the minimum periods of employment required by Section 3(b).

(e) An employer may provide substantive and procedural rights in addition to those provided by this [Act], either to one or more specific employees by express oral or written agreement, or to employees generally by a written personnel policy or statement, and may provide that those rights are enforceable under the procedures of this [Act].

(f) An employing person and an employee not otherwise subject to this [Act] may become subject to its provisions to the extent provided by express written agreement, in which case the employing person is deemed to be an employer.

(g) An agreement between an employer and an employee subject to this [Act] imposes a duty of good faith in its formation, performance, and enforcement.

(h) By express written agreement, an employer and an employee may settle at any time a claim arising under this [Act].

(i) By express written agreement before or after a dispute or claim arises under this [Act], an employer and an employee may agree to private arbitration or other alternative dispute-resolution procedure for resolving the dispute or claim.

(j) By express written agreement after a dispute or claim arises under this [Act], an employer and an employee may agree to judicial resolution of the dispute or claim.

(k) The substantive provisions of this [Act] apply under an agreement authorized by subsections (i) and (j).

§ 5. Procedure and Limitations.

(The Appendix following this Act contains Alternatives A and B to sections 5 through 8 of the Act.)

(a) An employee whose employment is terminated may file a complaint and demand for arbitration under this [Act] with the [Commission; Department; Service] not later than 180 days after the effective date of the termination, the date of the breach of an agreement for severance pay under Section 4(c), or the date the employee learns or should have learned of the facts forming the basis of the claim, whichever is latest. The time for filing is suspended while the employee is pursuing the employer's internal remedies and has not been notified in writing by the employer that the internal procedures have been concluded. Resort to an employer's internal procedures is not a condition for filing a complaint under this [Act].

(b) Except when an employee quits, an employer, within 10 business days after a termination, shall mail or deliver to the terminated employee a written statement of the reasons for the termination and a copy of this [Act] or a summary approved by the [Commission; Department; Service].

(c) An employer may file a complaint and demand for arbitration under this [Act] with the [Commission; Department; Service] to determine whether there is good cause for the termination of a named employee. At least 15 business days before filing, the employer shall mail or deliver to the employee a written statement of the employer's intention to file and the factors alleged to constitute good cause for a termination.

(d) The [Commission; Department; Service] shall promptly mail or deliver to the respondent a copy of the complaint and demand for arbitration. Within 21 days after receipt of a complaint, the respondent must file an answer with the [Commission; Department; Service] and mail a copy of the answer to the complainant. The answer of a respondent employer must include a copy of the statement of the reasons for the termination furnished the employee.

[(e) When a complaint is filed, a complainant employee or employer shall pay a filing fee to the [Commission; Department; Service] in [the amount of $________] [an amount not exceeding the maximum filing fee for a civil action in the courts of general jurisdiction of this State]. The [Commission; Department; Service] may waive or defer payment of the filing fee upon a showing of the complainant employee's indigency.]

§ 6. Arbitration; Selection and Powers of Arbitrator; Hearings; Burden of Proof.

(The Appendix following this Act contains Alternatives A and B to sections 5 through 8 of the Act.)

(a) Except as otherwise provided in this [Act], the [Uniform Arbitration Act] [______ arbitration act of this State] applies to proceedings under this [Act] as if the parties had agreed to arbitrate under that statute. The [Commission; Department; Service] shall adopt procedural rules to regulate arbitration under this [Act]. The [Administrative Procedure Act and other] statutes of this State applicable to the procedures of state agencies do not apply to arbitration under this [Act].

(b) The [Commission; Department; Service] shall adopt rules specifying the qualifications, method of selection, and appointment of arbitrators. An arbitrator serving under this [Act] exercises the authority of the state.

(c) Subject to rules adopted by the [Commission; Department; Service], all forms of discovery [provided by applicable state statute, rule, or regulation] are available in the discretion of the arbitrator, who shall ensure there is no undue delay, expense, or inconvenience. Upon request, the employer shall provide the complainant or respondent employee a complete copy of the employee's personnel file.

(d) A party may be represented in arbitration by an attorney or other person authorized under the laws of this State to represent an individual in arbitration.

(e) A complainant employee has the burden of proving that a termination was without good cause or that an employer breached an agreement for severance pay under Section 4(c). A complainant employer has the burden of proving that there is good cause for a termination. In all arbitrations, the employer shall present its case first unless the employee alleges that a quitting or retirement was a termination within the meaning of Section 1(8)(iii).

(f) If an employee establishes that a termination was motivated in part by impermissible grounds, the employer, to avoid liability, must establish by a preponderance of the evidence that it would have terminated the employment even in the absence of the impermissible grounds.

§ 7. Awards.

(The Appendix following this Act contains Alternatives A and B to sections 5 through 8 of the Act.)

(a) Within 30 days after the close of an arbitration hearing or at a later time agreeable to the parties, the arbitrator shall mail or deliver to the parties a written award sustaining or dismissing the complaint, in whole or in part, and specifying appropriate remedies, if any.

(b) An arbitrator may make one or more of the following awards for a termination in violation of this [Act]:

(1) reinstatement to the position of employment the employee held when employment was terminated or, if that is impractical, to a comparable position;

(2) full or partial backpay and reimbursement for lost fringe benefits, with interest, reduced by interim earnings from employment elsewhere, benefits received, and amounts that could have been received with reasonable diligence;

(3) if reinstatement is not awarded, a lump-sum severance payment at the employee's rate of pay in effect before the termination, for a period not exceeding [36 months] after the date of the award, together with the value of fringe benefits lost during that period, reduced by likely earnings and benefits from employment elsewhere, and taking into account such equitable considerations as the employee's length of service with the employer and the reasons for the termination; and

(4) reasonable attorney's fees and costs.

(c) An arbitrator may make either or both of the following awards for a violation of an agreement for severance pay under Section 4(c):

(1) enforcement of the severance pay and other applicable provisions of the agreement, with interest; and

(2) reasonable attorney's fees and costs.

(d) An arbitrator may not make an award except as provided in subsections (b) and (c). The arbitrator may not award damages for pain and suffering, emotional distress, defamation, fraud, or other injury under the common law; punitive damages; compensatory damages; or any other monetary award. In making a monetary award under this section, the arbitrator shall reduce the award by the amount of any monetary award to the employee in another forum for the same conduct of the employer. In making an award, the arbitrator is subject to the rules of issue, fact, and judgment preclusion applicable in courts of record in this State.

(e) If an arbitrator dismisses an employee's complaint and finds it frivolous, unreasonable, or without foundation, the arbitrator may award reasonable attorney's fees and costs to the prevailing employer.

(f) An arbitrator may sustain an employer's complaint and make an award declaring that there is good cause for the termination of a named employee. If the arbitrator dismisses the employer's complaint, the arbitrator may award reasonable attorney's fees and costs to the prevailing employee.

§ 8. Judicial Review and Enforcement.

(The Appendix following this Act contains Alternatives A and B to sections 5 through 8 of the Act.)

(a) Either party to an arbitration may seek vacation, modification, or enforcement of the arbitrator's award in the [court of general jurisdiction] for the [county] in which the termination occurred or in which the employee resides.

(b) An application for vacation or modification must be filed within [90] days after issuance of the arbitrator's award. An application for enforcement may be filed at any time after issuance of the arbitrator's award.

(c) The court may vacate or modify an arbitrator's award only if the court finds that:

(1) the award was procured by corruption, fraud, or other improper means;

(2) there was evident partiality by the arbitrator or misconduct prejudicing the rights of a party;

(3) the arbitrator exceeded the powers of an arbitrator;

(4) the arbitrator committed a prejudicial error of law; or

(5) another ground exists for vacating the award under the [Uniform Arbitration Act] [_______ arbitration act of this State].

(d) In an application for vacation, modification, or enforcement of an arbitrator's award, the court may award a prevailing employee reasonable attorney's fees and costs. In an application by an employee for vacation of an arbitrator's award, the court may award a prevailing employer reasonable attorney's fees and costs if the court finds the employee's application is frivolous, unreasonable, or without foundation.

§ 9. Posting.

An employer shall post a copy of this [Act] or a summary approved by the [Commission; Department; Service] in a prominent place in the work area. An employer who violates this section is subject to a civil penalty not exceeding [$_______]. The [Attorney General] may bring a civil action, on behalf of this State, to impose and collect any civil penalty arising under this section.

§ 10. Retaliation Prohibited and Civil Action Created.

An employer or other employing person may not directly or indirectly take adverse action in retaliation against an individual for filing a complaint, giving testimony, or otherwise lawfully participating in proceedings under this [Act], whether or not the individual is an employee having rights under this [Act]. An employer or other employing person who violates this section is liable to the individual subjected to the adverse action in retaliation for damage caused by the action, punitive damages when appropriate, and reasonable attorney's fees. A separate civil action may be brought to enforce this liability. The employer is also subject to applicable procedures and remedies provided by Sections 5 through 8.

§ 11. Severability Clause.

If any provision of this [Act] or its application to any person or circumstance is held invalid, the invalidity does not affect other provisions or applications of this [Act] which can be given effect without the invalid provision or application, and to this end the provisions of this [Act] are severable.

§ 12. Effective Date. * * *

§ 13. Repeals. * * *

§ 14. Savings and Transitional Provisions.

This [Act] does not apply to the termination of an employee within six months after the effective date of this [Act] based upon the employee's refusal to enter into an agreement meeting the minimum standards of Section 4(c), which the employer, in the exercise of good faith business judgment, may impose as a condition of continued employment.

APPENDIX TO MODEL EMPLOYMENT TERMINATION ACT

[Note: Instead of the arbitration system provided by Sections 5 through 8 of the preceding text, states may select the following Alternative A or Alternative B as the means of enforcement.]

ALTERNATIVE A

§ 5. Administrative Proceedings.

[Insert provisions consigning enforcement of the [Act] to a new or existing administrative agency, staffed by civil service or other governmental personnel, operating under applicable state statutes. Delete Sections 5 through 8 of the preceding text and renumber the remaining sections and any cross references accordingly.]

§ 6. Remedies.

(a) The [Commission; Department; Service] may provide one or more of the following remedies for a termination in violation of this [Act]:

(1) reinstatement to the position of employment the employee held when employment was terminated or, if that is impractical, to a comparable position;

(2) full or partial backpay and reimbursement for lost fringe benefits, with interest, reduced by interim earnings from employment elsewhere, benefits received, and amounts that could have been received with reasonable diligence;

(3) if reinstatement is not ordered, a lump-sum severance payment at the employee's rate of pay in effect before the termination, for a period not exceeding [36 months] from the date of the order, together with the value of fringe benefits lost during that period, reduced by likely earnings and benefits from employment elsewhere, and taking into account such equitable considerations as the employee's length of service with the employer and the reasons for the termination; and

(4) reasonable attorney's fees and costs.

(b) The [Commission; Department; Service] may grant either or both of the following remedies for a violation of an agreement for severance pay under Section 4(c):

(1) enforcement of the severance pay and other applicable provisions of the agreement, with interest; and

(2) reasonable attorney's fees and costs.

(c) The [Commission; Department; Service] may not make an award except as provided in subsections (a) and (b). The [Commission; Department; Service] may not award damages for pain and suffering, emotional distress, defamation, fraud, or other injury under the common law; punitive damages; compensatory damages; or any other monetary award under this [Act]. In making a monetary award under this section, the [Commission; Department; Service] shall reduce the award by the amount of any monetary award to the employee in another forum for the same conduct of the employer. In making an award, the [Commission; Department; Service] is subject to the rules of issue, fact, and judgment preclusion applicable in courts of record in this State.

(d) If the [Commission; Department; Service] dismisses an employee's complaint and finds it frivolous, unreasonable, or without foundation, the [Commission; Department; Service] may award reasonable attorney's fees and costs to the prevailing employer.

(e) Upon the complaint of an employer, the [Commission; Department; Service] may issue an order declaring whether there is good cause for the termination of a named employee. If the [Commission; Department; Service] dismisses the employer's complaint, the [Commission; Department; Service] may award reasonable attorney's fees and costs to the prevailing employee.

ALTERNATIVE B

[Alternative B would leave the enforcement of the statute to the civil courts. Delete Sections 5 through 8 of the preceding text and renumber the remaining sections and any cross references accordingly.]

§ 5. Judicial Remedies.

(a) The court may grant one or more of the following remedies for a termination in violation of this [Act]:

(1) reinstatement to the position of employment the employee held when employment was terminated or, if that is impractical, to a comparable position;

(2) full or partial backpay and reimbursement for lost fringe benefits, with interest, reduced by interim earnings from employment elsewhere, benefits received, and amounts that could have been received with reasonable diligence;

(3) if reinstatement is not awarded, a lump-sum severance payment at the employee's rate of pay in effect before the termination, for a period not exceeding [36 months] from the date of the award, together with the value of fringe benefits lost during that period, reduced by likely earnings and benefits from employment elsewhere, and taking into account such equitable considerations as the employee's length of service with the employer and the reasons for the termination; and

(4) reasonable attorney's fees and costs.

(b) The court may grant either or both of the following remedies for a violation of an agreement for severance pay under Section 4(c):

(1) enforcement of the severance pay and other applicable provisions of the agreement, with interest; and

(2) reasonable attorney's fees and costs.

(c) The court may not make an award except as provided in subsections (a) and (b). The court may not award damages for pain and suffering, emotional distress, defamation, fraud, or other injury under the common law; punitive damages; compensatory damages; or any other monetary award under this [Act]. In making a monetary award under this section, the court shall reduce the award by the amount of any monetary award to the employee in another forum for the same conduct of the employer. In making an award, the court is subject to the rules of issue, fact, and judgment preclusion applicable in courts of record in this State.

(d) If the court dismisses an employee's complaint and finds it frivolous, unreasonable, or without foundation, the court may award reasonable attorney's fees and costs to the prevailing employer.

(e) Upon the complaint of an employer, the court may enter a judgment declaring whether there is good cause for the termination of a named employee. If the court dismisses the employer's complaint, the court may award reasonable attorney's fees and costs to the prevailing employee.

NEW JERSEY EMPLOYMENT PROTECTION ACT

34:19–1. Short title

This act shall be known and may be cited as the "Conscientious Employee Protection Act."

34:19–2. Definitions

As used in this act:

a. "Employer" means any individual, partnership, association, corporation or any person or group of persons acting directly or indirectly on behalf of or in the interest of an employer with the employer's consent and shall include all branches of State Government, or the several counties and municipalities thereof, or any other political subdivision of the State, or a school district, or any special district, or any authority, commission, or board or any other agency or instrumentality thereof.

b. "Employee" means any individual who performs services for and under the control and direction of an employer for wages or other remuneration.

c. "Public body" means:

(1) the United States Congress, and State legislature, or any popularly-elected local governmental body, or any member or employee thereof;

(2) any federal, State, or local judiciary, or any member or employee thereof, or any grand or petit jury;

(3) any federal, State, or local regulatory, administrative, or public agency or authority, or instrumentality thereof;

(4) any federal, State, or local law enforcement agency, prosecutorial office, or police or peace officer;

(5) any federal, State or local department of an executive branch of government; or

(6) any division, board, bureau, office, committee or commission of any of the public bodies described in the above paragraphs of this subsection.

d. "Supervisor" means any individual with an employer's organization who has the authority to direct and control the work performance of the affected employee, who has authority to take corrective action regarding the violation of the law, rule or regulation of which the employee complains, or who has been designated by the employer on the notice required under section 7 of this act.

e. "Retaliatory action" means the discharge, suspension or demotion of an employee, or other adverse employment action taken against an employee in the terms and conditions of employment.

f. "Improper quality of patient care" means, with respect to patient care, any practice, procedure, action or failure to act of an employer that is a health care provider which violates any law or any rule, regulation or declaratory ruling adopted pursuant to law, or any professional code of ethics.

34:19–3. Retaliatory action prohibited

An employer shall not take any retaliatory action against an employee because the employee does any of the following:

a. Discloses, or threatens to disclose to a supervisor or to a public body an activity, policy or practice of the employer, or another employer, with whom there is a business relationship, that the employee reasonably believes:

(1) is in violation of a law, or a rule or regulation promulgated pursuant to law, including any violation involving deception of, or misrepresentation to, any shareholder, investor, client, patient, customer, employee, former employee, retiree or pensioner of the employer or any governmental entity, or, in the case of an employee who is a licensed or certified health care professional, reasonably believes constitutes improper quality of patient care; or

(2) is fraudulent or criminal, including any activity, policy or practice of deception or misrepresentation which the employee reasonably believes may defraud any shareholder, investor, client, patient, customer, employee, former employee, retiree or pensioner of the employer or any governmental entity;

b. Provides information to, or testifies before, any public body conducting an investigation, hearing or inquiry into any violation of law, or a rule or regulation promulgated pursuant to law by the employer, or another employer, with whom there is a business relationship, including any violation involving deception of, or misrepresentation to, any shareholder, investor, client, patient, customer, employee, former employee, retiree or pensioner of the employer or any governmental entity, or, in the case of an employee who is a licensed or certified health care professional, provides information to, or testifies before, any public body conducting an investigation, hearing or inquiry into the quality of patient care; or

c. Objects to, or refuses to participate in any activity, policy or practice which the employee reasonably believes:

(1) is in violation of a law, or a rule or regulation promulgated pursuant to law, including any violation involving deception of, or misrepresentation to, any shareholder, investor, client, patient, customer, employee, former employee, retiree or pensioner of the employer or any governmental entity, or, if the employee is a licensed or certified health care professional, constitutes improper quality of patient care;

(2) is fraudulent or criminal, including any activity, policy or practice of deception or misrepresentation which the employee reasonably believes may defraud any shareholder, investor, client, patient, customer, employee, former employee, retiree or pensioner of the employer or any governmental entity; or

(3) is incompatible with a clear mandate of public policy concerning the public health, safety or welfare or protection of the environment.

34:19–4. Written notice required

The protection against retaliatory action provided by this act pertaining to disclosure to a public body shall not apply to an employee who makes a disclosure to a public body unless the employee has brought the activity, policy or practice in violation of a law, or a rule or regulation promulgated pursuant to law to the attention of a supervisor of the employee by written notice and has afforded the employer a reasonable opportunity to correct the activity, policy or practice. Disclosure shall not be required where the employee is reasonably certain that the activity, policy or practice is known to one or more supervisors of the employer or where the employee reasonably fears physical harm as a result of the disclosure provided, however, that the situation is emergency in nature.

34:19–5. Civil action, jury trial; remedies

Upon a violation of any of the provisions of this act, an aggrieved employee or former employee may, within one year, institute a civil action in a court of competent jurisdiction. Upon the application of any party, a jury trial shall be directed to try the validity of any claim under this act specified in the suit. All remedies available in common law tort actions shall be available to prevailing plaintiffs. These remedies are in addition to any legal or equitable relief provided by this act or any other statute. The court shall also order, where appropriate and to the fullest extent possible:

a. An injunction to restrain any violation of this act which is continuing at the time that the court issues its order;

b. The reinstatement of the employee to the same position held before the retaliatory action, or to an equivalent position;

c. The reinstatement of full fringe benefits and seniority rights;

d. The compensation for all lost wages, benefits and other remuneration; and

e. The payment by the employer of reasonable costs, and attorney's fees.

In Addition, the court or jury may order: the assessment of a civil fine of not more than $10,000 for the first violation of the act and not more than $20,000 for each subsequent violation, which shall be paid to the State Treasurer for deposit in the General Fund; punitive damages; or both a civil fine and punitive damages. In determining the amount of punitive damages, the court or jury shall consider not only the amount of compensatory damages awarded to the employee, but also the amount of all damages caused to shareholders, investors, clients, patients, customers, employees, former employees, retirees or pensioners of the employer, or to the public or any governmental entity, by the activities, policies or practices of the employer which the employee disclosed, threatened to disclose, provided testimony regarding, objected to, or refused to participate in.

34:19–6. Fee, costs to employer

A court, upon notice of motion in accordance with the Rules Governing the Courts of the State of New Jersey, may also order that reasonable attorneys' fees and court costs be awarded to an employer if the court determines that an action brought by an employee under this act was without basis in law or in fact. However, an employee shall not be assessed attorneys' fees under this section if, after exercising reasonable and diligent efforts after filing a suit, the employee files a voluntary dismissal concerning the employer, within a reasonable time after determining that the employer would not be found to be liable for damages.

34:19–7. Posting of notices

An employer shall conspicuously display, and annually distribute to all employees, written or electronic notices of its employees' protections, obligations, rights and procedures under this act, and use other appropriate means to keep its employees so informed. Each notice posted or distributed pursuant to this section shall be in English, Spanish and at the employer's discretion, any other language spoken by the majority of the employer's employees. The notice shall include the name of the person or persons the employer has designated to receive written notifications pursuant to section 4 of this act. The Commissioner of Labor and Workforce Development shall make available to employers a text of a notice fulfilling the requirements of this section and provide copies of the notice suitable for display and distribution to any employers who request the copies, charging them as much as is needed to pay the costs of the department. The commissioner shall also provide notices printed in a language other than English and Spanish, at the request of the employer.

The requirement that an employer annually distribute to all employees written notices of the protections, obligations, rights and procedures provided to the employees by the provisions of P.L. 1986, c. 105 (C.34:19–1 et seq.) shall not apply to any employer who has less than 10 employees.

34:19–8. Other rights, remedies unaffected

Nothing in this act shall be deemed to diminish the rights, privileges, or remedies of any employee under any other federal or State law or regulation or under any collective bargaining agreement or employment contract; except that the institution of an action in accordance with this act shall be deemed a waiver of the rights and remedies available under any other contract, collective bargaining agreement, State law, rule or regulation or under the common law.

34:19–9. Definitions relative to employer communications on religious, political matters to employees

For the purposes of this act:

"Employer" means a person engaged in business who has employees, including the State and any political subdivision or other instrumentality of the State.

"Employee" means any person engaged in service to an employer for wages, salary or other compensation.

"Political matters" include political party affiliation and decisions to join or not join or participate in any lawful political, social, or community organization or activity.

34:19–10. Required participation by employee in meetings, communications prohibited; exception

No employer or employer's agent, representative or designee may, except as provided in section 3 of this act, require its employees to attend an employer-sponsored meeting or participate in any communications with the employer or its agents or representatives, the purpose of which is to communicate the employer's opinion about religious or political matters.

This act shall not be construed as prohibiting an employer from permitting its employees to voluntarily attend employer-sponsored meetings or providing other communications to the employees, if the employer notifies the employees that they may refuse to attend the meetings or accept the communications without penalty.

34:19–11. Permitted communication about religious, political matters

a. An employer or its agent, representative or designee may communicate to employees information about religious or political matters that the employer is required by law to communicate, but only to the extent required by law.

b. Nothing in this act shall prohibit:

(1) A religious organization from requiring its employees to attend an employer-sponsored meeting or to participate in any communications with the employer or its agents or representatives, the purpose of which is to communicate the employer's religious beliefs, practices or tenets;

(2) A political organization or party from requiring its employees to attend an employer-sponsored meeting or to participate in any communications with the employer or its agents or representatives, the purpose of which is to communicate the employer's political tenets or purposes; or

(3) An educational institution from requiring a student or instructor to attend lectures on political or religious matters that are part of the regular course work at the institution.

34:19–12. Retaliation against complaining employee prohibited

No employer or employer's agent, representative or designee shall discharge, discipline or otherwise penalize or threaten to discharge, discipline or otherwise penalize any employee because the employee, or a person acting on behalf of the employee, makes a good faith report, verbally or in writing, of a violation or suspected violation of this act.

34:19–13. Civil action by aggrieved employee

Any aggrieved employee may enforce the provisions of this act by means of a civil action brought no later than ninety days after the date of the alleged violation in a court of competent jurisdiction. The court shall award a prevailing employee all appropriate relief, including any of the following which are applicable to the violation:

a. A restraining order against any continuing violation;

b. The reinstatement of the employee to the employee's former position or an equivalent position and the reestablishment of any employee benefits and seniority rights;

c. The payment of any lost wages, benefits or other remuneration; and

d. The payment of reasonable attorneys' fees and costs of the action.

In addition, the court may award the prevailing employee punitive damages not greater than treble damages, or an assessment of a civil fine of not more than $1,000 for a first violation of the act and not more than $5,000 for each subsequent violation, which shall be paid to the State Treasurer for deposit in the General Fund.

34:19–14. Construction of act

Nothing in this act shall be construed to limit an employee's right to bring a common law cause of action against an employer for wrongful termination or to diminish or impair the rights of a person under any collective bargaining agreement.

Worker Adjustment and Retraining Notification Act (Title 29 U.S.C.)

§ 2101. Definitions; exclusions from definition of loss of employment

(a) Definitions

As used in this chapter:

(1) the term "employer" means any business enterprise that employs—

(A) 100 or more employees, excluding part-time employees; or

(B) 100 or more employees who in the aggregate work at least 4,000 hours per week (exclusive of hours of overtime);

(2) the term "plant closing" means the permanent or temporary shutdown of a single site of employment, or one or more facilities or operating units within a single site of employment, if the shutdown results in an employment loss at the single site of employment during any 30-day period for 50 or more employees excluding any part-time employees;

(3) the term "mass layoff" means a reduction in force which:

(A) is not the result of a plant closing; and

(B) results in an employment loss at the single site of employment during any 30-day period for:

(i)(I) at least 33 percent of the employees (excluding any part-time employees); and

(II) at least 50 employees (excluding any part-time employees); or

(ii) at least 500 employees (excluding any part-time employees);

(4) the term "representative" means an exclusive representative of employees within the meaning of section 159(a) or 158(f) of this title or section 152 of Title 45;

(5) the term "affected employees" means employees who may reasonably be expected to experience an employment loss as a consequence of a proposed plant closing or mass layoff by their employer;

(6) subject to subsection (b) of this section, the term "employment loss" means (A) an employment termination, other than a discharge for cause, voluntary departure, or retirement, (B) a layoff exceeding 6 months, or (C) a reduction in hours of work of more than 50 percent during each month of any 6-month period;

(7) the term "unit of local government" means any general purpose political subdivision of a State which has the power to levy taxes and spend funds, as well as general corporate and police powers; and

(8) the term "part-time employee" means an employee who is employed for an average of fewer than 20 hours per week or who has been employed for fewer than 6 of the 12 months preceding the date on which notice is required.

(b) Exclusions from definition of employment loss

(1) In the case of a sale of part or all of an employer's business, the seller shall be responsible for providing notice for any plant closing or mass layoff in accordance with section 2102 of this title, up to and including the effective date of the sale. After the effective date of the sale of part or all of an employer's business, the purchaser shall be responsible for providing notice for any plant closing or mass layoff in accordance with section 2102 of this title. Notwithstanding any other provision of this chapter, any person who is an employee of the seller (other than a part-time employee) as of the effective date of the sale shall be considered an employee of the purchaser immediately after the effective date of the sale.

(2) Notwithstanding subsection (a)(6) of this section, an employee may not be considered to have experienced an employment loss if the closing or layoff is the result of the relocation or consolidation of part or all of the employer's business and, prior to the closing or layoff:

(A) the employer offers to transfer the employee to a different site of employment within a reasonable commuting distance with no more than a 6-month break in employment; or

(B) the employer offers to transfer the employee to any other site of employment regardless of distance with no more than a 6-month break in employment, and the employee accepts within 30 days of the offer or of the closing or layoff, whichever is later.

§ 2102. Notice required before plant closings and mass layoffs

(a) Notice to employees, state dislocated worker units, and local governments

An employer shall not order a plant closing or mass layoff until the end of a 60-day period after the employer serves written notice of such an order—

(1) to each representative of the affected employees as of the time of the notice or, if there is no such representative at that time, to each affected employee; and

(2) to the State or entity designated by the State to carry out rapid response activities under section 3174(a)(2)(A) of this title, and the chief elected official of the unit of local government within such closing or layoff is to occur.

If there is more than one such unit, the unit of local government which the employer shall notify is the unit of local government to which the employer pays the highest taxes for the year preceding the year for which the determination is made.

(b) Reduction of notification period

(1) An employer may order the shutdown of a single site of employment before the conclusion of the 60-day period if as of the time that notice would have been required the employer was actively seeking capital or business which, if obtained, would have enabled the employer to avoid or postpone the shutdown and the employer reasonably and in good faith believed that giving the notice required would have precluded the employer from obtaining the needed capital or business.

(2)(A) An employer may order a plant closing or mass layoff before the conclusion of the 60-day period if the closing or mass layoff is caused by business circumstances that were not reasonably foreseeable as of the time that notice would have been required.

(B) No notice under this chapter shall be required if the plant closing or mass layoff is due to any form of natural disaster, such as a flood, earthquake, or the drought currently ravaging the farmlands of the United States.

(3) An employer relying on this subsection shall give as much notice as is practicable and at that time shall give a brief statement of the basis for reducing the notification period.

(c) Extension of layoff period

A layoff of more than 6 months which, at its outset, was announced to be a layoff of 6 months or less, shall be treated as an employment loss under this chapter unless—

(1) the extension beyond 6 months is caused by business circumstances (including unforeseeable changes in price or cost) not reasonably foreseeable at the time of the initial layoff; and

(2) notice is given at the time it becomes reasonably foreseeable that the extension beyond 6 months will be required.

(d) Determinations with respect to employment loss

For purposes of this section, in determining whether a plant closing or mass layoff has occurred or will occur, employment losses for 2 or more groups at a single site of employment, each of which is less than the minimum number of employees specified in section 2101(a)(2) or (3) of this title but which in the aggregate exceed that minimum number, and which occur within any 90-day period shall be considered to be a plant closing or mass layoff unless the employer demonstrates that the employment losses are the result of separate and distinct actions and causes and are not an attempt by the employer to evade the requirements of this chapter.

§ 2103. Exemptions

This chapter shall not apply to a plant closing or mass layoff if—

(1) the closing is of a temporary facility or the closing or layoff is the result of the completion of a particular project or undertaking, and the affected employees were hired with the understanding that their employment was limited to the duration of the facility or the project or undertaking; or

(2) the closing or layoff constitutes a strike or constitutes a lockout not intended to evade the requirements of this chapter. Nothing in this chapter shall require an employer to serve written notice pursuant to section 2102(a) of this title when permanently replacing a person who is deemed to be an economic striker under the National Labor Relations Act [29 U.S.C.A § 151 et seq.]: Provided, that nothing in this chapter shall be deemed to validate or invalidate any judicial or administrative ruling relating to the hiring of permanent replacements for economic strikers under the National Labor Relations Act.

§ 2104. Administration and enforcement of requirements

(a) Civil actions against employers

(1) Any employer who orders a plant closing or mass layoff in violation of section 2102 of this title shall be liable to each aggrieved employee who suffers an employment loss as a result of such closing or layoff for—

(A) back pay for each day of violation at a rate of compensation not less than the higher of:

(i) the average regular rate received by such employee during the last 3 years of the employee's employment; or

(ii) the final regular rate received by such employee; and

(B) benefits under an employee benefit plan described in section 1002(3) of this title, including the cost of medical expenses incurred during the employment loss which would have been covered under an employee benefit plan if the employment loss had not occurred.

Such liability shall be calculated for the period of the violation, up to a maximum of 60 days, but in no event for more than one-half the number of days the employee was employed by the employer.

(2) The amount for which an employer is liable under paragraph (1) shall be reduced by—

(A) any wages paid by the employer to the employee for the period of the violation;

(B) any voluntary and unconditional payment by the employer to the employee that is not required by any legal obligation; and

(C) any payment by the employer to a third party or trustee (such as premiums for health benefits or payments to a defined contribution pension plan) on behalf of and attributable to the employee for the period of the violation.

In addition, any liability incurred under paragraph (1) with respect to a defined benefit pension plan may be reduced by crediting the employee with service for all purposes under such a plan for the period of the violation.

(3) Any employer who violates the provisions of section 2102 of this title with respect to a unit of local government shall be subject to a civil penalty of not more than $500 for each day of such violation, except that such penalty shall not apply if the employer pays to each aggrieved employee the amount for which the employer is liable to that employee within 3 weeks from the date the employer orders the shutdown or layoff.

(4) If an employer which has violated this chapter proves to the satisfaction of the court that the act or omission that violated this chapter was in good faith and that the employer had reasonable grounds for believing that the act or omission was not a violation of this chapter the court may, in its discretion, reduce the amount of the liability or penalty provided for in this section.

(5) A person seeking to enforce such liability, including a representative of employees or a unit of local government aggrieved under paragraph (1) or (3), may sue either for such person or for other persons similarly situated, or both, in any district court of the United States for any district in which the violation is alleged to have occurred, or in which the employer transacts business.

(6) In any such suit, the court, in its discretion, may allow the prevailing party a reasonable attorney's fee as part of the costs.

(7) For purposes of this subsection, the term, "aggrieved employee" means an employee who has worked for the employer ordering the plant closing or mass layoff and who, as a result of the failure by the employer to comply with section 2102 of this title, did not receive timely notice either directly or through his or her representative as required by section 2102 of this title.

(b) Exclusivity of remedies

The remedies provided for in this section shall be the exclusive remedies for any violation of this chapter. Under this chapter, a Federal court shall not have authority to enjoin a plant closing or mass layoff.

§ 2105. Procedures in addition to other rights of employees

The rights and remedies provided to employees by this chapter are in addition to, and not in lieu of, any other contractual or statutory rights and remedies of the employees, and are not intended to alter or affect such rights and remedies, except that the period of notification required by this chapter shall run concurrently with any period of notification required by contract or by any other statute.

§ 2106. Procedures encouraged where not required

It is the sense of Congress that an employer who is not required to comply with the notice requirements of section 2102 of this title should, to the extent possible, provide notice to its employees about a proposal to close a plant or permanently reduce its workforce.

§ 2107. Authority to prescribe regulations

(a) The Secretary of Labor shall prescribe such regulations as may be necessary to carry out this chapter. Such regulations shall, at a minimum, include interpretative regulations describing the methods by which employers may provide for appropriate service of notice as required by this chapter.

(b) The mailing of notice to an employee's last known address or inclusion of notice in the employee's paycheck will be considered acceptable methods for fulfillment of the employer's obligation to give notice to each affected employee under this chapter.

§ 2108. Effect on other laws

The giving of notice pursuant to this chapter, if done in good faith compliance with this chapter, shall not constitute a violation of the National Labor Relations Act [29 U.S.C.A. § 151 et seq.] or the Railway Labor Act [45 U.S.C.A. § 151 et seq.].

FAIR LABOR STANDARDS ACT (TITLE 29 U.S.C.)

§ 201. Short title

This chapter may be cited as the "Fair Labor Standards Act of 1938".

§ 202. Congressional finding and declaration of policy

(a) The Congress finds that the existence, in industries engaged in commerce or in the production of goods for commerce, of labor conditions detrimental to the maintenance of the minimum standard of living necessary for health, efficiency, and general well-being of workers

(1) causes commerce and the channels and instrumentalities of commerce to be used to spread and perpetuate such labor conditions among the workers of the several States;

(2) burdens commerce and the free flow of goods in commerce;

(3) constitutes an unfair method of competition in commerce;

(4) leads to labor disputes burdening and obstructing commerce and the free flow of goods in commerce; and

(5) interferes with the orderly and fair marketing of goods in commerce. That Congress further finds that the employment of persons in domestic service in households affects commerce.

(b) It is declared to be the policy of this chapter, through the exercise by Congress of its power to regulate commerce among the several States and with foreign nations, to correct and as rapidly as practicable to eliminate the conditions above referred to in such industries without substantially curtailing employment or earning power.

§ 203. Definitions

As used in this Act:

(a) "Person" means an individual, partnership, association, corporation, business trust, legal representative, or any organized group of persons.

(b) "Commerce" means trade, commerce, transportation, transmission, or communication among the several States or between any State and any place outside thereof.

(c) "State" means any State of the United States or the District of Columbia or any Territory or possession of the United States.

(d) "Employer" includes any person acting directly or indirectly in the interest of an employer in relation to an employee and includes a public agency, but does not include any labor organization (other than when acting as an employer) or anyone acting in the capacity of officer or agent of such labor organization.

(e)(1) Except as provided in paragraphs (2), (3), and (4), the term "employee" means any individual employed by an employer.

(2) In the case of an individual employed by a public agency, such term means—

(A) any individual employed by the Government of the United States:

(i) as a civilian in the military departments (as defined in section 102 of title 5),

(ii) in any executive agency (as defined in section 105 of such title),

(iii) in any unit of the judicial branch of the Government which has positions in the competitive service,

(iv) in a nonappropriated fund instrumentality under the jurisdiction of the Armed Forces,

(v) in the Library of Congress, or

(vi) the Government Printing Office;

(B) any individual employed by the United States Postal Service or the Postal Regulatory Commission; and

(C) any individual employed by a State, political subdivision of a State, or an interstate governmental agency, other than such an individual—

(i) who is not subject to the civil service laws of the State, political subdivision, or agency which employs him; and

(ii) who—

(I) holds a public elective office of that State, political subdivision, or agency,

(II) is selected by the holder of such an office to be a member of his personal staff,

(III) is appointed by such an officeholder to serve on a policymaking level,

(IV) is an immediate adviser to such an officeholder with respect to the constitutional or legal powers of his office, or

(V) is an employee in the legislative branch or legislative body of that State, political subdivision, or agency and is not employed by the legislative library of such State, political subdivision, or agency.

(3) For purposes of subsection (u) of this section, such term does not include any individual employed by an employer engaged in agriculture if such individual is the parent, spouse, child, or other member of the employer's immediate family.

(4)(A) The term "employee" does not include any individual who volunteers to perform services for a public agency which is a State, a political subdivision of a State, or an interstate governmental agency, if:

(i) the individual receives no compensation or is paid expenses, reasonable benefits, or a nominal fee to perform the services for which the individual volunteered; and

(ii) such services are not the same type of services which the individual is employed to perform for such public agency.

(B) An employee of a public agency which is a State, political subdivision of a State, or an interstate governmental agency may volunteer to perform services for any other State, political subdivision, or interstate governmental agency, including a State, political subdivision or agency with which the employing State, political subdivision, or agency has a mutual aid agreement.

(5) The term "employee" does not include individuals who volunteer their services solely for humanitarian purposes to private non-profit food banks and who receive from the food banks groceries.

(f) "Agriculture" includes farming in all its branches and among other things includes the cultivation and tillage of the soil, dairying, the production, cultivation, growing, and harvesting of any agricultural or horticultural commodities (including commodities defined as agricultural commodities in section 1141j(g) of Title 12), the raising of livestock, bees, fur-bearing animals, or poultry, and any practices (including any forestry or lumbering operations) performed by a farmer or on a farm as incident to or in conjunction with such farming operations, including preparation for market, delivery to storage or to market or to carriers for transportation to market.

(g) "Employ" includes to suffer or permit to work.

(h) "Industry" means a trade, business, industry, or other activity, or branch or group thereof, in which individuals are gainfully employed.

(i) "Goods" means goods (including ships and marine equipment), wares, products, commodities, merchandise, or articles or subjects of commerce of any character, or any part or ingredient thereof, but does not include goods after their delivery into the actual physical possession of the ultimate consumer thereof other than a producer, manufacturer or processor thereof.

(j) "Produced" means produced, manufactured, mined, handled, or in any other manner worked on in any State; and for the purposes of this chapter an employee shall be deemed to have been engaged in the production of goods if such employee was employed in producing, manufacturing, mining, handling, transporting, or in any other manner working on such goods, or in any closely related process or occupation directly essential to the production thereof, in any State.

(k) "Sale" or "sell" includes any sale, exchange, contract to sell, consignment for sale, shipment for sale, or other disposition.

(*l*) "Oppressive child labor" means a condition of employment under which (1) any employee under the age of sixteen years is employed by an employer (other than a parent or a person standing in place of a parent employing his own child or a child in his custody under the age of sixteen years in an occupation other than manufacturing or mining or an occupation found by the Secretary of Labor to be particularly hazardous for the employment of children between the ages of sixteen and eighteen years or detrimental to their health or well-being) in any occupation, or (2) any employee between the ages of sixteen and eighteen years is employed by an employer in any occupation which the Secretary of Labor shall find and by order declare to be particularly hazardous for the employment of children between such ages or detrimental to their health or well-being; but oppressive child labor shall not be deemed to exist by virtue of the employment in any occupation of any person with respect to whom the employer shall have on file an unexpired certificate issued and held pursuant to regulations of the Secretary of Labor certifying that such person is above the oppressive child-labor age. The Secretary of Labor shall provide by regulation or by order that the employment of employees between the ages of fourteen and sixteen years in occupations other than manufacturing and mining shall not be deemed to constitute oppressive child labor if and to the extent that the Secretary of Labor determines that such employment is confined to periods which will not interfere with their schooling and to conditions which will not interfere with their health and well-being.

(m)(1) "Wage" paid to any employee includes the reasonable cost, as determined by the Administrator, to the employer of furnishing such employee with board, lodging, or other facilities, if such board, lodging, or other facilities are customarily furnished by such employer to his employees: Provided, That the cost of board, lodging, or other facilities shall not be included as a part of the wage paid to any employee to the extent it is excluded therefrom under the terms of a bona fide collective-bargaining agreement applicable to the particular employee: Provided further, That the Secretary is authorized to determine the fair value of such board, lodging, or other facilities for defined classes of employees and in defined areas, based on average cost to the employer or to groups of employers similarly situated, or average value to groups of employees, or other appropriate measures of fair value. Such evaluations, where applicable and pertinent, shall be used in lieu of actual measure of cost in determining the wage paid to any employee.

(2)(A) In determining the wage an employer is required to pay a tipped employee, the amount paid such employee by the employee's employer shall be an amount equal to—

(i) the cash wage paid such employee which for purposes of such determination shall be not less than the cash wage required to be paid such an employee on August 20, 1996; and

(ii) an additional amount on account of the tips received by such employee which amount is equal to the difference between the wage specified in clause (i) and the wage in effect under section 206(a)(1) of this title.

The additional amount on account of tips may not exceed the value of the tips actually received by an employee. The preceding 2 sentences shall not apply with respect to any tipped employee unless such employee has been informed by the employer of the provisions of this subsection, and all tips received by such employee have been retained by the employee, except that this subsection shall not be construed to prohibit the pooling of tips among employees who customarily and regularly receive tips.

(B) An employer may not keep tips received by its employees for any purposes, including allowing managers or supervisors to keep any portion of employees' tips, regardless of whether or not the employer takes a tip credit.

(n) "Resale" shall not include the sale of goods to be used in residential or farm building construction, repair, or maintenance: Provided, That the sale is recognized as a bona fide retail sale in the industry.

(*o*) Hours Worked. In determining for the purposes of sections 206 and 207 the hours for which an employee is employed, there shall be excluded any time spent in changing clothes or washing at the beginning or end of each workday which was excluded from measured working time during the week involved by the express terms of or by custom or practice under a bona fide collective-bargaining agreement applicable to the particular employee.

(p) "American vessel" includes any vessel which is documented or numbered under the laws of the United States.

(q) "Secretary" means the Secretary of Labor.

(r)(1) "Enterprise" means the related activities performed (either through unified operation or common control) by any person or persons for a common business purpose, and includes all such activities whether performed in one or more establishments or by one or more corporate or other organizational units including departments of an establishment operated through leasing arrangements, but shall not include the related activities performed for such enterprise by an independent contractor. Within the meaning of this subsection, a retail or service establishment which is under independent ownership shall not be deemed to be so operated or controlled as to be other than a separate and distinct enterprise by reason of any arrangement, which includes, but is not necessarily limited to, an agreement, (A) that it will sell, or sell only, certain goods specified by a particular manufacturer, distributor, or advertiser, or (B) that it will join with other such establishments in the same industry for the purpose of collective purchasing, or (C) that it will have the exclusive right to sell the goods or use the brand name of a manufacturer, distributor, or advertiser within a specified area, or by reason of the fact that it occupies premises leased to it by a person who also leases premises to other retail or service establishments.

(2) For purposes of paragraph (1), the activities performed by any person or persons:

(A) in connection with the operation of a hospital, an institution primarily engaged in the care of the sick, the aged, the mentally ill or defective who reside on the premises of such institution, a school for mentally or physically handicapped or gifted children, a preschool, elementary or secondary school, or an institution of higher education (regardless of whether or not such hospital, institution, or school is operated for profit or not for profit), or

(B) in connection with the operation of a street, suburban or interurban electric railway, or local trolley or motorbus carrier, if the rates and services of such railway or carrier are subject to regulation by a State or local agency (regardless of whether or not such railway or carrier is public or private or operated for profit or not for profit), or

(C) in connection with the activities of a public agency, shall be deemed to be activities performed for a business purpose.

(s)(1) "Enterprise engaged in commerce or in the production of goods for commerce" means an enterprise that:

(A)(i) has employees engaged in commerce or in the production of goods for commerce, or that has employees handling, selling, or otherwise working on goods or materials that have been moved in or produced for commerce by any person; and

(ii) is an enterprise whose annual gross volume of sales made or business done is not less than $500,000 (exclusive of excise taxes at the retail level that are separately stated);

(B) is engaged in the operation of a hospital, an institution primarily engaged in the care of the sick, the aged, or the mentally ill or defective who reside on the premises of such institution, a school for mentally or physically handicapped or gifted children, a preschool, elementary or secondary school, or an institution of higher education (regardless of whether or not such hospital, institution, or school is public or private or operated for profit or not for profit); or

(C) is an activity of a public agency.

(2) Any establishment that has as its only regular employees the owner thereof or the parent, spouse, child, or other member of the immediate family of such owner shall not be considered to be an enterprise engaged in commerce or in the production of goods for commerce or a part of such an enterprise. The sales of such an establishment shall not be included for the purpose of determining the annual gross volume of sales of any enterprise for the purpose of this subsection.

(t) "Tipped employee" means any employee engaged in an occupation in which he customarily and regularly receives more than $30 a month in tips.

(u) "Man-day" means any day during which an employee performs any agricultural labor for not less than one hour.

(v) "Elementary school" means a day or residential school which provides elementary education, as determined under State law.

(w) "Secondary school" means a day or residential school which provides secondary education, as determined under State law.

(x) "Public agency" means the Government of the United States; the government of a State or political subdivision thereof; any agency of the United States (including the United States Postal Service and Postal Regulatory Commission), a State, or a political subdivision of a State; or any interstate governmental agency.

(y) "Employee in fire protection activities" means an employee, including a firefighter, paramedic, emergency medical technician, rescue worker, ambulance personnel, or hazardous materials worker, who—

(1) is trained in fire suppression, has the legal authority and responsibility to engage in fire suppression, and is employed by a fire department of a municipality, county, fire district, or State; and

(2) is engaged in the prevention, control, and extinguishment of fires or response to emergency situations where life, property, or the environment is at risk.

§ 204. Administration

(a) Creation of Wage and Hour Division in Department of Labor; Administrator

There is created in the Department of Labor a Wage and Hour Division which shall be under the direction of an Administrator, to be known as the Administrator of the Wage and Hour Division (in this chapter referred to as the "Administrator"). The Administrator shall be appointed by the President, by and with the advice and consent of the Senate.

(b) Appointment, selection, classification, and promotion of employees by Administrator

The Administrator may, subject to the civil-service laws, appoint such employees as he deems necessary to carry out his functions and duties under this chapter and shall fix their compensation in accordance with chapter 51 and subchapter III of chapter 53 of Title 5. The Administrator may establish and utilize such regional, local, or other agencies, and utilize such voluntary and uncompensated services, as may from time to time be needed. Attorneys appointed under this section may appear for and represent the Administrator in any litigation, but all such litigation shall be subject to the direction and control of the Attorney General. In the appointment, selection, classification, and promotion of officers and employees of the Administrator, no political test or qualification shall be permitted or given consideration, but all such appointments and promotions shall be given and made on the basis of merit and efficiency.
* * *

§ 205. [Repealed]

§ 206. Minimum wage

(a) Employees engaged in commerce; home workers in Puerto Rico and Virgin Islands; employees in American Samoa; seamen on American vessels; agricultural employees

Every employer shall pay to each of his employees who in any workweek is engaged in commerce or in the production of goods for commerce, or is employed in an enterprise engaged in commerce or in the production of goods for commerce, wages at the following rates:

(1) except as otherwise provided in this section, not less than—

(A) $5.85 an hour, beginning on the 60th day after May 25, 2007;

(B) $6.55 an hour, beginning 12 months after that 60th day; and

(C) $7.25 an hour, beginning 24 months after that 60th day;

(2) if such employee is a home worker in Puerto Rico or the Virgin Islands, not less than the minimum piece rate prescribed by regulation or order; or, if no such minimum piece rate is in effect, any piece rate adopted by such employer which shall yield, to the proportion or class of employees prescribed by regulation or order, not less than the applicable minimum hourly wage rate. Such minimum piece rates or employer piece rates shall be commensurate with, and shall be paid in lieu of, the minimum hourly wage rate applicable under the provisions of this section. The Administrator, or his authorized representative, shall have power to make such regulations or orders as are necessary or appropriate to carry out any of the provisions of this paragraph, including the power without limiting the generality of the foregoing, to define any operation or occupation which is performed by such home work employees in Puerto Rico or the Virgin Islands; to establish minimum piece rates for any operation or occupation so defined; to prescribe the method and procedure for ascertaining and promulgating minimum piece rates; to prescribe standards for employer piece rates, including the proportion or class of employees who shall receive not less than the minimum hourly wage rates; to define the term "home worker"; and to prescribe the conditions under which employers, agents, contractors, and subcontractors shall cause goods to be produced by home workers;

(3) if such employee is employed as a seaman on an American vessel, not less than the rate which will provide to the employee, for the period covered by the wage payment, wages equal to compensation at the hourly rate prescribed by paragraph (1) of this subsection for all hours during such period when he was actually on duty (including periods aboard ship when the employee was on watch or was, at the direction of a superior officer, performing work or standing by, but not including off-duty periods which are provided pursuant to the employment agreement); or

(4) if such employee is employed in agriculture, not less than the minimum wage rate in effect under paragraph (1) after December 31, 1977.

(b) Additional applicability to employees pursuant to subsequent amendatory provisions

Every employer shall pay to each of his employees (other than an employee to whom subsection (a)(5) applies) who in any workweek is engaged in commerce or in the production of goods for commerce, or is employed in an enterprise engaged in commerce or in the production of goods for commerce, and who in such workweek is brought within the purview of this section by the amendments made to this chapter by the Fair Labor Standards Amendments of 1966, title IX of the Education Amendments of 1972, or the Fair Labor Standards Amendments of 1974, wages at the following rate: Effective after December 31, 1977, not less than the minimum wage rate in effect under subsection (a)(1).

(c) Repealed. Pub.L. 104–188, [Title II], § 2104(c), Aug. 20, 1996, 110 Stat. 1929

(d) Prohibition of sex discrimination

(1) No employer having employees subject to any provisions of this section shall discriminate, within any establishment in which such employees are employed, between employees on the basis of sex by paying wages to employees in such establishment at a rate less than the rate at which he pays wages to employees of the opposite sex in such establishment for equal work on jobs the performance of which requires equal skill, effort, and responsibility, and which are performed under similar working conditions, except where such payment is made pursuant to (i) a seniority system; (ii) a merit system; (iii) a system which measures earnings by quantity or quality of production; or (iv) a differential based on any other factor other than sex: Provided, that an employer who is paying a wage rate differential in violation of this subsection shall not, in order to comply with the provisions of this subsection, reduce the wage rate of any employee.

(2) No labor organization, or its agents, representing employees of an employer having employees subject to any provisions of this section shall cause or attempt to cause such an employer to discriminate against an employee in violation of paragraph (1) of this subsection.

(3) For purposes of administration and enforcement, any amounts owing to any employee which have been withheld in violation of this subsection shall be deemed to be unpaid minimum wages or unpaid overtime compensation under this chapter.

(4) As used in this subsection, the term "labor organization" means any organization of any kind, or any agency or employee representation committee or plan, in which employees participate and which exists for the purpose, in whole or in part, or dealing with employers concerning grievances, labor disputes, wages, rates of pay, hours of employment, or conditions of work.

(e) Employees of employers providing contract services to United States

(1) Notwithstanding the provisions of section 213 of this title (except subsections (a)(1) and (f) thereof), every employer providing any contract services (other than linen supply services) under a contract with the United States or any subcontract thereunder shall pay to each of his employees whose rate of pay is not governed by chapter 67 of Title 41) or to whom subsection (a)(1) of this section is not applicable, wages at rates not less than the rates provided for in subsection (b) of this section.

(2) Notwithstanding the provisions of section 213 of this title (except subsections (a)(1) and (f) thereof) and the provisions of chapter 67 of Title 41, every employer in an establishment providing linen supply services to the United States under a contract with the United States or any subcontract thereunder shall pay to each of his employees in such establishment wages at rates not less than those prescribed in subsection (b), except that if more than 50 per centum of the gross annual dollar volume of sales made or business done by such establishment is derived from providing such linen supply services under any such contracts or subcontracts, such employer shall pay to each of his employees in such establishment wages at rates not less than those prescribed in subsection (a)(1) of this section.

(f) Employees in domestic service.

Any employee:

(1) who in any workweek is employed in domestic service in a household shall be paid wages at a rate not less than the wage rate in effect under subsection (b) unless such employee's compensation for such service would not because of section 209(a)(6) of the Social Security Act constitute wages for the purposes of title II of such Act, or

(2) who in any workweek:

(A) is employed in domestic service in one or more households, and

(B) is so employed for more than 8 hours in the aggregate,

shall be paid wages for such employment in such workweek at a rate not less than the wage rate in effect under section (b).

(g) Newly Hired Employees who are less than 20 years old

(1) In lieu of the rate prescribed by subsection (a)(1) of this section, any employer may pay any employee of such employer, during the first 90 consecutive calendar days after such employee is initially employed by such employer, a wage which is not less than $4.25 an hour.

(2) In lieu of the rate prescribed by subsection (a)(1), the Governor of Puerto Rico, subject to the approval of the Financial Oversight and Management Board established pursuant to section 2121 of Title 48, may designate a time period not to exceed four years during which employers in Puerto Rico may pay employees who are initially employed after June 30, 2016, a wage which is not less than the wage described in paragraph (1). Notwithstanding the time period designated, such wage shall not continue in effect after such Board terminates in accordance with section 2149 of Title 48.

(3) No employer may take any action to displace employees (including partial displacements such as reduction in hours, wages, or employment benefits) for purposes of hiring individuals at the wage authorized in paragraph (1) or (2).

(4) Any employer who violates this subsection shall be considered to have violated section 215(a)(3) of this title.

(5) This subsection shall only apply to an employee who has not attained the age of 20 years, except in the case of the wage applicable in Puerto Rico, 25 years, until such times as the Board described in paragraph (2) terminates in accordance with section 2149 of Title 48.

§ 207. Maximum hours

(a) Employees engaged in interstate commerce; additional applicability to employees pursuant to subsequent amendatory provisions

(1) Except as otherwise provided in this section, no employer shall employ any of his employees who in any workweek is engaged in commerce or in the production of goods for commerce, or is employed in an enterprise engaged in commerce or in the production of goods for commerce, for a workweek longer than forty hours unless such employee receives compensation for his employment in excess of the hours above specified at a rate not less than one and one-half times the regular rate at which he is employed.

(2) No employer shall employ any of his employees who in any workweek is engaged in commerce or in the production of goods for commerce, or is employed in an enterprise engaged in commerce or in the production of goods for commerce, and who in such workweek is brought within the purview of this subsection by the amendments made to this chapter by the Fair Labor Standards Amendments of 1966:

(A) for a workweek longer than forty-four hours during the first year from the effective date of the Fair Labor Standards Amendments of 1966,

(B) for a workweek longer than forty-two hours during the second year from such date, or

(C) for a workweek longer than forty hours after the expiration of the second year from such date, unless such employee receives compensation for his employment in excess of the hours above specified at a rate not less than one and one-half times the regular rate at which he is employed.

(b) Employment pursuant to collective bargaining agreement; employment by independently owned and controlled local enterprise engaged in distribution of petroleum products

No employer shall be deemed to have violated subsection (a) of this section by employing any employee for a workweek in excess of that specified in such subsection without paying the compensation for overtime employment prescribed therein if such employee is so employed—

(1) in pursuance of an agreement, made as a result of collective bargaining by representatives of employees certified as bona fide by the National Labor Relations Board, which provides that no employee shall be employed more than one thousand and forty hours during any period of twenty-six consecutive weeks; or

(2) in pursuance of an agreement, made as a result of collective bargaining by representatives of employees certified as bona fide by the National Labor Relations Board, which provides that during a specified period of fifty-two consecutive weeks the employee shall be employed not more than two thousand two hundred and forty hours and shall be guaranteed not less than one thousand eight hundred and forty hours (or not less than forty-six weeks at the normal number of hours worked per week, but not less than thirty hours per week) and not more than two thousand and eighty hours of employment for which he shall receive compensation for all hours guaranteed or worked at rates not less than those applicable under the agreement to the work performed and for all hours in excess of the guaranty which are also in excess of the maximum workweek applicable to such employee under subsection (a) or two thousand and eighty in such period at rates not less than one and one-half times the regular rate at which he is employed; or

(3) by an independently owned and controlled local enterprise (including an enterprise with more than one bulk storage establishment) engaged in the wholesale or bulk distribution of petroleum products if—

(A) the annual gross volume of sales of such enterprise is less than $1,000,000 exclusive of excise taxes,

(B) more than 75 per centum of such enterprise's annual dollar volume of sales is made within the State in which such enterprise is located, and

(C) not more than 25 per centum of the annual dollar volume of sales of such enterprise is to customers who are engaged in the bulk distribution of such products for resale, and such employee receives compensation for employment in excess of forty hours in any work-week at a rate not less than one and one-half times the minimum wage rate applicable to him under section 206 of this title, and if such employee receives compensation for employment in excess of twelve hours in any workday, or for employment in excess of fifty-six hours in any workweek, as the case may be, at a rate not less than one and one-half times the regular rate at which he is employed.

(c), (d) [Repealed] Pub.L. 93–259, § 19(e), Apr. 8, 1974, 88 Stat. 66

(e) "Regular rate" defined

As used in this section the "regular rate" at which an employee is employed shall be deemed to include all remuneration for employment paid to, or on behalf of, the employee, but shall not be deemed to include—

(1) sums paid as gifts; payments in the nature of gifts made at Christmas time or on other special occasions, as a reward for service, the amounts of which are not measured by or dependent on hours worked, production, or efficiency;

(2) payments made for occasional periods when no work is performed due to vacation, holiday, illness, failure of the employer to provide sufficient work, or other similar cause; reasonable payments for traveling expenses, or other expenses, incurred by an employee in the furtherance of his employer's interests and properly reimbursable by the employer; and other similar payments to an employee which are not made as compensation for his hours of employment;

(3) Sums paid in recognition of services performed during a given period if either, (a) both the fact that payment is to be made and the amount of the payment are determined at the sole discretion of the employer at or near the end of the period and not pursuant to any prior contract, agreement, or promise causing the employee to expect such payments regularly; or (b) the payments are made pursuant to a bona fide profit-sharing plan or trust or bona fide thrift or savings plan, meeting the requirements of the Administrator set forth in appropriate regulations which he shall issue, having due regard among other relevant factors, to the extent to which the amounts paid to the employee are determined without regard to hours of work,

production, or efficiency; or (c) the payments are talent fees (as such talent fees are defined and delimited by regulations of the Administrator) paid to performers, including announcers, on radio and television programs;

(4) contributions irrevocably made by an employer to a trustee or third person pursuant to a bona fide plan for providing old-age, retirement, life, accident, or health insurance or similar benefits for employees;

(5) extra compensation provided by a premium rate paid for certain hours worked by the employee in any day or workweek because such hours are hours worked in excess of eight in a day or in excess of the maximum workweek applicable to such employee under subsection (a) of this section or in excess of the employee's normal working hours or regular working hours, as the case may be;

(6) extra compensation provided by a premium rate paid for work by the employee on Saturdays, Sundays, holidays, or regular days of rest, or on the sixth or seventh day of the workweek, where such premium rate is not less than one and one-half times the rate established in good faith for like work performed in nonovertime hours on other days;

(7) extra compensation provided by a premium rate paid to the employee, in pursuance of an applicable employment contract or collective-bargaining agreement, for work outside of the hours established in good faith by the contract or agreement as the basic, normal, or regular workday (not exceeding eight hours) or workweek (not exceeding the maximum workweek applicable to such employee under subsection (a) of this section), where such premium rate is not less than one and one-half times the rate established in good faith by the contract or agreement for like work performed during such workday or workweek; or

(8) any value or income derived from employer-provided grants or rights provided pursuant to a stock option, stock appreciation right, or bona fide employee stock purchase program which is not otherwise excludable under any of paragraphs (1) through (7) if—

(A) grants are made pursuant to a program, the terms and conditions of which are communicated to participating employees either at the beginning of the employee's participation in the program or at the time of the grant;

(B) in the case of stock options and stock appreciation rights, the grant or right cannot be exercisable for a period of at least 6 months after the time of grant (except that grants or rights may become exercisable because of an employee's death, disability, retirement, or a change in corporate ownership, or other circumstances permitted by regulation), and the exercise price is at least 85 percent of the fair market value of the stock at the time of grant;

(C) exercise of any grant or right is voluntary; and

(D) any determinations regarding the award of, and the amount of, employer-provided grants or rights that are based on performance are—

(i) made based upon meeting previously established performance criteria (which may include hours of work, efficiency, or productivity) of any business unit consisting of at least 10 employees or of a facility, except that, any determinations may be based on length of service or minimum schedule of hours or days of work; or

(ii) made based upon the past performance (which may include any criteria) of one or more employees in a given period so long as the determination is in the sole discretion of the employer and not pursuant to any prior contract.

(f) Employment necessitating irregular hours of work

No employer shall be deemed to have violated subsection (a) of this section by employing any employee for a workweek in excess of the maximum workweek applicable to such employee under subsection (a) of this section if such employee is employed pursuant to a bona fide individual contract, or pursuant to an agreement made as a result of collective bargaining by representatives of employees, if the duties of such employee necessitate irregular hours of work, and the contract or agreement (1) specifies a regular rate of pay of not less than the minimum hourly rate provided in subsection (a) or (b) of section 206 of this title (whichever may be applicable) and compensation at not less than one and one-half times such rate for all hours worked in excess of such maximum workweek, and (2) provides a weekly guaranty of pay for not more than sixty hours based on the rates so specified.

(g) Employment at piece rates

No employer shall be deemed to have violated subsection (a) of this section by employing any employee for a workweek in excess of the maximum workweek applicable to such employee under such subsection if, pursuant to an agreement or understanding arrived at between the employer and the employee before performance of the work, the amount paid to the employee for the number of hours worked by him in such workweek in excess of the maximum workweek applicable to such employee under such subsection—

(1) in the case of an employee employed at piece rates, is computed at piece rates not less than one and one-half times the bona fide piece rates applicable to the same work when performed during nonovertime hours; or

(2) in the case of an employee performing two or more kinds of work for which different hourly or piece rates have been established, is computed at rates not less than one and one-half times such bona fide rates applicable to the same work when performed during non-overtime hours; or

(3) is computed at a rate not less than one and one-half times the rate established by such agreement or understanding as the basic rate to be used in computing overtime compensation thereunder: Provided, that the rate so established shall be authorized by regulation by the Administrator as being substantially equivalent to the average hourly earnings of the employee, exclusive of overtime premiums, in the particular work over a representative period of time; and if (i) the employee's average hourly earnings for the workweek exclusive of payments described in paragraphs (1) through (7) of subsection (e) of this section are not less than the minimum hourly rate required by applicable law, and (ii) extra overtime compensation is properly computed and paid on other forms of additional pay required to be included in computing the regular rate.

(h) Credit toward minimum wage or overtime compensation of amounts excluded from regular rate

(1) Except as provided in paragraph (2), sums excluded from the regular rate pursuant to subsection (e) shall not be creditable toward wages required under section 6 or overtime compensation required under this section.

(2) Extra compensation paid as described in paragraphs (5), (6), and (7) of subsection (e) of this section shall be creditable toward overtime compensation payable pursuant to this section.

(i) Employment by retail or service establishment

No employer shall be deemed to have violated subsection (a) of this section by employing any employee at a retail or service establishment for a workweek in excess of the applicable workweek specified therein, if (1) the regular rate of pay of such employee is in excess of one and one-half times the minimum hourly rate applicable to him under section 206 of this title, and (2) more than half his compensation for a representative period (not less than one month) represents commissions on goods or services. In determining the proportion of compensation representing commissions, all earnings resulting from the application of a bona fide commission rate shall be deemed commissions on goods or services without regard to whether the computed commissions exceed the draw or guarantee.

(j) Employment in hospital or establishment engaged in care of sick, aged, or mentally ill

No employer engaged in the operation of a hospital or an establishment which is an institution primarily engaged in the care of the sick, the aged, or the mentally ill or defective who reside on the premises shall be deemed to have violated subsection (a) of this section if, pursuant to an agreement or understanding arrived at between the employer and the employee before performance of the work, a work period of fourteen consecutive days is accepted in lieu of the workweek of seven consecutive days for purposes of overtime computation and if, for his employment in excess of eight hours in any workday and in excess of eighty hours in such fourteen-day period, the employee receives compensation at a rate not less than one and one-half times the regular rate at which he is employed.

(k) Employment by public agency engaged in fire protection or law enforcement activities

No public agency shall be deemed to have violated subsection (a) of this section with respect to the employment of any employee in fire protection activities or any employee in law enforcement activities (including security personnel in correctional institutions) if:

(1) in a work period of 28 consecutive days the employee receives for tours of duty which in the aggregate exceed the lesser of (A) 216 hours, or (B) the average number of hours (as determined by the Secretary pursuant to section 6(c)(3) of the Fair Labor Standards Amendments of 1974) in tours of duty of employees engaged in such activities in work periods of 28 consecutive days in calendar year 1975; or

(2) in the case of such an employee to whom a work period of at least 7 but less than 28 days applies, in his work period the employee receives for tours of duty which in the aggregate exceed a number of hours which bears the same ratio to the number of consecutive days in his work period as 216 hours (or if lower, the number of hours referred to in clause(B) of paragraph (1)) bears to 28 days, compensation at a rate not less than one and one-half times the regular rate at which he is employed.

(*l*) Employment in domestic service in one or more households

No employer shall employ any employee in domestic service in one or more households for a workweek longer than forty hours unless such employee receives compensation for such employment in accordance with subsection (a) of this section.

(m) Employment in tobacco industry

For a period or periods of not more than fourteen workweeks in the aggregate in any calendar year, any employer may employ any employee for a workweek in excess of that specified in subsection (a) of this section without paying the compensation for overtime employment prescribed in such subsection, if such employee—

(1) is employed by such employer:

(A) to provide services (including stripping and grading) necessary and incidental to the sale at auction of green leaf tobacco of type 11, 12, 13, 14, 21, 22, 23, 24, 31, 35, 36, or 37 (as such types are defined by the Secretary of Agriculture), or in auction sale, buying, handling, stemming, redrying, packing, and storing of such tobacco,

(B) in auction sale, buying, handling, sorting, grading, packing, or storing green leaf tobacco of type 32 (as such type is defined by the Secretary of Agriculture), or

(C) in auction sale, buying, handling, stripping, sorting, grading, sizing, packing, or stemming prior to packing, of perishable cigar leaf tobacco of type 41, 42, 43, 44, 45, 46, 51, 52, 53, 54, 55, 61, or 62 (as such types are defined by the Secretary of Agriculture); and

(2) receives for:

(A) such employment by such employer which is in excess of ten hours in any workday, and

(B) such employment by such employer which is in excess of forty-eight hours in any workweek, compensation at a rate not less than one and one-half times the regular rate at which he is employed. An employer who receives an exemption under this subsection shall not be eligible for any other exemption under this section.

(n) Employment by street, suburban, or interurban electric railway, or local trolley or motorbus carrier

In the case of an employee of an employer engaged in the business of operating a street, suburban or interurban electric railway, or local trolley or motorbus carrier (regardless of whether or not such railway or carrier is public or private or operated for profit or not for profit), in determining the hours of employment of such an employee to which the rate prescribed by subsection (a) of this section applies there shall be excluded the hours such employee was employed in charter activities by such employer if (1) the employee's employment in such activities was pursuant to an agreement or understanding with his employer arrived at before engaging in such employment, and (2) if employment in such activities is not part of such employee's regular employment.

(*o*) Compensatory time

(1) Employees of a public agency which is a State, a political subdivision of a State, or an interstate governmental agency may receive, in accordance with this subsection and in lieu of overtime compensation, compensatory time off at a rate not less than one and one-half hours for each hour of employment for which overtime compensation is required by this section.

(2) A public agency may provide compensatory time under paragraph (1) only—

(A) pursuant to:

(i) applicable provisions of a collective bargaining agreement, memorandum of understanding, or any other agreement between the public agency and representatives of such employees; or

(ii) in the case of employees not covered by subclause (i), an agreement or understanding arrived at between the employer and employee before the performance of the work; and

(B) if the employee has not accrued compensatory time in excess of the limit applicable to the employee prescribed by paragraph (3). In the case of employees described in clause (A)(ii) hired prior to April 15, 1986, the regular practice in effect on April 15, 1986, with respect to compensatory time off for such employees in lieu of the receipt of overtime compensation, shall constitute an agreement or understanding under such clause (A)(ii). Except as provided in the previous sentence, the provision of compensatory time off to such employees for hours worked after April 14, 1986, shall be in accordance with this subsection.

(3)(A) If the work of an employee for which compensatory time may be provided included work in a public safety activity, an emergency response activity, or a seasonal activity, the employee engaged in such work may accrue not more than 480 hours of compensatory time for hours worked after April 15, 1986. If such work was any other work, the employee engaged in such work may accrue not more than 240 hours of compensatory time for hours worked after April 15, 1986. Any such employee who, after April 15, 1986, has accrued 480 or 240 hours, as the case may be, of compensatory time off shall, for additional overtime hours of work, be paid overtime compensation.

(B) If compensation is paid to an employee for accrued compensatory time off, such compensation shall be paid at the regular rate earned by the employee at the time the employee receives such payment.

(4) An employee who has accrued compensatory time off authorized to be provided under paragraph (1) shall, upon termination of employment, be paid for the unused compensatory time at a rate of compensation not less than—

(A) the average regular rate received by such employee during the last 3 years of the employee's employment, or

(B) the final regular rate received by such employee, whichever is higher.

(5) An employee of a public agency which is a State, political subdivision of a State, or an interstate governmental agency:

(A) who has accrued compensatory time off authorized to be provided under paragraph (1), and

(B) who has requested the use of such compensatory time, shall be permitted by the employee's employer to use such time within a reasonable period after making the request if the use of the compensatory time does not unduly disrupt the operations of the public agency.

(6) The hours an employee of a public agency performs court reporting transcript preparation duties shall not be considered as hours worked for the purposes of subsection (a) of this section if:

(A) such employee is paid at a per-page rate which is not less than:

(i) the maximum rate established by State law or local ordinance for the jurisdiction of such public agency,

(ii) the maximum rate otherwise established by a judicial or administrative officer and in effect on July 1, 1995, or

(iii) the rate freely negotiated between the employee and the party requesting the transcript, other than the judge who presided over the proceedings being transcribed, and

(B) the hours spent performing such duties are outside of the hours such employee performs other work (including hours for which the agency requires the employee's attendance) pursuant to the employment relationship with such public agency.

For purposes of this section, the amount paid such employee in accordance with subparagraph (A) for the performance of court reporting transcript preparation duties, shall not be considered in the calculation of the regular rate at which such employee is employed.

(7) For purposes of this subsection:

(A) the term "overtime compensation" means the compensation required by subsection (a), and

(B) the terms "compensatory time" and "compensatory time off" mean hours during which an employee is not working, which are not counted as hours worked during the applicable workweek or other work period for purposes of overtime compensation, and for which the employee is compensated at the employee's regular rate.

(p) Special detail work for fire protection and law enforcement employees; occasional or sporadic employment; substitution

(1) If an individual who is employed by a State, political subdivision of a State, or an interstate governmental agency in fire protection or law enforcement activities (including activities of security personnel in correctional institutions) and who, solely at such individual's option, agrees to be employed on a special detail by a separate or independent employer in fire protection, law enforcement, or related activities, the hours such individual was employed by such separate and independent employer shall be excluded by the public agency employing such individual in the calculation of the hours for which the employee is entitled to overtime compensation under this section if the public agency:

(A) requires that its employees engaged in fire protection, law enforcement, or security activities be hired by a separate and independent employer to perform the special detail,

(B) facilitates the employment of such employees by a separate and independent employer, or

(C) otherwise affects the condition of employment of such employees by a separate and independent employer.

(2) If an employee of a public agency which is a State, political subdivision of a State, or an interstate governmental agency undertakes, on an occasional or sporadic basis and solely at the employee's option, part-time employment for the public agency which is in a different capacity from any capacity in which the employee is regularly employed with the public agency, the hours such employee was employed in performing the different employment shall be excluded by the public agency in the calculation of the hours for which the employee is entitled to overtime compensation under this section.

(3) If an individual who is employed in any capacity by a public agency which is a State, political subdivision of a State, or an interstate governmental agency, agrees, with the approval of the public agency and solely at the option of such individual, to substitute during scheduled work hours for another individual who is employed by such agency in the same capacity, the hours such employee worked as a substitute shall be excluded by the public agency in the calculation of the hours for which the employee is entitled to overtime compensation under this section.

(q) Maximum hour exemption for employees receiving remedial education

Any employer may employ any employee for a period or periods of not more than 10 hours in the aggregate in any workweek in excess of the maximum workweek specified in subsection (a) of this section without paying the compensation for overtime employment prescribed in such subsection, if during such period or periods the employee is receiving remedial education that is:

(1) provided to employees who lack a high school diploma or educational attainment at the eighth grade level;

(2) designed to provide reading and other basic skills at an eighth grade level or below; and

(3) does not include job specific training.

(r) [Repealed]

§ 208. [Repealed]

§ 209. Attendance of witnesses

For the purpose of any hearing or investigation provided for in this chapter, the provisions of sections 49 and 50 of Title 15 (relating to the attendance of witnesses and the production of books, papers, and documents), are made applicable to the jurisdiction, powers, and duties of the Administrator, the Secretary of Labor, and the industry committees.

§ 210. Court review of wage orders in Puerto Rico and the Virgin Islands * * *

§ 211. Collection of data

(a) Investigations and inspections

The Administrator or his designated representatives may investigate and gather data regarding the wages, hours, and other conditions and practices of employment in any industry subject to this chapter, and may enter and inspect such places and such records (and make such transcriptions thereof), question such employees, and investigate such facts, conditions, practices, or matters as he may deem necessary or appropriate to determine whether any person has violated any provision of this chapter, or which may aid in the enforcement of the provisions of this chapter. Except as provided in section 212 of this title and in subsection (b) of this section, the Administrator shall utilize the bureaus and divisions of the Department of Labor for all the investigations and inspections necessary under this section. Except as provided in section 212 of this title, the Administer shall bring all actions under section 217 of this title to restrain violations of this chapter.

(b) State and local agencies and employees

With the consent and cooperation of State agencies charged with the administration of State labor laws, the Administrator and the Secretary of Labor may, for the purpose of carrying out their respective functions and duties under this chapter, utilize the services of State and local agencies and their employees and, notwithstanding any other provision of law, may reimburse such State and local agencies and their employees for services rendered for such purposes.

(c) Records

Every employer subject to any provision of this chapter or of any order issued under this chapter shall make, keep, and preserve such records of the persons employed by him and of the wages, hours, and other conditions and practices of employment maintained by him, and shall preserve such records for such periods of time, and shall make such reports therefrom to the Administrator as he shall prescribe by regulation or order as necessary or appropriate for the enforcement of the provisions of this chapter or the regulations or orders thereunder. The employer of an employee who performs substitute work described in section 207(p)(3) of this title may not be required under this subsection to keep a record of the hours of the substitute work.

(d) Homework regulations

The Administrator is authorized to make such regulations and orders regulating, restricting, or prohibiting industrial homework as are necessary or appropriate to prevent the circumvention or evasion of and to safeguard the minimum wage rate prescribed in this chapter, and all existing regulations or orders of the Administrator relating to industrial homework are continued in full force and effect.

§ 212. Child labor provisions

(a) Restrictions on shipment of goods; prosecution; conviction

No producer, manufacturer, or dealer shall ship or deliver for shipment in commerce any goods produced in an establishment situated in the United

States in or about which within thirty days prior to the removal of such goods therefrom any oppressive child labor has been employed: Provided, that any such shipment or delivery for shipment of such goods by a purchaser who acquired them in good faith in reliance on written assurance from the producer, manufacturer, or dealer that the goods were produced in compliance with the requirements of this section, and who acquired such goods for value without notice of any such violation, shall not be deemed prohibited by this subsection: And provided further, that a prosecution and conviction of a defendant for the shipment or delivery for shipment of any goods under the conditions herein prohibited shall be a bar to any further prosecution against the same defendant for shipments or deliveries for shipment of any such goods before the beginning of said prosecution.

(b) Investigations and inspections

The Secretary of Labor or any of his authorized representatives, shall make all investigations and inspections under section 211(a) of this title with respect to the employment of minors, and, subject to the direction and control of the Attorney General, shall bring all actions under section 217 of this title to enjoin any act or practice which is unlawful by reason of the existence of oppressive child labor, and shall administer all other provisions of this chapter relating to oppressive child labor.

(c) Oppressive child labor

No employer shall employ any oppressive child labor in commerce or in the production of goods for commerce or in any enterprise engaged in commerce or in the production of goods for commerce.

(d) Proof of age

In order to carry out the objectives of this section, the Secretary may by regulation require employers to obtain from any employee proof of age.

§ 213. Exemptions*

(a) Minimum wage and maximum hour requirements.

The provisions of sections 206 (except subsection (d) in the case of paragraph (1) of this subsection) and section 207 of this title shall not apply with respect to—

(1) any employee employed in a bona fide executive, administrative, or professional capacity (including any employee employed in the capacity of academic administrative personnel or teacher in elementary or secondary schools), or in the capacity of outside salesman (as such terms are defined and delimited from time to time by regulations of the Secretary, subject to the provisions of the subchapter II of chapter 5 of Title 5, except that an employee of a retail

* Gaps in number sequence occur due to the repeal of some subsections.

or service establishment shall not be excluded from the definition of employee employed in a bona fide executive or administrative capacity because of the number of hours in his workweek which he devotes to activities not directly or closely related to the performance of executive or administrative activities, if less than 40 per centum of his hours worked in the workweek are devoted to such activities); or

(2) [Repealed]

(3) any employee employed by an establishment which is an amusement or recreational establishment, organized camp, or religious or non-profit educational conference center, if (A) it does not operate for more than seven months in any calendar year, or (B) during the preceding calendar year, its average receipts for any six months of such year were not more than 33 1/3 per centum of its average receipts for the other six months of such year, except that the exemption from sections 206 and 207 of this title provided by this paragraph does not apply with respect to any employee of a private entity engaged in providing services or facilities (other than, in the case of the exemption from section 6, a private entity engaged in providing services and facilities directly related to skiing) in a national park or a national forest, or on land in the National Wildlife Refuge System, under a contract with the Secretary of the Interior or the Secretary of Agriculture; or

(4) [Repealed]

(5) any employee employed in the catching, taking, propagating, harvesting, cultivating, or farming of any kind of fish, shellfish, crustacea, sponges, seaweeds, or other aquatic forms of animal and vegetable life, or in the first processing, canning or packing such marine products at sea as an incident to, or in conjunction with, such fishing operations, including the going to and returning from work and loading and unloading when performed by any such employee; or

(6) any employee employed in agriculture (A) if such employee is employed by an employer who did not, during any calendar quarter during the preceding calendar year, use more than five hundred man-days of agriculture labor, (B) if such employee is the parent, spouse, child, or other member of his employer's immediate family, (C) if such employee (i) is employed as a hand harvest laborer and is paid on a piece rate basis in an operation which has been, and is customarily and generally recognized as having been, paid on a piece rate basis in the region of employment, (ii) commutes daily from his permanent residence to the farm on which he is so employed, and (iii) has been employed in agriculture less than thirteen weeks during the preceding calendar year, (D) if such employee (other than an employee described in clause (C) of this subsection) (i) is sixteen years of age or under and

is employed as a hand harvest laborer, is paid on a piece rate basis in an operation which has been, and is customarily and generally recognized as having been, paid on a piece rate basis in the region of employment, (ii) is employed on the same farm as his parent or person standing in the place of his parent, and (iii) is paid at the same piece rate as employees over age sixteen are paid on the same farm, or (E) if such employee is principally engaged in the range production of livestock; or

(7) any employee to the extent that such employee is exempt by regulations, order, or certificate of the Secretary issued under section 214 of this title; or

(8) any employee employed in connection with the publication of any weekly, semiweekly, or daily newspaper with a circulation of less than four thousand the major part of which circulation is within the county where published or counties contiguous thereto; or

(9) [Repealed]

(10) any switchboard operator employed by an independently owned public telephone company which has not more than seven hundred and fifty stations; or

(11) [Repealed]

(12) any employee employed as a seaman on a vessel other than an American vessel; or

(13), (14) [Repealed]

(15) any employee employed on a casual basis in domestic service employment to provide babysitting services or any employee employed in domestic service employment to provide companionship services for individuals who (because of age or infirmity) are unable to care for themselves (as such terms are defined and delimited by regulations of the Secretary); or

(16) a criminal investigator who is paid availability pay under section 5545a of title 5; or

(17) any employee who is a computer systems analyst, computer programmer, software engineer, or other similarly skilled worker, whose primary duty is—

(A) the application of systems analysis techniques and procedures, including consulting with users, to determine hardware, software, or system functional specifications;

(B) the design, development, documentation, analysis, creation, testing, or modification of computer systems or programs, including prototypes, based on and related to user or system design specifications;

(C) the design, documentation, testing, creation, or modification of computer programs related to machine operating systems; or

(D) a combination of duties described in subparagraphs (A), (B), and (C) the performance of which requires the same level of skills, and who, in the case of an employee who is compensated on an hourly basis, is compensated at a rate of not less than $27.63 an hour; or

(18) any employee who is a border patrol agent, as defined in section 5550(a) of Title 5; or

(19) any employee employed to play baseball who is compensated pursuant to a contract that provides for a weekly salary for services performed during the league's championship season (but not spring training or the off season) at a rate that is not less than a weekly salary equal to the minimum wage under section 206(a) of this title for a workweek of 40 hours, irrespective of the number of hours the employee devotes to baseball related activities.

(b) Maximum hour requirements. The provisions of section 207 of this title shall not apply with respect to:

(1) any employee with respect to whom the Secretary of Transportation has power to establish qualifications and maximum hours of service pursuant to the provisions of section 31502 of Title 49; or

(2) any employee of an employer engaged in the operation of a rail carrier subject to part A of subtitle IV of title 49; or

(3) any employee of a carrier by air subject to the provisions of Title II of the Railway Labor Act [45 U.S.C.A. § 181 et seq.]; or

(4) [Repealed]

(5) any individual employed as an outside buyer of poultry, eggs, cream, or milk, in their raw or natural state; or

(6) any employee employed as a seaman; or

(7), (8) [Repealed]

(9) any employee employed as an announcer, news editor, or chief engineer by a radio or television station the major studio of which is located

(A) in a city or town of one hundred thousand population or less according to the latest available decennial census figures as compiled by the Bureau of the Census, except where such city or town is part of a standard metropolitan statistical area, as defined and designated by the Office of Management and Budget, which has a total population in excess of one hundred thousand, or

(B) in a city or town of twenty-five thousand population or less, which is part of such an area but is at least 40 airline miles from the principal city in such area; or

(10)(A) any salesman, partsman, or mechanic primarily engaged in selling or servicing automobiles, trucks, or farm implements, if he is employed by a nonmanufacturing establishment primarily engaged in the business of selling such vehicles or implements to ultimate purchasers; or

(B) any salesman primarily engaged in selling trailers, boats, or aircraft, if he is employed by a nonmanufacturing establishment primarily engaged in the business of selling trailers, boats, or aircraft to ultimate purchasers; or

(11) any employee employed as a driver or driver's helper making local deliveries, who is compensated for such employment on the basis of trip rates, or other delivery payment plan, if the Secretary shall find that such plan has the general purpose and effect of reducing hours worked by such employees to, or below, the maximum workweek applicable to them under section 207(a) of this title; or

(12) any employee employed in agriculture or in connection with the operation or maintenance of ditches, canals, reservoirs, or waterways, not owned or operated for profit, or operated on a sharecrop basis, and which are used exclusively for supply and storing of water, at least 90 percent of which was ultimately delivered for agricultural purposes during the preceding calendar year; or

(13) any employee with respect to his employment in agriculture by a farmer, notwithstanding other employment of such employee in connection with livestock auction operations in which such farmer is engaged as an adjunct to the raising of livestock, either on his own account or in conjunction with other farmers, if such employee (A) is primarily employed during his workweek in agriculture by such farmer, and (B) is paid for his employment in connection with such livestock auction operations at a wage rate not less than that prescribed by section 206(a)(1) of this title; or

(14) any employee employed within the area of production (as defined by the Secretary) by an establishment commonly recognized as a country elevator, including such an establishment which sells products and services used in the operation of a farm, if no more than

five employees are employed in the establishment in such operations; or

(15) any employee engaged in the processing of maple sap into sugar (other than refined sugar) or syrup; or

(16) any employee engaged (A) in the transportation and preparation for transportation of fruits or vegetables, whether or not performed by the farmer, from the farm to a place of first processing or first marketing within the same State, or (B) in transportation, whether or not performed by the farmer, between the farm and any point within the same State of persons employed or to be employed in the harvesting of fruits or vegetables; or

(17) any driver employed by an employer engaged in the business of operating taxicabs; or

(18), (19) [Repealed]

(20) any employee of a public agency who in any workweek is employed in fire protection activities or any employee of a public agency who in any workweek is employed in law enforcement activities (including security personnel in correctional institutions), if the public agency employs during the workweek less than 5 employees in fire protection or law enforcement activities, as the case may be; or

(21) any employee who is employed in domestic service in a household and who resides in such household; or

(22), (23) [Repealed]

(24) any employee who is employed with his spouse by a nonprofit educational institution to serve as the parents of children—

(A) who are orphans or one of whose natural parents is deceased, or

(B) who are enrolled in such institution and reside in residential facilities of the institution, while such children are in residence at such institution, if such employee and his spouse reside in such facilities, receive, without cost, board and lodging from such institution, and are together compensated, on a cash basis, at an annual rate of not less than $10,000; or

(25), (26) [Repealed]

(27) any employee employed by an establishment which is a motion picture theater; or

(28) any employee employed in planting or tending trees, cruising, surveying, or felling timber, or in preparing or transporting logs or other forestry products to the mill, processing plant, railroad, or other transportation terminal, if the number of employees employed by his

employer in such forestry or lumbering operations does not exceed eight;

(29) any employee of an amusement or recreational establishment located in a national park or national forest or on land in the National Wildlife Refuge System if such employee (A) is an employee of a private entity engaged in providing services or facilities in a national park or national forest, or on land in the National Wildlife Refuge System, under a contract with the Secretary of the Interior or the Secretary of Agriculture, and (B) receives compensation for employment in excess of fifty-six hours in any workweek at a rate not less than one and one-half times the regular rate at which he is employed; or

(30) a criminal investigator who is paid availability pay under section 5545a of title 5.

(c) Child labor requirements

(1) Except as provided in paragraph (2) or (4), the provisions of section 212 of this title relating to child labor shall not apply to any employee employed in agriculture outside of school hours for the school district where such employee is living while he is so employed, if such employee—

(A) is less than twelve years of age and (i) is employed by his parent, or by a person standing in the place of his parent, on a farm owned or operated by such parent or person, or (ii) is employed, with the consent of his parent or person standing in the place of his parent, on a farm, none of the employees of which are (because of section (a)(6)(A) of this section) required to be paid at the wage rate prescribed by section 206(a)(5) of this title,

(B) is twelve years or thirteen years of age and (i) such employment is with the consent of his parent or person standing in the place of his parent, or (ii) his parent or such person is employed on the same farm as such employee, or

(C) is fourteen years of age or older.

(2) The provisions of section 212 of this title relating to child labor shall apply to an employee below the age of sixteen employed in agriculture in an occupation that the Secretary of Labor finds and declares to be particularly hazardous for the employment of children below the age of sixteen, except where such employee is employed by his parent or by a person standing in the place of his parent on a farm owned or operated by such parent or person.

(3) The provisions of section 212 of this title relating to child labor shall not apply to any child employed as an actor or performer in

motion pictures or theatrical productions, or in radio or television productions.

(4)(A) An employer or group of employers may apply to the Secretary for a waiver of the application of section 212 of this title to the employment for not more than eight weeks in any calendar year of individuals who are less than twelve years of age, but not less than ten years of age, as hand harvest laborers in an agricultural operation which has been, and is customarily and generally recognized as being, paid on a piece rate basis in the region in which such individuals would be employed. The Secretary may not grant such a waiver unless he finds, based on objective data submitted by the applicant, that—

(i) the crop to be harvested is one with a particularly short harvesting season and the application of section 212 of this title would cause severe economic disruption in the industry of the employer or group of employers applying for the waiver;

(ii) the employment of the individuals to whom the waiver would apply would not be deleterious to their health or well-being;

(iii) the level and type of pesticides and other chemicals used would not have an adverse effect on the health or well-being of the individuals to whom the waiver would apply;

(iv) individuals age twelve and above are not available for such employment; and

(v) the industry of such employer or group of employers has traditionally and substantially employed individuals under twelve years of age without displacing substantial job opportunities for individuals over sixteen years of age.

(B) Any waiver granted by the Secretary under subparagraph (A) shall require that—

(i) the individuals employed under such waiver be employed outside of school hours for the school district where they are living while so employed;

(ii) such individuals while so employed commute daily from their permanent residence to the farm on which they are so employed; and

(iii) such individuals be employed under such waiver (I) for not more than eight weeks between June 1 and October 15 of any calendar year, and (II) in accordance with such other terms and conditions as the Secretary shall prescribe for such individuals' protection.

(5)(A) In the administration and enforcement of the child labor provisions of this chapter, employees who are 16 and 17 years of age shall be permitted to load materials into, but not operate or unload materials from, scrap paper balers and paper box compactors:

(i) that are safe for 16- and 17-year-old employees loading the scrap paper balers or paper box compactors; and

(ii) that cannot be operated while being loaded.

(B) For purposes of subparagraph (A), scrap paper balers and paper box compactors shall be considered safe for 16- or 17-year-old employees to load only if:

(i)(I) the scrap paper balers and paper box compactors meet the American National Standards Institute's Standard ANSI Z245.5–1990 for scrap paper balers and Standard ANSI Z245.2–1992 for paper box compactors; or

(II) the scrap paper balers and paper box compactors meet an applicable standard that is adopted by the American National Standards Institute after August 6, 1996, and that is certified by the Secretary to be at least as protective of the safety of minors as the standard described in subclause (I);

(ii) the scrap paper balers and paper box compactors include an on-off switch incorporating a key-lock or other system and the control of the system is maintained in the custody of employees who are 18 years of age or older;

(iii) the on-off switch of the scrap paper balers and paper box compactors is maintained in an off position when the scrap paper balers and paper box compactors are not in operation; and

(iv) the employer of 16- and 17-year-old employees provides notice, and posts a notice, on the scrap paper balers and paper box compactors stating that—

(I) the scrap paper balers and paper box compactors meet the applicable standard described in clause (i);

(II) 16- and 17-year-old employees may only load the scrap paper balers and paper box compactors; and

(III) any employee under the age of 18 may not operate or unload the scrap paper balers and paper box compactors.

The Secretary shall publish in the Federal Register a standard that is adopted by the American National

Standards Institute for scrap paper balers or paper box compactors and certified by the Secretary to be protective of the safety of minors under clause (i)(II).

(C)(i) Employers shall prepare and submit to the Secretary reports—

(I) on any injury to an employee under the age of 18 that requires medical treatment (other than first aid) resulting from the employee's contact with a scrap paper baler or paper box compactor during the loading, operation, or unloading of the baler or compactor; and

(II) on any fatality of an employee under the age of 18 resulting from the employee's contact with a scrap paper baler or paper box compactor during the loading, operation, or unloading of the baler or compactor.

(ii) The reports described in clause (i) shall * * *

(v) The Secretary may not rely solely on the reports described in clause (i) as the basis for making a determination that any of the employers described in clause (i) has violated a provision of section 212 of this title relating to oppressive child labor or a regulation or order issued pursuant to section 12. The Secretary shall, prior to making such a determination, conduct an investigation and inspection in accordance with section 212(b) of this title.

(vi) The reporting requirements of this subparagraph shall expire 2 years after August 6, 1996.

(6) In the administration and enforcement of the child labor provisions of this chapter, employees who are under 17 years of age may not drive automobiles or trucks on public roadways. Employees who are 17 years of age may drive automobiles or trucks on public roadways only if—

(A) such driving is restricted to daylight hours;

(B) the employee holds a State license valid for the type of driving involved in the job performed and has no records of any moving violation at the time of hire;

(C) the employee has successfully completed a State approved driver education course;

(D) the automobile or truck is equipped with a seat belt for the driver and any passengers and the employee's employer has instructed the employee that the seat belts must be used when driving the automobile or truck;

(E) the automobile or truck does not exceed 6,000 pounds of gross vehicle weight;

(F) such driving does not involve:

(i) the towing of vehicles;

(ii) route deliveries or route sales;

(iii) the transportation for hire of property, goods, or passengers;

(iv) urgent, time-sensitive deliveries;

(v) more than two trips away from the primary place of employment in any single day for the purpose of delivering goods of the employee's employer to a customer (other than urgent, time-sensitive deliveries);

(vi) more than two trips away from the primary place of employment in any single day for the purpose of transporting passengers (other than employees of the employer);

(vii) transporting more than three passengers (including employees of the employer); or

(viii) driving beyond a 30 mile radius from the employee's place of employment; and

(G) such driving is only occasional and incidental to the employee's employment. For purposes of subparagraph (G), the term "occasional and incidental" is no more than one-third of an employee's worktime in any workday and no more than 20 percent of an employee's worktime in any workweek.

(7)(A)(i) Subject to subparagraph (B), in the administration and enforcement of the child labor provisions of this chapter, it shall not be considered oppressive child labor for a new entrant into the workforce to be employed inside or outside places of business where machinery is used to process wood products.

(ii) In this paragraph, the term "new entrant into the workforce" means an individual who

(I) is under the age of 18 and at least the age of 14, and

(II) by statute or judicial order is exempt from compulsory school attendance beyond the eighth grade.

(B) The employment of a new entrant into the workforce under subparagraph (A) shall be permitted

(i) if the entrant is supervised by an adult relative of the entrant or is supervised by an adult member of the same religious sect or division as the entrant;

(ii) if the entrant does not operate or assist in the operation of power-driven woodworking machines;

(iii) if the entrant is protected from wood particles or other flying debris within the workplace by a barrier appropriate to the potential hazard of such wood particles or flying debris or by maintaining a sufficient distance from machinery in operation; and

(iv) if the entrant is required to use personal protective equipment to prevent exposure to excessive levels of noise and saw dust.

(d) Delivery of newspapers and wreathmaking

The provisions of sections 206, 207 and 212 of this tittle shall not apply with respect to any employee engaged in the delivery of newspapers to the consumer or to any homeworker engaged in the making of wreaths composed primarily of natural holly, pine, cedar, or other evergreens (including the harvesting of the evergreens or other forest products used in making such wreaths).

(e) Maximum hour requirements and minimum wage employees

The provisions of section 207 of this title shall not apply with respect to employees for whom the Secretary of Labor is authorized to establish minimum wage rates as provided in section 206(a)(3) of this title, except with respect to employees for whom such rates are in effect; and with respect to such employees the Secretary may make rules and regulations providing reasonable limitations and allowing reasonable variations, tolerances, and exemptions to and from any or all of the provisions of section 207 of this title if he shall find, after a public hearing on the matter, and taking into account the factors set forth in section 206(a)(3) of this title, that economic conditions warrant such action.

(f) Employment in foreign countries and certain United States territories

The provisions of sections 206, 207, 211, and 212 of this title shall not apply with respect to any employee whose services during the workweek are performed in a workplace within a foreign country or within territory under the jurisdiction of the United States other than the following: a State of the United States; the District of Columbia; Puerto Rico; the Virgin Islands; outer Continental Shelf lands defined in the Outer Continental Shelf Lands Act (ch. 345, 67 stat. 462) [43 U.S.C.A. § 1331 et seq.];

American Samoa; Guam; Wake Island; Eniwetok Atoll; Kwajalein Atoll; and Johnston Island.

(g) Certain employment in retail or service establishments, agriculture

The exemption from section 206 of this title provided by paragraph (6) of subsection (a) of this section shall not apply with respect to any employee employed by an establishment (1) which controls, is controlled by, or is under common control with, another establishment the activities of which are not related for a common business purpose to, but materially support the activities of the establishment employing such employee; and (2) whose annual gross volume of sales made or business done, when combined with the annual gross volume of sales made or business done by each establishment which controls, is controlled by, or is under common control with, the establishment employing such employee, exceeds $10,000,000 (exclusive of excise taxes at the retail level which are separately stated).

(h) Maximum hour requirement; fourteen workweek limitation

The provisions of section 207 of this title shall not apply for a period or periods of not more than fourteen workweeks in the aggregate in any calendar year to any employee who—

(1) is employed by such employer—

(A) exclusively to provide services necessary and incidental to the ginning of cotton in an establishment primarily engaged in the ginning of cotton;

(B) exclusively to provide services necessary and incidental to the receiving, handling, and storing of raw cotton and the compressing of raw cotton when performed at a cotton warehouse or compress-warehouse facility, other than one operated in conjunction with a cotton mill, primarily engaged in storing and compressing;

(C) exclusively to provide services necessary and incidental to the receiving, handling, storing, and processing of cottonseed in an establishment primarily engaged in the receiving, handling, storing, and processing of cottonseed; or

(D) exclusively to provide services necessary and incidental to the processing of sugar cane or sugar beets in an establishment primarily engaged in the processing of sugar cane or sugar beets; and

(2) receives for:

(A) such employment by such employer which is in excess of ten hours in any workday, and

(B) such employment by such employer which is in excess of forty-eight hours in any workweek, compensation at a rate not less than one and one-half times the regular rate at which he is employed. Any employer who receives an exemption under this subsection shall not be eligible for any other exemption under this section or section 207 of this title.

(i) Cotton ginning

The provisions of section 207 of this title shall not apply for a period or periods of not more than fourteen workweeks in the aggregate in any period of fifty-two consecutive weeks to any employee who—

(1) is engaged in the ginning of cotton for market in any place of employment located in a county where cotton is grown in commercial quantities; and

(2) receives for any such employment during such workweeks—

(A) in excess of ten hours in any workday, and

(B) in excess of forty-eight hours in any workweek, compensation at a rate not less than one and one-half times the regular rate at which he is employed. No week included in any fifty-two week period for purposes of the preceding sentence may be included for such purposes in any other fifty-two week period.

(j) Processing of sugar beets, sugar beet molasses, or sugar cane

The provisions of section 207 of this title shall not apply for a period or periods of not more than fourteen workweeks in the aggregate in any period of fifty-two consecutive weeks to any employee who—

(1) is engaged in the processing of sugar beets, sugar beet molasses, or sugar cane into sugar (other than refined sugar) or syrup; and * * *

§ 214. Employment under special certificates

(a) Learners, apprentices, messengers

The Secretary, to the extent necessary in order to prevent curtailment of opportunities for employment, shall by regulations or by orders provide for the employment of learners, of apprentices, and of messengers employed primarily in delivering letters and messages, under special certificates issued pursuant to regulations of the Secretary, at such wages lower than the minimum wage applicable under section 206 of this title and subject to such limitations as to time, number, proportion, and length of service as the Secretary shall prescribe.

(b) Students

(1)(A) The Secretary, to the extent necessary in order to prevent curtailment of opportunities for employment, shall by special certificate issued under a regulation or order provide, in accordance with subparagraph (B), for the employment, at a wage rate not less than 85 per centum of the otherwise applicable wage rate in effect under section 206 of this title or not less than $1.60 an hour, whichever is the higher, of full-time students (regardless of age but in compliance with applicable child labor laws) in retail or service establishments.

(B) Except as provided in paragraph (4)(B), during any month in which full-time students are to be employed in any retail or service establishment under certificates issued under this subsection the proportion of student hours of employment to the total hours of employment of all employees in such establishment may not exceed

(i) in the case of a retail or service establishment whose employees (other than employees engaged in commerce or in the production of goods for commerce) were covered by this chapter before the effective date of the Fair Labor Standards Amendments of 1974

(I) the proportion of student hours of employment to the total hours of employment of all employees in such establishment for the corresponding month of the immediately preceding twelve-month period,

(II) the maximum proportion for any corresponding month of student hours of employment to the total hours of employment of all employees in such establishment applicable to the issuance of certificates under this section at any time before the effective date of the Fair Labor Standards Amendments of 1974 for the employment of students by such employer, or

(III) a proportion equal to one-tenth of the total hours of employment of all employees in such establishment, whichever is greater;

(ii) in the case of retail or service establishment whose employees (other than employees engaged in commerce or in the production of goods for commerce) are covered for the first time on or after the effective date of the Fair Labor Standards Amendments of 1974

(I) the proportion of hours of employment of students in such establishment to the total hours of employment of all employees in such establishment for the corresponding month of the twelve-month period immediately prior to the effective date of such Amendments,

(II) the proportion of student hours of employment to the total hours of employment of all employees in such establishment for the corresponding month of the immediately preceding twelve-month period, or

(III) a proportion equal to one-tenth of the total hours of employment of all employees in such establishment, whichever is greater; or

(iii) in the case of a retail or service establishment for which records of student hours worked are not available, the proportion of student hours of employment to the total hours of employment of all employees based on the practice during the immediately preceding twelve-month period in (I) similar establishments of the same employer in the same general metropolitan area in which such establishment is located, (II) similar establishments of the same or nearby communities if such establishment is not in a metropolitan area, or (III) other establishments of the same general character operating in the community or the nearest comparable community.

For purpose of clauses (i), (ii), and (iii) of this subparagraph, the term "student hours of employment" means hours during which students are employed in a retail or service establishment under certificates issued under this subsection.

(2) The Secretary, to the extent necessary in order to prevent curtailment of opportunities for employment, shall by special certificate issued under a regulation or order provide for the employment, at a wage rate not less than 85 per centum of the wage rate in effect under section 206(a)(5) of this title or not less than $1.30 an hour, whichever is the higher, of full-time students (regardless of age but in compliance with applicable child labor laws) in any occupation in agriculture.

(3) The Secretary, to the extent necessary in order to prevent curtailment of opportunities for employment, shall by special certificate issued under a regulation or order provide for the employment by an institution of higher education, at a wage rate not less than 85 per centum of the otherwise applicable wage rate in effect under section 206 of this title or not less than $1.60 an hour, whichever is the higher, of full-time students (regardless of age but in compliance with applicable child labor laws) who are enrolled in such institution. The Secretary shall by regulation prescribe standards and requirements to insure that this paragraph will not create a substantial probability of reducing the full-time employment

opportunities of persons other than those to whom the minimum wage rate authorized by this paragraph is applicable.

(4)(A) A special certificate issued under paragraph (1), (2), or (3) shall provide that the student or students for whom it is issued shall, except during vacation periods, be employed on a part-time basis and not in excess of twenty hours in any workweek.

(B) If the issuance of a special certificate under paragraph (1) or (2) for an employer will cause the number of students employed by such employer under special certificates issued under this subsection to exceed six, the Secretary may not issue such a special certificate for the employment of a student by such employer unless the Secretary finds employment of such student will not create a substantial probability of reducing the full-time employment opportunities of persons other than those employed under special certificates issued under this subsection. If the issuance of a special certificate under paragraph (1) or (2) for an employer will not cause the number of students employed by such employer under special certificates issued under this subsection to exceed six

(i) the Secretary may issue a special certificate under paragraph (1) or (2) for the employment of a student by such employer if such employer certifies to the Secretary that the employment of such student will not reduce the full-time employment opportunities of persons other than those employed under special certificates issued under this subsection, and

(ii) in the case of an employer which is a retail or service establishment, subparagraph (B) of paragraph (1) shall not apply with respect to the issuance of special certificates for such employer under such paragraph.

The requirement of this subparagraph shall not apply in the case of the issuance of special certificates under paragraph (3) for the employment of full-time students by institutions of higher education; except that if the Secretary determines that an institution of higher education is employing students under certificates issued under paragraph (3) but in violation of the requirements of that paragraph or of regulations issued thereunder, the requirements of this subparagraph shall apply with respect to the issuance of special certificates under paragraph (3) for the employment of students by such institution.

(C) No special certificate may be issued under this subsection unless the employer for whom the certificate is to be issued provides evidence satisfactory to the Secretary of the student status of the employees to be employed under such special certificate.

(D) To minimize paperwork for, and to encourage, small businesses to employ students under special certificates issued under paragraphs (1) and (2), the Secretary shall, by regulation or order, prescribe a simplified application form to be used by employers in applying for such a certificate for the employment of not more than six full-time students. Such an application shall require only

(i) a listing of the name, address, and business of the applicant employer,

(ii) a listing of the date the applicant began business, and

(iii) the certification that the employment of such full-time students will not reduce the full-time employment opportunities of persons other than persons employed under special certificates.

(c) Handicapped workers

(1) The Secretary, to the extent necessary to prevent curtailment of opportunities for employment, shall by regulation or order provide for the employment, under special certificates, of individuals (including individuals employed in agriculture) whose earning or productive capacity is impaired by age, physical or mental deficiency, or injury, at wages which are—

(A) lower than the minimum wage applicable under section 206 of this title,

(B) commensurate with those paid to nonhandicapped workers, employed in the vicinity in which the individuals under the certificates are employed, for essentially the same type, quality, and quantity of work, and

(C) related to the individual's productivity.

(2) The Secretary shall not issue a certificate under paragraph (1) unless the employer provides written assurances to the Secretary that

(A) in the case of individuals paid on an hourly rate basis, wages paid in accordance with paragraph (1) will be reviewed by the employer at periodic intervals at least once every six months, and

(B) wages paid in accordance with paragraph (1) will be adjusted by the employer at periodic intervals, at least once each year, to reflect changes in the prevailing wage paid to experienced nonhandicapped individuals employed in the locality for essentially the same type of work.

(3) Notwithstanding paragraph (1), no employer shall be permitted to reduce the hourly wage rate prescribed by certificate under this subsection in effect on June 1, 1986, of any handicapped individual for a period of two years from such date without prior authorization of the Secretary.

(4) Nothing in this subsection shall be construed to prohibit an employer from maintaining or establishing work activities centers to provide therapeutic activities for handicapped clients.

(5)(A) Notwithstanding any other provision of this subsection, any employee receiving a special minimum wage at a rate specified pursuant to this subsection or the parent or guardian of such an employee may petition the Secretary to obtain a review of such special minimum wage rate. An employee or the employee's parent or guardian may file such a petition for and in behalf of the employee or in behalf of the employee and other employees similarly situated. No employee may be a party to any such action unless the employee or the employee's parent or guardian gives consent in writing to become such a party and such consent is filed with the Secretary.

(B) Upon receipt of a petition filed in accordance with subparagraph (A), the Secretary within ten days shall assign the petition to an administrative law judge appointed pursuant to section 3105 of Title 5. The administrative law judge shall conduct a hearing on the record in accordance with section 554 of Title 5 with respect to such petition within thirty days after assignment.

(C) In any such proceeding, the employer shall have the burden of demonstrating that the special minimum wage rate is justified as necessary in order to prevent curtailment of opportunities for employment.

(D) In determining whether any special minimum wage rate is justified pursuant to subparagraph (C), the administrative law judge shall consider

(i) the productivity of the employee or employees identified in the petition and the conditions under which such productivity was measured; and

(ii) the productivity of other employees performing work of essentially the same type and quality for other employers in the same vicinity.

(E) The administrative law judge shall issue a decision within thirty days after the hearing provided for in subparagraph (B).

Such action shall be deemed to be a final agency action unless within thirty days the Secretary grants a request to review the decision of the administrative law judge. Either the petitioner or the employer may request review by the Secretary within fifteen days of the date of issuance of the decision by the administrative law judge.

(F) The Secretary, within thirty days after receiving a request for review, shall review the record and either adopt the decision of the administrative law judge or issue exceptions. The decision of the administrative law judge, together with any exceptions, shall be deemed to be a final agency action.

(G) A final agency action shall be subject to judicial review pursuant to chapter 7 of Title 5. An action seeking such review shall be brought within thirty days of a final agency action described in subparagraph (F).

(d) Employment by schools

The Secretary may by regulation or order provide that sections 206 and 207 of this title shall not apply with respect to the employment by any elementary or secondary school of its students if such employment constitutes, as determined under regulations prescribed by the Secretary, an integral part of the regular education program provided by such school and such employment is in accordance with applicable child labor laws.

§ 215. Prohibited acts; prima facie evidence

(a) After the expiration of one hundred and twenty days from June 25, 1938, it shall be unlawful for any person—

(1) to transport, offer for transportation, ship, deliver, or sell in commerce, or to ship, deliver, or sell with knowledge that shipment or delivery or sale thereof in commerce is intended, any goods in the production of which any employee was employed in violation of section 206 or section 207 of this title, or in violation of any regulation or order of the Secretary issued under section 214 of this title; except that no provision of this chapter shall impose any liability upon any common carrier for the transportation in commerce in the regular course of its business of any goods not produced by such common carrier, and no provision of this chapter shall excuse any common carrier from its obligation to accept any goods for transportation; and except that any such transportation, offer, shipment, delivery, or sale of such goods by a purchaser who acquired them in good faith in reliance on written assurance from the producer that the goods were produced in compliance with the requirements of this chapter, and who acquired such goods for value without notice of any such violation, shall not be deemed unlawful;

(2) to violate any of the provisions of section 206 or section 207 of this title, or any of the provisions of any regulation or order of the Administrator issued under section 214 of this title;

(3) to discharge or in any other manner discriminate against any employee because such employee has filed any complaint or instituted or caused to be instituted any proceeding under or related to this chapter, or has testified or is about to testify in any such proceeding, or has served or is about to serve on an industry committee;

(4) to violate any of the provisions of section 212 of this title;

(5) to violate any of the provisions of section 211(c) of this title, or any regulation or order made or continued in effect under the provisions of section 211(d) of this title, or to make any statement, report, or record filed or kept pursuant to the provisions of such section or of any regulation or order thereunder, knowing such statement, report, or record to be false in a material respect.

(b) For the purposes of subsection (a)(1) of this section proof that any employee was employed in any place of employment where goods shipped or sold in commerce were produced, within ninety days prior to the removal of the goods from such place of employment, shall be prima facie evidence that such employee was engaged in the production of such goods.

§ 216. Penalties

(a) Fines and imprisonment

Any person who willfully violates any of the provisions of section 215 of this title shall upon conviction thereof be subject to a fine of not more than $10,000, or to imprisonment for not more than six months, or both. No person shall be imprisoned under this subsection except for an offense committed after the conviction of such person for a prior offense under this subsection.

(b) Damages; right of action; attorney's fees and costs; termination of right of action

Any employer who violates the provisions of section 206 or section 207 of this title shall be liable to the employee or employees affected in the amount of their unpaid minimum wages, or their unpaid overtime compensation, as the case may be, and in an additional equal amount as liquidated damages. Any employer who violates the provisions of section 215(a)(3) of this title shall be liable for such legal or equitable relief as may be appropriate to effectuate the purposes of section 215(a)(3) of this title, including without limitation employment, reinstatement, promotion, and the payment of wages lost and an additional equal amount as liquidated damages. Any employer who violates section 203(m)(2)(B) of this title shall be liable to the employee or employees affected in the amount of the sum of any tip credit taken by the employer and all such tips unlawfully kept by the employer, and in an additional equal amount as liquidated damages. An action to recover the liability prescribed in the preceding sentences may be maintained against any employer (including a public agency) in any Federal or State court of competent jurisdiction by any one or more employees for and in behalf of himself or themselves and other employees similarly situated. No employee shall be a party plaintiff to any such action unless he gives his consent in writing to become such a party and such consent is filed in the court in which such action is brought. The court in such action shall, in addition to any judgment awarded to the plaintiff or plaintiffs, allow a reasonable attorney's fee to be paid by the defendant, and costs of the action. The right provided by this subsection to bring an action by or on behalf of any employee, and the right of any employee to become a party plaintiff to any such action, shall terminate upon the filing of a complaint by the Secretary of Labor in an action under section 217 of this title in which (1) restraint is sought of any further delay in the payment of unpaid minimum wages, or the amount of unpaid overtime compensation, as the case may be, owing to such employee under section 206 or section 207 of this title by an employer liable therefor under the provisions of this subsection or (2) legal or equitable relief is sought as a result of alleged violations of section 215(a)(3) of this title.

(c) Payment of wages and compensation; waiver of claims; actions by the Secretary; limitation of actions

The Secretary is authorized to supervise the payment of the unpaid minimum wages or the unpaid overtime compensation owing to any employee or employees under section 206 or 207 of this title, and the agreement of any employee to accept such payment shall upon payment in full constitute a waiver by such employee of any right he may have under subsection (b) of this section to such unpaid minimum wages or unpaid overtime compensation and an additional equal amount as liquidated damages. The Secretary may bring an action in any court of competent jurisdiction to recover the amount of the unpaid minimum wages or overtime compensation and an equal amount as liquidated damages. The right provided by subsection (b) of this section to bring to recover the liability specified in the first sentence of such subsection and of any employee to become a party plaintiff to any such action shall terminate upon the filing of a complaint by the Secretary in an action under this subsection in which a recovery is sought of unpaid minimum wages or unpaid overtime compensation under sections 206 and 207 of this title or liquidated or other damages provided by this subsection owing to such employee by an employer liable under the provisions of subsection (b) of this section, unless such action is dismissed without prejudice on motion of the Secretary. Any sums thus recovered by the Secretary of Labor on behalf of an employee pursuant to this subsection shall be held in a special deposit account and shall be paid, on order of the Secretary of Labor, directly to the employee or employees affected. Any such sums not paid to an employee because of inability to do so within a period of three years shall be covered into the Treasury of the United States as miscellaneous receipts. In determining when an action is commenced by the Secretary of Labor under this subsection for the purposes of the statutes of limitations provided in section 255(a) of this title, it shall be considered to be commenced in the case of any individual claimant on the date when the complaint is filed if he is specifically named as a party plaintiff in the complaint, or if his name did not so appear, on the subsequent date on which his name is added as a party plaintiff in such action. The authority and requirements described in this subsection shall apply with respect to a violation of section 203(m)(2)(B) of this title, as appropriate, and the employer shall be liable for the amount of the sum of any tip credit taken by the employer and all such tips unlawfully kept by the employer, and an additional equal amount as liquidated damages.

(d) Savings provision

In any action or proceeding commenced prior to, on, or after August 8, 1956, no employer shall be subject to any liability or punishment under this chapter, or the Portal-to-Portal Act of 1947 [29 U.S.C.A. § 251 et seq.] on account of his failure to comply with any provision or provisions of such Acts (1) with respect to work heretofore or hereafter performed in a workplace to which the exemption in section 213(f) of this title is applicable, (2) with respect to work performed in Guam, the Canal Zone or Wake Island before the effective date of this amendment of subsection (d), or (3) with respect to work performed in a possession named in section 206(a)(3) of this title at any time prior to the establishment by the Secretary, as provided therein, of a minimum wage rate applicable to such work.

(e)(1)(A) Any person who violates the provisions of section 212 or section 213(c)(5) of this title, relating to child labor, or any regulation issued pursuant to such sections, shall be subject to a civil penalty of not to exceed

(i) $11,000 for each employee who was the subject of such a violation; or

(ii) $50,000 with regard to each such violation that causes the death or serious injury of any employee under the age of 18 years, which penalty may be doubled where the violation is a repeated or willful violation.

(B) For purposes of subparagraph (A), the term "serious injury" means—

(i) permanent loss or substantial impairment of one of the senses (sight, hearing, taste, smell, tactile sensation);

(ii) permanent loss or substantial impairment of the function of a bodily member, organ, or mental faculty, including the loss of all or part of an arm, leg, foot, hand or other body part; or

(iii) permanent paralysis or substantial impairment that causes loss of movement or mobility of an arm, leg, foot, hand or other body part.

(2) Any person who repeatedly or willfully violates section 206 or 207, relating to wages, shall be subject to a civil penalty not to exceed $1,100 for each such violation. Any person who violates section 203(m)(2)(B) of this title shall be subject to a civil penalty not to exceed $1,100 for each such violation, as the Secretary determines appropriate, in addition to being liable to the employee or employees affected for all tips unlawfully kept, and an additional equal amount as liquidated damages, as described in subsection (b).

(3) In determining the amount of any penalty under this subsection, the appropriateness of such penalty to the size of the business of the person charged and the gravity of the violation shall be considered. The amount of any penalty under this subsection, when finally determined, may be—

(A) deducted from any sums owing by the United States to the person charged;

(B) recovered in a civil action brought by the Secretary in any court of competent jurisdiction, in which litigation the Secretary shall be represented by the Solicitor of Labor; or

(C) ordered by the court, in an action brought for a violation of section 215(a)(4) of this title or a repeated or willful violation of section 215(a)(2) of this title, to be paid to the Secretary.

(4) Any administrative determination by the Secretary of the amount of any penalty under this subsection shall be final, unless within fifteen days after receipt of notice thereof by certified mail the person charged with the violation takes exception to the determination that the violation for which the penalty is imposed occurred, in which event final determination of the penalty shall be made in an administrative proceeding after opportunity for hearing in accordance with section 554 of title 5, and regulations to be promulgated by the Secretary.

(5) Except for civil penalties collected for violations of section 212 of this title, sums collected as penalties pursuant to this section shall be applied toward reimbursement of the costs of determining the violations and assessing and collecting such penalties, in accordance with the provisions of section 9a of this title. Civil penalties collected

for violations of section 212 of this title shall be deposited in the general fund of the Treasury.

§ 216a. [Repealed]

§ 216b. Liability for overtime work performed prior to July 20, 1949 * * *

§ 217. Injunction proceedings

The district courts, together with the United States District Court for the District of the Canal Zone, the District Court of the Virgin Islands, and the District Court of Guam shall have jurisdiction, for cause shown, to restrain violations of section 215 of this title, including in the case of violations of section 215(a)(2) of this title the restraint of any withholding of payment of minimum wages or overtime compensation found by the court to be due to employees under this chapter (except sums which employees are barred from recovering, at the time of the commencement of the action to restrain the violations, by virtue of the provisions of section 255 of this title).

§ 218. Relation to other laws

(a) No provision of this chapter or of any order thereunder shall excuse noncompliance with any Federal or State law or municipal ordinance establishing a minimum wage higher than the minimum wage established under this chapter or a maximum workweek lower than the maximum workweek established under this chapter, and no provision of this chapter relating to the employment of child labor shall justify noncompliance with any Federal or State law or municipal ordinance establishing a higher standard than the standard established under this chapter. No provision of this chapter shall justify any employer in reducing a wage paid by him which is in excess of the applicable minimum wage under this chapter, or justify any employer in increasing hours of employment maintained by him which are shorter than the maximum hours applicable under this chapter.

(b) Notwithstanding any other provision of this chapter (other than section 213(f) of this title) or any other law:

(1) any Federal employee in the Canal Zone engaged in employment of the kind described in section 5102(c)(7) of Title 5, or

(2) any employee employed in a nonappropriated fund instrumentality under the jurisdiction of the Armed Forces, shall have his basic compensation fixed or adjusted at a wage rate that is not less than the appropriate wage rate provided for in section 206(a)(1) of this title (except that the wage rate provided for in section 206(b) of this title shall apply to any employee who performed services during the

workweek in a work place within the Canal Zone), and shall have his overtime compensation set at an hourly rate not less than the overtime rate provided for in section 207(a)(1) of this title.

§ 218a. [Repealed]

§ 218b Notice to employees

(a) In general

In accordance with regulations promulgated by the Secretary, an employer to which this chapter applies, shall provide to each employee at the time of hiring (or with respect to current employees, not later than March 1, 2013), written notice—

(1) informing the employee of the existence of an Exchange, including a description of the services provided by such Exchange, and the manner in which the employee may contact the Exchange to request assistance;

(2) if the employer plan's share of the total allowed costs of benefits provided under the plan is less than 60 percent of such costs, that the employee may be eligible for a premium tax credit under section 36B of the Title 26 and a cost sharing reduction under section 18071 of Title 42 if the employee purchases a qualified health plan through the Exchange; and

(3) if the employee purchases a qualified health plan through the Exchange, the employee may lose the employer contribution (if any) to any health benefits plan offered by the employer and that all or a portion of such contribution may be excludable from income for Federal income tax purposes.

(b) Effective date

Subsection (a) shall take effect with respect to employers in a State beginning on March 1, 2013.

§ 218c. Protection for employees

(a) Prohibition

No employer shall discharge or in any manner discriminate against any employee with respect to his or her compensation, terms, conditions, or other privileges of employment because the employee (or an individual acting at the request of the employee) has—

(1) received a credit under section 36B of Title 26 or a subsidy under section 18071 of Title 42;

(2) provided, caused to be provided, or is about to provide or cause to be provided to the employer, the Federal Government, or the

attorney general of a State information relating to any violation of, or any act or omission the employee reasonably believes to be a violation of, any provision of this title (or an amendment made by this title);

(3) testified or is about to testify in a proceeding concerning such violation;

(4) assisted or participated, or is about to assist or participate, in such a proceeding; or

(5) objected to, or refused to participate in, any activity, policy, practice, or assigned task that the employee (or other such person) reasonably believed to be in violation of any provision of this title (or amendment), or any order, rule, regulation, standard, or ban under this title (or amendment).

(b) Complaint procedure

(1) In general

An employee who believes that he or she has been discharged or otherwise discriminated against by any employer in violation of this section may seek relief in accordance with the procedures, notifications, burdens of proof, remedies, and statutes of limitation set forth in section 2087(b) of Title 15.

(2) No limitation on rights

Nothing in this section shall be deemed to diminish the rights, privileges, or remedies of any employee under any Federal or State law or under any collective bargaining agreement. The rights and remedies in this section may not be waived by any agreement, policy, form, or condition of employment.

§ 219. Separability

If any provision of this chapter or the application of such provision to any person or circumstance is held invalid, the remainder of this chapter and the application of such provision to other persons or circumstances shall not be affected thereby.

PORTAL-TO-PORTAL PAY ACT (TITLE 29 U.S.C.)

§ 251. Congressional findings and declaration of policy

(a) The Congress finds that the Fair Labor Standards Act of 1938, as amended [29 U.S.C.A § 201 et seq.], has been interpreted judicially in disregard of long-established customs, practices, and contracts between employers and employees, thereby creating wholly unexpected liabilities, immense in amount and retroactive in operation, upon employers with the results that, if said Act as so interpreted or claims arising under such interpretations were permitted to stand, (1) the payment of such liabilities would bring about financial ruin of many employers and seriously impair the capital resources of many others, thereby resulting in the reduction of industrial operations, halting of expansion and development, curtailing employment, and the earning power of employees; (2) the credit of many employers would be seriously impaired; (3) there would be created both an extended and continuous uncertainty on the part of industry, both employer and employee, as to the financial condition of productive establishments and a gross inequality of competitive conditions between employers and between industries; (4) employees would receive windfall payments, including liquidated damages, of sums for activities performed by them without any expectation of reward beyond that included in their agreed rates of pay; (5) there would occur the promotion of increasing demands for payment to employees for engaging in activities no compensation for which had been contemplated by either the employer or employee at the time they were engaged in; (6) voluntary collective bargaining would be interfered with and industrial disputes between employees and employers and between employees and employees would be created; (7) the courts of the country would be burdened with excessive and needless litigation and champertous practices would be encouraged; (8) the Public Treasury would be deprived of large sums of revenues and public finances would be seriously deranged by claims against the Public Treasury for refunds of taxes already paid; (9) the cost to the Government of goods and services heretofore and hereafter purchased by its various departments and agencies would be unreasonably increased and the Public Treasury would be seriously affected by consequent increased cost of war contracts; and (10) serious and adverse effects upon the revenues of Federal, State, and local governments would occur.

The Congress further hereby finds that all of the foregoing constitutes a substantial burden on commerce and a substantial obstruction to the free flow of goods in commerce.

The Congress, therefore, further finds and declares that it is in the national public interest and for the general welfare, essential to national defense, and necessary to aid, protect, and foster commerce, that this chapter be enacted.

The Congress further finds that the varying and extended periods of time for which, under the laws of the several States, potential retroactive liability may be imposed upon employers, have given and will give rise to great difficulties in the sound and orderly conduct of business and industry.

The Congress further finds and declares that all of the results which have arisen or may arise under the Fair Labor Standards Act of 1938, as amended, as aforesaid, may (except as to liability for liquidated damages) arise with respect to the Walsh-Healey and Bacon-Davis Acts and that it is, therefore, in the national public interest and for the general welfare, essential to national defense, and necessary to aid, protect, and foster commerce, that this chapter shall apply to the Walsh-Healey Act and the Bacon-Davis Act.

(b) It is declared to be the policy of the Congress in order to meet the existing emergency and to correct existing evils (1) to relieve and protect interstate commerce from practices which burden and obstruct it; (2) to protect the right of collective bargaining; and (3) to define and limit the jurisdiction of the courts.

§ 254. Relief from liability and punishment under the Fair Labor Standards Act of 1938, the Walsh-Healy Act, and the Bacon-Davis Act for failure to pay minimum wage or overtime compensation

(a) Activities not compensable

Except as provided in subsection (b) of this section, no employer shall be subject to any liability or punishment under the Fair Labor Standards Act of 1938, as amended [29 U.S.C.A § 201 et seq.], the Walsh-Healey Act, or the Bacon-Davis Act, on account of the failure of such employer to pay an employee minimum wages, or to pay an employee overtime compensation, for or on account of any of the following activities of such employee engaged in on or after enacted May 14, 1947—

(1) walking, riding, or traveling to and from the actual place of performance of the principal activity or activities which such employee is employed to perform, and

(2) activities which are preliminary to or postliminary to said principal activity or activities, which occur either prior to the time on any particular workday at which such employee commences, or subsequent to the time on any particular workday at which he ceases, such principal activity or activities. For purposes of this subsection,

the use of an employer's vehicle for travel by an employee and activities performed by an employee which are incidental to the use of such vehicle for commuting shall not be considered part of the employee's principal activities if the use of such vehicle for travel is within the normal commuting area for the employer's business or establishment and the use of the employer's vehicle is subject to an agreement on the part of the employer and the employee or representative of such employee.

(b) Compensability by contract or custom

Notwithstanding the provisions of subsection (a) of this section which relieve an employer from liability and punishment with respect to an activity, the employer shall not be so relieved if such activity is compensable by either—

(1) an express provision of a written or nonwritten contract in effect, at the time of such activity, between such employee, his agent, or collective-bargaining representative and his employer; or

(2) a custom or practice in effect, at the time of such activity, at the establishment or other place where such employee is employed, covering such activity, not inconsistent with a written or nonwritten contract, in effect at the time of such activity, between such employee, his agent, or collective-bargaining representative and his employer.

(c) Restriction of time employed with respect to activities

For the purposes of subsection (b) of this section, an activity shall be considered as compensable under such contract provision or such custom or practice only when it is engaged in during the portion of the day with respect to which it is so made compensable.

(d) Determination of time employed with respect to activities

In the application of the minimum wage and overtime compensation provisions of the Fair Labor Standards Act of 1938, as amended [29 U.S.C.A. § 201 et seq.], of the Walsh-Healey Act, or of the Bacon-Davis Act, in determining the time for which an employer employs an employee with respect to walking, riding, traveling, or other preliminary or postliminary activities described in subsection (a) of this section, there shall be counted all that time, but only that time, during which the employee engages in any such activity which is compensable within the meaning of subsections (b) and (c) of this section.

§ 255. Statute of limitations

Any action commenced on or after May 14, 1947, to enforce any cause of action for unpaid minimum wages, unpaid overtime compensation, or liquidated damages, under the Fair Labor Standards Act of 1938, as amended [29 U.S.C.A. § 201 et seq.], or the Bacon-Davis Act.

(a) if the cause of action accrues on or after May 14, 1947 may be commenced within two years after the cause of action accrued, and every such action shall be forever barred unless commenced within two years after the cause of action accrued, except that a cause of action arising out of a willful violation may be commenced within three years after the cause of action accrued;

* * *

§ 256. Determination of commencement of future actions

In determining when an action is commenced for the purposes of section 255 of this title, an action commenced on or after May 14, 1947 under the Fair Labor Standards Act of 1938, as amended [29 U.S.C.A. § 201 et seq.], the Walsh-Healey Act, or the Bacon-Davis Act, shall be considered to be commenced on the date when the complaint is filed; except that in the case of a collective or class action instituted under the Fair Labor Standards Act of 1938, as amended, or the Bacon-Davis Act, it shall be considered to be commenced in the case of any individual claimant—

(a) on the date when the complaint is filed, if he is specifically named as a party plaintiff in the complaint and his written consent to become a party plaintiff is filed on such date in the court in which the action is brought; or

(b) if such written consent was not so filed or if his name did not so appear—on the subsequent date on which such written consent is filed in the court in which the action was commenced.

* * *

§ 259. Reliance in future on administrative rulings, etc.

(a) In any action or proceeding based on any act or omission on or after May 14, 1947, no employer shall be subject to any liability or punishment for or on account of the failure of the employer to pay minimum wages or overtime compensation under the Fair Labor Standards Act of 1938, as amended [29 U.S.C.A. § 201 et seq.], the Walsh-Healey Act, or the Bacon-Davis Act, if he pleads and proves that the act or omission complained of was in good faith in conformity with and in reliance on any written administrative regulation, order, ruling, approval, or interpretation, of the agency of the United States specified in subsection (b) of this section, or any administrative practice or enforcement policy of such agency with respect to the class of employers to which he belonged. Such a defense, if established, shall be a bar to the action or proceeding, notwithstanding that after such act or omission, such administrative regulation, order, ruling, approval, interpretation, practice, or enforcement policy is modified or rescinded or is determined by judicial authority to be invalid or of no legal effect.

(b) The agency referred to in subsection (a) of this section shall be—

(1) in the case of the Fair Labor Standards Act of 1938, as amended [29 U.S.C.A. § 201 et seq.]—the Administrator of the Wage and Hour Division of the Department of Labor;

(2) in the case of the Walsh-Healey Act—the Secretary of Labor, or any Federal officer utilized by him in the administration of such Act; and

(3) in the case of the Bacon-Davis Act [40 U.S.C.A. § 276a et seq.]—the Secretary of Labor.

§ 260. Liquidated damages

In any action commenced prior to or on or after May 14, 1947 to recover unpaid minimum wages, unpaid overtime compensation, or liquidated damages, under the Fair Labor Standards Act of 1938, as amended [29 U.S.C.A. § 201 et seq.], if the employer shows to the satisfaction of the court that the act or omission giving rise to such action was in good faith and that he had reasonable grounds for believing that his act or omission was not a violation of the Fair Labor Standards Act of 1938, as amended, the court may, in its sound discretion, award no liquidated damages or award any amount thereof not to exceed the amount specified in section 216 of this title.

§ 262. Definitions

(a) When the terms "employer", "employee", and "wage" are used in this chapter in relation to the Fair Labor Standards Act of 1938, as amended [29 U.S.C.A. § 201 et seq.], they shall have the same meaning as when used in such Act of 1938.

(b) When the term "employer" is used in this chapter in relation to the Walsh-Healey Act or Bacon-Davis Act it shall mean the contractor or subcontractor covered by such Act.

(c) When the term "employee" is used in this chapter in relation to the Walsh-Healey Act or the Bacon-Davis Act it shall mean any individual employed by the contractor or subcontractor covered by such Act in the performance of his contract or subcontract.

* * *

(e) As used in section 255 of this title the term "State" means any State of the United States or the District of Columbia or any Territory or possession of the United States.

* * *

CONSUMER CREDIT PROTECTION ACT RESTRICTIONS ON GARNISHMENT (TITLE 15 U.S.C.)

§ 1671. Congressional findings and declaration of purpose

(a) Disadvantages of garnishment

The Congress finds:

(1) The unrestricted garnishment of compensation due for personal services encourages the making of predatory extensions of credit. Such extensions of credit divert money into excessive credit payments and thereby hinder the production and flow of goods in interstate commerce.

(2) The application of garnishment as a creditors' remedy frequently results in loss of employment by the debtor, and the resulting disruption of employment, production, and consumption constitutes a substantial burden on interstate commerce.

(3) The great disparities among the laws of the several States relating to garnishment have, in effect, destroyed the uniformity of the bankruptcy laws and frustrated the purposes thereof in many areas of the country.

(b) Necessity for regulation

On the basis of the findings stated in subsection (a) of this section, the Congress determines that the provisions of this subchapter are necessary and proper for the purpose of carrying into execution the powers of the Congress to regulate commerce and to establish uniform bankruptcy laws.

§ 1672. Definitions

For the purposes of this subchapter:

(a) The term "earnings" means compensation paid or payable for personal services, whether denominated as wages, salary, commission, bonus, or otherwise, and includes periodic payments pursuant to a pension or retirement program.

(b) The term "disposable earnings" means that part of the earnings of any individual remaining after the deduction from those earnings of any amounts required by law to be withheld.

(c) The term "garnishment" means any legal or equitable procedure through which the earnings of any individual are required to be withheld for payment of any debt.

§ 1673. Restriction on garnishment

(a) Maximum allowable garnishment

Except as provided in subsection (b) of this section and in section 1675 of this title, the maximum part of the aggregate disposable earnings of an individual for any workweek which is subjected to garnishment may not exceed

(1) 25 per centum of his disposable earnings for that week, or

(2) the amount by which his disposable earnings for that week exceed thirty times the Federal minimum hourly wage prescribed by section 206(a)(1) of Title 29 in effect at the time the earnings are payable, whichever is less. In the case of earnings for any pay period other than a week, the Secretary of Labor shall by regulation prescribe a multiple of the Federal minimum hourly wage equivalent in effect to that set forth in paragraph (2).

(b) Exceptions

(1) The restrictions of subsection (a) of this section do not apply in the case of

(A) any order for the support of any person issued by a court of competent jurisdiction or in accordance with an administrative procedure, which is established by State law, which affords substantial due process, and which is subject to judicial review.

(B) any order of any court of the United States having jurisdiction over cases under chapter 13 of Title 11.

(C) any debt due for any State or Federal tax.

(2) The maximum part of the aggregate disposable earnings of an individual for any workweek which is subject to garnishment to enforce any order for the support of any person shall not exceed—

(A) where such individual is supporting his spouse or dependent child (other than a spouse or child with respect to whose support such order is used), 50 per centum of such individual's disposable earnings for that week; and

(B) where such individual is not supporting such a spouse or dependent child described in clause (A), 60 per centum of such individual's disposable earnings for that week; except that, with respect to the disposable earnings of any individual for any workweek, the 50 per centum specified in clause (A) shall be deemed to be 55 per centum and the 60 per centum specified in clause (B) shall be deemed to be 65 per centum, if and to the extent that such earnings are subject to garnishment to enforce a support order with respect to a period which is prior to the twelve-week period which ends with the beginning of such workweek.

(c) Execution or enforcement of garnishment order or process prohibited

No court of the United States or any State, and no State (or officer or agency thereof), may make, execute, or enforce any order or process in violation of this section.

§ 1674. Restriction on discharge from employment by reason of garnishment

(a) Termination of employment

No employer may discharge any employee by reason of the fact that his earnings have been subjected to garnishment for any one indebtedness.

(b) Penalties

Whoever willfully violates subsection (a) of this section shall be fined not more than $1,000, or imprisoned not more than one year, or both.

§ 1675. Exemption for State-regulated garnishments

The Secretary of Labor may by regulation exempt from the provisions of section 1673(a) and (b)(2) of this title garnishments issued under the laws of any State if he determines that the laws of that State provide restrictions on garnishment which are substantially similar to those provided in section 1673(a) and (b)(2) of this title.

§ 1676. Enforcement by Secretary of Labor

The Secretary of Labor, acting through the Wage and Hour Division of the Department of Labor, shall enforce the provisions of this subchapter.

§ 1677. Effect on State Laws

This subchapter does not annul, alter, or affect, or exempt any person from complying with, the laws of any State

(1) prohibiting garnishments or providing for more limited garnishment than are allowed under this subchapter, or

(2) prohibiting the discharge of any employee by reason of the fact that his earnings have been subjected to garnishment for more than one indebtedness.

FEDERAL EMPLOYERS' LIABILITY ACT (TITLE 45 U.S.C.)

§ 51. Liability of common carriers by railroad, in interstate or foreign commerce, for injuries to employees from negligence; employee defined

Every common carrier by railroad while engaging in commerce between any of the several States or Territories, or between any of the States and Territories, or between the District of Columbia and any of the States or Territories, or between the District of Columbia or any of the States or Territories and any foreign nation or nations, shall be liable in damages to any person suffering injury while he is employed by such carrier in such commerce, or, in case of the death of such employee, to his or her personal representative, for the benefit of the surviving widow or husband and children of such employee; and, if none, then of such employee's parents; and, if none, then of the next of kin dependent upon such employee, for such injury or death resulting in whole or in part from the negligence of any of the officers, agents, or employees of such carrier, or by reason of any defect or insufficiency, due to its negligence, in its cars, engines, appliances, machinery, track, roadbed, works, boats, wharves, or other equipment.

Any employee of a carrier, any part of whose duties as such employee shall be the furtherance of interstate or foreign commerce; or shall, in any way directly or closely and substantially, affect such commerce as above set forth shall, for the purposes of this chapter, be considered as being employed by such carrier in such commerce and shall be considered as entitled to the benefits of this chapter.

§ 52. Carriers in Territories or other possessions of United States

Every common carrier by railroad in the Territories, the District of Columbia, the Panama Canal Zone, or other possessions of the United States shall be liable in damages to any person suffering injury while he is employed by such carrier in any of said jurisdictions, or, in case of the death of such employee, to his or her personal representative, for the benefit of the surviving widow or husband and children of such employee; and, if none, then of such employee's parents; and, if none, then of the next of kin dependent upon such employee, for such injury or death resulting in whole or in part from the negligence of any of the officers, agents, or employees of such carrier, or by reason of any defect or insufficiency, due to its negligence, in its cars, engines, appliances, machinery, track, roadbed, works, boats, wharves, or other equipment.

§ 53. Contributory negligence; diminution of damages

In all actions on and after April 22, 1908 brought against any such common carrier by railroad under or by virtue of any of the provisions of this chapter to recover damages for personal injuries to an employee, or where such injuries have resulted in his death, the fact that the employee may have been guilty of contributory negligence shall not bar a recovery, but the damages shall be diminished by the jury in proportion to the amount of negligence attributable to such employee: Provided, That no such employee who may be injured or killed shall be held to have been guilty of contributory negligence in any case where the violation by such common carrier of any statute enacted for the safety of employees contributed to the injury or death of such employee.

§ 54. Assumption of risks of employment

In any action brought against any common carrier under or by virtue of any of the provisions of this chapter to recover damages for injuries to, or the death of, any of its employees, such employee shall not be held to have assumed the risks of his employment in any case where such injury or death resulted in whole or in part from the negligence of any of the officers, agents, or employees of such carrier; and no employee shall be held to have assumed the risks of his employment in any case where the violation by such common carrier of any statute enacted for the safety of employees contributed to the injury or death of such employee.

§ 54a. Certain Federal and State regulations deemed statutory authority

A regulation, standard, or requirement in force, or prescribed by the Secretary of Transportation under Chapter 201 of Title 49, or by a State agency that is participating in investigative and surveillance activities under section 20105 of Title 49 is deemed to be a statute under sections 53 and 54 of this title.

§ 55. Contract, rule, regulation, or device exempting from liability; set-off

Any contract, rule, regulation, or device whatsoever, the purpose or intent of which shall be to enable any common carrier to exempt itself from any liability created by this chapter, shall to that extent be void: Provided, That in any action brought against any such common carrier under or by virtue of any of the provisions of this chapter, such common carrier may set off therein any sum it has contributed or paid to any insurance, relief benefit, or indemnity that may have been paid to the injured employee or the person entitled thereto on account of the injury or death for which said action was brought.

§ 56. Actions; limitations; concurrent jurisdiction of courts

No action shall be maintained under this chapter unless commenced within three years from the day the cause of action accrued. Under this chapter an action may be brought in a district court of the United States, in the district of the residence of the defendant, or in which the cause of action arose, or in which the defendant shall be doing business at the time of commencing such action. The jurisdiction of the courts of the United States under this chapter shall be concurrent with that of the courts of the several States.

§ 57. Who included in term "common carrier"

The term "common carrier" as used in this chapter shall include the receiver or receivers or other persons or corporations charged with the duty of the management and operation of the business of a common carrier.

§ 58. Duty or liability of common carriers and rights of employees under other acts not impaired

Nothing in this chapter shall be held to limit the duty or liability of common carriers or to impair the rights of their employees under any other Act or Acts of Congress.

§ 59. Survival of right of action of person injured

Any right of action given by this chapter to a person suffering injury shall survive to his or her personal representative, for the benefit of the surviving widow or husband and children of such employee, and, if none, then of such employee's parents; and, if none, then of the next of kin dependent upon such employee, but in such cases there shall be only one recovery for the same injury.

§ 60. Penalty for suppression of voluntary information incident to accidents; separability of provisions

Any contract, rule, regulation, or device whatsoever, the purpose, intent, or effect of which shall be to prevent employees of any common carrier from furnishing voluntarily information to a person in interest as to the facts incident to the injury or death of any employee, shall be void, and whoever, by threat, intimidation, order, rule, contract, regulation, or device whatsoever, shall attempt to prevent any person from furnishing voluntarily such information to a person in interest, or whoever discharges or otherwise disciplines or attempts to discipline any employee for furnishing voluntarily such information to a person in interest, shall, upon conviction thereof, be punished by a fine of not more than $1,000 or imprisoned for not more than one year, or by both such fine and imprisonment, for each offense: Provided, That nothing herein contained shall be construed to void any contract, rule, or regulation with respect to any information contained in the files of the carrier, or other privileged or confidential reports.

If any provision of this chapter is declared unconstitutional or the applicability thereof to any person or circumstances is held invalid, the validity of the remainder of the chapter and the applicability of such provision to other persons and circumstances shall not be affected thereby.

LONGSHORE AND HARBOR WORKERS' COMPENSATION ACT (TITLE 33 U.S.C.)

§ 901. Short title

This Act may be cited as "Longshore and Harbor Workers' Compensation Act."

§ 902. Definitions

When used in this Act—

(1) The term "person" means individual, partnership, corporation, or association.

(2) The term "injury" means accidental injury or death arising out of and in the course of employment, and such occupational disease or infection as arises naturally out of such employment or as naturally or unavoidably results from such accidental injury, and includes an injury caused by the willful act of a third person directed against an employee because of his employment.

(3) The term "employee" means any person engaged in maritime employment, including any longshoreman or other person engaged in longshoring operations, and any harbor-worker including a ship repairman, shipbuilder, and ship-breaker, but such term does not include—

(A) individuals employed exclusively to perform office clerical, secretarial, security, or data processing work;

(B) individuals employed by a club, camp, recreational operation, restaurant, museum, or retail outlet;

(C) individuals employed by a marina and who are not engaged in construction, replacement, or expansion of such marina (except for routine maintenance);

(D) individuals who (i) are employed by suppliers, transporters, or vendors, (ii) are temporarily doing business on the premises of an employer described in paragraph (4), and (iii) are not engaged in work normally performed by employees of that employer under this chapter;

(E) aquaculture workers;

(F) individuals employed to build any recreational vessel under sixty-five feet in length, or individuals employed to repair any recreational vessel, or to dismantle any part of a recreational vessel in connection with the repair of such vessel;

(G) a master or member of a crew of any vessel; or

(H) any person engaged by a master to load or unload or repair any small vessel under eighteen tons net;

if individuals described in clauses (A) through (F) are subject to coverage under a State workers' compensation law.

(4) The term "employer" means an employer any of whose employees are employed in maritime employment, in whole or in part, upon the navigable waters of the United States (including any adjoining pier, wharf, dry dock, terminal, building way, marine railway, or other adjoining area customarily used by an employer in loading, unloading, repairing, or building a vessel).

(5) The term "carrier" means any person or fund authorized under section 932 of this title to insure under this chapter and includes self-insurers.

(6) The term "Secretary" means the Secretary of Labor.

(7) The term "deputy commissioner" means the deputy commissioner having jurisdiction in respect of an injury or death.

(8) The term "State" includes a Territory and the District of Columbia.

(9) The term "United States" when used in a geographical sense means the several States and Territories and the District of Columbia, including the territorial waters thereof.

(10) "Disability" means incapacity because of injury to earn the wages which the employee was receiving at the time of injury in the same or any other employment; but such term shall mean permanent impairment, determined (to the extent covered thereby) under the guides to the evaluation of permanent impairment promulgated and modified from time to time by the American Medical Association, in the case of an individual whose claim is described in section 910(d)(2) of this title.

(11) "Death" as a basis for a right to compensation means only death resulting from an injury.

(12) "Compensation" means the money allowance payable to an employee or to his dependents as provided for in this chapter, and includes funeral benefits provided therein.

(13) The term "wages" means the money rate at which the service rendered by an employee is compensated by an employer under the contract of hiring in force at the time of the injury, including the

reasonable value of any advantage which is received from the employer and included for purposes of any withholding of tax under subtitle C of title 26 (relating to employment taxes). The term wages does not include fringe benefits, including (but not limited to) employer payments for or contributions to a retirement, pension, health and welfare, life insurance, training, social security or other employee or dependent benefit plan for the employee's or dependent's benefit, or any other employee's dependent entitlement.

(14) "child" shall include a posthumous child, a child legally adopted prior to the injury of the employee, a child in relation to whom the deceased employee stood in loco parentis for at least one year prior to the time of injury, and a stepchild or acknowledged illegitimate child dependent upon the deceased, but does not include married children unless wholly dependent on him. "Grandchild" means a child as above defined of a child as above defined. "Brother" and "sister" include stepbrothers and stepsisters, half brothers and half sisters, and brothers and sisters by adoption, but does not include married brothers nor married sisters unless wholly dependent on the employee. "Child", "grandchild", "brother", and "sister" include only a person who is under eighteen years of age, or who, though eighteen years of age or over, is (1) wholly dependent upon the employee and incapable of self-support by reason of mental or physical disability, or (2) a student as defined in paragraph (19) of this section.

(15) The term "parent" includes step-parents and parents by adoption, parents-in-law, and any person who for more than three years prior to the death of the deceased employee stood in the place of a parent to him, if dependent on the injured employee.

(16) The terms "widow or widower" includes only the decedent's wife or husband living with or dependent for support upon him or her at the time of his or her death; or living apart for justifiable cause or by reason of his or her desertion at such time.

(17) The terms "adoption" or "adopted" mean legal adoption prior to the time of the injury.

(18) The term "student" means a person regularly pursuing a full-time course of study or training at an institution which is—

(A) a school or college or university operated or directly supported by the United States, or by any State or local government or political subdivision thereof,

(B) a school or college or university which has been accredited by a State or by a State recognized or nationally recognized accrediting agency or body,

(C) a school or college or university not so accredited but whose credits are accepted, on transfer, by not less than three institutions which are so accredited, for credit on the same basis as if transferred from an institution so accredited, or

(D) an additional type of educational or training institution as defined by the Secretary,

but not after he reaches the age of twenty-three or has completed four years of education beyond the high school level, except that, where his twenty-third birthday occurs during a semester or other enrollment period, he shall continue to be considered a student until the end of such semester or other enrollment period. A child shall not be deemed to have ceased to be a student during any interim between school years if the interim does not exceed five months and if he shows to the satisfaction of the Secretary that he has a bona fide intention of continuing to pursue a full-time course of education or training during the semester or other enrollment period immediately following the interim or during periods of reasonable duration during which, in the judgment of the Secretary, he is prevented by factors beyond his control from pursuing his education. A child shall not be deemed to be a student under this chapter during a period of service in the Armed Forces of the United States.

(19) The term "national average weekly wage" means the national average weekly earnings of production or nonsupervisory workers on private nonagricultural payrolls.

(20) The term "Board" shall mean the Benefits Review Board.

(21) Unless the context requires otherwise, the term "vessel" means any vessel upon which or in connection with which any person entitled to benefits under this chapter suffers injury or death arising out of or in the course of his employment, and said vessel's owner, owner pro hac vice, agent, operator, charter or bare boat charterer, master, officer, or crew member.

(22) The singular includes the plural and the masculine includes the feminine and neuter.

§ 903. Coverage

(a) Disability or death; injuries occurring upon navigable waters of United States

Except as otherwise provided in this section, compensation shall be payable under this chapter in respect of disability or death of an employee, but only if the disability or death results from an injury occurring upon the navigable waters of the United States (including any adjoining pier, wharf, dry dock, terminal, building way, marine railway, or other adjoining area customarily used by an employer in loading, unloading, repairing, dismantling, or building a vessel).

(b) Governmental officers and employees

No compensation shall be payable in respect of the disability or death of an officer or employee of the United States, or any agency thereof, or of any State or foreign government, or any subdivision thereof.

(c) Intoxication; willful intention to kill

No compensation shall be payable if the injury was occasioned solely by the intoxication of the employee or by the willful intention of the employee to injure or kill himself or another.

(d) Small vessels

(1) No compensation shall be payable to an employee employed at a facility of an employer if, as certified by the Secretary, the facility is engaged in the business of building, repairing, or dismantling exclusively small vessels (as defined in paragraph (3) of this subsection), unless the injury occurs while upon the navigable waters of the United States or while upon any adjoining pier, wharf, dock, facility over land for launching vessels, or facility over land for hauling, lifting, or drydocking vessels.

(2) Notwithstanding paragraph (1), compensation shall be payable to an employee—

(A) who is employed at a facility which is used in the business of building, repairing, or dismantling small vessels if such facility receives Federal maritime subsidies; or

(B) if the employee is not subject to coverage under a State workers' compensation law.

(3) For purposes of this subsection, a small vessel means—

(A) a commercial barge which is under 900 lightship displacement tons; or

(B) a commercial tugboat, towboat, crew boat, supply boat, fishing vessel, or other work vessel which is under 1,600 tons gross as measured under section 14502 of title 46, United States Code, or an alternate tonnage measured under section 14302 of that title as prescribed by the Secretary under section 14104 of that title.

(e) Credit for benefits paid under other laws

Notwithstanding any other provision of law, any amounts paid to an employee for the same injury, disability, or death for which benefits are claimed under this chapter pursuant to any other workers' compensation law or section 30104 of Title 46 shall be credited against any liability imposed by this chapter.

§ 904. Liability for compensation

(a) Every employer shall be liable for and shall secure the payment to his employees of the compensation payable under sections 907, 908, and 909 of this title. In the case of an employer who is a subcontractor, only if such subcontractor fails to secure the payment of compensation shall the contractor be liable for and be required to secure the payment of compensation. A subcontractor shall not be deemed to have failed to secure the payment of compensation if the contractor has provided insurance for such compensation for the benefit of the subcontractor.

(b) Compensation shall be payable irrespective of fault as a cause for the injury.

§ 905. Exclusiveness of liability

(a) Employer liability; failure of employer to secure payment of compensation

The liability of an employer prescribed in section 904 of this title shall be exclusive and in place of all other liability of such employer to the employee, his legal representative, husband or wife, parents, dependents, next of kin, and anyone otherwise entitled to recover damages from such employer at law or in admiralty on account of such injury or death, except that if an employer fails to secure payment of compensation as required by this chapter, an injured employee, or his legal representative in case death results from the injury, may elect to claim compensation under the chapter, or to maintain an action at law or in admiralty for damages on account of such injury or death. In such action the defendant may not plead as a defense that the injury was caused by the negligence of a fellow servant, or that the employee assumed the risk of his employment, or that the injury was due to the contributory negligence of the employee. For purposes of this subsection, a contractor shall be deemed the employer of a subcontractor's employees only if the subcontractor fails to secure the payment of compensation as required by section 904 of this title.

(b) Negligence of vessel

In the event of injury to a person covered under this chapter caused by the negligence of a vessel, then such person, or anyone otherwise entitled to recover damages by reason thereof, may bring an action against such vessel as a third party in accordance with the provisions of section 933 of this title, and the employer shall not be liable to the vessel for such damages directly or indirectly and any agreements or warranties to the contrary shall be void. If such person was employed by the vessel to provide stevedoring services, no such action shall be permitted if the injury was caused by the negligence of persons engaged in providing stevedoring services to the vessel. If such person was employed to provide shipbuilding, repairing, or breaking services and such person's employer was the owner, owner pro hac vice, agent, operator, or charterer of the vessel, no such action shall be permitted, in whole or in part or directly or indirectly, against the injured person's employer (in any capacity, including as the vessel's owner, owner pro hac vice, agent, operator, or charterer) or against the employees of the employer. The liability of the vessel under this subsection shall not be based upon the warranty of seaworthiness or a breach thereof at the time the injury occurred. The remedy provided in this subsection shall be exclusive of all other remedies against the vessel except remedies available under this chapter.

(c) Outer Continental Shelf

In the event that the negligence of a vessel causes injury to a person entitled to receive benefits under this Act by virtue of section 1333 of Title 43, then such person, or anyone otherwise entitled to recover damages by reason thereof, may bring an action against such vessel in accordance with the provisions of subsection (b) of this section. Nothing contained in subsection (b) of this section shall preclude the enforcement according to its terms of any reciprocal indemnity provision whereby the employer of a person entitled to receive benefits under this Act by virtue of section 1333 of title 43 and the vessel agree to defend and indemnify the other for cost of defense and loss or liability for damages arising out of or resulting from death or bodily injury to their employees.

§ 906. Compensation

(a) Time for commencement. No compensation shall be allowed for the first three days of the disability, except the benefits provided for in section 907 of this title: Provided, however, That in case the injury results in disability of more than Fourteen days the compensation shall be allowed from the date of the disability.

(b) Maximum rate of compensation.

(1) Compensation for disability or death (other than compensation for death required by this Act to be paid in a lump sum) shall not exceed an amount equal to 200 per centum of the applicable national average weekly wage, as determined by the Secretary under paragraph (3).

(2) Compensation for total disability shall not be less than 50 per centum of the applicable national average weekly wage determined by the Secretary under paragraph (3), except that if the employee's average weekly wages as computed under section 910 of this title are less than 50 per centum of such national average weekly wage, he shall receive his average weekly wages as compensation for total disability.

(3) As soon as practicable after June 30 of each year, and in any event prior to October 1 of such year, the Secretary shall determine the national average weekly wage for the three consecutive calendar quarters ending June 30. Such determination shall be the applicable national average weekly wage for the period beginning with October 1 of that year and ending with September 30 of the next year. The initial determination under this paragraph shall be made as soon as practicable after October 27, 1972.

(c) Applicability of determinations. Determinations under subsection (b)(3) with respect to a period shall apply to employees or survivors currently receiving compensation for permanent total disability or death benefits during such period, as well as those newly awarded compensation during such period.

(d) [Redesignated]

§ 907. Medical services and supplies

(a) General requirement. The employer shall furnish such medical, surgical, and other attendance or treatment, nurse and hospital service, medicine, crutches, and apparatus, for such period as the nature of the injury or the process of recovery may require.

(b) Physician selection; administrative supervision; change of physicians and hospitals. The employee shall have the right to choose an attending physician authorized by the Secretary to provide medical care under this Act as hereinafter provided. If, due to the nature of the injury, the employee is unable to select his physician and the nature of the injury requires immediate medical treatment and care, the employer shall select a physician for him. The Secretary shall actively supervise the medical care rendered to injured employees, shall require periodic reports as to the medical care being rendered to injured employees, shall have authority to determine the necessity, character, and sufficiency of any medical aid furnished or to be furnished, and may, on his own initiative or at the request of the employer, order a change of physicians or hospitals when in his judgment such change is desirable or necessary in the interest of the employee or where the charges exceed those prevailing within the community for the same or similar services or exceed the provider's customary charges. Change of physicians at the request of employees shall be permitted in accordance with regulations of the Secretary.

(c) Physicians and health care providers not authorized to render medical care or provide medical services

(1)(A) The Secretary shall annually prepare a list of physicians and health care providers in each compensation district who are not authorized to render medical care or provide medical services under this chapter. The names of physicians and health care providers contained on the list required under this subparagraph shall be made available to employees and employers in each compensation district through posting and in such other forms as the Secretary may prescribe.

(B) Physicians and health care providers shall be included on the list of those not authorized to provide medical care and medical services pursuant to subparagraph (A) when the Secretary determines under this section, in accordance with the procedures provided in subsection (j) of this section, that such physician or health care provider—

(i) has knowingly and willfully made, or caused to be made, any false statement or misrepresentation of a material fact for use in a claim for compensation or claim for reimbursement of medical expenses under this chapter;

(ii) has knowingly and willfully submitted, or caused to be submitted, a bill or request for payment under this chapter containing a charge which the Secretary finds to be substantially in excess of the charge for the service, appliance, or supply prevailing within the community or in excess of the provider's customary charges, unless the Secretary finds there is good cause for the bill or request containing the charge;

(iii) has knowingly and willfully furnished a service, appliance, or supply which is determined by the Secretary to be substantially in excess of the need of the recipient thereof or to be of a quality which substantially fails to meet professionally recognized standards;

(iv) has been convicted under any criminal statute (without regard to pending appeal thereof) for fraudulent activities in connection with any Federal or State program for which payments are made to physicians or providers of similar services, appliances, or supplies; or

(v) has otherwise been excluded from participation in such program.

(C) Medical services provided by physicians or health care providers who are named on the list published by the Secretary pursuant to subparagraph (A) of this section shall not be reimbursable under this chapter; except that the Secretary shall direct the reimbursement of medical claims for services rendered by such physicians or health care providers in cases where the services were rendered in an emergency.

(D) A determination under subparagraph (B) shall remain in effect for a period of not less than three years and until the Secretary finds and gives notice to the public that there is reasonable assurance that the basis for the determination will not reoccur.

(E) A provider of a service, appliance, or supply shall provide to the Secretary such information and certification as the Secretary may require to assure that this subsection is enforced.

(2) Whenever the employer or carrier acquires knowledge of the employee's injury, through written notice or otherwise as prescribed by the chapter, the employer or carrier shall forthwith authorize medical treatment and care from a physician selected by an employee pursuant to subsection (b) of this section. An employee may not select a physician who is on the list required by paragraph (1) of this subsection. An employee may not change physicians after his initial choice unless the employer, carrier, or deputy commissioner has given prior consent for such change. Such consent shall be given in cases where an employee's initial choice was not of a specialist whose services are necessary for and appropriate to the proper care and treatment of the compensable injury or disease. In all other cases, consent may be given upon a showing of good cause for change.

(d) Request of treatment or services prerequisite to recovery of expenses; formal report of injury and treatment; suspension of compensation for refusal of treatment or examination; justification.

(1) An employee shall not be entitled to recover any amount expended by him for medical or other treatment or services unless—

(A) the employer shall have refused or neglected a request to furnish such services and the employee has complied with subsections (b) and (c) of this section and the applicable regulations; or

(B) the nature of the injury required such treatment and services and the employer or his superintendent or foreman having knowledge of such injury shall have neglected to provide or authorize same.

(2) No claim for medical or surgical treatment shall be valid and enforceable against such employer unless, within ten days following the first treatment, the physician giving such treatment furnishes to the employer and the deputy commissioner a report of such injury or treatment, on a form prescribed by the Secretary. The Secretary may excuse the failure to furnish such report within the ten-day period whenever he finds it to be in the interest of justice to do so.

(3) The Secretary may, upon application by a party in interest, make an award for the reasonable value of such medical or surgical treatment so obtained by the employee.

(4) If at any time the employee unreasonably refuses to submit to medical or surgical treatment, or to an examination by a physician selected by the employer, the Secretary or administrative law judge may, by order, suspend the payment of further compensation during such time as such refusal continues, and no compensation shall be paid at any time during the period of such suspension, unless the circumstances justified the refusal.

(e) Physical examination; medical questions; report of physical impairment; review or reexamination; costs. In the event that medical questions are raised in any case, the Secretary shall have the power to cause the employee to be examined by a physician employed or selected by the Secretary and to obtain from such physician a report containing his estimate of the employee's physical impairment and such other information as may be appropriate. Any party who is dissatisfied with such report may request a review or reexamination of the employee by one or more different physicians employed or selected by the Secretary. The Secretary shall order such review or reexamination unless he finds that it is clearly unwarranted. Such review or reexamination shall be completed within two weeks from the date ordered unless the Secretary finds that because of extraordinary circumstances a longer period is required. The Secretary shall have the power in his discretion to charge the cost of examination or review under this subsection to the employer, if he is a self-insurer, or to the insurance company which is carrying the risk, in appropriate cases, or to the special fund in section 944 of this title.

(f) Place of examination; exclusion of physicians other than examining physician of Secretary; good cause for conclusions of other physicians respecting impairment; examination by employer's physician; suspension of proceedings and compensation for refusal of examination. An employee shall submit to a physical examination under subsection (e) of this section at such place as the Secretary may require. The place, or places, shall be designated by the Secretary and shall be reasonably convenient for the employee. No physician selected by the employer, carrier, or employee shall be present at or participate in any manner in such examination, nor shall conclusions of such physicians as to the nature or extent of impairment or the cause of impairment be available to the examining physician unless otherwise ordered, for good cause, by the Secretary. Such employer or carrier shall, upon request, be entitled to have the employee examined immediately thereafter and upon the same premises by a qualified physician or physicians in the presence of such physician as the employee may select, if any. Proceedings shall be suspended and no compensation shall be payable for any period during which the employee may refuse to submit to examination.

(g) Fees and charges for examinations, treatment, or service; limitation; regulations. All fees and other charges for medical examinations, treatment, or service shall be limited to such charges as prevail in the community for such treatment, and shall be subject to regulation by the Secretary. The Secretary shall issue regulations limiting the nature and extent of medical expenses chargeable against the employer without authorization by the employer or the Secretary.

(h) Third party liability. The liability of an employer for medical treatment as herein provided shall not be affected by the fact that his employee was injured through the fault or negligence of a third party not in the same employ, or that suit has been brought against such third party. The employer shall, however, have a cause of action against such third party to recover any amounts paid by him for such medical treatment in like manner as provided in section 933(b) of this title.

(i) Physicians' ineligibility for subsection (e) physical examinations and reviews because of workmen's compensation claim employment or fee acceptance or participation. Unless the parties to the claim agree, the Secretary shall not employ or select any physician for the purpose of making examinations or reviews under subsection (e) of this section who, during such employment, or during the period of two years prior to such employment, has been employed by, or accepted or participated in any fee relating to a workmen's compensation claim from any insurance carrier or any self-insurer.

(j) Rules and regulations; notice of findings; hearing; judicial review.

(1) The Secretary shall have the authority to make rules and regulations and to establish procedures, not inconsistent with the provisions of this chapter, which are necessary or appropriate to carry out the provisions of subsection (c) of this section, including the nature and extent of the proof and evidence necessary for actions under this section and the methods of taking and furnishing such proof and evidence.

(2) Any decision to take action with respect to a physician or health care provider under this section shall be based on specific findings of fact by the Secretary. The Secretary shall provide notice of these findings and an opportunity for a hearing pursuant to section 556 of title 5 for a provider who would be affected by a decision under this section. A request for a hearing must be filed with the Secretary within thirty days after notice of the findings is received by the provider making such request. If a hearing is held, the Secretary shall, on the basis of evidence adduced at the hearing, affirm, modify, or reverse the findings of fact and proposed action under this section.

(3) For the purpose of any hearing, investigation, or other proceeding authorized or directed under this section, the provisions of section 49 and 50 of Title 15 (relating to the attendance of witnesses and the production of books, papers, and documents) shall apply to the jurisdiction, powers, and duties of the Secretary or any officer designated by him.

(4) Any physician or health care provider, after any final decision of the Secretary made after a hearing to which he was a party, irrespective of the amount in controversy, may obtain a review of such decision by a civil action commenced within sixty days after the mailing to him of notice of such decision, but the pendency of such review shall not operate as a stay upon the effect of such decision. Such action shall be brought in the court of appeals of the United States for the judicial circuit in which the plaintiff resides or has his principal place of business, or the Court of Appeals for the District of Columbia. As part of his answer, the Secretary shall file a certified copy of the transcript of the record of the hearing, including all evidence submitted in connection therewith. The findings of fact of the Secretary, if based on substantial evidence in the record as a whole, shall be conclusive.

(k) Refusal of treatment on religious grounds

(1) Nothing in this chapter prevents an employee whose injury or disability has been established under this chapter from relying in good faith on treatment by prayer or spiritual means alone, in accordance with the tenets and practice of a recognized church or religious denomination, by an accredited practitioner of such recognized church or religious denomination, and on nursing services rendered in accordance with such tenets and practice, without suffering loss or diminution of the compensation or benefits under this chapter. Nothing in this subsection shall be construed to except an employee from all physical examinations required by this chapter.

(2) If an employee refuses to submit to medical or surgical services solely because, in adherence to the tenets and practice of a recognized church or religious denomination, the employee relies upon prayer or spiritual means alone for healing, such employee shall not be considered to have unreasonably refused medical or surgical treatment under subsection (d) of this section.

§ 908. Compensation for disability

Compensation for disability shall be paid to the employee as follows:

(a) Permanent total disability: In case of total disability adjudged to be permanent 66 2/3 per centum of the average weekly wages shall be paid to the employee during the continuance of such total disability. Loss of both hands, or both arms, or both feet, or both legs or both eyes, or of any two thereof shall, in the absence of conclusive proof to the contrary, constitute permanent total disability. In all other cases permanent total disability shall be determined in accordance with the facts.

(b) Temporary total disability: In case of disability total in character but temporary in quality 66 2/3 per centum of the average weekly wages shall be paid to the employee during the continuance thereof.

(c) Permanent partial disability: In case of disability partial in character but permanent in quality the compensation shall be 66 2/3 per centum of the average weekly wages, which shall be in addition to compensation for temporary total disability or temporary partial disability paid in accordance with subdivision (b) or subdivision (e) of this section, respectively, and shall be paid to the employee, as follows:

(1) Arm lost, three hundred and twelve weeks' compensation.

(2) Leg lost, two hundred and eighty-eight weeks' compensation.

(3) Hand lost, two hundred and forty-four weeks' compensation.

(4) Foot lost, two hundred and five weeks' compensation.

(5) Eye lost, one hundred and sixty weeks' compensation.

(6) Thumb lost, seventy-five weeks' compensation.

(7) First finger lost, forty-six weeks' compensation.

(8) Great toe lost, thirty-eight weeks' compensation.

(9) Second finger lost, thirty weeks' compensation.

(10) Third finger lost, twenty-five weeks' compensation.

(11) Toe other than great toe lost, sixteen weeks' compensation.

(12) Fourth finger lost, fifteen weeks' compensation.

(13) Loss of hearing:

(A) Compensation for loss of hearing in one ear, fifty-two weeks.

(B) Compensation for loss of hearing in both ears, two-hundred weeks.

(C) An audiogram shall be presumptive evidence of the amount of hearing loss sustained as of the date thereof, only if (i) such audiogram was administered by a licensed or certified audiologist or a physician who is certified in otolaryngology, (ii) such audiogram, with the report thereon, was provided to the employee at the time it was administered, and (iii) no contrary audiogram made at that time is produced.

(D) The time for filing a notice of injury, under section 912 of this title, or a claim for compensation, under section 913 of this title, shall not begin to run in connection with any claim for loss of hearing under this section, until the employee has received an audiogram, with the accompanying report thereon, which indicates that the employee has suffered a loss of hearing.

(E) Determinations of loss of hearing shall be made in accordance with the guides for the evaluation of permanent impairment as promulgated and modified from time to time by the American Medical Association.

(14) Phalanges: Compensation for loss of more than one phalange of a digit shall be the same as for loss of the entire digit. Compensation for loss of the first phalange shall be one-half of the compensation for loss of the entire digit.

(15) Amputated arm or leg: Compensation for an arm or a leg, if amputated at or above the elbow or the knee, shall be the same as for a loss of the arm or leg; but, if amputated between the elbow and the wrist or the knee and the ankle, shall be the same as for loss of a hand or foot.

(16) Binocular vision or per centum of vision: Compensation for loss of binocular vision or for 80 per centum or more of the vision of an eye shall be the same as for loss of the eye.

(17) Two or more digits: Compensation for loss of two or more digits, or one or more phalanges of two or more digits, of a hand or foot may be proportioned to the loss of use of the hand or foot occasioned thereby, but shall not exceed the compensation for loss of a hand or foot.

(18) Total loss of use: Compensation for permanent total loss of use of a member shall be the same as for loss of the member.

(19) Partial loss or partial loss of use: Compensation for permanent partial loss or loss of use of a member may be for proportionate loss or loss of use of the member.

(20) Disfigurement: Proper and equitable compensation not to exceed $7,500 shall be awarded for serious disfigurement of the face, head, or neck or of other normally exposed areas likely to handicap the employee in securing or maintaining employment.

(21) Other cases: In all other cases in the class of disability, the compensation shall be 66 2/3 per centum of the difference between the average weekly wages of the employee and the employee's wage-earning capacity thereafter in the same employment or otherwise, payable during the continuance of partial disability.

(22) In any case in which there shall be a loss of, or loss of use of, more than one member or parts of more than one member set forth in paragraphs (1) to (19) of this subsection, not amounting to permanent total disability, the award of compensation shall be for the loss of, or loss of use of, each such member or part thereof, which awards shall run consecutively, except that where the injury affects only two or more digits of the same hand or foot, paragraph (17) of this subsection shall apply.

(23) Notwithstanding paragraphs (1) through (22), with respect to a claim for permanent partial disability for which the average weekly wages are determined under section 910(d)(2) of this title, the compensation shall be 66 2/3 per centum of such average weekly wages multiplied by the percentage of permanent impairment, as determined under the guides referred to in section 902(10) of this title, payable during the continuance of such impairment.

(d)(1) If an employee who is receiving compensation for permanent partial disability pursuant to subsection (c)(1)–(20) of this section dies from causes other than the injury, the total amount of the award unpaid at the time of death shall be payable to or for the benefit of his survivors, as follows:

(A) if the employee is survived only by a widow or widower, such unpaid amount of the award shall be payable to such widow or widower,

(B) if the employee is survived only by a child or children, such unpaid amount of the award shall be paid to such child or children in equal shares,

(C) if the employee is survived by a widow or widower and a child or children, such unpaid amount of the award shall be payable to such survivors in equal shares,

(D) if there be no widow or widower and no surviving child or children, such unpaid amount of the award shall be paid to the survivors specified in section 909(d) of this title (other than a wife, husband, or child); and the amount to be paid each such survivor shall be determined by multiplying such unpaid amount of the award by the appropriate percentage specified in section 909(d) of this title, but if the aggregate amount to which all such survivors are entitled, as so determined, is less than such unpaid amount of the award, the excess amount shall be divided among such survivors pro rata according to the amount otherwise payable to each under this subparagraph.

(2) Notwithstanding any other limitation in section 909 of this title, the total amount of any award for permanent partial disability

pursuant to subsection (c)(1)–(20) of this section unpaid at time of death shall be payable in full in the appropriate distribution.

(3) An award for disability may be made after the death of the injured employee. Except where compensation is payable under subsection (c)(21) of this section if there be no survivors as prescribed in this section, then the compensation payable under this subsection shall be paid to the special fund established under section 944(a) of this title.

(e) Temporary partial disability: In case of temporary partial disability resulting in decrease of earning capacity the compensation shall be two-thirds of the difference between the injured employee's average weekly wages before the injury and his wage-earning capacity after the injury in the same or another employment, to be paid during the continuance of such disability, but shall not be paid for a period exceeding five years.

(f) Injury increasing disability:

(1) In any case in which an employee having an existing permanent partial disability suffers injury, the employer shall provide compensation for such disability as is found to be attributable to that injury based upon the average weekly wages of the employee at the time of the injury. If following an injury falling within the provisions of subsection (c)(1)–(20) of this section, the employee is totally and permanently disabled, and the disability is found not to be due solely to that injury, the employer shall provide compensation for the applicable prescribed period of weeks provided for in that section for the subsequent injury, or for one hundred and four weeks, whichever is the greater, except that, in the case of an injury falling within the provisions of subsection (c)(13) of this section, the employer shall provide compensation for the lesser of such periods. In all other cases of total permanent disability or of death, found not to be due solely to that injury, of an employee having an existing permanent partial disability, the employer shall provide in addition to compensation under paragraphs (b) and (e) of this section, compensation payments or death benefits for one hundred and four weeks only. If following an injury falling within the provisions of subsection (c)(1)–(20) of this section, the employee has a permanent partial disability and the disability is found not to be due solely to that injury, and such disability is materially and substantially greater than that which would have resulted from the subsequent injury alone, the employer shall provide compensation for the applicable period of weeks provided for in that section for the subsequent injury, or for one hundred and four weeks, whichever is the greater, except that, in the case of an injury falling within the provisions of subsection (c)(13) of this section, the employer shall provide compensation for the lesser of such periods.

In all other cases in which the employee has a permanent partial disability, found not to be due solely to that injury, and such disability is materially and substantially greater than that which would have resulted from the subsequent injury alone, the employer shall provide in addition to compensation under paragraphs (b) and (e) of this section, compensation for one hundred and four weeks only.

(2)(A) After cessation of the payments for the period of weeks provided for herein, the employee or his survivor entitled to benefits shall be paid the remainder of the compensation that would be due out of the special fund established in section 944 of this title, except that the special fund shall not assume responsibility with respect to such benefits (and such payments shall not be subject to cessation) in the case of any employer who fails to comply with section 932(a) of this title.

(B) After cessation of payments for the period of weeks provided for in this subsection, the employer or carrier responsible for payment of compensation shall remain a party to the claim, retain access to all records relating to the claim, and in all other respects retain all rights granted under this chapter prior to cessation of such payments.

(3) Any request, filed after September 28, 1984, for apportionment of liability to the special fund established under section 944 of this title for the payment of compensation benefits, and a statement of the grounds therefore, shall be presented to the deputy commissioner prior to the consideration of the claim by the deputy commissioner. Failure to present such request prior to such consideration shall be an absolute defense to the special fund's liability for the payment of any benefits in connection with such claim, unless the employer could not have reasonably anticipated the liability of the special fund prior to the issuance of a compensation order.

(g) Maintenance for employees undergoing vocational rehabilitation: An employee who as a result of injury is or may be expected to be totally or partially incapacitated for a remunerative occupation and who, under the direction of the Secretary as provided by section 939(c) of this title, is being rendered fit to engage in a remunerative occupation, shall receive additional compensation necessary for his maintenance, but such additional compensation shall not exceed $25 a week. The expense shall be paid out of the special fund established in section 944 of this title.

(h) The wage-earning capacity of an injured employee in cases of partial disability under subsection (c)(21) of this section or under subsection (e) of this section shall be determined by his actual earnings if such actual earnings fairly and reasonably represent his wage-earning capacity: Provided, however, That if the employee has no actual earnings or his actual earnings do not fairly and reasonably represent his wage-earning capacity, the deputy commissioner may, in the interest of justice, fix such wage-earning capacity as shall be reasonable, having due regard to the nature of his injury, the degree of physical impairment, his usual employment, and any other factors or circumstances in the case which may affect his capacity to earn wages in his disabled condition, including the effect of disability as it may naturally extend into the future.

(i)(1) Whenever the parties to any claim for compensation under this Act, including survivors benefits, agree to a settlement, the deputy commissioner or administrative law judge shall approve the settlement within thirty days unless it is found to be inadequate or procured by duress. Such settlement may include future medical benefits if the parties so agree. No liability of any employer, carrier, or both for medical, disability, or death benefits shall be discharged unless the application for settlement is approved by the deputy commissioner or administrative law judge. If the parties to the settlement are represented by counsel, then agreements shall be deemed approved unless specifically disapproved within thirty days after submission for approval.

(2) If the deputy commissioner disapproves an application for settlement under paragraph (1), the deputy commissioner shall issue a written statement within thirty days containing the reasons for disapproval. Any party to the settlement may request a hearing before an administrative law judge in the manner prescribed by this chapter. Following such hearing, the administrative law judge shall enter an order approving or rejecting the settlement.

(3) A settlement approved under this section shall discharge the liability of the employer or carrier, or both. Settlements may be agreed upon at any stage of the proceeding including after entry of a final compensation order.

(4) The special fund shall not be liable for reimbursement of any sums paid or payable to an employee or any beneficiary under such settlement, or otherwise voluntarily paid prior to such settlement by the employer or carrier, or both.

(j)(1) The employer may inform a disabled employee of his obligation to report to the employer not less than semiannually any earnings from employment or self-employment, on such forms as the Secretary shall specify in regulations.

(2) An employee who—

(A) fails to report the employee's earnings under paragraph (1) when requested, or

(B) knowingly and willfully omits or understates any part of such earnings, and who is determined by the deputy commissioner to have violated clause (A) or (B) of this paragraph, forfeits his right to compensation with respect to any period during which the employee was required to file such report.

(3) Compensation forfeited under this subsection, if already paid, shall be recovered by a deduction from the compensation payable to the employee in any amount and on such schedule as determined by the deputy commissioner.

§ 909. Compensation for death

If the injury causes death, the compensation therefore shall be known as a death benefit and shall be payable in the amount and to or for the benefit of the persons following:

(a) Reasonable funeral expenses not exceeding $3,000.

(b) If there be a widow or widower and no child of the deceased, to such widow or widower 50 per centum of the average wages of the deceased, during widowhood, or dependent widowerhood, with two years' compensation in one sum upon remarriage; and if there be a surviving child or children of the deceased, the additional amount of 16 2/3 per centum of such wages for each such child; in case of the death or remarriage of such widow or widower, if there be one surviving child of the deceased employee, such child shall have his compensation increased to 50 per centum of such wages, and if there be more than one surviving child of the deceased employee, to such children, in equal parts, 50 per centum of such wages increased by 16 2/3 per centum of such wages for each child in excess of one: Provided, That the total amount payable shall in no case exceed 66 2/3 per centum of such wages. The deputy commissioner having jurisdiction over the claim may, in his discretion, require the appointment of a guardian for the purpose of receiving the compensation of a minor child. In the absence of such a requirement the appointment of a guardian for such purposes shall not be necessary.

(c) If there be one surviving child of the deceased, but no widow or widower, then for the support of such child 50 per centum of the wages of the deceased; and if there be more than one surviving child of the deceased, but no widow or dependent husband, then for the support of such children, in equal parts 50 per centum of such wages increased by 16 2/3 per centum of such wages for each child in excess of one: Provided, That the total amount payable shall in no case exceed 66 2/3 per centum of such wages.

(d) If there be no widow or widower or child, or if the amount payable to a widow or widower and to children shall be less in the aggregate than 66 2/3 per centum of the average wages of the deceased; then for the support of grandchildren or brothers and sisters, if dependent upon the deceased at the time of the injury, and any other persons who satisfy the definition of the term "dependent" in section 152 of title 26, but are not otherwise eligible under this section, 20 per centum of such wages for the support of each such person during such dependency and for the support of each parent, or grandparent, of the deceased if dependent upon him at the time of the injury, 25 per centum of such wages during such dependency. But in no case shall the aggregate amount payable under this subdivision exceed the difference between 66 2/3 per centum of such wages and the amount payable as hereinbefore provided to widow or widower and for the support of surviving child or children.

(e) In computing death benefits, the average weekly wages of the deceased shall not be less than the national average weekly wage as prescribed in section 906(b) of this title, but—

(1) the total weekly benefits shall not exceed the lesser of the average weekly wages of the deceased or the benefit which the deceased employee would have been eligible to receive under section 906(b)(1) of this title; and

(2) in the case of a claim based on death due to an occupational disease for which the time of injury (as determined under section 910(i) of this title) occurs after the employee has retired, the total weekly benefits shall not exceed one fifty-second part of the employee's average annual earnings during the 52-week period preceding retirement.

(f) All questions of dependency shall be determined as of the time of the injury.

(g) Aliens: Compensation under this chapter to aliens not residents (or about to become nonresidents) of the United States or Canada shall be the same in amount as provided for residents, except that dependents in any foreign country shall be limited to surviving wife and child or children, or if there be no surviving wife or child or children, to surviving father or mother whom the employee has supported, either wholly or in part, for the period of one year prior to the date of the injury, and except that the Secretary may, at its option or upon the application of the insurance carrier shall, commute all future installments of compensation to be paid to such aliens by paying or causing to be paid to them one-half of the commuted amount of such future installments of compensation as determined by the Secretary.

§ 910. Determination of pay

Except as otherwise provided in this chapter, the average weekly wage of the injured employee at the time of the injury shall be taken as the basis upon which to compute compensation and shall be determined as follows:

(a) If the injured employee shall have worked in the employment in which he was working at the time of the injury, whether for the same or another employer, during substantially the whole of the year immediately preceding his injury, his average annual earnings shall consist of three hundred times the average daily wage or salary for a six-day worker and two hundred and sixty times the average daily wage or salary for a five-day worker, which he shall have earned in such employment during the days when so employed.

(b) If the injured employee shall not have worked in such employment during substantially the whole of such year, his average annual earnings, if a six-day worker, shall consist of three hundred times the average daily wage or salary, and, if a five-day worker, two hundred and sixty times the average daily wage or salary, which an employee of the same class working substantially the whole of such immediately preceding year in the same or in similar employment in the same or a neighboring place shall have earned in such employment during the days when so employed.

(c) If either of the foregoing methods of arriving at the average annual earnings of the injured employee cannot reasonably and fairly be applied, such average annual earnings shall be such sum as, having regard to the previous earnings of the injured employee in the employment in which he was working at the time of the injury, and of other employees of the same or most similar class working in the same or most similar employment in the same or neighboring locality, or other employment of such employee, including the reasonable value of the services of the employee if engaged in self-employment, shall reasonably represent the annual earning capacity of the injured employee.

(d)(1) The average weekly wages of an employee shall be one fifty-second part of his average annual earnings.

(2) Notwithstanding paragraph (1), with respect to any claim based on a death or disability due to an occupational disease for which the time of injury (as determined under subsection (i) of this section) occurs—

(A) within the first year after the employee has retired, the average weekly wages shall be one fifty-second part of his average annual earnings during the 52-week period preceding retirement; or

(B) more than one year after the employee has retired, the average weekly wage shall be deemed to be the national average weekly wage (as determined by the Secretary pursuant to section 906(b) of this title) applicable at the time of the injury.

(e) If it be established that the injured employee was a minor when injured, and that under normal conditions his wages should be expected to increase during the period of disability the fact may be considered in arriving at his average weekly wages.

(f) Effective October 1 of each year, the compensation or death benefits payable for permanent total disability or death arising out of injuries subject to this chapter shall be increased by the lesser of—

(1) a percentage equal to the percentage (if any) by which the applicable national weekly wage for the period beginning on such October 1, as determined under section 906(b) of this title, exceeds the applicable national average weekly wage, as so determined, for the period beginning with the preceding October 1; or

(2) 5 per centum.

(g) The weekly compensation after adjustment under subsection (f) of this section shall be fixed at the nearest dollar. No adjustment of less than $1 shall be made, but in no event shall compensation or death benefits be reduced.

(h)(1) Not later than ninety days after October 27, 1972, the compensation to which an employee or his survivor is entitled due to total permanent disability or death which commenced or occurred prior to October 27, 1972, shall be adjusted. The amount of such adjustment shall be determined in accordance with regulations of the Secretary by designating as the employee's average weekly wage the applicable national average weekly wage determined under section 906(b) of this title and (A) computing the compensation to which such employee or survivor would be entitled if the disabling injury or death had occurred on the day following October 27, 1972, and (B) subtracting therefrom the compensation to which such employee or survivor was entitled on October 27, 1972; except that no such employee or survivor shall receive total compensation amounting to less than that to which he was entitled on October 27, 1972. Notwithstanding the foregoing sentence, where such an employee or his survivor was awarded compensation as the result of death or permanent total disability at less than the maximum rate that was provided in this chapter at the time of the injury which resulted in the death or disability, then his average weekly wage shall be determined by increasing his average weekly wage at the time of such injury by the percentage which the applicable national average weekly wage has increased between the year in which the injury occurred and the first day of the first month following October 27, 1972. Where such injury occurred prior to 1947, the Secretary shall determine, on the basis of such economic data as he deems relevant, the amount by which the employee's average weekly wage shall be increased for the pre-1947 period.

(2) Fifty per centum of any additional compensation or death benefit paid as a result of the adjustment required by paragraphs (1) and (3) of this subsection shall be paid out of the special fund established under section 944 of this title, and 50 per centum shall be paid from appropriations.

(3) For the purposes of subsections (f) and (g) of this section an injury which resulted in permanent total disability or death which occurred prior to October 27, 1972, shall be considered to have occurred on the day following such date.

(i) For purposes of this section with respect to a claim for compensation for death or disability due to an occupational disease which does not immediately result in death or disability, the time of injury shall be deemed to be the date on which the employee or claimant becomes aware, or in the exercise of reasonable diligence or by reason of medical advice should have been aware, of the relationship between the employment, the disease, and the death or disability.

§ 911. Guardian for minor or incompetent

The deputy commissioner may require the appointment by a court of competent jurisdiction, for any person who is mentally incompetent or a minor, of a guardian or other representative to receive compensation payable to such person under this chapter and to exercise the powers granted to or to perform the duties required of such person under this chapter.

§ 912. Notice of injury or death

(a) Time limitation; to whom notice given. Notice of an injury or death in respect of which compensation is payable under this chapter shall be given within thirty days after the date of such injury or death, or thirty days after the employee or beneficiary is aware, or in the exercise of reasonable diligence or by reason of medical advice should have been aware, of a relationship between the injury or death and the employment, except that in the case of an occupational disease which does not immediately result in a disability or death, such notice shall be given within one year after the employee or claimant becomes aware, or in the exercise of reasonable diligence or by reason of medical advice should have been aware, of the relationship between the employment, the disease, and the death or disability. Notice shall be given (1) to the deputy commissioner in the compensation district in which the injury or death occurred, and (2) to the employer.

(b) Form and content. Such notice shall be in writing, shall contain the name and address of the employee and a statement of the time, place, nature, and cause of the injury or death, and shall be signed by the employee or by some person on his behalf, or in case of death, by any person claiming to be entitled to compensation for such death or by a person on his behalf.

(c) Delivery requirements; designation of agents. Notice shall be given to the deputy commissioner by delivering it to him or sending it by mail addressed to his office, and to the employer by delivering it to him or by sending it by mail addressed to him at his last known place of business. If the employer is a partnership, such notice may be given to any partner, or if a corporation, such notice may be given to any agent or officer thereof upon whom legal process may be served or who is in charge of the business in the place where the injury occurred. Each employer shall designate those agents or other responsible officials to receive such notice, except that the employer shall designate as its representatives individuals among first line supervisors, local plant management, and personnel office officials. Such designations shall be made in accordance with regulations prescribed by the Secretary and the employer shall notify his employees and the Secretary of such designation in a manner prescribed by the Secretary in regulations.

(d) Failure to give notice. Failure to give such notice shall not bar any claim under this chapter (1) if the employer (or his agent or agents or other responsible official or officials designated by the employer pursuant to subsection (c)) or the carrier had knowledge of the injury or death, (2) the deputy commissioner determines that the employer or carrier has not been prejudiced by failure to give such notice, or (3) if the deputy commissioner excuses such failure on the ground that (i) notice, while not given to a responsible official designated by the employer pursuant to subsection (c) of this section, was given to an official of the employer or the employer's insurance carrier, and that the employer or carrier was not prejudiced due to the failure to provide notice to a responsible official designated by the employer pursuant to subsection (c), or (ii) for some satisfactory reason such notice could not be given; nor unless objection to such failure is raised before the deputy commissioner at the first hearing of a claim for compensation in respect of such injury or death.

§ 913. Filing of claims

(a) Time to file. Except as otherwise provided in this section, the right to compensation for disability or death under this chapter shall be barred unless a claim therefore is filed within one year after the injury or death. If payment of compensation has been made without an award on account of such injury or death, a claim may be filed within one year after the date of the last payment. Such claim shall be filed with the deputy commissioner in the compensation district in which such injury or death occurred. The time for filing a claim shall not begin to run until the employee or beneficiary is aware, or by the exercise of reasonable diligence should have been aware, of the relationship between the injury or death and the employment.

(b) Failure to file.

(1) Notwithstanding the provisions of subsection (a) of this section, failure to file a claim within the period prescribed in such

subdivision shall not be a bar to such right unless objection to such failure is made at the first hearing of such claim in which all parties in interest are given reasonable notice and opportunity to be heard.

(2) Notwithstanding the provisions of subsection (a) of this section, a claim for compensation for death or disability due to an occupational disease which does not immediately result in such death or disability shall be timely if filed within two years after the employee or claimant becomes aware, or in the exercise of reasonable diligence or by reason of medical advice should have been aware, of the relationship between the employment, the disease, and the death or disability, or within one year of the date of the last payment of compensation, whichever is later.

(c) Effect on incompetents and minors. If a person who is entitled to compensation under this chapter is mentally incompetent or a minor, the provisions of subsection (a) of this section, shall not be applicable so long as such person has no guardian or other authorized representative, but shall be applicable in the case of a person who is mentally incompetent or a minor from the date of appointment of such guardian or other representative, or in the case of a minor, if no guardian is appointed before he becomes of age, from the date he becomes of age.

(d) Tolling provision. Where recovery is denied to any person, in a suit brought at law or in admiralty to recover damages in respect of injury or death, on the ground that such person was an employee and that the defendant was an employer within the meaning of this chapter and that such employer had secured compensation to such employee under this Act the limitation of time prescribed in subsection (a) of this section shall begin to run only from the date of termination of such suit.

§ 914. Payment of compensation

(a) Manner of payment. Compensation under this chapter shall be paid periodically, promptly, and directly to the person entitled thereto, without an award, except where liability to pay compensation is controverted by the employer.

(b) Period of installment payments. The first installment of compensation shall become due on the fourteenth day after the employer has been notified pursuant to section 912 of this title, or the employer has knowledge of the injury or death, on which date all compensation then due shall be paid. Thereafter compensation shall be paid in installments, semimonthly, except where the deputy commissioner determines that payment in installments should be made monthly or at some other period.

(c) Notification of commencement or suspension of payment. Upon making the first payment, and upon suspension of payment for any cause, the employer shall immediately notify the deputy commissioner, in accordance with a form prescribed by the Secretary, that payment of compensation has begun or has been suspended, as the case may be.

(d) Right to compensation controverted. If the employer controverts the right to compensation he shall file with the deputy commissioner on or before the fourteenth day after he has knowledge of the alleged injury or death, a notice, in accordance with a form prescribed by the commission, stating that the right to compensation is controverted, the name of the claimant, the name of the employer, the date of the alleged injury or death, and the grounds upon which the right to compensation is controverted.

(e) Additional compensation for overdue installment payments payable without award. If any installment of compensation payable without an award is not paid within fourteen days after it becomes due, as provided in subdivision (b) of this section, there shall be added to such unpaid installment an amount equal to 10 per centum thereof, which shall be paid at the same time as, but in addition to, such installment, unless notice is filed under subdivision (d) of this section, or unless such nonpayment is excused by the deputy commissioner after a showing by the employer that owing to conditions over which he had no control such installment could not be paid within the period prescribed for the payment.

(f) Additional compensation for overdue installment payments payable under terms of award. If any compensation, payable under the terms of an award, is not paid within ten days after it becomes due, there shall be added to such unpaid compensation an amount equal to 20 per centum thereof, which shall be paid at the same time as, but in addition to, such compensation, unless review of the compensation order making such award is had as provided in section 921 of this title and an order staying payment has been issued by the Board or court.

(g) Notice of payment; penalty. Within sixteen days after final payment of compensation has been made, the employer shall send to the deputy commissioner a notice, in accordance with a form prescribed by the Secretary, stating that such final payment has been made, the total amount of compensation paid, the name of the employee and of any other person to whom compensation has been paid, the date of the injury or death, and the date to which compensation has been paid. If the employer fails to so notify the deputy commissioner within such time the Secretary shall assess against such employer a civil penalty in the amount of $100.

(h) Investigations, examinations, and hearings for controverted, stopped or suspended payments. The deputy commissioner (1) may upon his own initiative at any time in a case in which payments are being made without an award, and (2) shall in any case where right to compensation is controverted, or where payments of compensation have been stopped or suspended, upon receipt of notice from any person entitled to compensation, or from the employer, that the right to compensation is controverted, or that payments of compensation have been stopped or suspended, make such investigations, cause such medical examinations to be made, or hold such hearings, and take such further action as he considers will properly protect the rights of all parties.

(i) Deposit by employer. Whenever the deputy commissioner deems it advisable he may require any employer to make a deposit with the Treasury of the United States to secure the prompt and convenient payment of such compensation, and payments therefrom upon any awards shall be made upon order of the deputy commissioner.

(j) Reimbursement for advance payments. If the employer has made advance payments of compensation, he shall be entitled to be reimbursed out of any unpaid installment or installments of compensation due.

(k) Receipt for payment. An injured employee, or in case of death his dependents or personal representative, shall give receipts for payment of compensation to the employer paying the same and such employer shall produce the same for inspection by the deputy commissioner, whenever required.

§ 915. Invalid agreements

(a) No agreement by an employee to pay any portion of premium paid by his employer to a carrier or to contribute to a benefit fund or department maintained by such employer for the purpose of providing compensation or medical services and supplies as required by this chapter shall be valid, and any employer who makes a deduction for such purpose from the pay of any employee entitled to the benefits of this act shall be guilty of a misdemeanor and upon conviction thereof shall be punished by a fine of not more than $1,000.

(b) No agreement by an employee to waive his right to compensation under this chapter shall be valid.

§ 916. Assignment and exemption from claims of creditors

No assignment, release, or commutation of compensation or benefits due or payable under this chapter, except as provided by this chapter, shall be valid, and such compensation and benefits shall be exempt from all claims of creditors and from levy, execution, and attachment or other remedy for recovery or collection of a debt, which exemption may not be waived.

§ 917. Compensation a lien against assets

Where a trust fund which complies with section 186(c) of Title 29 established pursuant to a collective-bargaining agreement in effect between an employer and an employee covered under this chapter has paid disability benefits to an employee which the employee is legally obligated to repay by reason of his entitlement to compensation under this chapter or under a settlement, the Secretary shall authorize a lien on such compensation in favor of the trust fund for the amount of such payments.

§ 918. Collection of defaulted payments; special fund

(a) In case of default by the employer in the payment of compensation due under any award of compensation for a period of thirty days after the compensation is due and payable, the person to whom such compensation is payable may, within one year after such default, make application to the deputy commissioner making the compensation order or a supplementary order declaring the amount of the default. After investigation, notice, and hearing, as provided in section 919 of this title, the deputy commissioner shall make a supplementary order, declaring the amount of the default, which shall be filed in the same manner as the compensation order. In case the payment in default is an installment of the award, the deputy commissioner may, in his discretion, declare the whole of the award as the amount in default. The applicant may file a certified copy of such supplementary order with the clerk of the Federal district court for the judicial district in which the employer has his principal place of business or maintains an office, or for the judicial district in which the injury occurred. In case such principal place of business or office or place where the injury occurred is in the District of Columbia, a copy of such supplementary order may be filed with the clerk of the Supreme Court of the District of Columbia [United States District Court for the District of Columbia]. Such supplementary order of the deputy commissioner shall be final, and the court shall upon the filing of the copy enter judgment for the amount declared in default by the supplementary order if such supplementary order is in accordance with law. Review of the judgment so entered may be had as in civil suits for damages at common law. Final proceedings to execute the judgment may be had by writ of execution in the form used by the court in suits at common law in actions of assumpsit. No fee shall be required for filing the supplementary order nor for entry of judgment thereon, and the applicant shall not be liable for costs in a proceeding for review of the judgment unless the court shall otherwise direct. The court shall modify such judgment to conform to any later compensation order upon presentation of a certified copy thereof to the court.

(b) In cases where judgment cannot be satisfied by reason of the employer's insolvency or other circumstances precluding payment, the Secretary of Labor may, in his discretion and to the extent he shall determine advisable after consideration of current commitments payable from the special fund established in section 944 of this title, make payment from such fund upon any award made under this chapter and in addition, provide any necessary medical, surgical, and other treatment required by section 907 of this title in any case of disability where there has been a default in furnishing medical treatment by reason of the insolvency of the employer. Such an employer shall be liable for payment into such fund of the amounts paid therefrom by the Secretary of Labor under this subsection; and for the purpose of enforcing his liability, the Secretary of Labor for the benefit of the fund shall be subrogated to all the rights of the person receiving such payment or benefits as against the employer and may by a proceeding in the name of the Secretary of Labor under subsection (c) of section 921 of this title, or both, seek to recover the amount of the default or so much thereof as in the judgment of the Secretary is possible, or the Secretary may settle and compromise any such claim.

§ 919. Procedure in respect of claims

(a) Filing of claim. Subject to the provisions of section 913 of this title a claim for compensation may be filed with the deputy commissioner in accordance with regulations prescribed by the Secretary at any time after the first seven days of disability following any injury, or at any time after death, and the deputy commissioner shall have full power and authority to hear and determine all questions in respect of such claim.

(b) Notice of claim. Within ten days after such claim is filed the deputy commissioner, in accordance with regulations prescribed by the Secretary, shall notify the employer and any other person (other than the claimant), whom the deputy commissioner considers an interested party, that a claim has been filed. Such notice may be served personally upon the employer or other person, or sent to such employer or person by registered mail.

(c) Investigations; order for hearing; notice; rejection or award. The deputy commissioner shall make or cause to be made such investigations as he considers necessary in respect of the claim, and upon application of any interested party shall order a hearing thereon. If a hearing on such claim is ordered the deputy commissioner shall give the claimant and other interested parties at least ten days' notice of such hearing, served personally upon the claimant and other interested parties or sent to such claimant and other interested parties by registered mail or by certified mail, and shall within twenty days after such hearing is had, by order, reject the claim or make an award in respect of the claim. If no hearing is ordered within twenty days after notice if given as provided in subdivision (b) of this section, the deputy commissioner shall, by order, reject the claim or make an award in respect of the claim.

(d) Provisions governing conduct of hearing; hearing examiners. Notwithstanding any other provisions of this Act, any hearing held under this Act shall be conducted in accordance with the provisions of section 554 of title 5. Any such hearing shall be conducted by a administrative law judge qualified under section 3105 of that title. All powers, duties, and responsibilities vested by this chapter, on October 27, 1972], in the deputy commissioners with respect to such hearings shall be vested in such administrative law judges.

(e) Filing and mailing of order rejecting claim or making award. The order rejecting the claim or making the award (referred to in this chapter as a compensation order) shall be filed in the office of the deputy commissioner, and a copy thereof shall be sent by registered mail or by certified mail to the claimant and to the employer at the last known address of each.

(f) Awards after death of employee. An award of compensation for disability may be made after the death of an injured employee.

(g) Transfer of case. At any time after a claim has been filed with him, the deputy commissioner may, with the approval of the Secretary, transfer such case to any other deputy commissioner for the purpose of making investigation, taking testimony, making physical examinations or taking such other necessary action therein as may be directed.

(h) Physical examination of injured employee. An injured employee claiming or entitled to compensation shall submit to such physical examination by a medical officer of the United States or by a duly qualified physician designated or approved by the Secretary as the deputy commissioner may require. The place or places shall be reasonably convenient for the employee. Such physician or physicians as the employee, employer, or carrier may select and pay for may participate in an examination if the employee, employer, or carrier so requests. Proceedings shall be suspended and no compensation be payable for any period during which the employee may refuse to submit to examination.

§ 920. Presumptions

In any proceeding for the enforcement of a claim for compensation under this chapter it shall be presumed, in the absence of substantial evidence to the contrary—

(a) That the claim comes within the provisions of this chapter.

(b) That sufficient notice of such claim has been given.

(c) That the injury was not occasioned solely by the intoxication of the injured employee.

(d) That the injury was not occasioned by the willful intention of the injured employee to injure or kill himself or another.

§ 921. Review of compensation orders

(a) Effectiveness and finality of order. A compensation order shall become effective when filed in the office of the deputy commissioner as provided in section 919 of this title, and, unless proceedings for the suspension or setting aside of such order are instituted as provided in subdivision (b) of this section, shall become final at the expiration of the thirtieth day thereafter.

(b) Benefits Review Board; establishment; members; chairman; quorum; voting; questions reviewable; record; conclusiveness of findings; stay of payments; remand.

(1) There is hereby established a Benefits Review Board which shall be composed of five members appointed by the Secretary from among individuals who are especially qualified to serve on such Board. The Secretary shall designate one of the members of the Board to serve as chairman. The Chairman shall have the authority, as delegated by the Secretary, to exercise all administrative functions necessary to operate the Board.

(2) For the purpose of carrying out its functions under this chapter, three members of the Board shall constitute a quorum and official action can be taken only on the affirmative vote of at least three members.

(3) The Board shall be authorized to hear and determine appeals raising a substantial question of law or fact taken by any party in interest from decisions with respect to claims of employees under this chapter and the extensions thereof. The Board's orders shall be based upon the hearing record. The findings of fact in the decision under review by the Board shall be conclusive if supported by substantial evidence in the record considered as a whole. The payment of the amounts required by an award shall not be stayed pending final decision in any such proceeding unless ordered by the Board. No stay shall be issued unless irreparable injury would otherwise ensue to the employer or carrier.

(4) The Board may, on its own motion or at the request of the Secretary, remand a case to the administrative law judge for further appropriate action. The consent of the parties in interest shall not be a prerequisite to a remand by the Board.

(5) Notwithstanding paragraphs (1) through (4), upon application of the Chairman of the Board, the Secretary may designate up to four Department of Labor administrative law judges to serve on the Board temporarily, for not more than one year. The Board is authorized to delegate to panels of three members any or all of the powers which the Board may exercise. Each such panel shall have no more than one temporary member. Two members shall constitute a quorum of a panel. Official adjudicative action may be taken only on the affirmative vote of at least two members of a panel. Any party aggrieved by a decision of a panel of the Board may, within thirty days after the date

of entry of the decision, petition the entire permanent Board for review of the panel's decision. Upon affirmative vote of the majority of the permanent members of the Board, the petition shall be granted. The Board shall amend its Rules of Practice to conform with this paragraph. Temporary members, while serving as members of the Board, shall be compensated at the same rate of compensation as regular members.

(c) Court of appeals; jurisdiction; persons entitled to review; petition; record; determination and enforcement; service of process; stay of payments. Any person adversely affected or aggrieved by a final order of the Board may obtain a review of that order in the United States court of appeals for the circuit in which the injury occurred, by filing in such court within sixty days following the issuance of such Board order a written petition praying that the order be modified or set aside. A copy of such petition shall be forthwith transmitted by the clerk of the court, to the Board, and to the other parties, and thereupon the Board shall file in the court the record in the proceedings as provided in section 2112 of title 28. Upon such filing, the court shall have jurisdiction of the proceeding and shall have the power to give a decree affirming, modifying, or setting aside, in whole or in part, the order of the Board and enforcing same to the extent that such order is affirmed or modified. The orders, writs, and processes of the court in such proceedings may run, be served, and be returnable anywhere in the United States. The payment of the amounts required by an award shall not be stayed pending final decision in any such proceeding unless ordered by the court. No stay shall be issued unless irreparable injury would otherwise ensue to the employer or carrier. The order of the court allowing any stay shall contain a specific finding, based upon evidence submitted to the court and identified by reference thereto, that irreparable damage would result to the employer, and specifying the nature of the damage.

(d) District Court; jurisdiction; enforcement of orders; application of beneficiaries of awards or deputy commissioner; process for compliance with orders. If any employer or his officers or agents fails to comply with a compensation order making an award, that has become final, any beneficiary of such award or the deputy commissioner making the order, may apply for the enforcement of the order to the Federal district court for the judicial district in which the injury occurred (or to the United States District Court for the District of Columbia if the injury occurred in the District). If the court determines that the order was made and served in accordance with law, and that such employer or his officers or agents have failed to comply therewith, the court shall enforce obedience to the order by writ of injunction or by other proper process, mandatory or otherwise, to enjoin upon such person and his officers and agents compliance with the order.

(e) Institution of proceedings for suspension, setting aside, or enforcement of compensation orders. Proceedings for suspending, setting aside, or enforcing a compensation order, whether rejecting a claim or making an award, shall not be instituted otherwise than as provided in this section and section 918 of this title.

§ 922. Modification of awards

Upon his own initiative, or upon the application of any party in interest (including an employer or carrier which has been granted relief under section 908(f) of this title), on the ground of a change in conditions or because of a mistake in a determination of fact by the deputy commissioner, the deputy commissioner may, at any time prior to one year after the date of the last payment of compensation, whether or not a compensation order has been issued, or at any time prior to one year after the rejection of a claim, review a compensation case (including a case under which payments are made pursuant to section 944(i) of this title in accordance with the procedure prescribed in respect of claims in section 919 of this title), and in accordance with such section issue a new compensation order which may terminate, continue, reinstate, increase, or decrease such compensation, or award compensation. Such new order shall not affect any compensation previously paid, except that an award increasing the compensation rate may be made effective from the date of the injury, and if any part of the compensation due or to become due is unpaid, an award decreasing the compensation rate may be made effective from the date of the injury, and any payment made prior thereto in excess of such decreased rate shall be deducted from any unpaid compensation, in such manner and by such method as may be determined by the deputy commissioner with the approval of the Secretary. This section does not authorize the modification of settlements.

§ 923. Procedure before deputy commissioner or Board

(a) In making an investigation or inquiry or conducting a hearing the deputy commissioner or Board shall not be bound by common law or statutory rules of evidence or by technical or formal rules of procedure, except as provided by this chapter; but may make such investigation or inquiry or conduct such hearing in such manner as to best ascertain the rights of the parties. Declarations of a deceased employee concerning the injury in respect of which the investigation or inquiry is being made or the hearing conducted shall be received in evidence and shall, if corroborated by other evidence, be sufficient to establish the injury.

(b) Hearings before a deputy commissioner or Board shall be open to the public and shall be stenographically reported, and the deputy commissioners or Board, subject to the approval of the Secretary, are authorized to contract for the reporting of such hearings. The Secretary shall by regulation provide for the preparation of a record of the hearings and other proceedings before the deputy commissioners or Board.

§ 924. Witnesses

No person shall be required to attend as a witness in any proceeding before a deputy commissioner at a place outside of the State of his residence and more than one hundred miles from his place of residence unless his lawful mileage and fee for one day's attendance shall be first paid or tendered to him; but the testimony of any witness may be taken by deposition or interrogatories according to the rules of practice of the Federal district court for the judicial district in which the case is pending (or of the Supreme Court of the District of Columbia [United States District Court for the District of Columbia] if the case is pending in the District).

§ 925. Witness fees

Witnesses summoned in a proceeding before a deputy commissioner or whose depositions are taken shall receive the same fees and mileage as witnesses in courts of the United States.

§ 926. Costs in proceedings brought without reasonable grounds

If the court having jurisdiction of proceedings in respect of any claim or compensation order determines that the proceedings in respect of such claim or order have been instituted or continued without reasonable ground, the costs of such proceedings shall be assessed against the party who has so instituted or continued such proceedings.

§ 927. Powers of deputy commissioners or Board

(a) The deputy commissioner or Board shall have power to preserve and enforce order during any such proceedings; to issue subpoenas for, to administer oaths to, and to compel the attendance and testimony of witnesses, or the production of books, papers, documents, and other evidence, or the taking of depositions before any designated individual competent to administer oaths; to examine witnesses; and to do all things conformable to law which may be necessary to enable him effectively to discharge the duties of his office.

(b) If any person in proceedings before a deputy commissioner or Board disobeys or resists any lawful order or process, or misbehaves during a hearing or so near the place thereof as to obstruct the same, or neglects to produce, after having been ordered to do so, any pertinent book, paper, or document, or refuses to appear after having been subpoenaed, or upon appearing refuses to take the oath as a witness, or after having taken the oath refuses to be examined according to law, the deputy commissioner or

Board shall certify the facts to the district court having jurisdiction in the place in which he is sitting (or to the United State District Court for the District of Columbia if he is sitting in such District) which shall thereupon in a summary manner hear the evidence as to the acts complained of, and, if the evidence so warrants, punish such person in the same manner and to the same extent as for a contempt committed before the court, or commit such person upon the same conditions as if the doing of the forbidden act had occurred with reference to the process of or in the presence of the court.

§ 928. Fees for services

(a) Attorney's fee; successful prosecution of case. If the employer or carrier declines to pay any compensation on or before the thirtieth day after receiving written notice of a claim for compensation having been filed from the deputy commissioner, on the ground that there is no liability for compensation within the provisions of this chapter, and the person seeking benefits shall thereafter have utilized the services of an attorney at law in the successful prosecution of his claim, there shall be awarded, in addition to the award of compensation, in a compensation order, a reasonable attorney's fee against the employer or carrier in an amount approved by the deputy commissioner, Board, or court, as the case may be, which shall be paid directly by the employer or carrier to the attorney for the claimant in a lump sum after the compensation order becomes final.

(b) Attorney's fee; successful prosecution for additional compensation; independent medical evaluation of disability controversy; restriction of other assessments. If the employer or carrier pays or tenders payment of compensation without an award pursuant to section 914(a) and (b) of this title, and thereafter a controversy develops over the amount of additional compensation, if any, to which the employee may be entitled, the deputy commissioner or Board shall set the matter for an informal conference and following such conference the deputy commissioner or Board shall recommend in writing a disposition of the controversy. If the employer or carrier refuse to accept such written recommendation, within fourteen days after its receipt by them, they shall pay or tender to the employee in writing the additional compensation, if any, to which they believe the employee is entitled. If the employee refuses to accept such payment or tender of compensation, and thereafter utilizes the services of an attorney at law, and if the compensation thereafter awarded is greater than the amount paid or tendered by the employer or carrier, a reasonable attorney's fee based solely upon the difference between the amount awarded and the amount tendered or paid shall be awarded in addition to the amount of compensation. The foregoing sentence shall not apply if the controversy relates to degree or length of disability, and if the employer or carrier offers to submit the case for evaluation by physicians employed or selected by the Secretary, as authorized in section 907(e) of this title and offers to tender an amount of compensation based upon the degree or length of disability found by the independent medical report at such time as an evaluation of disability can be made. If the claimant is successful in review proceedings before the Board or court in any such case an award may be made in favor of the claimant and against the employer or carrier for a reasonable attorney's fee for claimant's counsel in accord with the above provisions. In all other cases any claim for legal services shall not be assessed against the employer or carrier.

(c) Approval; payment; lien. In all cases fees for attorneys representing the claimant shall be approved in the manner herein provided. If any proceedings are had before the Board or any court for review of any action, award, order, or decision, the Board or court may approve an attorney's fee for the work done before it by the attorney for the claimant. An approved attorney's fee, in cases in which the obligation to pay the fee is upon the claimant, may be made a lien upon the compensation due under an award; and the deputy commissioner, Board, or court shall fix in the award approving the fee, such lien and manner of payment.

(d) Costs; witnesses' fees and mileage; prohibition against diminution of compensation to claimant. In cases where an attorney's fee is awarded against an employer or carrier there may be further assessed against such employer or carrier as costs, fees and mileage for necessary witnesses attending the hearing at the instance of claimant. Both the necessity for the witness and the reasonableness of the fees of expert witnesses must be approved by the hearing officer, the Board, or the court, as the case may be. The amounts awarded against an employer or carrier as attorney's fees, costs, fees and mileage for witnesses shall not in any respect affect or diminish the compensation payable under this chapter.

(e) Unapproved fees; solicitation; penalty. A person who receives a fee, gratuity, or other consideration on account of services rendered as a representative of a claimant, unless the consideration is approved by the deputy commissioner, administrative law judge, Board, or court, or who makes it a business to solicit employment for a lawyer, or for himself, with respect to a claim or award for compensation under this chapter, shall, upon conviction thereof, for each offense be punished by a fine of not more than $1,000 or be imprisoned for not more than one year, or both.

§ 929. Record of injury or death

Every employer shall keep a record in respect of any injury to an employee. Such record shall contain such information of disease, other disability, or death in respect of such injury as the Secretary may be regulation require, and shall be available to inspection by the Secretary or by any State authority at such times and under such conditions as the Secretary may by regulation prescribe.

§ 930. Reports to Secretary

(a) Time for sending; contents; copy to deputy commissioner. Within ten days from the date of any injury, which causes loss of one or more shifts of work, or death or from the date that the employer has knowledge of a disease or infection in respect of such injury, the employer shall send to the Secretary a report setting forth (1) the name, address, and business of the employer; (2) the name, address, and occupation of the employee; (3) the cause and nature of the injury or death; (4) the year, month, day, and hour when and the particular locality where the injury or death occurred; and (5) such other information as the Secretary may require. A copy of such report shall be sent at the same time to the deputy commissioner in the compensation district in which the injury occurred. Notwithstanding the requirements of this subsection, each employer shall keep a record of each and every injury regardless of whether such injury results in the loss of one or more shifts of work.

(b) Additional reports. Additional reports in respect of such injury and of the condition of such employee shall be sent by the employer to the Secretary and to such deputy commissioner at such times and in such manner as the Secretary may prescribe.

(c) Use as evidence. Any report provided for in subsection (a) or (b) of this section shall not be evidence of any fact stated in such report in any proceeding in respect of such injury or death on account of which the report is made.

(d) Compliance by mailing. The mailing of any such report and copy in a stamped envelope, within the time prescribed in subsections (a) or (b) of this section, to the Secretary and deputy commissioner, respectively, shall be a compliance with this section.

(e) Penalty for failure or refusal to send report. Any employer, insurance carrier, or self-insured employer who knowingly and willfully fails or refuses to send any report required by this section or knowingly or willfully makes a false statement or misrepresentation in any such report shall be subject to a civil penalty not to exceed $10,000 for each such failure, refusal, false statement, or misrepresentation.

(f) Tolling provision. Where the employer or the carrier has been given notice, or the employer (or his agent in charge of the business in the place where the injury occurred) or the carrier has knowledge, of any injury or death of an employee and fails, neglects, or refuses to file report thereof as required by the provisions of subsection (a) of this section, the limitations in subsection (a) of section 913 of this title shall not begin to run against the claim of the injured employee or his dependents entitled to compensation, or in favor of either the employer or the carrier, until such report shall have been furnished as required by the provisions of subsection (a) of this section.

§ 931. Penalty for misrepresentation; prosecution of claims

(a)(1) Any claimant or representative of a claimant who knowingly and willfully makes a false statement or representation for the purpose of obtaining a benefit or payment under this chapter shall be guilty of a felony, and on conviction thereof shall be punished by a fine not to exceed $10,000, by imprisonment not to exceed five years, or by both.

(2) The United States attorney for the district in which the injury is alleged to have occurred shall make every reasonable effort to promptly investigate each complaint made under this subsection.

(b)(1) No representation fee of a claimant's representative shall be approved by the deputy commissioner, an administrative law judge, the Board, or a court pursuant to section 928 of this title, if the claimant's representative is on the list of individuals who are disqualified from representing claimants under this chapter maintained by the Secretary pursuant to paragraph (2) of this subsection.

(2)(A) The Secretary shall annually prepare a list of those individuals in each compensation district who have represented claimants for a fee in cases under this chapter and who are not authorized to represent claimants. The names of individuals contained on the list required under this subparagraph shall be made available to employees and employers in each compensation district through posting and in such other forms as the Secretary may prescribe.

(B) Individuals shall be included on the list of those not authorized to represent claimants under this chapter if the Secretary determines under this section, in accordance with the procedure provided in subsection (j) of section 907 of this title, that such individual—

(i) has been convicted (without regard to pending appeal) of any crime in connection with the representation of a claimant under this chapter or any workers' compensation statute;

(ii) has engaged in fraud in connection with the presentation of a claim under this or any workers' compensation statute, including, but not limited to, knowingly making false representations, concealing or attempting to conceal material facts with respect to a claim, or soliciting or otherwise procuring false testimony;

(iii) has been prohibited from representing claimants before any other workers' compensation agency for reasons of professional misconduct which are similar in nature to those which would be grounds for disqualification under this paragraph; or

(iv) has accepted fees for representing claimants under this chapter which were not approved, or which were in excess of the amount approved pursuant to section 928 of this title.

(C) Notwithstanding subparagraph (B), no individual who is on the list required to be maintained by the Secretary pursuant to this section shall be prohibited from presenting his or her own claim or from representing without fee, a claimant who is a spouse, mother, father, sister, brother, or child of such individual.

(D) A determination under subparagraph (A) shall remain in effect for a period of not less than three years and until the Secretary finds and gives notice to the public that there is reasonable assurance that the basis for the determination will not reoccur.

(3) No employee shall be liable to pay a representation fee to any representative whose fee has been disallowed by reason of the operation of this paragraph.

(4) The Secretary shall issue such rules and regulations as are necessary to carry out this section.

(c) A person including, but not limited to, an employer, his duly authorized agent, or an employee of an insurance carrier who knowingly and willfully makes a false statement or representation for the purpose of reducing, denying, or terminating benefits to an injured employee, or his dependents pursuant to section 909 of this title if the injury results in death, shall be punished by a fine not to exceed $10,000, by imprisonment not to exceed five years, or by both.

§ 932. Security for compensation

(a) Every employer shall secure the payment of compensation under this chapter—

(1) By insuring and keeping insured the payment of such compensation with any stock company or mutual company or association, or with any other person or fund, while such person or fund is authorized (A) under the laws of the United States or of any State, to insure workmen's compensation, and (B) by the Secretary, to insure payment of compensation under this chapter; or

(2) By furnishing satisfactory proof to the Secretary of his financial ability to pay such compensation and receiving an authorization from the Secretary to pay such compensation directly. The Secretary may, as a condition to such authorization, require such employer to deposit in a depository designated by the Secretary either an indemnity bond or securities (at the option of the employer) of a

kind and in an amount determined by the Secretary, based on the employer's financial condition, the employer's previous record of payments, and other relevant factors, and subject to such conditions as the Secretary may prescribe, which shall include authorization to the Secretary in case of default to sell any such securities sufficient to pay compensation awards or to bring suit upon such bonds, to procure prompt payment of compensation under this chapter. Any employer securing compensation in accordance with the provisions of this paragraph shall be known as a self-insurer.

(b) In granting authorization to any carrier to insure payment of compensation under this chapter, the Secretary may take into consideration the recommendation of any State authority having supervision over carriers or over workmen's compensation, and may authorize any carrier to insure the payment of compensation under this chapter in a limited territory. Any marine protection and indemnity mutual insurance corporation or association, authorized to write insurance against liability for loss or damage from personal injury and death, and for other losses and damages, incidental to or in respect of the ownership, operation, or chartering of vessels on a mutual assessment plan, shall be deemed a qualified carrier to insure compensation under this chapter. The Secretary may suspend or revoke any such authorization for good cause shown after a hearing at which the carrier shall be entitled to be heard in person or by counsel and to present evidence. No suspension or revocation shall affect the liability of any carrier already incurred.

§ 933. Compensation for injuries where third persons are liable

(a) Election of remedies. If on account of a disability or death for which compensation is payable under this chapter, the person entitled to such compensation determines that some person other than the employer or a person or persons in his employ is liable in damages, he need not elect whether to receive such compensation or to recover damages against such third person.

(b) Acceptance of compensation acting as assignment. Acceptance of compensation under an award in a compensation order filed by the deputy commissioner, an administrative law judge, or the Board shall operate as an assignment to the employer of all rights of the person entitled to compensation to recover damages against such third person unless such person shall commence an action against such third person within six months after such acceptance. If the employer fails to commence an action against such third person within ninety days after the cause of action is assigned under this section, the right to bring such action shall revert to the person entitled to compensation. For the purpose of this subsection, the term "award" with respect to a compensation order means a formal order issued by the deputy commissioner, an administrative law judge, or Board.

(c) Payment into section 944 fund operating as assignment. The payment of such compensation into the fund established in section 944 of this title shall operate as an assignment to the employer of all right of the legal representative of the deceased (hereinafter referred to as "representative") to recover damages against such third person.

(d) Institution of proceedings or compromise by assignee. Such employer on account of such assignment may either institute proceedings for the recovery of such damages or may compromise with such third person either without or after instituting such proceeding.

(e) Recoveries by assignee. Any amount recovered by such employer on account of such assignment, whether or not as the result of a compromise, shall be distributed as follows:

(1) The employer shall retain an amount equal to—

(A) the expenses incurred by him in respect to such proceedings or compromise (including a reasonable attorney's fee as determined by the deputy commissioner or Board);

(B) the cost of all benefits actually furnished by him to the employee under section 907 of this title;

(C) all amounts paid as compensation;

(D) the present value of all amounts thereafter payable as compensation, such present value to be computed in accordance with a schedule prepared by the Secretary, and the present value of the cost of all benefits thereafter to be furnished under section 907 of this title, to be estimated by the deputy commissioner, and the amounts so computed and estimated to be retained by the employer as a trust fund to pay such compensation and the cost of such benefits as they become due, and to pay any sum finally remaining in excess thereof to the person entitled to compensation or to the representative; and

(2) The employer shall pay any excess to the person entitled to compensation or to the representative.

(f) Institution of proceedings by person entitled to compensation. If the person entitled to compensation institutes proceedings within the period prescribed in subsection (b) of this section the employer shall be required to pay as compensation under this chapter, a sum equal to the excess of the amount which the Secretary determines is payable on account of such injury or death over the net amount recovered against such third person. Such net amount shall be equal to the actual amount recovered less the expenses reasonably incurred by such person in respect to such proceedings (including reasonable attorneys' fees).

(g) Settlement with third person.

(1) If the person entitled to compensation (or the person's representative) enters into a settlement with a third person referred to in subsection (a) of this section for an amount less than the compensation to which the person (or the person's representative) would be entitled under this chapter, the employer shall be liable for compensation as determined under subsection (f) of this section only if written approval of the settlement is obtained from the employer and the employer's carrier, before the settlement is executed, and by the person entitled to compensation (or the person's representative). The approval shall be made on a form provided by the Secretary and shall be filed in the office of the deputy commissioner within thirty days after the settlement is entered into.

(2) If no written approval of the settlement is obtained and filed as required by paragraph (1), or if the employee fails to notify the employer of any settlement obtained from or judgment rendered against a third person, all rights to compensation and medical benefits under this chapter shall be terminated, regardless of whether the employer or the employer's insurer has made payments or acknowledged entitlement to benefits under this chapter.

(3) Any payments by the special fund established under section 944 of this section shall be a lien upon the proceeds of any settlement obtained from or judgment rendered against a third person referred to under subsection (a) of this section. Notwithstanding any other provision of law, such lien shall be enforceable against such proceeds, regardless of whether the Secretary on behalf of the special fund has agreed to or has received actual notice of the settlement or judgment.

(4) Any payments by a trust fund described in section 917 of this title shall be a lien upon the proceeds of any settlement obtained from or judgment recorded against a third person referred to under subsection (a) of this section. Such lien shall have priority over a lien under paragraph (3) of this subsection.

(h) Subrogation. Where the employer is insured and the insurance carrier has assumed the payment of the compensation, the insurance carrier shall be subrogated to all the rights of the employer under this section.

(i) Right to compensation as exclusive remedy. The right to compensation or benefits under this chapter shall be the exclusive remedy to an employee when he is injured, or to his eligible survivors or legal representatives if he is killed, by the negligence or wrong of any other person or persons in the same employ: Provided, That this provision shall not affect the liability of a person other than an officer or employee of the employer.

§ 934. Compensation notice

Every employer who has secured compensation under the provisions of this chapter shall keep posted in a conspicuous place or places in and about his place or places of business typewritten or printed notices, in accordance with a form prescribed by the Secretary, stating that such employer has secured the payment of compensation in accordance with the provisions of this chapter. Such notices shall contain the name and address of the carrier, if any, with whom the employer has secured payment of compensation and the date of the expiration of the policy.

§ 935. Substitution of carrier for employer

In any case where the employer is not a self-insurer, in order that the liability for compensation imposed by this chapter may be most effectively discharged by the employer, and in order that the administration of this chapter in respect of such liability may be facilitated, the Secretary shall by regulation provide for the discharge, by the carrier for such employer, of such obligations and duties of the employer in respect of such liability, imposed by this chapter upon the employer, as it considers proper in order to effectuate the provisions of this chapter. For such purposes (1) notice to or knowledge of an employer of the occurrence of the injury shall be notice to or knowledge of the carrier, (2) jurisdiction of the employer by a deputy commissioner, the Board, or the Secretary, or any court under this chapter shall be jurisdiction of the carrier, and (3) any requirement by a deputy commissioner, the Board, or the Secretary, or any court under any compensation order, finding, or decision shall be binding upon the carrier in the same manner and to the same extent as upon the employer.

§ 936. Insurance policies

(a) Every policy or contract of insurance issued under authority of this chapter shall contain (1) a provision to carry out the provisions of section 935 of this title, and (2) a provision that insolvency or bankruptcy of the employer and/or discharge therein shall not relieve the carrier from payment of compensation for disability or death sustained by an employee during the life of such policy or contract.

(b) No contract or policy of insurance issued by a carrier under this chapter shall be canceled prior to the date specified in such contract or policy for its expiration until at least thirty days have elapsed after a notice of cancellation has been sent to the deputy commissioner and to the employer in accordance with the provisions of subsection (c) of section 912 of this title.

§ 937. Certificate of compliance with this Act

No stevedoring firm shall be employed in any compensation district by a vessel or by hull owners until it presents to such vessel or hull owners a certificate issued by a deputy commissioner assigned to such district that it has complied with the provisions of this chapter requiring the securing of compensation to its employees. Any person violating the provisions of this section shall be punished by a fine of not more than $1,000, or by imprisonment for not more than one year, or by both such fine and imprisonment.

§ 938. Penalty for failure to secure payment of compensation

(a) Failure to secure payment of compensation. Any employer required to secure the payment of compensation under this chapter who fails to secure such compensation shall be guilty of a misdemeanor and, upon conviction thereof, shall be punished by a fine of not more than $10,000, or by imprisonment for not more than one year, or by both such fine and imprisonment; and in any case where such employer is a corporation, the president, secretary, and treasurer thereof shall be also severally liable to such fine or imprisonment as herein provided for the failure of such corporation to secure the payment of compensation; and such president, secretary, and treasurer shall be severally personally liable, jointly with such corporation, for any compensation or other benefit which may accrue under the said chapter in respect to any injury which may occur to any employee of such corporation while it shall so fail to secure the payment of compensation as required by section 932 of this title.

(b) Avoiding payment of compensation. Any employer who knowingly transfers, sells, encumbers, assigns, or in any manner disposes of, conceals, secretes, or destroys any property belonging to such employer, after one of his employees has been injured within the purview of this chapter, and with intent to avoid the payment of compensation under this chapter to such employee or his dependents, shall be guilty of a misdemeanor and, upon conviction thereof, shall be punished by a fine of not more than $10,000, or by imprisonment for not more than one year, or by both such fine and imprisonment; and in any case where such employer is a corporation, the president, secretary, and treasurer thereof shall be also severally liable to such penalty of imprisonment as well as jointly liable with such corporation for such fine.

(c) Effect on other liability of employer. This section shall not affect any other liability of the employer under this chapter.

§ 939. Administration by Secretary

(a) Prescribing rules and regulations; appointing and fixing compensation of employees; making expenditures. Except as otherwise specifically provided, the Secretary shall administer the provisions of this chapter, and for such purpose the Secretary is authorized (1) to make such rules and regulations; (2) to appoint and fix the compensation of such temporary technical assistants and medical advisers, and, subject to the provisions of the civil service laws, to appoint, and, in accordance with chapter 51 and subchapter III of chapter 53 of Title 5, to fix the compensation of such deputy commissioners (except deputy commissioners appointed under subdivision (a) of section 940 of this title) and other officers and employees; and (3) to make such expenditures (including expenditures for personal services and rent at the seat of government and elsewhere, for law books, books of reference, periodicals, and for printing and binding) as may be necessary in the administration of this chapter. All expenditures of the Secretary in the administration of this Act shall be allowed and paid as provided in section 945 of this title upon the presentation of itemized vouchers therefor approved by the Secretary.

(b) Establishing compensation districts. The Secretary shall establish compensation districts, to include the high seas and the areas within the United States to which this chapter applies, and shall assign to each such district one or more deputy commissioners, as the Secretary deems advisable. Judicial proceedings under sections 918 and 921 of this title in respect of any injury or death occurring on the high seas shall be instituted in the district court within whose territorial jurisdiction is located the office of the deputy commissioner having jurisdiction in respect of such injury or death (or in the Supreme Court of the District of Columbia [United States District Court for the District of Columbia] if such office is located in such District).

(c) Furnishing information and assistance; directing vocational rehabilitation.

(1) The Secretary shall, upon request, provide persons covered by this chapter with information and assistance relating to the chapter's coverage and compensation and the procedures for obtaining such compensation and including assistance in processing a claim. The Secretary may, upon request, provide persons covered by this chapter with legal assistance in processing a claim. The Secretary shall also provide employees receiving compensation information on medical, manpower, and vocational rehabilitation services and assist such employees in obtaining the best such services available.

(2) The Secretary shall direct the vocational rehabilitation of permanently disabled employees and shall arrange with the appropriate public or private agencies in State or Territories, possessions, or the District of Columbia for such rehabilitation. The Federal Board for Vocational Education shall cooperate with the Secretary in such educational work. The Secretary may in its

discretion furnish such prosthetic appliances or other apparatus made necessary by an injury upon which an award has been made under this chapter to render a disabled employee fit to engage in a remunerative occupation. Where necessary rehabilitation services are not available otherwise, the Secretary of Labor may, in his discretion, use the fund provided for in section 944 of this title in such amounts as may be necessary to procure such services, including necessary prosthetic appliances or other apparatus. This fund shall also be available in such amounts as may be authorized in annual appropriations for the Department of Labor for the costs of administering this subsection.

§ 940. Deputy commissioners

(a) Appointment; use of personnel and facilities of boards, commissions, or other agencies; expenses and salaries. The Secretary may appoint as deputy commissioners any member of any board, commission, or other agency of a State to act as deputy commissioner for any compensation district or part thereof in such State, and may make arrangements with such board, commission, or other agency for the use of the personnel and facilities thereof in the administration of this chapter. The Secretary may make such arrangements as may be deemed advisable by it for the payment of expenses of such board, commission, or other agency, incurred in the administration of this chapter pursuant to this section, and for the payment of salaries to such board, commission, or other agency, or the members thereof, and may pay any amounts agreed upon to the proper officers of the State, upon vouchers approved by the Secretary.

(b) Appointment in Territories and District of Columbia; compensation. In any Territory of the United States or in the District of Columbia a person holding an office under the United States may be appointed deputy commissioner and for services rendered as deputy commissioner may be paid compensation, in addition to that he is receiving from the United States, in an amount fixed by the Secretary in accordance with chapter 51 and subchapter III of chapter 53 of Title 5.

(c) Transfers to other districts; temporary details. Deputy commissioners (except deputy commissioners appointed under subsection (a) of this section) may be transferred from one compensation district to another and may be temporarily detailed from one compensation district for service in another in the discretion of the Secretary.

(d) Maintaining offices. Each deputy commissioner shall maintain and keep open during reasonable business hours an office, at a place designated by the Secretary, for the transaction of business under this chapter, at which office he shall keep his official records and papers. Such office shall be furnished and equipped by the Secretary, who shall also furnish the deputy commissioner with all necessary clerical and, other assistants, records, books, blanks, and supplies. Wherever practicable such office shall be located in a building owned or leased by the United States; otherwise the Secretary shall rent suitable quarters.

(e) Records and papers. If any deputy commissioner is removed from office, or for any reason ceases to act as such deputy commissioner, all of his official records and papers and office equipment shall be transferred to his successor in office or, if there be no successor, then to the Secretary or to a deputy commissioner designated by the Secretary.

(f) Conflict of interest. Neither a deputy commissioner or Board member nor any business associate of a deputy commissioner shall appear as attorney in any proceeding under this chapter, and no deputy commissioner or Board member shall act in any such case in which he is interested, or when he is employed by any party in interest or related to any party in interest by consanguinity or affinity within the third degree, as determined by the common law.

§ 941. Safety rules and regulations

(a) Safe place of employment; installation of safety devices and safeguards. Every employer shall furnish and maintain employment and places of employment which shall be reasonably safe for his employees in all employments covered by this chapter and shall install, furnish, maintain, and use such devices and safeguards with particular reference to equipment used by and working conditions established by such employers as the Secretary may determine by regulation or order to be reasonably necessary to protect the life, health, and safety of such employees, and to render safe such employment and places of employment, and to prevent injury to his employees. However, the Secretary may not make determinations by regulation or order under this section as to matters within the scope of title 52 of the Revised Statutes and Acts supplementary or amendatory thereto, the Act of June 15, 1917 (ch. 30, 40 Stat. 220), as amended or section 1333(e) of Title 43.

(b) Studies and investigations by the Secretary. The Secretary, in enforcing and administering the provisions of this section, is authorized in addition to such other powers and duties as are conferred upon him—

(1) to make studies and investigations with respect to safety provisions and the causes and prevention of injuries in employments covered by this chapter, and in making such studies and investigations to cooperate with any agency of the United States or with any State agency engaged in similar work;

(2) to utilize the services of any agency of the United States or any State agency engaged in similar work (with the consent of such agency) in connection with the administration of this section;

(3) to promote uniformity in safety standards in employments covered by this chapter through cooperative action with any agency of the United States or with any State agency engaged in similar work;

(4) to provide for the establishment and supervision of programs for the education and training of employers and employees in the recognition, avoidance, and prevention of unsafe working conditions in employments covered by this chapter, and to consult with and advise employers as to the best means of preventing injuries;

(5) to hold such hearings, issue such orders, and make such decisions, based upon findings of fact, as are deemed to be necessary to enforce the provisions of this section, and for such purposes the Secretary and the district courts shall have the authority and jurisdiction provided by subsections (b) to (f) of section 6507 of Title 41, and the Secretary shall be represented in any court proceedings as provided in section 921a of this title.

(c) Inspection of places and practices of employment. The Secretary or his authorized representative may inspect such places of employment, question such employees, and investigate such conditions, practices, or matters in connection with employment subject to this chapter, as he may deem appropriate to determine whether any person has violated any provision of this section, or any rule or regulation issued thereunder, or which may aid in the enforcement of the provisions of this section. No employer or other person shall refuse to admit the Secretary or his authorized representatives to any such place or shall refuse to permit any such inspection.

(d) Requests for advice; variations from safety rules and regulations. Any employer may request the advice of the Secretary or his authorized representative, in complying with the requirements of any rule or regulation adopted to carry out the provisions of this section. In case of practical difficulties or unnecessary hardships, the Secretary in his discretion may grant variations from any such rule or regulation, or particular provisions thereof, and permit the use of other or different devices if he finds that the purpose of the rule or regulation will be observed by the variation and the safety of employees will be equally secured thereby. Any person affected by such rule or regulation, or his agent, may request the Secretary to grant such variation, stating in writing the grounds on which his request is based. Any authorization by the Secretary of a variation shall be in writing, shall describe the conditions under which the variation shall be permitted, and shall be published as provided in section 552 of Title 5. A properly indexed record of all variations shall be kept in the office of the Secretary and open to public inspection.

(e) Jurisdiction to restrain violations. The United States district courts, together with the District Court for the Territory of Alaska, shall have jurisdiction for cause shown, in any action brought by the Secretary, represented as provided in section 921a of this title, to restrain violations of this section or of any rule, regulation, or order of the Secretary adopted to carry out the provisions of this section.

(f) Violations and penalties. Any employer who, willfully, violates or fails or refuses to comply with the provisions of subsection (a) of this section, or with any lawful rule, regulation, or order adopted to carry out the provisions of this section, and any employer or other person who willfully interferes with, hinders, or delays the Secretary or his authorized representative in carrying out his duties under subsection (c) of this section by refusing to admit the Secretary or his authorized representative to any place, or to permit the inspection or examination of any employment or place of employment, or who willfully hinders or delays the Secretary or his authorized representative in the performance of his duties in the enforcement of this section, shall be guilty of an offense, and, upon conviction thereof, shall be punished for each offense by a fine of not less than $100 nor more than $3,000; and in any case where such employer is a corporation, the officer who willfully permits any such violation to occur shall be guilty of an offense, and, upon conviction thereof, shall be punished also for each offense by a fine of not less than $100 nor more than $3,000. The liability hereunder shall not affect any other liability of the employer under this chapter.

(g) Inapplicability to certain employments.

(1) The provisions of this section shall not apply in the case of any employment relating to the operations for the exploration, production, or transportation by pipeline of mineral resources upon the navigable waters of the United States, nor under the authority of the Act of August 7, 1953 (ch. 345, 67 Stat. 462) [43 USC §§ 1331 et seq.], nor in the case of any employment in connection with lands (except filled in, made or reclaimed lands) beneath the navigable waters as defined in the Act of May 22, 1953 (ch. 65, 67 Stat. 29) [43 USC §§ 1301 et seq.] nor in the case of any employment for which compensation in case of disability or death is provided for employees under the authority of the Act of May 17, 1928 (ch. 612, 45 Stat. 600), as amended, nor under the authority of the Act of August 16, 1941 (ch. 357, 55 Stat. 622), as amended [42 USC §§ 1651 et seq.].

(2) The provisions of this section, with the exception of paragraph (1) of subsection (b) of this section, shall not be applied under the authority of subchapter I of chapter 81 of Title 5.

§ 942. Annual report

The Secretary shall make to Congress at the end of each fiscal year, a report of the administration of this title for the preceding fiscal year, including a detailed statement of receipts of and expenditures from the fund established in section 944 of this title, together with such recommendations as the Secretary deems advisable. Such report shall include the annual report required under section 936(b) of Title 30 and shall be identified as the Annual Report of the Office of Workers' Compensation Programs.

§ 943. [Repealed]

§ 944. Special fund

(a) Establishment; administration; custody, trust. There is hereby established in the Treasury of the United States a special fund. Such fund shall be administered by the Secretary. The Treasurer of the United States shall be the custodian of such fund, and all moneys and securities in such fund shall be held in trust by such Treasurer and shall not be money or property of the United States.

(b) Disbursements; bond of custodian. The Treasurer is authorized to disburse moneys from such fund only upon order of the Secretary. He shall be required to give bond in an amount to be fixed and with securities to be approved by the Secretary of the Treasury and the Comptroller General of the United States conditioned upon the faithful performance of his duty as custodian of such fund.

(c) Payments into fund. Payments into such fund shall be made as follows:

(1) Whenever the Secretary determines that there is no person entitled under this chapter to compensation for the death of an employee which would otherwise be compensable under this chapter, the appropriate employer shall pay $5,000 as compensation for the death of such an employee.

(2) At the beginning of each calendar year the Secretary shall estimate the probable expenses of the fund during that calendar year and the amount of payments required (and the schedule therefor) to maintain adequate reserves in the fund. Each carrier and self-insurer shall make payments into the fund on a prorated assessment by the Secretary determined by—

(A) computing the ratio (expressed as a percent) of (i) the carrier's or self-insured's workers' compensation payments under this chapter during the preceding calendar year, to (ii) the total of such payments by all carriers and self-insureds under this chapter during such year;

(B) computing the ratio (expressed as a percent) of (i) the payments under section 908(f) of this title during the preceding calendar year which are attributable to the carrier or self-insured, to (ii) the total of such payments during such year attributable to all carriers and self-insureds;

(C) dividing the sum of the percentages computed under subparagraphs (A) and (B) for the carrier or self-insured by two; and

(D) multiplying the percent computed under subparagraph (C) by such probable expenses of the fund (as determined under the first sentence of this paragraph).

(3) All amounts collected as finds and penalties under the provisions of this chapter shall be paid into such fund.

(d) Investigations; records, availability; recordkeeping; provisions of sections 49 and 50 of title 15 applicable to Secretary.

(1) For the purpose of making rules, regulations, and determinations under this section under and for providing enforcement thereof, the Secretary may investigate and gather appropriate data from each carrier and self-insurer. For that purpose, the Secretary may enter and inspect such places and records (and make such transcriptions thereof), question such employees, and investigate such facts, conditions, practices, or matters as he may deem necessary or appropriate.

(2) Each carrier and self-insurer shall make, keep, and preserve such records, and make such reports and provide such additional information, as prescribed by regulation or order of the Secretary, as the Secretary deems necessary or appropriate to carry out his responsibilities under this section.

(3) For the purpose of any hearing or investigation related to determinations or the enforcement of the provisions of this section, the provisions of sections 49 and 50 of Title 50 (relating to the attendance of witnesses and the production of books, papers, and documents) are hereby made applicable to the jurisdiction, powers, and duties of the Secretary of Labor.

(e) Depositories; investments. The Treasurer of the United States shall deposit any moneys paid into such fund into such depository banks as the Secretary may designate and may invest any portion of the funds which, in the opinion of the Secretary, is not needed for current requirements, in bonds or notes of the United States or of any Federal land bank.

(f) Limitation of liability. Neither the United States nor the Secretary shall be liable in respect of payments authorized under section 908 of this title in an amount greater than the money or property deposited in or belonging to such fund.

(g) Audit by Comptroller General; finality of payment determinations; credits of disbursing officers. The Comptroller General of the United States shall audit the account for such fund, but the action of the Secretary in making payments from such fund shall be final and not subject to review, and the Comptroller General is authorized and directed to allow credit in the accounts of any disbursing officer of the Secretary for payments made from such fund authorized by the Secretary.

(h) Civil actions for civil penalties. All civil penalties and unpaid assessments provided for in this chapter shall be collected by civil suit brought by the Secretary.

(i) Proceeds available for certain payments. The proceeds of this fund shall be available for payments:

(1) Pursuant to section 910 of this title with respect to certain initial and subsequent annual adjustments in compensation for total permanent disability or death.

(2) Under section 908(f) and (g), under section 918(b), and under section 939(c) of this title.

(3) To repay the sums deposited in the fund pursuant to subsection (d) of this section.

(4) To defray the expense of making examinations as provided in section 907(e) of this title.

(j) Audit to be included in report. The fund shall be audited annually and the results of such audit shall be included in the annual report required by section 942 of this title.

§ 945. [Repealed]

§ 948. Laws inapplicable

Nothing in sections 183, 184 to 186, 188, or 189 of Title 46, Appendix, shall be held to limit the amount for which recovery may be had (1) in any suit at law or in admiralty where an employer has failed to secure compensation as required by this chapter, or (2) in any proceeding for compensation, any addition to compensation, or any civil penalty.

§ 948a. Discrimination against employees who bring proceedings; penalties; deposit of payments in special funds; civil actions; entitlement to restoration of employment and compensation, qualifications requirement; liability of employer for penalties and payments; insurance policy exemption from liability

It shall be unlawful for any employer or his duly authorized agent to discharge or in any other manner discriminate against an employee as to his employment because such employee has claimed or attempted to claim compensation from such employer, or because he has testified or is about to testify in a proceeding under this chapter. The discharge or refusal to employ a person who has been adjudicated to have filed a fraudulent claim for compensation is not a violation of this section. Any employer who violates this section shall be liable to a penalty of not less than $1,000 or more than $5,000, as may be determined by the deputy commissioner. All such penalties shall be paid to the deputy commissioner for deposit in the special fund as described in section 944 of this title, and if not paid may be recovered in a civil action brought in the appropriate United States district court. Any employee so discriminated against shall be restored to his employment and shall be compensated by his employer for any loss of wages arising out of such discrimination: Provided, That if such employee shall cease to be qualified to perform the duties of his employment, he shall not be entitled to such restoration and compensation. The employer alone and not his carrier shall be liable for such penalties and payments. Any provision in an insurance policy undertaking to relieve the employer from the liability for such penalties and payments shall be void.

§ 949. Effect of unconstitutionality

If any part of this chapter is adjudged unconstitutional by the courts, and such adjudication has the effect of invalidating any payment of compensation under this chapter, the period intervening between the time the injury was sustained and the time of such adjudication shall not be computed as a part of the time prescribed by law for the commencement of any action against the employer in respect of such injury; but the amount of any compensation paid under this chapter on account of such injury shall be deducted from the amount of damages awarded in such action in respect of such injury.

§ 950. Separability

If any provision of this chapter is declared unconstitutional or the applicability thereof to any person or circumstances is held invalid, the validity of the remainder of the chapter and the applicability of such provision to other persons and circumstances shall not be affected thereby.

§ 951. [Reserved]

Maximum Workers' Compensation Benefit for Lost Wages by Scheduled Injury and Jurisdiction (2023)
Source: U.S. Chamber of Commerce, Analysis of Workers' Compensation Laws (2023)

Jurisdiction	Arm at Shoulder	Hand	Thumb	First Finger	Second Finger	Third Finger	Fourth Finger	Leg at Hip	Foot	Great Toe	Other Toes	One Eye	One Ear	Both Ears
In this group of jurisdictions, compensation for temporary disability is allowed in addition to allowances for scheduled injury.														
Alabama	48,840	37,400	13,640	9,460	6,820	4,840	3,520	44,000	30,580	7,040	2,420	27,280	11,660	35,860
Alaska	No schedule. Benefits are $177,000 multiplied by the percentage of the whole person rating according to AMA *Guides to the Evaluation of Permanent Impairement,* 6th edition.													
Arizona	165,964	138,303	41,491	24,895	19,362	13,830	11,064	138,303	110,642	19,362	6,915	82,982	55,321	165,964
Arkansas	179,584	134,688	53,728	31,648	27,232	17,664	13,984	135,454	96,416	23,552	8,096	77,280	30,912	116,288
California	228,916	214,012	53,165	22,615	22,615	10,117	10,117	149,428	88,674	13,357	2,381	92,906	18,647	139,492
Colorado	75,650	37,825	18,185	9,456	6,547	4,728	4,728	75,650	37,825	9,456	4,001	37,825	12,729	50,554
Connecticut	224,192	197,232	73,962	42,264	34,046	24,654	19,958	181,970	146,750	32,872	10,566	184,318	41,090	122,096
Delaware	186,915	164,485	56,074	37,383	29,906	22,430	14,953	186,915	119,626	29,906	11,215	149,532	56,074	130,840
Dist. of Col.	323,764	253,203	78,859	48,418	31,823	26,291	16,611	298,856	213,082	40,121	16,611	166,031	53,966	207,534
Florida	No schedule; benefits are paid according to degree of impairment.													
Georgia	disability (PPD) is scheduled and is not payable if the employee is receiving income benefits. When it is paid, it is based on a rating assigned by the treating physician pursuant to the AMA													
Hawaii	340,080	265,960	81,750	50,140	32,700	27,250	16,350	313,920	223,450	41,420	17,440	152,600	56,680	218,000
Idaho	149,820	134,838	54,934	34,958	27,467	12,485	7,491	99,880	69,916	20,975	3,496	8,395	N/A	87,395
Illinois	502,519	320,459	175,850	42,915	737,925	21,956	21,956	450,406	166,669	37,925	12,974	161,679	54,893	214,574
Iowa	505,750	384,370	121,380	70,805	60,690	50,575	40,460	445,060	303,450	80,920	30,345	283,220	101,150	354,025
Maine	work or not; employer may offset specific loss amount of incapacity benefits previously paid.													
Maryland	(see note 19)													
Massachusetts	Benefits are paid according to degree of impairment in §36 of Gen. Laws Chapter 152 (Massachussetts Workers' Comp. Act).													
Minnesota	Benefits are paid according to degree of impairment, mostly set out in PP schedule rules													
Mississippi	117,164	87,873	35,149	20,504	17,575	11,716	8,787	102,518	73,227	17,575	5,858	58,582	23,433	87,873
Missouri	144,190	108,764	37,291	21,753	21,753	21,753	13,673	128,653	93,226	24,860	8,710	87,011	30,454	111,872
Montana	No schedule; benefits are paid according to degree of impairment, age, education, wage loss, and lifting restriction.													
Nebraska	231,525	180,075	61,740	36,015	30,870	20,580	15,435	221,235	154,350	30,870	10,290	128,625	25,725	51,450
Nevada	No schedule for injuries arising after 1973.													
New Hampshire	435,540	391,986	157,624	97,478	78,812	39,406	18,666	290,360	203,252	37,332	6,222	174,216	62,220	255,102
New Jersey	265,980	3,219,900	23,440	617,580	14,560	11,720	8,790	253,890	208,905	11,720	4,395	102,600	17,580	102,600
New Mexico	influence of drugs contributes to the accident.													
North Carolina	298,800	249,000	93,375	56,025	49,800	31,125	24,900	249,000	179,280	43,575	12,450	149,400	87,150	186,750
North Dakota	Benefits are paid according to degree of impairment, mostly set out in PP schedule rules 65-05-12.													

Maximum Workers' Compensation Benefit for Lost Wages by Scheduled Injury and Jurisdiction (2023) (Continued)

Source: U.S. Chamber of Commerce, Analysis of Workers' Compensation Laws (2023)

Jurisdiction	Arm at Shoulder	Hand	Thumb	First Finger	Second Finger	Third Finger	Fourth Finger	Leg at Hip	Foot	Great Toe	Other Toes	One Eye	One Ear	Both Ears
Ohio	258,525	201,075	68,940	40,215	34,470	22,980	17,235	229,800	172,350	34,470	11,490	143,625	28,725	143,625
Oklahoma	91,990	73,592	22,077	13,046	11,039	7,359	5,687	91,990	73,592	11,039	3,680	91,990	36,796	110,388
Oregon	77,736	60,893	19,434	10,365	9,069	3,887	2,591	60,893	54,415	7,774	1,296	38,868	24,616	77,736
Rhode Island	Benefits are paid based on number of weeks set out in RIGL §28-33-19.													
South Carolina	520 weeks	185 weeks	65 weeks	40 weeks	35 weeks	25 weeks	20 weeks	475 weeks	140 weeks	35 weeks	10 weeks	140 weeks	80 weeks	165 weeks
South Dakota	205,800	154,350	51,450	36,015	30,870	20,580	15,435	164,640	128,625	30,870	10,290	154,350	51,450	154,350
Tennessee	No scheduled injuries for injuries on or after 7/1/14.													
Texas	No schedule; benefits are paid according to degree of impairment as calculated based on AMA *Guides to the Evaluation of Permanent Impairment,* 4th edition.													
Utah	153,340	137,760	54,940	34,440	27,880	13,940	6,560	102,500	72,160	21,320	3,280	82,000	32,001	89,380
Vermont	No schedule; benefits are paid according to degree of impairment as calculated based on AMA *Guides to the Evaluation of Permanent Impairment,* 5 th edition.													
Virginia	268,600	201,450	80,580	47,005	40,290	26,860	30,145	235,025	111,917	26,860	8,953	134,300	67,150	134,300
Washington	136,932	123,239	49,295	30,810	24,648	12,324	6,162	136,932	95,852	28,756	10,498	55,773	18,257	109,546
West Virginia	Benefits for PP shall be paid at 66⅔% of employee's AWW, not to exceed 70 % of state AWW, in accordance with statutory schedule.													
Wisconsin	500 weeks	400 weeks	160 weeks	60 weeks	45 weeks	26 weeks	28 weeks	500 weeks	250 weeks	83⅓ wks	25 weeks	275 wks	55 weeks	330 weeks
Wyoming	No schedule; benefits are paid as calculated based on AMA *Guides to the Evaluation of Permanent Impairment.*													
Amer. Samoa	312 weeks	244 weeks	75 weeks	46 weeks	30 weeks	25 weeks	15 weeks	288 weeks	205 weeks	38 weeks	16 weeks	160 weeks	N/A	N/A
Virgin Islands	Benefits for PP shall be 66 2/3% of AWW pursuant to statutory schedule in accordance with degree of impairment.													
FECA	312 weeks	244 weeks	75 weeks	46 weeks	30 weeks	25 weeks	15 weeks	288 weeks	205 weeks	38 weeks	16 weeks	160 weeks	52 weeks	200 weeks
Longshore Act	471,357	368,625	113,307	69,495	45,323	37,769	22,661	435,099	309,706	57,409	24,172	241,722	78,560	302,152
In this group of jurisdictions, compensation for temporary disability is allowed in addition to scheduled injury, with certain limitations as to period.														
Indiana	108,590	82,480	21,404	14,000	12,250	10,500	7,000	92,660	666,550	21,404	14,600	66,550	27,260	79,730
New York	312 weeks	244 weeks	75 weeks	46 weeks	30 weeks	25 weeks	15 weeks	288 weeks	205 weeks	38 weeks	16 weeks	160 weeks	60 weeks	150 weeks
Pennsylvania	The percent of hearing loss under the AMA impairment rating *Guides* multiplied by 60 weeks.													
In this group of jurisdictions, compensation for temporary disability is deducted from the allowance for scheduled injury.														
Kansas	210 weeks	150 weeks	60 weeks	37 weeks	30 weeks	20 weeks	15 weeks	200 weeks	125 weeks	30 weeks	10 weeks	120 weeks	30 weeks	110 weeks
Kentucky	No schedule; PP benefits are paid at 66⅔% of wages according to degree of disability - 425 weeks if disability is 50% or less, or 520 weeks if disability is greater than 50%.													
Louisiana	200 weeks	150 weeks	50 weeks	30 weeks	20 weeks	20 weeks	20 weeks	175 weeks	125 weeks	20 weeks	10 weeks	100 weeks	100 weeks	100 weeks
Michigan	269 weeks	215 weeks	65 weeks	38 weeks	33 weeks	22 weeks	16 weeks	215 weeks	162 weeks	33 weeks	11 weeks	562 weeks	Lost earnings.	Lost earnings.

OCCUPATIONAL SAFETY AND HEALTH ACT (TITLE 29 U.S.C.)

§ 651. Congressional statement of findings and declaration of purpose and policy

(a) The Congress finds that personal injuries and illnesses arising out of work situations impose a substantial burden upon, and are a hindrance to, interstate commerce in terms of lost production, wage loss, medical expenses, and disability compensation payments.

(b) The Congress declares it to be its purpose and policy, through the exercise of its powers to regulate commerce among the several States and with foreign nations and to provide for the general welfare, to assure so far as possible every working man and woman in the Nation safe and healthful working conditions and to preserve our human resources-

(1) by encouraging employers and employees in their efforts to reduce the number of occupational safety and health hazards at their places of employment, and to stimulate employers and employees to institute new and to perfect existing programs for providing safe and healthful working conditions;

(2) by providing that employers and employees have separate but dependent responsibilities and rights with respect to achieving safe and healthful working conditions;

(3) by authorizing the Secretary of Labor to set mandatory occupational safety and health standards applicable to businesses affecting interstate commerce, and by creating an Occupational Safety and Health Review Commission for carrying out adjudicatory functions under this chapter;

(4) by building upon advances already made through employer and employee initiative for providing safe and healthful working conditions;

(5) by providing for research in the field of occupational safety and health, including the psychological factors involved, and by developing innovative methods, techniques, and approaches for dealing with occupational safety and health problems;

(6) by exploring ways to discover latent diseases, establishing causal connections between diseases and work in environmental conditions, and conducting other research relating to health problems, in recognition of the fact that occupational health standards present problems often different from those involved in occupational safety;

(7) by providing medical criteria which will assure insofar as practicable that no employee will suffer diminished health, functional capacity, or life expectancy as a result of his work experience;

(8) by providing for training programs to increase the number and competence of personnel engaged in the field of occupational safety and health;

(9) by providing for the development and promulgation of occupational safety and health standards;

(10) by providing an effective enforcement program which shall include a prohibition against giving advance notice of any inspection and sanctions for any individual violating this prohibition;

(11) by encouraging the States to assume the fullest responsibility for the administration and enforcement of their occupational safety and health laws by providing grants to the States to assist in identifying their needs and responsibilities in the area of occupational safety and health, to develop plans in accordance with the provisions of this chapter, to improve the administration and enforcement of State occupational safety and health laws, and to conduct experimental and demonstration projects in connection therewith;

(12) by providing for appropriate reporting procedures with respect to occupational safety and health which procedures will help achieve the objectives of this chapter and accurately describe the nature of the occupational safety and health problem;

(13) by encouraging joint labor-management efforts to reduce injuries and disease arising out of employment.

§ 652. Definitions

For the purposes of this chapter-

(1) The term "Secretary" mean[s] the Secretary of Labor.

(2) The term "Commission" means the Occupational Safety and Health Review Commission established under this chapter.

(3) The term "commerce" means trade, traffic, commerce, transportation, or communication among the several States, or between a State and any place outside thereof, or within the District of Columbia, or a possession of the United States (other than the Trust Territory of the Pacific Islands), or between points in the same State but through a point outside thereof.

(4) The term "person" means one or more individuals, partnerships, associations, corporations, business trusts, legal representatives, or any organized group of persons.

(5) The term "employer" means a person engaged in a business affecting commerce who has employees, but does not include the United States (not including the United States Postal Service) or any State or political subdivision of a State.

(6) The term "employee" means an employee of an employer who is employed in a business of his employer which affects commerce.

(7) The term "State" includes a State of the United States, the District of Columbia, Puerto Rico, the Virgin Islands, American Samoa, Guam, and the Trust Territory of the Pacific Islands.

(8) The term "occupational safety and health standard" means a standard which requires conditions, or the adoption or use of one or more practices, means, methods, operations, or processes, reasonably necessary or appropriate to provide safe or healthful employment and places of employment.

(9) The term "national consensus standard" means any occupational safety and health standard or modification thereof which (1) has been adopted and promulgated by a nationally recognized standards-producing organization under procedures whereby it can be determined by the Secretary that persons interested and affected by the scope or provisions of the standard have reached substantial agreement on its adoption, (2) was formulated in a manner which afforded an opportunity for diverse views to be considered and (3) has been designated as such a standard by the Secretary, after consultation with other appropriate Federal agencies.

(10) The term "established Federal standard" means any operative occupational safety and health standard established by any agency of the United States and presently in effect, or contained in any Act of Congress in force on December 29, 1970.

(11) The term "Committee" means the National Advisory Committee on Occupational Safety and Health established under this chapter.

(12) The term "Director" means the Director of the National Institute for Occupational Safety and Health.

(13) The term "Institute" means the National Institute for Occupational Safety and Health established under this chapter.

(14) The term "Workmen's Compensation Commission" means the National Commission on State Workmen's Compensation Laws established under this chapter.

§ 653. Geographic applicability; judicial enforcement; applicability to existing standards; report to Congress on duplication and coordination of Federal laws; workmen's compensation law or common law or statutory rights, duties, or liabilities of employers and employees unaffected

(a) This chapter shall apply with respect to employment performed in a workplace in a State, the District of Columbia, the Commonwealth of Puerto Rico, the Virgin Islands, American Samoa, Guam, the Trust Territory of the Pacific Islands, Wake Island, Outer Continental Shelf lands defined in the Outer Continental Shelf Lands Act [43 U.S.C. § 1331 *et seq.*], Johnston Island, and the Canal Zone. The Secretary of the Interior shall, by regulation, provide for judicial enforcement of this chapter by the courts established for areas in which there are no United States district courts having jurisdiction.

(b)(1) Nothing in this chapter shall apply to working conditions of employees with respect to which other Federal agencies, and State agencies acting under section 2021 of title 42 [42 U.S.C. § 2021], exercise statutory authority to prescribe or enforce standards or regulations affecting occupational safety or health.

(2) The safety and health standards promulgated under the Act of June 30, 1936, commonly known as the Walsh-Healey Act [41 U.S.C. §§ 6501 et seq.], the Service Contract Act of 1965, Public Law 91–54, Act of August 9, 1969 [40 U.S.C. §§ 3704, 3705], Public Law 85–742, Act of August 23, 1958 [33 U.S.C. § 941], and the National Foundation on Arts and Humanities Act [20 U.S.C. § 951 et seq.] are superseded on the effective date of corresponding standards, promulgated under this chapter, which are determined by the Secretary to be more effective. Standards issued under the laws listed in this paragraph and in effect on or after the effective date of this chapter shall be deemed to be occupational safety and health standards issued under this chapter, as well as under such other Acts.

* * *

(4) Nothing in this chapter shall be construed to supersede or in any manner affect any workmen's compensation law or to enlarge or diminish or affect in any other manner the common law or statutory rights, duties, or liabilities of employers and employees under any law with respect to injuries, diseases, or death of employees arising out of, or in the course of, employment.

§ 654. Duties of employers and employees

(a) Each employer-

(1) shall furnish to each of his employees employment and a place of employment which are free from recognized hazards that are causing or are likely to cause death or serious physical harm to his employees;

(2) shall comply with occupational safety and health standards promulgated under this chapter.

(b) Each employee shall comply with occupational safety and health standards and all rules, regulations, and orders issued pursuant to this chapter which are applicable to his own actions and conduct.

§ 655. Standards

(a) Promulgation by Secretary of national consensus standards and established Federal standards; time for promulgation; conflicting standards

Without regard to chapter 5 of title 5 [5 U.S.C. §§ 500 et seq.] or to the other subsections of this section, the Secretary shall, as soon as practicable during the period beginning with the effective date of this chapter and ending two years after such date, by rule promulgate as an occupational safety or health standard any national consensus standard, and any established Federal standard, unless he determines that the promulgation of such a standard would not result in improved safety or health for specifically designated employees. In the event of conflict among any such standards, the Secretary shall promulgate the standard which assures the greatest protection of the safety or health of the affected employees.

(b) Procedure for promulgation, modification, or revocation of standards

The Secretary may by rule promulgate, modify, or revoke any occupational safety or health standard in the following manner:

(1) Whenever the Secretary, upon the basis of information submitted to him in writing by an interested person, a representative of any organization of employers or employees, a nationally recognized standards-producing organization, the Secretary of Health and Human Services, the National Institute for Occupational Safety and Health, or a State or political subdivision, or on the basis of information developed by the Secretary or otherwise available to him, determines that a rule should be promulgated in order to serve the objectives of this chapter, the Secretary may request the recommendations of an advisory committee appointed under section 656 of this title [29 U.S.C. § 656]. The Secretary shall provide such an advisory committee with any proposals of his own or of the Secretary of Health and Human Services, together with all pertinent factual information developed by the Secretary or the Secretary of Health and

Human Services, or otherwise available, including the results of research, demonstrations, and experiments. An advisory committee shall submit to the Secretary its recommendations regarding the rule to be promulgated within ninety days from the date of its appointment or within such longer or shorter period as may be prescribed by the Secretary, but in no event for a period which is longer than two hundred and seventy days.

(2) The Secretary shall publish a proposed rule promulgating, modifying, or revoking an occupational safety or health standard in the Federal Register and shall afford interested persons a period of thirty days after publication to submit written data or comments. Where an advisory committee is appointed and the Secretary determines that a rule should be issued, he shall publish the proposed rule within sixty days after the submission of the advisory committee's recommendations or the expiration of the period prescribed by the Secretary for such submission.

(3) On or before the last day of the period provided for the submission of written data or comments under paragraph (2), any interested person may file with the Secretary written objections to the proposed rule, stating the grounds therefor and requesting a public hearing on such objections. Within thirty days after the last day for filing such objections, the Secretary shall publish in the Federal Register a notice specifying the occupational safety or health standard to which objections have been filed and a hearing requested, and specifying a time and place for such hearing.

(4) Within sixty days after the expiration of the period provided for the submission of written data or comments under paragraph (2), or within sixty days after the completion of any hearing held under paragraph (3), the Secretary shall issue a rule promulgating, modifying, or revoking an occupational safety or health standard or make a determination that a rule should not be issued. Such a rule may contain a provision delaying its effective date for such period (not in excess of ninety days) as the Secretary determines may be necessary to insure that affected employers and employees will be informed of the existence of the standard and of its terms and that employers affected are given an opportunity to familiarize themselves and their employees with the existence of the requirements of the standard.

(5) The Secretary, in promulgating standards dealing with toxic materials or harmful physical agents under this subsection, shall set the standard which most adequately assures, to the extent feasible, on the basis of the best available evidence, that no employee will suffer material impairment of health or functional capacity even if such employee has regular exposure to the hazard dealt with by such

standard for the period of his working life. Development of standards under this subsection shall be based upon research, demonstrations, experiments, and such other information as may be appropriate. In addition to the attainment of the highest degree of health and safety protection for the employee, other considerations shall be the latest available scientific data in the field, the feasibility of the standards, and experience gained under this and other health and safety laws. Whenever practicable, the standard promulgated shall be expressed in terms of objective criteria and of the performance desired.

(6)(A) Any employer may apply to the Secretary for a temporary order granting a variance from a standard or any provision thereof promulgated under this section. Such temporary order shall be granted only if the employer files an application which meets the requirements of clause (B) and establishes that (i) he is unable to comply with a standard by its effective date because of unavailability of professional or technical personnel or of materials and equipment needed to come into compliance with the standard or because necessary construction or alteration of facilities cannot be completed by the effective date, (ii) he is taking all available steps to safeguard his employees against the hazards covered by the standard, and (iii) he has an effective program for coming into compliance with the standard as quickly as practicable. Any temporary order issued under this paragraph shall prescribe the practices, means, methods, operations, and processes which the employer must adopt and use while the order is in effect and state in detail his program for coming into compliance with the standard. Such a temporary order may be granted only after notice to employees and an opportunity for a hearing: Provided, That the Secretary may issue one interim order to be effective until a decision is made on the basis of the hearing. No temporary order may be in effect for longer than the period needed by the employer to achieve compliance with the standard or one year, whichever is shorter, except that such an order may be renewed not more than twice (I) so long as the requirements of this paragraph are met and (II) if an application for renewal is filed at least 90 days prior to the expiration date of the order. No interim renewal of an order may remain in effect for longer than 180 days.

(B) An application for a temporary order under this paragraph (6) shall contain:

(i) a specification of the standard or portion thereof from which the employer seeks a variance,

(ii) a representation by the employer, supported by representations from qualified persons having firsthand knowledge of the facts represented, that he is unable to comply with the standard or portion thereof and a detailed statement of the reasons therefor,

(iii) a statement of the steps he has taken and will take (with specific dates) to protect employees against the hazard covered by the standard,

(iv) a statement of when he expects to be able to comply with the standard and what steps he has taken and what steps he will take (with dates specified) to come into compliance with the standard, and

(v) a certification that he has informed his employees of the application by giving a copy thereof to their authorized representative, posting a statement giving a summary of the application and specifying where a copy may be examined at the place or places where notices to employees are normally posted, and by other appropriate means.

A description of how employees have been informed shall be contained in the certification. The information to employees shall also inform them of their right to petition the Secretary for a hearing.

(C) The Secretary is authorized to grant a variance from any standard or portion thereof whenever he determines, or the Secretary of Health and Human Services certifies, that such variance is necessary to permit an employer to participate in an experiment approved by him or the Secretary of Health and Human Services designed to demonstrate or validate new and improved techniques to safeguard the health or safety of workers.

(7) Any standard promulgated under this subsection shall prescribe the use of labels or other appropriate forms of warning as are necessary to insure that employees are apprised of all hazards to which they are exposed, relevant symptoms and appropriate emergency treatment, and proper conditions and precautions of safe use or exposure. Where appropriate, such standard shall also prescribe suitable protective equipment and control or technological procedures to be used in connection with such hazards and shall provide for monitoring or measuring employee exposure at such locations and intervals, and in such manner as may be necessary for the protection of employees. In addition, where appropriate, any such standard shall prescribe the type and frequency of medical examinations or other tests which shall be made available, by the employer or at his cost, to employees exposed to such hazards in order to most effectively determine whether the health of such employees is adversely affected by such exposure. In the event such medical examinations are in the nature of research, as determined by the Secretary of Health and

Human Services, such examinations may be furnished at the expense of the Secretary of Health and Human Services. The results of such examinations or tests shall be furnished only to the Secretary or the Secretary of Health and Human Services, and, at the request of the employee, to his physician. The Secretary, in consultation with the Secretary of Health and Human Services, may by rule promulgated pursuant to section 553 of title 5 [5 U.S.C. § 553], make appropriate modifications in the foregoing requirements relating to the use of labels or other forms of warning, monitoring or measuring, and medical examinations, as may be warranted by experience, information, or medical or technological developments acquired subsequent to the promulgation of the relevant standard.

(8) Whenever a rule promulgated by the Secretary differs substantially from an existing national consensus standard, the Secretary shall, at the same time, publish in the Federal Register a statement of the reasons why the rule as adopted will better effectuate the purposes of this chapter than the national consensus standard.

(c) Emergency temporary standards

(1) The Secretary shall provide, without regard to the requirements of chapter 5 of title 5 [5 U.S.C. § 500 et seq.], for an emergency temporary standard to take immediate effect upon publication in the Federal Register if he determines (A) that employees are exposed to grave danger from exposure to substances or agents determined to be toxic or physically harmful or from new hazards, and (B) that such emergency standard is necessary to protect employees from such danger.

(2) Such standard shall be effective until superseded by a standard promulgated in accordance with the procedures prescribed in paragraph (3) of this subsection.

(3) Upon publication of such standard in the Federal Register the Secretary shall commence a proceeding in accordance with subsection (b), and the standard as published shall also serve as a proposed rule for the proceeding. The Secretary shall promulgate a standard under this paragraph no later than six months after publication of the emergency standard as provided in paragraph (2) of this subsection.

(d) Variances from standards; procedure

Any affected employer may apply to the Secretary for a rule or order for a variance from a standard promulgated under this section. Affected employees shall be given notice of each such application and an opportunity to participate in a hearing. The Secretary shall issue such rule or order if he determines on the record, after opportunity for an inspection where appropriate and a hearing, that the proponent of the variance has demonstrated by a preponderance of the evidence that the conditions, practices, means, methods, operations, or processes used or proposed to be used by an employer will provide employment and places of employment to his employees which are as safe and healthful as those which would prevail if he complied with the standard. The rule or order so issued shall prescribe the conditions the employer must maintain, and the practices, means, methods, operations, and processes which he must adopt and utilize to the extent they differ from the standard in question. Such a rule or order may be modified or revoked upon application by an employer, employees, or by the Secretary on his own motion, in the manner prescribed for its issuance under this subsection at any time after six months from its issuance.

(e) Statement of reasons for Secretary's determinations; publication in Federal Register

Whenever the Secretary promulgates any standard, makes any rule, order, or decision, grants any exemption or extension of time, or compromises, mitigates, or settles any penalty assessed under this chapter, he shall include a statement of the reasons for such action, which shall be published in the Federal Register.

(f) Judicial review

Any person who may be adversely affected by a standard issued under this section may at any time prior to the sixtieth day after such standard is promulgated file a petition challenging the validity of such standard with the United States court of appeals for the circuit wherein such person resides or has his principal place of business, for a judicial review of such standard. A copy of the petition shall be forthwith transmitted by the clerk of the court to the Secretary. The filing of such petition shall not, unless otherwise ordered by the court, operate as a stay of the standard. The determinations of the Secretary shall be conclusive if supported by substantial evidence in the record considered as a whole.

(g) Priority for establishment of standards

In determining the priority for establishing standards under this section, the Secretary shall give due regard to the urgency of the need for mandatory safety and health standards for particular industries, trades, crafts, occupations, businesses, workplaces or work environments. The Secretary shall also give due regard to the recommendations of the Secretary of Health and Human Services regarding the need for mandatory standards in determining the priority for establishing such standards.

§ 656. Administration

(a) National Advisory Committee on Occupational Safety and Health; establishment; membership; appointment; Chairman;

functions; meetings; compensation; secretarial and clerical personnel

(1) There is hereby established a National Advisory Committee on Occupational Safety and Health consisting of twelve members appointed by the Secretary, four of whom are to be designated by the Secretary of Health and Human Services, without regard to the provisions of title 5 governing appointments in the competitive service, and composed of representatives of management, labor, occupational safety and occupational health professions, and of the public. The Secretary shall designate one of the public members as Chairman. The members shall be selected upon the basis of their experience and competence in the field of occupational safety and health.

(2) The Committee shall advise, consult with, and make recommendations to the Secretary and the Secretary of Health and Human Services on matters relating to the administration of this chapter. The Committee shall hold no fewer than two meetings during each calendar year. All meetings of the Committee shall be open to the public and a transcript shall be kept and made available for public inspection.

* * *

(b) Advisory committees; appointment; duties; membership; compensation; reimbursement to member's employer; meetings; availability of records; conflict of interest

An advisory committee may be appointed by the Secretary to assist him in his standard-setting functions under section 655 of this title [29 U.S.C. § 655]. Each such committee shall consist of not more than fifteen members and shall include as a member one or more designees of the Secretary of Health and Human Services, and shall include among its members an equal number of persons qualified by experience and affiliation to present the viewpoint of the employers involved, and of persons similarly qualified to present the viewpoint of the workers involved, as well as one or more representatives of health and safety agencies of the States. An advisory committee may also include such other persons as the Secretary may appoint who are qualified by knowledge and experience to make a useful contribution to the work of such committee, including one or more representatives of professional organizations of technicians or professionals specializing in occupational safety or health, and one or more representatives of nationally recognized standards-producing organizations, but the number of persons so appointed to any such advisory committee shall not exceed the number appointed to such committee as representatives of Federal and State agencies. Persons appointed to advisory committees from private life shall be compensated in the same manner as consultants or experts under section 3109 of title 5 [5

U.S.C. § 3109]. The Secretary shall pay to any State which is the employer of a member of such a committee who is a representative of the health or safety agency of that State, reimbursement sufficient to cover the actual cost to the State resulting from such representative's membership on such committee. Any meeting of such committee shall be open to the public and an accurate record shall be kept and made available to the public. No member of such committee (other than representatives of employers and employees) shall have an economic interest in any proposed rule.

(c) Use of services, facilities, and personnel of Federal, State, and local agencies; reimbursement; employment of experts and consultants or organizations; renewal of contracts; compensation; travel expenses

In carrying out his responsibilities under this chapter, the Secretary is authorized to-

(1) use, with the consent of any Federal agency, the services, facilities, and personnel of such agency, with or without reimbursement, and with the consent of any State or political subdivision thereof, accept and use the services, facilities, and personnel of any agency of such State or subdivision with reimbursement; and

(2) employ experts and consultants or organizations thereof as authorized by section 3109 of title 5 [5 U.S.C. § 3109], except that contracts for such employment may be renewed annually; compensate individuals so employed at rates not in excess of the rate specified at the time of service for grade GS—18 under section 5332 of title 5 [5 U.S.C. § 5332], including traveltime, and allow them while away from their homes or regular places of business, travel expenses (including per diem in lieu of subsistence) as authorized by section 5703 of title 5 [5 U.S.C. § 5703] for persons in the Government service employed intermittently, while so employed.

(d) Maritime Occupational Safety and Health Advisory Committee

There is established a Maritime Occupational Safety and Health Advisory Committee, which shall be a continuing body and shall provide advice to the Secretary in formulating maritime industry standards and regarding matters pertaining to the administration of this chapter related to the maritime industry. The composition of such advisory committee shall be consistent with the advisory committees established under subsection (b). A member of the advisory committee who is otherwise qualified may continue to serve until a successor is appointed. The Secretary may promulgate or amend regulations as necessary to implement this subsection.

§ 657. Inspections, investigations, and recordkeeping

(a) Authority of Secretary to enter, inspect, and investigate places of employment; time and manner

In order to carry out the purposes of this chapter, the Secretary, upon presenting appropriate credentials to the owner, operator, or agent in charge, is authorized-

(1) to enter without delay and at reasonable times any factory, plant, establishment, construction site, or other area, workplace or environment where work is performed by an employee of an employer; and

(2) to inspect and investigate during regular working hours and at other reasonable times, and within reasonable limits and in a reasonable manner, any such place of employment and all pertinent conditions, structures, machines, apparatus, devices, equipment, and materials therein, and to question privately any such employer, owner, operator, agent, or employee.

(b) Attendance and testimony of witnesses and production of evidence; enforcement of subpoena

In making his inspections and investigations under this chapter the Secretary may require the attendance and testimony of witnesses and the production of evidence under oath. Witnesses shall be paid the same fees and mileage that are paid witnesses in the courts of the United States. In case of a contumacy, failure, or refusal of any person to obey such an order, any district court of the United States or the United States courts of any territory or possession, within the jurisdiction of which such person is found, or resides or transacts business, upon the application by the Secretary, shall have jurisdiction to issue to such person an order requiring such person to appear to produce evidence if, as, and when so ordered, and to give testimony relating to the matter under investigation or in question, and any failure to obey such order of the court may be punished by said court as a contempt thereof.

(c) Maintenance, preservation, and availability of records; issuance of regulations; scope of records; periodic inspections by employer; posting of notices by employer; notification of employee of corrective action

(1) Each employer shall make, keep and preserve, and make available to the Secretary or the Secretary of Health and Human Services, such records regarding his activities relating to this chapter as the Secretary, in cooperation with the Secretary of Health and Human Services, may prescribe by regulation as necessary or appropriate for the enforcement of this chapter or for developing information regarding the causes and prevention of occupational

accidents and illnesses. In order to carry out the provisions of this paragraph such regulations may include provisions requiring employers to conduct periodic inspections. The Secretary shall also issue regulations requiring that employers, through posting of notices or other appropriate means, keep their employees informed of their protections and obligations under this chapter, including the provisions of applicable standards.

(2) The Secretary, in cooperation with the Secretary of Health and Human Services, shall prescribe regulations requiring employers to maintain accurate records of, and to make periodic reports on, work-related deaths, injuries and illnesses other than minor injuries requiring only first aid treatment and which do not involve medical treatment, loss of consciousness, restriction of work or motion, or transfer to another job.

(3) The Secretary, in cooperation with the Secretary of Health and Human Services, shall issue regulations requiring employers to maintain accurate records of employee exposures to potentially toxic materials or harmful physical agents which are required to be monitored or measured under section 655 of this title [29 U.S.C. § 655]. Such regulations shall provide employees or their representatives with an opportunity to observe such monitoring or measuring, and to have access to the records thereof. Such regulations shall also make appropriate provision for each employee or former employee to have access to such records as will indicate his own exposure to toxic materials or harmful physical agents. Each employer shall promptly notify any employee who has been or is being exposed to toxic materials or harmful physical agents in concentrations or at levels which exceed those prescribed by an applicable occupational safety and health standard promulgated under section 655 of this title [29 U.S.C. § 655], and shall inform any employee who is being thus exposed of the corrective action being taken.

(d) Obtaining of information

Any information obtained by the Secretary, the Secretary of Health and Human Services, or a State agency under this chapter shall be obtained with a minimum burden upon employers, especially those operating small businesses. Unnecessary duplication of efforts in obtaining information shall be reduced to the maximum extent feasible.

(e) Employer and authorized employee representatives to accompany Secretary or his authorized representative on inspection of workplace; consultation with employees where no authorized employee representative is present

Subject to regulations issued by the Secretary, a representative of the employer and a representative authorized by his employees shall be given an opportunity to accompany the Secretary or his authorized representative during the physical inspection of any workplace under subsection (a) for the purpose of aiding such inspection. Where there is no authorized employee representative, the Secretary or his authorized representative shall consult with a reasonable number of employees concerning matters of health and safety in the workplace.

(f) Request for inspection by employees or representative of employees; grounds; procedure; determination of request; notification of Secretary or representative prior to or during any inspection of violations; procedure for review of refusal by representative of Secretary to issue citation for alleged violations

(1) Any employees or representative of employees who believe that a violation of a safety or health standard exists that threatens physical harm, or that an imminent danger exists, may request an inspection by giving notice to the Secretary or his authorized representative of such violation or danger. Any such notice shall be reduced to writing, shall set forth with reasonable particularity the grounds for the notice, and shall be signed by the employees or representative of employees, and a copy shall be provided the employer or his agent no later than at the time of inspection, except that, upon the request of the person giving such notice, his name and the names of individual employees referred to therein shall not appear in such copy or on any record published, released, or made available pursuant to subsection (g) of this section. If upon receipt of such notification the Secretary determines there are reasonable grounds to believe that such violation or danger exists, he shall make a special inspection in accordance with the provisions of this section as soon as practicable, to determine if such violation or danger exists. If the Secretary determines there are no reasonable grounds to believe that a violation or danger exists he shall notify the employees or representative of the employees in writing of such determination.

(2) Prior to or during any inspection of a workplace, any employees or representative of employees employed in such workplace may notify the Secretary or any representative of the Secretary responsible for conducting the inspection, in writing, of any violation of this chapter which they have reason to believe exists in such workplace. The Secretary shall, by regulation, establish procedures for informal review of any refusal by a representative of the Secretary to issue a citation with respect to any such alleged violation and shall furnish the employees or representative of employees requesting such review a written statement of the reasons for the Secretary's final disposition of the case.

(g) Compilation, analysis, and publication of reports and information; rules and regulations

(1) The Secretary and Secretary of Health and Human Services are authorized to compile, analyze, and publish, either in summary or detailed form, all reports or information obtained under this section.

(2) The Secretary and the Secretary of Health and Human Services shall each prescribe such rules and regulations as he may deem necessary to carry out their responsibilities under this chapter, including rules and regulations dealing with the inspection of an employer's establishment.

(h) Use of results of enforcement activities

The Secretary shall not use the results of enforcement activities, such as the number of citations issued or penalties assessed, to evaluate employees directly involved in enforcement activities under this chapter or to impose quotas or goals with regard to the results of such activities.

§ 658. Citations

(a) Authority to issue; grounds; contents; notice in lieu of citation for de minimis violations

If, upon inspection or investigation, the Secretary or his authorized representative believes that an employer has violated a requirement of section 654 of this title [29 U.S.C. § 654], of any standard, rule or order promulgated pursuant to section 655 of this title [29 U.S.C. § 655], or of any regulations prescribed pursuant to this chapter, he shall with reasonable promptness issue a citation to the employer. Each citation shall be in writing and shall describe with particularity the nature of the violation, including a reference to the provision of the chapter, standard, rule, regulation, or order alleged to have been violated. In addition, the citation shall fix a reasonable time for the abatement of the violation. The Secretary may prescribe procedures for the issuance of a notice in lieu of a citation with respect to de minimis violations which have no direct or immediate relationship to safety or health.

(b) Posting

Each citation issued under this section, or a copy or copies thereof, shall be prominently posted, as prescribed in regulations issued by the Secretary, at or near each place a violation referred to in the citation occurred.

(c) Time for issuance

No citation may be issued under this section after the expiration of six months following the occurrence of any violation.

§ 659. Enforcement procedures

(a) Notification of employer of proposed assessment of penalty subsequent to issuance of citation; time for notification of Secretary by employer of contest by employer of citation or proposed assessment; citation and proposed assessment as final order upon failure of employer to notify of contest and failure of employees to file notice

If, after an inspection or investigation, the Secretary issues a citation under section 658(a) of this title [29 U.S.C. § 658(a)], he shall, within a reasonable time after the termination of such inspection or investigation, notify the employer by certified mail of the penalty, if any, proposed to be assessed under section 666 of this title [29 U.S.C. § 666] and that the employer has fifteen working days within which to notify the Secretary that he wishes to contest the citation or proposed assessment of penalty. If, within fifteen working days from the receipt of the notice issued by the Secretary the employer fails to notify the Secretary that he intends to contest the citation or proposed assessment of penalty, and no notice is filed by any employee or representative of employees under subsection (c) within such time, the citation and the assessment, as proposed, shall be deemed a final order of the Commission and not subject to review by any court or agency.

(b) Notification of employer of failure to correct in allotted time period violation for which citation was issued and proposed assessment of penalty for failure to correct; time for notification of Secretary by employer of contest by employer of notification of failure to correct or proposed assessment; notification or proposed assessment as final order upon failure of employer to notify of contest

If the Secretary has reason to believe that an employer has failed to correct a violation for which a citation has been issued within the period permitted for its correction (which period shall not begin to run until the entry of a final order by the Commission in the case of any review proceedings under this section initiated by the employer in good faith and not solely for delay or avoidance of penalties), the Secretary shall notify the employer by certified mail of such failure and of the penalty proposed to be assessed under section 666 of this title [29 U.S.C. § 666] by reason of such failure, and that the employer has fifteen working days within which to notify the Secretary that he wishes to contest the Secretary's notification or the proposed assessment of penalty. If, within fifteen working days from the receipt of notification issued by the Secretary, the employer fails to notify the Secretary that he intends to contest the notification or proposed assessment of penalty, the notification and assessment, as proposed, shall be deemed a final order of the Commission and not subject to review by any court or agency.

(c) Advisement of Commission by Secretary of notification of contest by employer of citation or notification or of filing of notice by any employee or representative of employees; hearing by Commission; orders of Commission and Secretary; rules of procedure

If an employer notifies the Secretary that he intends to contest a citation issued under section 658(a) of this title [29 U.S.C. § 658(a)] or notification issued under subsection (a) or (b) of this section, or if, within fifteen working days of the issuance of a citation under section 658(a) of this title, any employee or representative of employees files a notice with the Secretary alleging that the period of time fixed in the citation for the abatement of the violation is unreasonable, the Secretary shall immediately advise the Commission of such notification, and the Commission shall afford an opportunity for a hearing (in accordance with section 554 of title 5 [5 U.S.C. § 554] but without regard to subsection (a)(3) of such section). The Commission shall thereafter issue an order, based on findings of fact, affirming, modifying, or vacating the Secretary's citation or proposed penalty, or directing other appropriate relief, and such order shall become final thirty days after its issuance. Upon a showing by an employer of a good faith effort to comply with the abatement requirements of a citation, and that abatement has not been completed because of factors beyond his reasonable control, the Secretary, after an opportunity for a hearing as provided in this subsection, shall issue an order affirming or modifying the abatement requirements in such citation. The rules of procedure prescribed by the Commission shall provide affected employees or representatives of affected employees an opportunity to participate as parties to hearings under this subsection.

§ 660. Judicial review

(a) Filing of petition by persons adversely affected or aggrieved; orders subject to review; jurisdiction; venue; procedure; conclusiveness of record and findings of Commission; appropriate relief; finality of judgment

Any person adversely affected or aggrieved by an order of the Commission issued under subsection (c) of section 659 of this title [29 U.S.C. § 659] may obtain a review of such order in any United States court of appeals for the circuit in which the violation is alleged to have occurred or where the employer has its principal office, or in the Court of Appeals for the District of Columbia Circuit, by filing in such court within sixty days following the issuance of such order a written petition praying that the order be modified or set aside. A copy of such petition shall be forthwith transmitted by the clerk of the court to the Commission and to the other parties, and thereupon the Commission shall file in the court the record in the proceeding as provided in section 2112 of title 28 [28 U.S.C. § 2112]. Upon such filing, the court shall have jurisdiction of the proceeding and of the question determined therein, and shall have power to grant such temporary relief or restraining order as it deems just and proper, and to make and enter upon the pleadings, testimony, and proceedings set forth in such record a decree affirming, modifying, or setting aside in whole or in part, the order of the Commission and enforcing the same to the extent that such order is affirmed or modified. The commencement of proceedings under this subsection shall not, unless ordered by the court, operate as a stay of the order of the Commission. No objection that has not been urged before the Commission shall be considered by the court, unless the failure or neglect to urge such objection shall be excused because of extraordinary circumstances. The findings of the Commission with respect to questions of fact, if supported by substantial evidence on the record considered as a whole, shall be conclusive. If any party shall apply to the court for leave to adduce additional evidence and shall show to the satisfaction of the court that such additional evidence is material and that there were reasonable grounds for the failure to adduce such evidence in the hearing before the Commission, the court may order such additional evidence to be taken before the Commission and to be made a part of the record. The Commission may modify its findings as to the facts, or make new findings, by reason of additional evidence so taken and filed, and it shall file such modified or new findings, which findings with respect to questions of fact, if supported by substantial evidence on the record considered as a whole, shall be conclusive, and its recommendations, if any, for the modification or setting aside of its original order. Upon the filing of the record with it, the jurisdiction of the court shall be exclusive and its judgment and decree shall be final, except that the same shall be subject to review by the Supreme Court of the United States, as provided in section 1254 of title 28 [28 U.S.C. § 1254].

(b) Filing of petition by Secretary; orders subject to review; jurisdiction; venue; procedure; conclusiveness of record and findings of Commission; enforcement of orders; contempt proceedings

The Secretary may also obtain review or enforcement of any final order of the Commission by filing a petition for such relief in the United States court of appeals for the circuit in which the alleged violation occurred or in which the employer has its principal office, and the provisions of subsection (a) shall govern such proceedings to the extent applicable. If no petition for review, as provided in subsection (a), is filed within sixty days after service of the Commission's order, the Commission's findings of fact and order shall be conclusive in connection with any petition for enforcement which is filed by the Secretary after the expiration of such sixty-day period. In any such case, as well as in the case of a noncontested citation or notification by the Secretary which has become a final order of the Commission under subsection (a) or (b) of section 659 of this title [29 U.S.C. § 659], the clerk of the court, unless otherwise ordered by the court, shall forthwith enter a decree enforcing the order and shall transmit a copy of such decree to the Secretary and the employer named in the petition. In any contempt proceeding brought to enforce a decree of a court of appeals entered pursuant to this subsection or subsection (a), the court of appeals may assess the penalties provided in section 666 of this title [29 U.S.C. § 666], in addition to invoking any other available remedies.

(c) Discharge or discrimination against employee for exercise of rights under this chapter; prohibition; procedure for relief

(1) No person shall discharge or in any manner discriminate against any employee because such employee has filed any complaint or instituted or caused to be instituted any proceeding under or related to this chapter or has testified or is about to testify in any such proceeding or because of the exercise by such employee on behalf of himself or others of any right afforded by this chapter.

(2) Any employee who believes that he has been discharged or otherwise discriminated against by any person in violation of this subsection may, within thirty days after such violation occurs, file a complaint with the Secretary alleging such discrimination. Upon receipt of such complaint, the Secretary shall cause such investigation to be made as he deems appropriate. If upon such investigation, the Secretary determines that the provisions of this subsection have been violated, he shall bring an action in any appropriate United States district court against such person. In any such action the United States district courts shall have jurisdiction, for cause shown to restrain violations of paragraph (1) of this subsection and order all appropriate relief including rehiring or reinstatement of the employee to his former position with back pay.

(3) Within 90 days of the receipt of a complaint filed under this subsection the Secretary shall notify the complainant of his determination under paragraph (2) of this subsection.

§ 661. Occupational Safety and Health Review Commission

(a) Establishment; membership; appointment; Chairman

The Occupational Safety and Health Review Commission is hereby established. The Commission shall be composed of three members who shall be appointed by the President, by and with the advice and consent of the Senate, from among persons who by reason of training, education, or experience are qualified to carry out the functions of the Commission under this chapter. The President shall designate one of the members of the Commission to serve as Chairman.

(b) Terms of office; removal by President

The terms of members of the Commission shall be six years except that (1) the members of the Commission first taking office shall serve, as designated by the President at the time of appointment, one for a term of two years, one for a term of four years, and one for a term of six years, and (2) a vacancy caused by the death, resignation, or removal of a member prior to the expiration of the term for which he was appointed shall be filled only for the remainder of such unexpired term. A member of the Commission may be removed by the President for inefficiency, neglect of duty, or malfeasance in office.

* * *

(e) Functions and duties of Chairman; appointment and compensation of administrative law judges and other employees

The Chairman shall be responsible on behalf of the Commission for the administrative operations of the Commission and shall appoint such administrative law judges and other employees as he deems necessary to assist in the performance of the Commission's functions and to fix their compensation in accordance with the provisions of chapter 51 and subchapter III of chapter 53 of title 5 [5 U.S.C. §§ 5101 et seq., 5331 et seq.] relating to classification and General Schedule pay rates: Provided, That assignment, removal and compensation of administrative law judges shall be in accordance with sections 3105, 3344, 5372, and 7521 of title 5 [5 U.S.C. §§ 3105, 3344, 5372, 7521].

(f) Quorum; official action

For the purpose of carrying out its functions under this chapter, two members of the Commission shall constitute a quorum and official action can be taken only on the affirmative vote of at least two members.

(g) Hearings and records open to public; promulgation of rules; applicability of Federal Rules of Civil Procedure

Every official act of the Commission shall be entered of record, and its hearings and records shall be open to the public. The Commission is authorized to make such rules as are necessary for the orderly transaction of its proceedings. Unless the Commission has adopted a different rule, its proceedings shall be in accordance with the Federal Rules of Civil Procedure.

(h) Depositions and production of documentary evidence; fees

The Commission may order testimony to be taken by deposition in any proceedings pending before it at any state of such proceeding. Any person may be compelled to appear and depose, and to produce books, papers, or documents, in the same manner as witnesses may be compelled to appear and testify and produce like documentary evidence before the Commission. Witnesses whose depositions are taken under this subsection, and the persons taking such depositions, shall be entitled to the same fees as are paid for like services in the courts of the United States.

(i) Investigatory powers

For the purpose of any proceeding before the Commission, the provisions of section 161 of this title [29 U.S.C. § 161] are hereby made applicable to the jurisdiction and powers of the Commission.

(j) Administrative law judges; determinations; report as final order of Commission

A[n] administrative law judge appointed by the Commission shall hear, and make a determination upon, any proceeding instituted before the Commission and any motion in connection therewith, assigned to such administrative law judge by the Chairman of the Commission, and shall make a report of any such determination which constitutes his final disposition of the proceedings. The report of the administrative law judge shall become the final order of the Commission within thirty days after such report by the administrative law judge, unless within such period any Commission member has directed that such report shall be reviewed by the Commission.

(k) Appointment and compensation of administrative law judges

* * *

§ 662. Injunction proceedings

(a) Petition by Secretary to restrain imminent dangers; scope of order

The United States district courts shall have jurisdiction, upon petition of the Secretary, to restrain any conditions or practices in any place of employment which are such that a danger exists which could reasonably be expected to cause death or serious physical harm immediately or before the imminence of such danger can be eliminated through the enforcement procedures otherwise provided by this chapter. Any order issued under this section may require such steps to be taken as may be necessary to avoid, correct, or remove such imminent danger and prohibit the employment or presence of any individual in locations or under conditions where such imminent danger exists, except individuals whose presence is necessary to avoid, correct, or remove such imminent danger or to maintain the capacity of a continuous process operation to resume normal operations without a complete cessation of operations, or where a cessation of operations is necessary, to permit such to be accomplished in a safe and orderly manner.

(b) Appropriate injunctive relief or temporary restraining order pending outcome of enforcement proceeding; applicability of Rule 65 of Federal Rules of Civil Procedure

Upon the filing of any such petition the district court shall have jurisdiction to grant such injunctive relief or temporary restraining order pending the outcome of an enforcement proceeding pursuant to this chapter. The proceeding shall be as provided by Rule 65 of the Federal Rules, Civil Procedure, except that no temporary restraining order issued without notice shall be effective for a period longer than five days.

(c) Notification of affected employees and employers by inspector of danger and of recommendation to Secretary to seek relief

Whenever and as soon as an inspector concludes that conditions or practices described in subsection (a) exist in any place of employment, he shall inform the affected employees and employers of the danger and that he is recommending to the Secretary that relief be sought.

(d) Failure of Secretary to seek relief; writ of mandamus

If the Secretary arbitrarily or capriciously fails to seek relief under this section, any employee who may be injured by reason of such failure, or the representative of such employees, might bring an action against the Secretary in the United States district court for the district in which the imminent danger is alleged to exist or the employer has its principal office, or for the District of Columbia, for a writ of mandamus to compel the Secretary to seek such an order and for such further relief as may be appropriate.

§ 663. Representation in civil litigation

Except as provided in section 518(a) of title 28 [28 U.S.C. § 518(a)] relating to litigation before the Supreme Court, the Solicitor of Labor may appear for and represent the Secretary in any civil litigation brought under this chapter but all such litigations shall be subject to the direction and control of the Attorney General.

§ 664. Disclosure of trade secrets; protective orders

All information reported to or otherwise obtained by the Secretary or his representative in connection with any inspection or proceeding under this chapter which contains or which might reveal a trade secret referred to in section 1905 of title 18 [18 U.S.C. § 1905] shall be considered confidential for the purpose of that section, except that such information may be disclosed to other officers or employees concerned with carrying out this chapter or when relevant in any proceeding under this chapter. In any such proceeding the Secretary, the Commission, or the court shall issue such orders as may be appropriate to protect the confidentiality of trade secrets.

§ 665. Variations, tolerances, and exemptions from required provisions; procedure; duration

The Secretary, on the record, after notice and opportunity for a hearing may provide such reasonable limitations and may make such rules and regulations allowing reasonable variations, tolerances, and exemptions to and from any or all provisions of this chapter as he may find necessary and proper to avoid serious impairment of the national defense. Such action shall not be in effect for more than six months without notification to affected employees and an opportunity being afforded for a hearing.

§ 666. Civil and criminal penalties

(a) Willful or repeated violation

Any employer who willfully or repeatedly violates the requirements of section 654 of this title [29 U.S.C. § 654], any standard, rule, or order promulgated pursuant to section 655 of this title [29 U.S.C. § 655], or regulations prescribed pursuant to this chapter may be assessed a civil penalty of not more than $70,000 for each violation, but not less than $5,000 for each willful violation.

(b) Citation for serious violation

Any employer who has received a citation for a serious violation of the requirements of section 654 of this title [29 U.S.C. § 654], of any standard, rule, or order promulgated pursuant to section 655 of this title [29 U.S.C. § 655], or of any regulations prescribed pursuant to this chapter, shall be assessed a civil penalty of up to $7,000 for each such violation.

(c) Citation for violation determined not serious

Any employer who has received a citation for a violation of the requirements of section 654 of this title [29 U.S.C. § 654], of any standard, rule, or order promulgated pursuant to section 655 of this title [29 U.S.C. § 655], or of regulations prescribed pursuant to this chapter, and such violation is specifically determined not to be of a serious nature, may be assessed a civil penalty of up to $7,000 for each such violation.

(d) Failure to correct violation

Any employer who fails to correct a violation for which a citation has been issued under section 658(a) of this title [29 U.S.C. § 658(a)] within the period permitted for its correction (which period shall not begin to run until the date of the final order of the Commission in the case of any review proceeding under section 659 of this title [29 U.S.C. § 659] initiated by the employer in good faith and not solely for delay or avoidance of penalties), may be assessed a civil penalty of not more than $7,000 for each day during which such failure or violation continues.

(e) Willful violation causing death to employee

Any employer who willfully violates any standard, rule, or order promulgated pursuant to section 655 of this title [29 U.S.C. § 655], or of any regulations prescribed pursuant to this chapter, and that violation caused death to any employee, shall, upon conviction, be punished by a fine of not more than $10,000* or by imprisonment for not more than six months, or by both; except that if the conviction is for a violation committed after a first conviction of such person, punishment shall be by a fine of not more than $20,000* or by imprisonment for not more than one year, or by both.

(f) Giving advance notice of inspection

Any person who gives advance notice of any inspection to be conducted under this chapter, without authority from the Secretary or his designees, shall, upon conviction, be punished by a fine of not more than $1,000 or by imprisonment for not more than six months, or by both.

(g) False statements, representations or certification

Whoever knowingly makes any false statement, representation, or certification in any application, record, report, plan, or other document filed or required to be maintained pursuant to this chapter shall, upon conviction, be punished by a fine of not more than $10,000, or by imprisonment for not more than six months, or by both.

(h) [Omitted]

(i) Violation of posting requirements

Any employer who violates any of the posting requirements, as prescribed under the provisions of this chapter, shall be assessed a civil penalty of up to $7,000 for each violation.

(j) Authority of Commission to assess civil penalties

The Commission shall have authority to assess all civil penalties provided in this section, giving due consideration to the appropriateness of the penalty with respect to the size of the business of the employer being charged, the gravity of the violation, the good faith of the employer, and the history of previous violations.

(k) Determination of serious violation

---

* 18 U.S.C.A. § 3571(b) and (c) increase the maximum fines to $250,000 for an individual defendant and $500,000 for an organizational defendant. Individuals acting on behalf of or aiding and abetting organizations to commit criminal offenses are guilty of the same crime as the organization. 18 U.S.C.A. § 2.

For purposes of this section, a serious violation shall be deemed to exist in a place of employment if there is a substantial probability that death or serious physical harm could result from a condition which exists, or from one or more practices, means, methods, operations, or processes which have been adopted or are in use, in such place of employment unless the employer did not, and could not with the exercise of reasonable diligence, know of the presence of the violation.

(*l*) Procedure for payment of civil penalties

Civil penalties owed under this chapter shall be paid to the Secretary for deposit into the Treasury of the United States and shall accrue to the United States and may be recovered in a civil action in the name of the United States brought in the United States district court for the district where the violation is alleged to have occurred or where the employer has its principal office.

§ 667. State jurisdiction and plans

(a) Assertion of State standards in absence of applicable Federal standards

Nothing in this chapter shall prevent any State agency or court from asserting jurisdiction under State law over any occupational safety or health issue with respect to which no standard is in effect under section 655 of this title [29 U.S.C. § 655].

(b) Submission of State plan for development and enforcement of State standards to preempt applicable Federal standards

Any State which, at any time, desires to assume responsibility for development and enforcement therein of occupational safety and health standards relating to any occupational safety or health issue with respect to which a Federal standard has been promulgated under section 655 of this title [29 U.S.C. § 655] shall submit a State plan for the development of such standards and their enforcement.

(c) Conditions for approval of plan

The Secretary shall approve the plan submitted by a State under subsection (b), or any modification thereof, if such plan in his judgment-

(1) designates a State agency or agencies as the agency or agencies responsible for administering the plan throughout the State,

(2) provides for the development and enforcement of safety and health standards relating to one or more safety or health issues, which standards (and the enforcement of which standards) are or will be at least as effective in providing safe and healthful employment and places of employment as the standards promulgated under section 655 of this title [29 U.S.C. § 655] which relate to the same issues, and

which standards, when applicable to products which are distributed or used in interstate commerce, are required by compelling local conditions and do not unduly burden interstate commerce,

(3) provides for a right of entry and inspection of all workplaces subject to this chapter which is at least as effective as that provided in section 657 of this title [29 U.S.C. § 657], and includes a prohibition on advance notice of inspections,

(4) contains satisfactory assurances that such agency or agencies have or will have the legal authority and qualified personnel necessary for the enforcement of such standards,

(5) gives satisfactory assurances that such State will devote adequate funds to the administration and enforcement of such standards,

(6) contains satisfactory assurances that such State will, to the extent permitted by its law, establish and maintain an effective and comprehensive occupational safety and health program applicable to all employees of public agencies of the State and its political subdivisions, which program is as effective as the standards contained in an approved plan,

(7) requires employers in the State to make reports to the Secretary in the same manner and to the same extent as if the plan were not in effect, and

(8) provides that the State agency will make such reports to the Secretary in such form and containing such information, as the Secretary shall from time to time require.

(d) Rejection of plan; notice and opportunity for hearing

If the Secretary rejects a plan submitted under subsection (b), he shall afford the State submitting the plan due notice and opportunity for a hearing before so doing.

(e) Discretion of Secretary to exercise authority over comparable standards subsequent to approval of State plan; duration; retention of jurisdiction by Secretary upon determination of enforcement of plan by State

After the Secretary approves a State plan submitted under subsection (b), he may, but shall not be required to, exercise his authority under sections 657, 658, 659, 662, and 666 of this title [29 U.S.C. §§ 657, 658, 659, 662, 666] with respect to comparable standards promulgated under section 655 of this title [29 U.S.C.§ 655], for the period specified in the next sentence. The Secretary may exercise the authority referred to above until he determines, on the basis of actual operations under the State plan, that the criteria set forth in subsection (c) are being applied, but he shall not make such determination for at least three years after the plan's approval under subsection (c). Upon making the determination referred to in the preceding sentence, the provisions of sections 654(a)(2), 657 (except for the purpose of carrying out subsection (f) of this section), 658, 659, 662, and 666 of this title [29 U.S.C. §§ 654(a)(2), 657, 658, 659, 662], and standards promulgated under section 655 of this title [29 U.S.C. § 665], shall not apply with respect to any occupational safety or health issues covered under the plan, but the Secretary may retain jurisdiction under the above provisions in any proceeding commenced under section 658 or 659 of this title [29 U.S.C. §§ 658, 659] before the date of determination.

(f) Continuing evaluation by Secretary of State enforcement of approved plan; withdrawal of approval of plan by Secretary; grounds; procedure; conditions for retention of jurisdiction by State

The Secretary shall, on the basis of reports submitted by the State agency and his own inspections make a continuing evaluation of the manner in which each State having a plan approved under this section is carrying out such plan. Whenever the Secretary finds, after affording due notice and opportunity for a hearing, that in the administration of the State plan there is a failure to comply substantially with any provision of the State plan (or any assurance contained therein), he shall notify the State agency of his withdrawal of approval of such plan and upon receipt of such notice such plan shall cease to be in effect, but the State may retain jurisdiction in any case commenced before the withdrawal of the plan in order to enforce standards under the plan whenever the issues involved do not relate to the reasons for the withdrawal of the plan.

(g) Judicial review of Secretary's withdrawal of approval or rejection of plan; jurisdiction; venue; procedure; appropriate relief; finality of judgment

The State may obtain a review of a decision of the Secretary withdrawing approval of or rejecting its plan by the United States court of appeals for the circuit in which the State is located by filing in such court within thirty days following receipt of notice of such decision a petition to modify or set aside in whole or in part the action of the Secretary. A copy of such petition shall forthwith be served upon the Secretary, and thereupon the Secretary shall certify and file in the court the record upon which the decision complained of was issued as provided in section 2112 of title 28 [28 U.S.C. § 2112]. Unless the court finds that the Secretary's decision in rejecting a proposed State plan or withdrawing his approval of such a plan is not supported by substantial evidence the court shall affirm the Secretary's decision. The judgment of the court shall be subject to review by the Supreme Court of the United States upon certiorari or certification as provided in section 1254 of title 28 [28 U.S.C. § 1254].

(h) Temporary enforcement of State standards

* * *

§ 668. Programs of Federal agencies

(a) Establishment, development, and maintenance by head of each Federal agency

It shall be the responsibility of the head of each Federal agency (not including the Postal Service) to establish and maintain an effective and comprehensive occupational safety and health program which is consistent with the standards promulgated under section 655 of this title [29 U.S.C. § 655]. The head of each agency shall (after consultation with representatives of the employees thereof)-

(1) provide safe and healthful places and conditions of employment, consistent with the standards set under section 655 of this title [29 U.S.C. § 655];

(2) acquire, maintain, and require the use of safety equipment, personal protective equipment, and devices reasonably necessary to protect employees;

(3) keep adequate records of all occupational accidents and illnesses for proper evaluation and necessary corrective action;

(4) consult with the Secretary with regard to the adequacy as to form and content of records kept pursuant to subsection (a)(3) of this section; and

(5) make an annual report to the Secretary with respect to occupational accidents and injuries and the agency's program under this section. Such report shall include any report submitted under section 7902(e)(2) of title 5 [5 U.S.C. § 7902(e)(2)].

(b) Report by Secretary to President

* * *

(d) Access by Secretary to records and reports required of agencies

The Secretary shall have access to records and reports kept and filed by Federal agencies pursuant to subsections (a)(3) and (5) of this section unless those records and reports are specifically required by Executive order to be kept secret in the interest of the national defense or foreign policy, in which case the Secretary shall have access to such information as will not jeopardize national defense or foreign policy.

§ 669. Research and related activities

(a) Authority of Secretary of Health and Human Services to conduct research, experiments, and demonstrations, develop plans, establish criteria, promulgate regulations, authorize programs, and publish results and industrywide studies; consultations

(1) The Secretary of Health and Human Services after consultation with the Secretary and with other appropriate Federal departments or agencies, shall conduct (directly or by grants or contracts) research, experiments, and demonstrations relating to occupational safety and health, including studies of psychological factors involved, and relating to innovative methods, techniques, and approaches for dealing with occupational safety and health problems.

(2) The Secretary of Health and Human Services shall from time to time consult with the Secretary in order to develop specific plans for such research, demonstrations, and experiments as are necessary to produce criteria, including criteria identifying toxic substances, enabling the Secretary to meet his responsibility for the formulation of safety and health standards under this chapter; and the Secretary of Health and Human Services, on the basis of such research, demonstrations, and experiments and any other information available to him, shall develop and publish at least annually such criteria as will effectuate the purposes of this chapter.

(3) The Secretary of Health and Human Services, on the basis of such research, demonstrations, and experiments, and any other information available to him, shall develop criteria dealing with toxic materials and harmful physical agents and substances which will describe exposure levels that are safe for various periods of employment, including but not limited to the exposure levels at which no employee will suffer impaired health or functional capacities or diminished life expectancy as a result of his work experience.

(4) The Secretary of Health and Human Services shall also conduct special research, experiments, and demonstrations relating to occupational safety and health as are necessary to explore new problems, including those created by new technology in occupational safety and health, which may require ameliorative action beyond that which is otherwise provided for in the operating provisions of this chapter. The Secretary of Health and Human Services shall also conduct research into the motivational and behavioral factors relating to the field of occupational safety and health.

(5) The Secretary of Health and Human Services, in order to comply with his responsibilities under paragraph (2), and in order to develop needed information regarding potentially toxic substances or

harmful physical agents, may prescribe regulations requiring employers to measure, record, and make reports on the exposure of employees to substances or physical agents which the Secretary of Health and Human Services reasonably believes may endanger the health or safety of employees. The Secretary of Health and Human Services also is authorized to establish such programs of medical examinations and tests as may be necessary for determining the incidence of occupational illnesses and the susceptibility of employees to such illnesses. Nothing in this or any other provision of this chapter shall be deemed to authorize or require medical examination, immunization, or treatment for those who object thereto on religious grounds, except where such is necessary for the protection of the health or safety of others. Upon the request of any employer who is required to measure and record exposure of employees to substances or physical agents as provided under this subsection, the Secretary of Health and Human Services shall furnish full financial or other assistance to such employer for the purpose of defraying any additional expense incurred by him in carrying out the measuring and recording as provided in this subsection.

(6) The Secretary of Health and Human Services shall publish within six months of December 29, 1970, and thereafter as needed but at least annually a list of all known toxic substances by generic family or other useful grouping, and the concentrations at which such toxicity is known to occur. He shall determine following a written request by any employer or authorized representative of employees, specifying with reasonable particularity the grounds on which the request is made, whether any substance normally found in the place of employment has potentially toxic effects in such concentrations as used or found; and shall submit such determination both to employers and affected employees as soon as possible. If the Secretary of Health and Human Services determines that any substance is potentially toxic at the concentrations in which it is used or found in a place of employment, and such substance is not covered by an occupational safety or health standard promulgated under section 655 of this title [29 U.S.C. § 655], the Secretary of Health and Human Services shall immediately submit such determination to the Secretary, together with all pertinent criteria.

(7) Within two years of December 29, 1970, and annually thereafter the Secretary of Health and Human Services shall conduct and publish industrywide studies of the effect of chronic or low-level exposure to industrial materials, processes, and stresses on the potential for illness, disease, or loss of functional capacity in aging adults.

(b) Authority of Secretary of Health and Human Services to make inspections and question employers and employees

The Secretary of Health and Human Services is authorized to make inspections and question employers and employees as provided in section 657 of this title [29 U.S.C. § 657] in order to carry out his functions and responsibilities under this section.

(c) Contracting authority of Secretary of Labor; cooperation between Secretary of Labor and Secretary of Health and Human Services

The Secretary is authorized to enter into contracts, agreements, or other arrangements with appropriate public agencies or private organizations for the purpose of conducting studies relating to his responsibilities under this chapter. In carrying out his responsibilities under this subsection, the Secretary shall cooperate with the Secretary of Health and Human Services in order to avoid any duplication of efforts under this section.

(d) Dissemination of information to interested parties

Information obtained by the Secretary and the Secretary of Health and Human Services under this section shall be disseminated by the Secretary to employers and employees and organizations thereof.

(e) Delegation of functions of Secretary of Health and Human Services to Director of National Institute for Occupational Safety and Health

The functions of the Secretary of Health and Human Services under this chapter shall, to the extent feasible, be delegated to the Director of the National Institute for Occupational Safety and Health established by section 671 of this title [29 U.S.C. § 671].

§ 669a. Expanded research on worker health and safety

The Secretary of Health and Human Services (referred to in this section as the "Secretary"), acting through the Director of the National Institute of Occupational Safety and Health, shall enhance and expand research as deemed appropriate on the health and safety of workers who are at risk for bioterrorist threats or attacks in the workplace, including research on the health effects of measures taken to treat or protect such workers for diseases or disorders resulting from a bioterrorist threat or attack. Nothing in this section may be construed as establishing new regulatory authority for the Secretary or the Director to issue or modify any occupational safety and health rule or regulation.

§ 670. Training and employee education

(a) Authority of Secretary of Health and Human Services to conduct education and informational programs; consultations

The Secretary of Health and Human Services, after consultation with the Secretary and with other appropriate Federal departments and agencies, shall conduct, directly or by grants or contracts (1) education programs to provide an adequate supply of qualified personnel to carry out the purposes of this chapter, and (2) informational programs on the importance of and proper use of adequate safety and health equipment.

(b) Authority of Secretary of Labor to conduct short-term training of personnel

The Secretary is also authorized to conduct, directly or by grants or contracts, short-term training of personnel engaged in work related to his responsibilities under this chapter.

(c) Authority of Secretary of Labor to establish and supervise education and training programs and consult and advise interested parties

The Secretary, in consultation with the Secretary of Health and Human Services, shall (1) provide for the establishment and supervision of programs for the education and training of employers and employees in the recognition, avoidance, and prevention of unsafe or unhealthful working conditions in employments covered by this chapter, and (2) consult with and advise employers and employees, and organizations representing employers and employees as to effective means of preventing occupational injuries and illnesses.

(d) Compliance assistance program

(1) The Secretary shall establish and support cooperative agreements with the States under which employers subject to this chapter may consult with State personnel with respect to-

(A) the application of occupational safety and health requirements under this chapter or under State plans approved under section 667 of this title [29 U.S.C. § 667]; and

(B) voluntary efforts that employers may undertake to establish and maintain safe and healthful employment and places of employment.

Such agreements may provide, as a condition of receiving funds under such agreements, for contributions by States towards meeting the costs of such agreements.

(2) Pursuant to such agreements the State shall provide on-site consultation at the employer's worksite to employers who request such

assistance. The State may also provide other education and training programs for employers and employees in the State. The State shall ensure that on-site consultations conducted pursuant to such agreements include provision for the participation by employees.

(3) Activities under this subsection shall be conducted independently of any enforcement activity. If an employer fails to take immediate action to eliminate employee exposure to an imminent danger identified in a consultation or fails to correct a serious hazard so identified within a reasonable time, a report shall be made to the appropriate enforcement authority for such action as is appropriate.

(4) The Secretary shall, by regulation after notice and opportunity for comment, establish rules under which an employer-

(A) which requests and undergoes an on-site consultative visit provided under this subsection;

(B) which corrects the hazards that have been identified during the visit within the time frames established by the State and agrees to request a subsequent consultative visit if major changes in working conditions or work processes occur which introduce new hazards in the workplace; and

(C) which is implementing procedures for regularly identifying and preventing hazards regulated under this chapter and maintains appropriate involvement of, and training for, management and non-management employees in achieving safe and healthful working conditions,

may be exempt from an inspection (except an inspection requested under section 657(f) of this title [29 U.S.C. § 657(f)] or an inspection to determine the cause of a workplace accident which resulted in the death of one or more employees or hospitalization for three or more employees) for a period of 1 year from the closing of the consultative visit.

(5) A State shall provide worksite consultations under paragraph (2) at the request of an employer. Priority in scheduling such consultations shall be assigned to requests from small businesses which are in higher hazard industries or have the most hazardous conditions at issue in the request.

§ 671. National Institute for Occupational Safety and Health

(a) Statement of purpose

It is the purpose of this section to establish a National Institute for Occupational Safety and Health in the Department of Health and Human Services in order to carry out the policy set forth in section 651 of this title [29 U.S.C. § 651] and to perform the functions of the Secretary of Health and Human Services under sections 669 and 670 of this title [29 U.S.C. §§ 669, 670].

(b) Establishment; Director; appointment; term

There is hereby established in the Department of Health and Human Services a National Institute for Occupational Safety and Health. The Institute shall be headed by a Director who shall be appointed by the Secretary of Health and Human Services, and who shall serve for a term of six years unless previously removed by the Secretary of Health and Human Services.

(c) Development and establishment of standards; performance of functions of Secretary of Health and Human Services

The Institute is authorized to-

(1) develop and establish recommended occupational safety and health standards; and

(2) perform all functions of the Secretary of Health and Human Services under sections 669 and 670 of this title [29 U.S.C. §§ 669, 670].

(d) Authority of Director

Upon his own initiative, or upon the request of the Secretary or the Secretary of Health and Human Services, the Director is authorized (1) to conduct such research and experimental programs as he determines are necessary for the development of criteria for new and improved occupational safety and health standards, and (2) after consideration of the results of such research and experimental programs make recommendations concerning new or improved occupational safety and health standards. Any occupational safety and health standard recommended pursuant to this section shall immediately be forwarded to the Secretary of Labor, and to the Secretary of Health and Human Services.

(e) Additional authority of Director

In addition to any authority vested in the Institute by other provisions of this section, the Director, in carrying out the functions of the Institute, is authorized to-

(1) prescribe such regulations as he deems necessary governing the manner in which its functions shall be carried out;

(2) receive money and other property donated, bequeathed, or devised, without condition or restriction other than that it be used for the purposes of the Institute and to use, sell, or otherwise dispose of such property for the purpose of carrying out its functions;

(3) receive (and use, sell, or otherwise dispose of, in accordance with paragraph (2)), money and other property donated, bequeathed

or devised to the Institute with a condition or restriction, including a condition that the Institute use other funds of the Institute for the purposes of the gift;

(4) in accordance with the civil service laws, appoint and fix the compensation of such personnel as may be necessary to carry out the provisions of this section;

(5) obtain the services of experts and consultants in accordance with the provisions of section 3109 of title 5 [5 U.S.C. § 3109];

(6) accept and utilize the services of voluntary and noncompensated personnel and reimburse them for travel expenses, including per diem, as authorized by section 5703 of title 5 [5 U.S.C. § 5703];

(7) enter into contracts, grants or other arrangements, or modifications thereof to carry out the provisions of this section, and such contracts or modifications thereof may be entered into without performance or other bonds, and without regard to section 6101 of title 41 [41 U.S.C. § 6101] or any other provision of law relating to competitive bidding;

(8) make advance, progress, and other payments which the Director deems necessary under this title without regard to the provisions of section 3324(a) and (b) of title 31 [31 U.S.C. § 3324(a), (b)]; and

(9) make other necessary expenditures.

(f) Annual reports

* * *

(g) Lead-based paint activities

(1) Training Grant Program

* * *

(2) Evaluation of Programs

* * *

§ 671a. Workers' family protection

(a) Short title. This section may be cited as the "Workers' Family Protection Act".

(b) Findings and purposes

(1) Findings

Congress finds that-

(A) hazardous chemicals and substances that can threaten the health and safety of workers are being transported out of industries on workers' clothing and persons;

(B) these chemicals and substances have the potential to pose an additional threat to the health and welfare of workers and their families;

(C) additional information is needed concerning issues related to employee transported contaminant releases; and

(D) additional regulations may be needed to prevent future releases of this type.

(2) Purpose. It is the purpose of this section to-

(A) increase understanding and awareness concerning the extent and possible health impacts of the problems and incidents described in paragraph (1);

(B) prevent or mitigate future incidents of home contamination that could adversely affect the health and safety of workers and their families;

(C) clarify regulatory authority for preventing and responding to such incidents; and

(D) assist workers in redressing and responding to such incidents when they occur.

(c) Evaluation of employee transported contaminant releases

(1) Study

(A) In general. Not later than 18 months after October 26, 1992, the Director of the National Institute for Occupational Safety and Health (hereafter in this section referred to as the "Director"), in cooperation with the Secretary of Labor, the Administrator of the Environmental Protection Agency, the Administrator of the Agency for Toxic Substances and Disease Registry, and the heads of other Federal Government agencies as determined to be appropriate by the Director, shall conduct a study to evaluate the potential for, the prevalence of, and the issues related to the contamination of workers' homes with hazardous chemicals and substances, including infectious agents, transported from the workplaces of such workers.

(B) Matters to be evaluated. In conducting the study and evaluation under subparagraph (A), the Director shall-

(i) conduct a review of past incidents of home contamination through the utilization of literature and of records concerning past investigations and enforcement actions undertaken by-

(I) the National Institute for Occupational Safety and Health;

(II) the Secretary of Labor to enforce the Occupational Safety and Health Act of 1970 (29 U.S.C. 651 et seq.);

(III) States to enforce occupational safety and health standards in accordance with section 18 of such Act (29 U.S.C. 667); and

(IV) other government agencies (including the Department of Energy and the Environmental Protection Agency), as the Director may determine to be appropriate;

(ii) evaluate current statutory, regulatory, and voluntary industrial hygiene or other measures used by small, medium and large employers to prevent or remediate home contamination;

(iii) compile a summary of the existing research and case histories conducted on incidents of employee transported contaminant releases, including-

(I) the effectiveness of workplace housekeeping practices and personal protective equipment in preventing such incidents;

(II) the health effects, if any, of the resulting exposure on workers and their families;

(III) the effectiveness of normal house cleaning and laundry procedures for removing hazardous materials and agents from workers' homes and personal clothing;

(IV) indoor air quality, as the research concerning such pertains to the fate of chemicals transported from a workplace into the home environment; and

(V) methods for differentiating exposure health effects and relative risks associated with specific agents from other sources of exposure inside and outside the home;

(iv) identify the role of Federal and State agencies in responding to incidents of home contamination;

(v) prepare and submit to the Task Force established under paragraph (2) and to the appropriate committees of

Congress, a report concerning the results of the matters studied or evaluated under clauses (i) through (iv); and

(vi) study home contamination incidents and issues and worker and family protection policies and practices related to the special circumstances of firefighters and prepare and submit to the appropriate committees of Congress a report concerning the findings with respect to such study.

(2) Development of investigative strategy

* * *

(B) Investigative Strategy

(i) Content. The investigative strategy developed under subparagraph (A)(iv) shall identify data gaps that can and cannot be filled, assumptions and uncertainties associated with various components of such strategy, a timetable for the implementation of such strategy, and methodologies used to gather any required data.

* * *

(iii) Final strategy. After the peer review and public comment is conducted under clause (ii), the Director, in consultation with the heads of other government agencies, shall propose a final strategy for investigating issues related to home contamination that shall be implemented by the National Institute for Occupational Safety and Health and other Federal agencies for the period of time necessary to enable such agencies to obtain the information identified under subparagraph (A)(iii).

* * *

(d) Regulations

(1) In general. Not later than 4 years after October 26, 1992, and periodically thereafter, the Secretary of Labor, based on the information developed under subsection (c) and on other information available to the Secretary, shall-

(A) determine if additional education about, emphasis on, or enforcement of existing regulations or standards is needed and will be sufficient, or if additional regulations or standards are needed with regard to employee transported releases of hazardous materials; and

(B) prepare and submit to the appropriate committees of Congress a report concerning the result of such determination.

(2) Additional regulations or standards. If the Secretary of Labor determines that additional regulations or standards are needed under paragraph (1), the Secretary shall promulgate, pursuant to the Secretary's authority under the Occupational Safety and Health Act of 1970 (29 U.S.C. 651 et seq.), such regulations or standards as determined to be appropriate not later than 3 years after such determination.

* * *

§ 672. Grants to States

* * *

(g) Administration and enforcement of programs contained in approved State plans; Federal share

The Secretary is authorized to make grants to the States to assist them in administering and enforcing programs for occupational safety and health contained in State plans approved by the Secretary pursuant to section 667 of this title [29 U.S.C. § 667]. The Federal share for each State grant under this subsection may not exceed 50 per centum of the total cost to the State of such a program. The last sentence of subsection (f) shall be applicable in determining the Federal share under this subsection.

(h) Report to President and Congress

* * *

§ 673. Statistics

(a) Development and maintenance of program of collection, compilation, and analysis; employments subject to coverage; scope

In order to further the purposes of this chapter, the Secretary, in consultation with the Secretary of Health and Human Services, shall develop and maintain an effective program of collection, compilation, and analysis of occupational safety and health statistics. Such program may cover all employments whether or not subject to any other provisions of this chapter but shall not cover employments excluded by section 653 of this title [29 U.S.C. § 653]. The Secretary shall compile accurate statistics on work injuries and illnesses which shall include all disabling, serious, or significant injuries and illnesses, whether or not involving loss of time from work, other than minor injuries requiring only first aid treatment and which do not involve medical treatment, loss of consciousness, restriction of work or motion, or transfer to another job.

(b) Authority of Secretary to promote, encourage, or engage in programs, make grants, and grant or contract for research and investigations

To carry out his duties under subsection (a) of this section, the Secretary may-

(1) promote, encourage, or directly engage in programs of studies, information and communication concerning occupational safety and health statistics;

(2) make grants to States or political subdivisions thereof in order to assist them in developing and administering programs dealing with occupational safety and health statistics; and

(3) arrange, through grants or contracts, for the conduct of such research and investigations as give promise of furthering the objectives of this section.

(c) Federal share for grants

The Federal share for each grant under subsection (b) of this section may be up to 50 per centum of the State's total cost.

(d) Utilization by Secretary of State or local services, facilities, and employees; consent; reimbursement

The Secretary may, with the consent of any State or political subdivision thereof, accept and use the services, facilities, and employees of the agencies of such State or political subdivision, with or without reimbursement, in order to assist him in carrying out his functions under this section.

(e) Reports by employers

On the basis of the records made and kept pursuant to section 657(c) of this title [29 U.S.C. § 657(c)], employers shall file such reports with the Secretary as he shall prescribe by regulation, as necessary to carry out his functions under this chapter.

(f) Supersedure of agreements between Department of Labor and States for collection of statistics

* * *

§ 674. Audit of grant recipient; maintenance of records; contents of records; access to books, etc.

* * *

§ 675. Annual reports by Secretary of Labor and Secretary of Health and Human Services; contents

* * *

§ 677. Separability

If any provision of this chapter, or the application of such provision to any person or circumstance, shall be held invalid, the remainder of this chapter, or the application of such provision to persons or circumstances other than those as to which it is held invalid, shall not be affected thereby.

§ 678. Authorization of appropriations

There are authorized to be appropriated to carry out this chapter for each fiscal year such sums as the Congress shall deem necessary.

EMPLOYEE RETIREMENT INCOME SECURITY ACT (SELECTED SECTIONS)

Quick Guide for Case References

ERISA § 404 = 29 U.S.C. § 1104 (Fiduciary duties)

ERISA § 409 = 29 U.S.C. § 1109 (Liability for breach of fiduciary duty)

ERISA § 502 = 29 U.S.C. § 1132 (Civil enforcement)

ERISA § 510 = 29 U.S.C. § 1140 (Interference with protected rights)

(Title 29 U.S.C.)

§ 1001. Congressional findings and declaration of policy

(a) Benefit plans as affecting interstate commerce and the Federal taxing power

The Congress finds that the growth in size, scope, and numbers of employee benefit plans in recent years has been rapid and substantial; that the operational scope and economic impact of such plans is increasingly interstate; that the continued well-being and security of millions of employees and their dependents are directly affected by these plans; that they are affected with a national public interest; that they have become an important factor affecting the stability of employment and the successful development of industrial relations; that they have become an important factor in commerce because of the interstate character of their activities, and of the activities of their participants, and the employers, employee organizations, and other entities by which they are established or maintained; that a large volume of the activities of such plans are carried on by means of the mails and instrumentalities of interstate commerce; that owing to the lack of employee information and adequate safeguards concerning their operation, it is desirable in the interests of employees and their beneficiaries, and to provide for the general welfare and the free flow of commerce, that disclosure be made and safeguards be provided with respect to the establishment, operation, and administration of such plans; that they substantially affect the revenues of the United States because they are afforded preferential Federal tax treatment; that despite the enormous growth in such plans many employees with long years of employment are losing anticipated retirement benefits owing to the lack of vesting provisions in such plans; that owing to the inadequacy of current minimum standards, the soundness and stability of plans with respect to adequate funds to pay promised benefits may be endangered; that owing to the termination of plans before requisite funds have been accumulated, employees and their beneficiaries have been deprived of anticipated benefits; and that it is therefore desirable in the interests of employees and their beneficiaries, for the protection of the revenue of the United States, and to provide for the free flow of commerce, that minimum standards be provided assuring the equitable character of such plans and their financial soundness.

(b) Protection of interstate commerce and beneficiaries by requiring disclosure and reporting, setting standards of conduct, etc., for fiduciaries

It is hereby declared to be the policy of this chapter to protect interstate commerce and the interests of participants in employee benefit plans and their beneficiaries, by requiring the disclosure and reporting to participants and beneficiaries of financial and other information with respect thereto, by establishing standards of conduct, responsibility, and obligation for fiduciaries of employee benefit plans, and by providing for appropriate remedies, sanctions, and ready access to the Federal courts.

(c) Protection of interstate commerce, the Federal taxing power, and beneficiaries by vesting of accrued benefits, setting minimum standards of funding, requiring termination insurance

It is hereby further declared to be the policy of this chapter to protect interstate commerce, the Federal taxing power, and the interests of participants in private pension plans and their beneficiaries by improving the equitable character and the soundness of such plans by requiring them to vest the accrued benefits of employees with significant periods of service, to meet minimum standards of funding, and by requiring plan termination insurance.

(§ 1001a and § 1001b. Additional Congressional findings and declaration of policy, Omitted)

§ 1002. Definitions

For purposes of this subchapter:

(1) The terms "employee welfare benefit plan" and "welfare plan" mean any plan, fund, or program which was heretofore or is hereafter established or maintained by an employer or by an employee organization, or by both, to the extent that such plan, fund, or program was established or is maintained for the purpose of providing for its participants or their beneficiaries, through the purchase of insurance or otherwise, (A) medical, surgical, or hospital care or benefits, or benefits in the event of sickness, accident, disability, death or unemployment, or vacation benefits, apprenticeship or other training programs, or day care centers, scholarship funds, or prepaid legal services, or (B) any benefit described in section

186(c) of this title [29 U.S.C. § 186(c)] (other than pensions on retirement or death, and insurance to provide such pensions).

(2)(A) Except as provided in subparagraph (B), the terms "employee pension benefit plan" and "pension plan" mean any plan, fund, or program which was heretofore or is hereafter established or maintained by an employer or by an employee organization, or by both, to the extent that by its express terms or as a result of surrounding circumstances such plan, fund, or program-

(i) provides retirement income to employees, or

(ii) results in a deferral of income by employees for periods extending to the termination of covered employment or beyond,

regardless of the method of calculating the contributions made to the plan, the method of calculating the benefits under the plan or the method of distributing benefits from the plan. A distribution from a plan, fund, or program shall not be treated as made in a form other than retirement income or as a distribution prior to termination of covered employment solely because such distribution is made to an employee who has attained age 62 and who is not separated from employment at the time of such distribution.

(B) The Secretary may by regulation prescribe rules consistent with the standards and purposes of this chapter providing one or more exempt categories under which-

(i) severance pay arrangements, and

(ii) supplemental retirement income payments, under which the pension benefits of retirees or their beneficiaries are supplemented to take into account some portion or all of the increases in the cost of living (as determined by the Secretary of Labor) since retirement,

shall, for purposes of this subchapter, be treated as welfare plans rather than pension plans. In the case of any arrangement or payment a principal effect of which is the evasion of the standards or purposes of this chapter applicable to pension plans, such arrangement or payment shall be treated as a pension plan. An applicable voluntary early retirement incentive plan (as defined in section 457(e)(11)(D)(ii) of title 26 [26 U.S.C. § 457(e)(11)(D)(ii)]) making payments or supplements described in section 457(e)(11)(D)(i) of title 26 [26 U.S.C. § 457(e)(11(D)(i)], and an applicable employment retention plan (as defined in section 457(f)(4)(C) of title 26 [26 U.S.C. § 457(f)(4)(C)]) making payments of benefits described in section 457(f)(4)(A) of title 26 [26 U.S.C. § 457(f)(4)(C)], shall, for purposes of this subchapter, be treated as a welfare plan (and not a pension plan) with respect to such payments and supplements.

(C) A pooled employer plan shall be treated as-

(i) a single employee pension benefit plan or single pension plan; and

(ii) a plan to which section 1060(a) of this title [29 U.S.C. § 1060(a)] applies.

(3) The term "employee benefit plan" or "plan" means an employee welfare benefit plan or an employee pension benefit plan or a plan which is both an employee welfare benefit plan and an employee pension benefit plan.

(4) The term "employee organization" means any labor union or any organization of any kind, or any agency or employee representation committee, association, group, or plan, in which employees participate and which exists for the purpose, in whole or in part, of dealing with employers concerning an employee benefit plan, or other matters incidental to employment relationships; or any employees' beneficiary association organized for the purpose in whole or in part, of establishing such a plan.

(5) The term "employer" means any person acting directly as an employer, or indirectly in the interest of an employer, in relation to an employee benefit plan; and includes a group or association of employers acting for an employer in such capacity.

(6) The term "employee" means any individual employed by an employer.

(7) The term "participant" means any employee or former employee of an employer, or any member or former member of an employee organization, who is or may become eligible to receive a benefit of any type from an employee benefit plan which covers employees of such employer or members of such organization, or whose beneficiaries may be eligible to receive any such benefit.

(8) The term "beneficiary" means a person designated by a participant, or by the terms of an employee benefit plan, who is or may become entitled to a benefit thereunder.

(9) The term "person" means an individual, partnership, joint venture, corporation, mutual company, joint-stock company, trust, estate, unincorporated organization, association, or employee organization.

(10) The term "State" includes any State of the United States, the District of Columbia, Puerto Rico, the Virgin Islands, American Samoa, Guam, Wake Island, and the Canal Zone. The term "United States" when used in the geographic sense means the States and the Outer Continental

Shelf lands defined in the Outer Continental Shelf Lands Act (43 U.S.C. 1331–1343).

(11) The term "commerce" means trade, traffic, commerce, transportation, or communication between any State and any place outside thereof.

(12) The term "industry or activity affecting commerce" means any activity, business, or industry in commerce or in which a labor dispute would hinder or obstruct commerce or the free flow of commerce, and includes any activity or industry "affecting commerce" within the meaning of the Labor Management Relations Act, 1947 [29 U.S.C. §§ 141 et seq.], or the Railway Labor Act [45 U.S.C. §§ 151 et seq.].

(13) The term "Secretary" means the Secretary of Labor.

(14) The term "party in interest" means, as to an employee benefit plan-

(A) any fiduciary (including, but not limited to, any administrator, officer, trustee, or custodian), counsel, or employee of such employee benefit plan;

(B) a person providing services to such plan;

(C) an employer any of whose employees are covered by such plan;

(D) an employee organization any of whose members are covered by such plan;

(E) an owner, direct or indirect, of 50 percent or more of-

(i) the combined voting power of all classes of stock entitled to vote or the total value of shares of all classes of stock of a corporation.

(ii) the capital interest or the profits interest of a partnership, or

(iii) the beneficial interest of a trust or unincorporated enterprise,

which is an employer or an employee organization described in subparagraph (C) or (D);

(F) a relative (as defined in paragraph (15)) of any individual described in subparagraph (A), (B), (C), or (E);

(G) a corporation, partnership, or trust or estate of which (or in which) 50 percent or more of-

(i) the combined voting power of all classes of stock entitled to vote or the total value of shares of all classes of stock of such corporation,

(ii) the capital interest or profits interest of such partnership, or

(iii) the beneficial interest of such trust or estate,

is owned directly or indirectly, or held by persons described in subparagraph (A), (B), (C), (D), or (E);

(H) an employee, officer, director (or an individual having powers or responsibilities similar to those of officers or directors), or a 10 percent or more shareholder directly or indirectly, of a person described in subparagraph (B), (C), (D), (E), or (G), or of the employee benefit plan; or

(I) a 10 percent or more (directly or indirectly in capital or profits) partner or joint venturer of a person described in subparagraph (B), (C), (D), (E), or (G).

The Secretary, after consultation and coordination with the Secretary of the Treasury, may by regulation prescribe a percentage lower than 50 percent for subparagraph (E) and (G) and lower than 10 percent for subparagraph (H) or (I). The Secretary may prescribe regulations for determining the ownership (direct or indirect) of profits and beneficial interests, and the manner in which indirect stockholdings are taken into account. Any person who is a party in interest with respect to a plan to which a trust described in section 501(c)(22) of title 26 [26 U.S.C. § 501(c)(22)] is permitted to make payments under section 1403 of this title [26 U.S.C. § 1403] shall be treated as a party in interest with respect to such trust.

(15) The term "relative" means a spouse, ancestor, lineal descendant, or spouse of a lineal descendant.

(16)(A) The term "administrator" means-

(i) the person specifically so designated by the terms of the instrument under which the plan is operated;

(ii) if an administrator is not so designated, the plan sponsor; or

(iii) in the case of a plan for which an administrator is not designated and a plan sponsor cannot be identified, such other person as the Secretary may by regulation prescribe.

(B) The term "plan sponsor" means (i) the employer in the case of an employee benefit plan established or maintained by a single employer, (ii) the employee organization in the case of a plan established or maintained by an employee organization, (iii) in the case of a plan established or maintained by two or more employers or jointly by one or more employers and one or more employee organizations, the association, committee, joint board of trustees, or other similar group of representatives of the parties who establish or maintain the plan, or (iv) in the case of a pooled employer plan, the pooled plan provider.

(17) The term "separate account" means an account established or maintained by an insurance company under which income, gains, and losses, whether or not realized, from assets allocated to such account, are, in accordance with the applicable contract, credited to or charged against such account without regard to other income, gains, or losses of the insurance company.

(18) The term "adequate consideration" when used in part 4 of subtitle B [29 U.S.C. §§ 1101–1114] means (A) in the case of a security for which there is a generally recognized market, either (i) the price of the security prevailing on a national securities exchange which is registered under section 78f of title 15 [15 U.S.C. § 78f], or (ii) if the security is not traded on such a national securities exchange, a price not less favorable to the plan than the offering price for the security as established by the current bid and asked prices quoted by persons independent of the issuer and of any party in interest; and (B) in the case of an asset other than a security for which there is a generally recognized market, the fair market value of the asset as determined in good faith by the trustee or named fiduciary pursuant to the terms of the plan and in accordance with regulations promulgated by the Secretary.

(19) The term "nonforfeitable" when used with respect to a pension benefit or right means a claim obtained by a participant or his beneficiary to that part of an immediate or deferred benefit under a pension plan which arises from the participant's service, which is unconditional, and which is legally enforceable against the plan. For purposes of this paragraph, a right to an accrued benefit derived from employer contributions shall not be treated as forfeitable merely because the plan contains a provision described in section 1053(a)(3) of this title [29 U.S.C. § 1053(a)(3)].

(20) The term "security" has the same meaning as such term has under section 77a(1) of title 15 [15 U.S.C. § 77b(a)(1)].

(21)(A) Except as otherwise provided in subparagraph (B), a person is a fiduciary with respect to a plan to the extent (i) he exercises any discretionary authority or discretionary control respecting management of such plan or exercises any authority or control respecting management or disposition of its assets, (ii) he renders investment advice for a fee or other compensation, direct or indirect, with respect to any moneys or other property of such plan, or has any authority or responsibility to do so, or (iii) he has any discretionary authority or discretionary responsibility in the administration of such plan. Such term includes any person designated under section 1105(c)(1)(B) of this title [29 U.S.C. § 1105(c)(1)(B)].

(B) If any money or other property of an employee benefit plan is invested in securities issued by an investment company registered under the Investment Company Act of 1940 [15 U.S.C. §§ 80a–1 et seq.], such investment shall not by itself cause such investment company or such investment company's investment adviser or principal underwriter to be deemed to be a fiduciary or a party in interest as those terms are defined in this subchapter, except insofar as such investment company or its investment adviser or principal underwriter acts in connection with an employee benefit plan covering employees of the investment company, the investment adviser, or its principal underwriter. Nothing contained in this subparagraph shall limit the duties imposed on such investment company, investment adviser, or principal underwriter by any other law.

(22) The term "normal retirement benefit" means the greater of the early retirement benefit under the plan, or the benefit under the plan commencing at normal retirement age. The normal retirement benefit shall be determined without regard to-

(A) medical benefits, and

(B) disability benefits not in excess of the qualified disability benefit.

For purposes of this paragraph, a qualified disability benefit is a disability benefit provided by a plan which does not exceed the benefit which would be provided for the participant if he separated from the service at normal retirement age. For purposes of this paragraph, the early retirement benefit under a plan shall be determined without regard to any benefit under the plan which the Secretary of the Treasury finds to be a benefit described in section 1054(b)(1)(G) of this title [29 U.S.C. § 1054(b)(1)(G)].

(23) The term "accrued benefit" means-

(A) in the case of a defined benefit plan, the individual's accrued benefit determined under the plan and, except as provided in section 1054(c)(3) of this title [29 U.S.C. § 1054(c)(3)], expressed in the form of an annual benefit commencing at normal retirement age, or

(B) in the case of a plan which is an individual account plan, the balance of the individual's account.

The accrued benefit of an employee shall not be less than the amount determined under section 1054(c)(2)(B) of this title [29 U.S.C. § 1054(c)(2)(B)] with respect to the employee's accumulated contribution.

(24) The term "normal retirement age" means the earlier of-

(A) the time a plan participant attains normal retirement age under the plan, or

(B) the later of-

(i) the time a plan participant attains age 65, or

(ii) the 5th anniversary of the time a plan participant commenced participation in the plan.

(25) The term "vested liabilities" means the present value of the immediate or deferred benefits available at normal retirement age for participants and their beneficiaries which are nonforfeitable.

(26) The term "current value" means fair market value where available and otherwise the fair value as determined in good faith by a trustee or a named fiduciary (as defined in section 1102(a)(2) of this title [29 U.S.C. § 1102(a)(2)]) pursuant to the terms of the plan and in accordance with regulations of the Secretary, assuming an orderly liquidation at the time of such determination.

(27) The term "present value", with respect to a liability, means the value adjusted to reflect anticipated events. Such adjustments shall conform to such regulations as the Secretary of the Treasury may prescribe.

(28) The term "normal service cost" or "normal cost" means the annual cost of future pension benefits and administrative expenses assigned, under an actuarial cost method, to years subsequent to a particular valuation date of a pension plan. The Secretary of the Treasury may prescribe regulations to carry out this paragraph.

(29) The term "accrued liability" means the excess of the present value, as of a particular valuation date of a pension plan, of the projected future benefit costs and administrative expenses for all plan participants and beneficiaries over the present value of future contributions for the normal cost of all applicable plan participants and beneficiaries. The Secretary of the Treasury may prescribe regulations to carry out this paragraph.

(30) The term "unfunded accrued liability" means the excess of the accrued liability, under an actuarial cost method which so provides, over the present value of the assets of a pension plan. The Secretary of the Treasury may prescribe regulations to carry out this paragraph.

(31) The term "advance funding actuarial cost method" or "actuarial cost method" means a recognized actuarial technique utilized for establishing the amount and incidence of the annual actuarial cost of pension plan benefits and expenses. Acceptable actuarial cost methods shall include the accrued benefit cost method (unit credit method), the entry age normal cost method, the individual level premium cost method, the aggregate cost method, the attained age normal cost method, and the frozen initial liability cost method. The terminal funding cost method and the current funding (pay-as-you-go) cost method are not acceptable

actuarial cost methods. The Secretary of the Treasury shall issue regulations to further define acceptable actuarial cost methods.

(32) The term "governmental plan" means a plan established or maintained for its employees by the Government of the United States, by the government of any State or political subdivision thereof, or by any agency or instrumentality of any of the foregoing. The term "governmental plan" also includes any plan to which the Railroad Retirement Act of 1935, or 1937 [45 U.S.C. §§ 231 et seq.] applies, and which is financed by contributions required under that Act and any plan of an international organization which is exempt from taxation under the provisions of the International Organizations Immunities Act [22 U.S.C. §§ 288 et seq.]. The term "governmental plan" includes a plan which is established and maintained by an Indian tribal government (as defined in section 7701(a)(40) of title 26), a subdivision of an Indian tribal government (determined in accordance with section 7871(d) of title 26), or an agency or instrumentality of either, and all of the participants of which are employees of such entity substantially all of whose services as such an employee are in the performance of essential governmental functions but not in the performance of commercial activities (whether or not an essential government function).

(33)(A) The term "church plan" means a plan established and maintained (to the extent required in clause (ii) of subparagraph (B)) for its employees (or their beneficiaries) by a church or by a convention or association of churches which is exempt from tax under section 501 of title 26 [26 U.S.C. § 501].

(B) The term "church plan" does not include * * *

(34) The term "individual account plan" or "defined contribution plan" means a pension plan which provides for an individual account for each participant and for benefits based solely upon the amount contributed to the participant's account, and any income, expenses, gains and losses, and any forfeitures of accounts of other participants which may be allocated to such participant's account.

(35) The term "defined benefit plan" means a pension plan other than an individual account plan; except that a pension plan which is not an individual account plan and which provides a benefit derived from employer contributions which is based partly on the balance of the separate account of a participant-

(A) for the purposes of section 1052 of this title [29 U.S.C. § 1052], shall be treated as an individual account plan, and

(B) for the purposes of paragraph (23) of this section and section 1054 of this title [29 U.S.C. § 1054], shall be treated as an individual account plan to the extent benefits are based upon the separate account of a participant and as a defined benefit plan with respect to the remaining portion of benefits under the plan.

(36) The term "excess benefit plan" means a plan maintained by an employer solely for the purpose of providing benefits for certain employees in excess of the limitations on contributions and benefits imposed by section 415 of title 26 [26 U.S.C. § 415] on plans to which that section applies without regard to whether the plan is funded. To the extent that a separable part of a plan (as determined by the Secretary of Labor) maintained by an employer is maintained for such purpose, that part shall be treated as a separate plan which is an excess benefit plan.

(37)(A) The term "multiemployer plan" means a plan-

(i) to which more than one employer is required to contribute,

(ii) which is maintained pursuant to one or more collective bargaining agreements between one or more employee organizations and more than one employer, and

(iii) which satisfies such other requirements as the Secretary may prescribe by regulation.

(B) For purposes of this paragraph, all trades or businesses (whether or not incorporated) which are under common control within the meaning of section 1301(b)(1) of this title [29 U.S.C. § 1301(b)(1)] are considered a single employer.

(C) Notwithstanding subparagraph (A), a plan is a multiemployer plan on and after its termination date if the plan was a multiemployer plan under this paragraph for the plan year preceding its termination date.

(D) For purposes of this subchapter, notwithstanding the preceding provisions of this paragraph, for any plan year which began before September 26, 1980, the term "multiemployer plan" means a plan described in this paragraph (37) as in effect immediately before such date.

(E) Within one year after September 26, 1980, a multiemployer plan may irrevocably elect, pursuant to procedures established by the corporation and subject to the provisions of sections 1453(b) and (c) of this title [29 U.S.C. § 1453(b), (c)], that the plan shall not be treated as a multiemployer plan for all purposes under this chapter or the Internal Revenue Code of 1954 [26 U.S.C. §§ 1 et seq.] if for each of the last 3 plan years ending prior to the effective date of the Multiemployer Pension Plan Amendments Act of 1980-

(i) the plan was not a multiemployer plan because the plan was not a plan described in subparagraph (A)(iii) of this paragraph and section 414(f)(1)(C) of title 26 [26 U.S.C.

§ 414(f)(1)(C)] (as such provisions were in effect on the day before September 26, 1980); and

(ii) the plan had been identified as a plan that was not a multiemployer plan in substantially all its filings with the corporation, the Secretary of Labor and the Secretary of the Treasury.

(F)(i) For purposes of this subchapter a qualified football coaches plan-

(I) shall be treated as a multiemployer plan to the extent not inconsistent with the purposes of this subparagraph; and

(II) notwithstanding section 401(k)(4)(B) of title 26 [26 U.S.C. § 401(k)(4)(B)], may include a qualified cash and deferred arrangement.

(ii) For purposes of this subparagraph, the term "qualified football coaches plan" means * * *

(38) The term "investment manager" means any fiduciary (other than a trustee or named fiduciary, as defined in section 1102(a)(2) of this title [29 U.S.C. § 1102(a)(2)])—

(A) who has the power to manage, acquire, or dispose of any asset of a plan;

(B) who (i) is registered as an investment adviser under the Investment Advisers Act of 1940 [15 U.S.C. §§ 80b–1 et seq.]; (ii) is not registered as an investment adviser under such Act by reason of paragraph (1) of section 203A(a) of such Act [15 U.S.C. § 80b–3a(a)], is registered as an investment adviser under the laws of the State (referred to in such paragraph (1)) in which it maintains its principal office and place of business, and, at the time the fiduciary last filed the registration form most recently filed by the fiduciary with such State in order to maintain the fiduciary's registration under the laws of such State, also filed a copy of such form with the Secretary; (iii) is a bank, as defined in that Act; or (iv) is an insurance company qualified to perform services described in subparagraph (A) under the laws of more than one State; and

(C) has acknowledged in writing that he is a fiduciary with respect to the plan.

(39) The terms "plan year" and "fiscal year of the plan" mean, with respect to a plan, the calendar, policy, or fiscal year on which the records of the plan are kept.

(40)(A) The term "multiple employer welfare arrangement" means an employee welfare benefit plan, or any other arrangement (other than an employee welfare benefit plan), which is established or maintained for the purpose of offering or providing any benefit described in paragraph (1) to the employees of two or more employers (including one or more self-employed individuals), or to their beneficiaries, except that such term does not include any such plan or other arrangement which is established or maintained-

(i) under or pursuant to one or more agreements which the Secretary finds to be collective bargaining agreements,

(ii) by a rural electric cooperative, or

(iii) by a rural telephone cooperative association.

(B) For purposes of this paragraph-

(i) two or more trades or businesses, whether or not incorporated, shall be deemed a single employer if such trades or businesses are within the same control group,

(ii) the term "control group" means a group of trades or businesses under common control,

(iii) the determination of whether a trade or business is under "common control" with another trade or business shall be determined under regulations of the Secretary applying principles similar to the principles applied in determining whether employees of two or more trades or businesses are treated as employed by a single employer under section 1301(b) of this title [29 U.S.C. § 1301(b)], except that, for purposes of this paragraph, common control shall not be based on an interest of less than 25 percent,

(iv) the term "rural electric cooperative" means * * *

(v) the term "rural telephone cooperative association" means * * *

(41) Single-employer plan.

The term "single-employer plan" means an employee benefit plan other than a multiemployer plan.

(42) the term "plan assets" means plan assets as defined by such regulations as the Secretary may prescribe, except that under such regulations the assets of any entity shall not be treated as plan assets if, immediately after the most recent acquisition of any equity interest in the entity, less than 25 percent of the total value of each class of equity interest in the entity is held by benefit plan investors. For purposes of determinations pursuant to this paragraph, the value of any equity interest held by a person (other than such a benefit plan investor) who has discretionary authority or control with respect to the assets of the entity or any person who provides investment advice for a fee (direct or indirect)

with respect to such assets, or any affiliate of such a person, shall be disregarded for purposes of calculating the 25 percent threshold. An entity shall be considered to hold plan assets only to the extent of the percentage of the equity interest held by benefit plan investors. For purposes of this paragraph, the term "benefit plan investor" means an employee benefit plan subject to part 4 [29 U.S.C. §§ 1101–1114], any plan to which section 4975 of title 26 [26 U.S.C. § 4975] applies, and any entity whose underlying assets include plan assets by reason of a plan's investment in such entity.

(43) Pooled employer plan.

(A) In general.

The term "pooled employer plan" means a plan-

(i) which is an individual account plan established or maintained for the purpose of providing benefits to the employees of 2 or more employers;

(ii) which is a plan described in section 401(a) of title 26 [26 U.S.C. § 401(a)] which includes a trust exempt from tax under section 501(a) of title 26 [26 U.S.C. § 501(a)], a plan that consists of annuity contracts described in section 403(b) of title 26 [26 U.S.C. § 403(b)], or a plan that consists of individual retirement accounts described in section 408 of title 26 [26 U.S.C. § 408] (including by reason of subsection (c) thereof); and

(iii) the terms of which meet the requirements of subparagraph (B).

Such term shall not include a plan maintained by employers which have a common interest other than having adopted the plan, but such term shall include any plan (other than a plan excepted from the application of this title by section 1003(b)(2) of this title [29 U.S.C. § 1003(b)(2)]) maintained for the benefit of the employees of more than 1 employer that consists of annuity contracts described in section 403(b) of title 26 [26 U.S.C. § 403(b)] and that meets the requirements of subparagraph (B) of section 413(e)(1) of title 26 [26 U.S.C. § 413(e)(1)].

(B) Requirements for plan terms.

The requirement of this subparagraph are met with respect to any plan if the terms of the plan-

(i) designate a pooled plan provider and provide that the pooled plan provider is a named fiduciary of the plan;

(ii) designate a named fiduciary (other than an employer in the plan) to be responsible for collecting contributions to the plan and require such fiduciary to implement written contribution collection procedures that are reasonable, diligent, and systematic;

(iii) provide that each employer in the plan retains fiduciary responsibility for-

(I) the selection and monitoring in accordance with section 1104(a) of this title [29 U.S.C. § 1104(a)] of the person designated as the pooled plan provider and any other person who, in addition to the pooled plan provider, is designated as a named fiduciary of the plan; and

(II) to the extent not otherwise delegated to another fiduciary by the pooled plan provider and subject to the provisions of section 1104(c) of this title [29 U.S.C. § 1104(c)], the investment and management of the portion of the plan's assets attributable to the employees of the employer (or beneficiaries of such employees);

(iv) provide that employers in the plan, and participants and beneficiaries, are not subject to unreasonable restrictions, fees, or penalties with regard to ceasing participation, receipt of distributions, or otherwise transferring assets of the plan in accordance with section 1058 of this title [29 U.S.C. § 1058] or paragraph (44)(C)(i)(II) [(44)(C)(ii)(I)];

(v) require-

(I) the pooled plan provider to provide to employers in the plan any disclosures or other information which the Secretary may require, including any disclosures or other information to facilitate the selection or any monitoring of the pooled plan provider by employers in the plan; and

(II) each employer in the plan to take such actions as the Secretary or the pooled plan provider determines are necessary to administer the plan or for the plan to meet any requirement applicable under this chapter or title 26 to a plan described in section 401(a) of title 26 [26 U.S.C. § 401(a)], a plan that consists of annuity contracts described in section 403(b) of title 26 [26 U.S.C. § 403(b)], or to a plan that consists of individual retirement accounts described in section 408 of title 26 [26 U.S.C. § 408] (including by reason of subsection (c) thereof), whichever is applicable, including providing any disclosures or other information which the Secretary may require or which the pooled plan provider otherwise determines are necessary to administer the plan or to allow the plan to meet such requirements; and

(vi) provide that any disclosure or other information required to be provided under clause (v) may be provided in electronic form and will be designed to ensure only reasonable costs are imposed on pooled plan providers and employers in the plan.

(C) Exceptions.

The term "pooled employer plan" does not include-

(i) a multiemployer plan; or

(ii) a plan established before December 20, 2019, unless the plan administrator elects that the plan will be treated as a pooled employer plan and the plan meets the requirements of this subchapter applicable to a pooled employer plan established on or after such date.

(D) Treatment of employers as plan sponsors.

Except with respect to the administrative duties of the pooled plan provider described in paragraph (44)(A)(i), each employer in a pooled employer plan shall be treated as the plan sponsor with respect to the portion of the plan attributable to employees of such employer (or beneficiaries of such employees).

(44) Pooled plan provider.

(A) In general.

The term "pooled plan provider" means a person who-

(i) is designated by the terms of a pooled employer plan as a named fiduciary, as the plan administrator, and as the person responsible for the performance of all administrative duties (including conducting proper testing with respect to the plan and the employees of each employer in the plan) which are reasonably necessary to ensure that-

(I) the plan meets any requirement applicable under this chapter or title 26 to a plan described in section 401(a) of title 26 [26 U.S.C. § 401(a)], a plan that consists of annuity contracts described in section 403(b) of title 26 [26 U.S.C. § 403(b)], or to a plan that consists of individual retirement accounts described in section 408 of title 26 [26 U.S.C. § 408] (including by reason of subsection (c) thereof), whichever is applicable; and

(II) each employer in the plan takes such actions as the Secretary or pooled plan provider determines are necessary for the plan to meet the requirements described in subclause (I), including providing the disclosures and information described in paragraph (43)(B)(v)(II);

(ii) registers as a pooled plan provider with the Secretary, and provides to the Secretary such other information as the Secretary may require, before beginning operations as a pooled plan provider;

(iii) acknowledges in writing that such person is a named fiduciary, and the plan administrator, with respect to the pooled employer plan; and

(iv) is responsible for ensuring that all persons who handle assets of, or who are fiduciaries of, the pooled employer plan are bonded in accordance with section 1112 of this title [29 U.S.C. § 1112].

(B) Audits, examinations and investigations.

The Secretary may perform audits, examinations, and investigations of pooled plan providers as may be necessary to enforce and carry out the purposes of this paragraph and paragraph (43).

(C) Guidance.

The Secretary shall issue such guidance as the Secretary determines appropriate to carry out this paragraph and paragraph (43), including guidance-

(i) to identify the administrative duties and other actions required to be performed by a pooled plan provider under either such paragraph; and

(ii) which requires in appropriate cases that if an employer in the plan fails to take the actions required under subparagraph (A)(i)(II)-

(I) the assets of the plan attributable to employees of such employer (or beneficiaries of such employees) are transferred to a plan maintained only by such employer (or its successor), to an eligible retirement plan as defined in section 402(c)(8)(B) of title 26 [26 U.S.C. § 402(c)(8)(B)] for each individual whose account is transferred, or to any other arrangement that the Secretary determines is appropriate in such guidance; and

(II) such employer (and not the plan with respect to which the failure occurred or any other employer in such plan) shall, except to the extent provided in such guidance, be liable for any liabilities with respect to such plan attributable to employees of such employer (or beneficiaries of such employees).

The Secretary shall take into account under clause (ii) whether the failure of an employer or pooled plan provider to provide any disclosures or other information, or to take any other action, necessary to administer a plan or to allow a plan to meet requirements described in subparagraph (A)(i)(II) has continued over a period of time that demonstrates a lack of commitment to compliance. The Secretary may waive the requirements of subclause (ii)(I) in appropriate circumstances if the Secretary determines it is in the best interests of the employees of the employer referred to in such clause (and the beneficiaries of such employees) to retain the assets in the plan with respect to which the employer's failure occurred.

(D) Good faith compliance with law before guidance.

An employer or pooled plan provider shall not be treated as failing to meet a requirement of guidance issued by the Secretary under subparagraph (C) if, before the issuance of such guidance, the employer or pooled plan provider complies in good faith with a reasonable interpretation of the provisions of this paragraph, or paragraph (43), to which such guidance relates.

(E) Aggregation Rules.

For purposes of this paragraph, in determining whether a person meets the requirements of this paragraph to be a pooled plan provider with respect to any plan, all persons who perform services for the plan and who are treated as a single employer under subsection (b), (c), (m), or (*o*) of section 414 of title 26 [26 U.S.C. § 414] shall be treated as one person.

§ 1003. Coverage

(a) In general

Except as provided in subsection (b) or (c) and in sections 1051, 1081, and 1101 of this title [29 U.S.C. §§ 1051, 1081, 1101], this subchapter shall apply to any employee benefit plan if it is established or maintained-

(1) by any employer engaged in commerce or in any industry or activity affecting commerce; or

(2) by any employee organization or organizations representing employees engaged in commerce or in any industry or activity affecting commerce; or

(3) by both.

(b) Exceptions for certain plans

The provisions of this subchapter shall not apply to any employee benefit plan if-

(1) such plan is a governmental plan (as defined in section 1002(32) of this title [29 U.S.C. § 1002(32)]);

(2) such plan is a church plan (as defined in section 1002(33) of this title [29 U.S.C. § 1002(33)]) with respect to which no election has been made under section 410(d) of title 26 [26 U.S.C. § 410(d)];

(3) such plan is maintained solely for the purpose of complying with applicable workmen's compensation laws or unemployment compensation or disability insurance laws;

(4) such plan is maintained outside of the United States primarily for the benefit of persons substantially all of whom are nonresident aliens; or

(5) such plan is an excess benefit plan (as defined in section 1002(36) of this title [29 U.S.C. § 1002(36)]) and is unfunded.

The provisions of part 7 of subtitle B of this subchapter [29 U.S.C. §§ 1181–1191d] shall not apply to a health insurance issuer (as defined in section 1191b(b)(2) of this title [29 U.S.C. § 1191b(b)(2)]) solely by reason of health insurance coverage (as defined in section 1191b(b)(1) of this title [29 U.S.C. § 1191b(b)(1)]) provided by such issuer in connection with a group health plan (as defined in section 1191b(a)(1) of this title [29 U.S.C. § 1191b(a)(1)]) if the provisions of this subchapter do not apply to such group health plan.

(c) Voluntary employee contributions to accounts and annuities

If a pension plan allows an employee to elect to make voluntary employee contributions to accounts and annuities as provided in section 408(q) of title 26 [26 U.S.C. § 408(q)], such accounts and annuities (and contributions thereto) shall not be treated as part of such plan (or as a separate pension plan) for purposes of any provision of this subchapter other than section 1103(c), 1104, or 1105 of this title [29 U.S.C. §§ 1103(c), 1104, 1105] (relating to exclusive benefit, and fiduciary and co-fiduciary responsibilities) and part 5 of subtitle B of this subchapter [29 U.S.C. §§ 1131–1153] (relating to administration and enforcement). Such provisions shall apply to such accounts and annuities in a manner similar to their application to a simplified employee pension under section 408(k) of title 26 [26 U.S.C. § 408(k)].

§ 1021. Duty of disclosure and reporting

(a) Summary plan description and information to be furnished to participants and beneficiaries

The administrator of each employee benefit plan shall cause to be furnished in accordance with section 1024(b) of this title [29 U.S.C. § 1024(b)] to each participant covered under the plan and to each beneficiary who is receiving benefits under the plan—

(1) a summary plan description described in section 1022(a)(1) of this title [29 U.S.C. § 1022(a)]; and

(2) the information described in subsection (f) and sections 1024(b)(3) and 1025(a) and (c) of this title [29 U.S.C. §§ 1024(b)(3), 1025(a), 1025(c)].

(b) Reports to be filed with Secretary of Labor

The administrator shall, in accordance with section 1024(a) of this title [29 U.S.C. § 1024(a)], file with the Secretary—

(1) the annual report containing the information required by section 1023 of this title [29 U.S.C. § 1023]; and

(2) terminal and supplementary reports as required by subsection (c) of this section.

(c) Terminal and supplementary reports

(1) Each administrator of an employee pension benefit plan which is winding up its affairs (without regard to the number of participants remaining in the plan) shall, in accordance with regulations prescribed by the Secretary, file such terminal reports as the Secretary may consider necessary. A copy of such report shall also be filed with the Pension Benefit Guaranty Corporation.

(2) The Secretary may require terminal reports to be filed with regard to any employee welfare benefit plan which is winding up its affairs in accordance with regulations promulgated by the Secretary.

(3) The Secretary may require that a plan described in paragraph (1) or (2) file a supplementary or terminal report with the annual report in the year such plan is terminated and that a copy of such supplementary or terminal report in the case of a plan described in paragraph (1) be also filed with the Pension Benefit Guaranty Corporation.

(d) Notice of failure to meet minimum funding standards

(1) In general

If an employer maintaining a plan other than a multiemployer plan fails to make a required installment or other payment required to meet the minimum funding standard under section 1082 of this title [29 U.S.C. § 1082] to a plan before the 60th day following the due date for such installment or other payment, the employer shall notify each participant and beneficiary (including an alternate payee as defined in section 1056(d)(3)(K) of this title [29 U.S.C. § 1056(d)(3)(K)]) of such plan of such failure. Such notice shall be made at such time and in such manner as the Secretary may prescribe.

(2) Subsection not to apply if waiver pending

This subsection shall not apply to any failure if the employer has filed a waiver request under section 1083 or 1085a of this title [29 U.S.C. §§ 1083, 1085a] with respect to the plan year to which the required installment relates, except that if the waiver request is denied, notice under paragraph (1) shall be provided within 60 days after the date of such denial.

(3) Definitions

For purposes of this subsection, the terms "required installment" and "due date" have the same meanings given such terms by section 1083(j) or 1085a(f) of this title [29 U.S.C. §§ 1083(j), 1085a(f)], whichever is applicable.

(e) Notice of transfer of excess pension assets to health benefits accounts

(1) Notice to participants

Not later than 60 days before the date of a qualified transfer by an employee pension benefit plan of excess pension assets to a health benefits account or applicable life insurance account, the administrator of the plan shall notify (in such manner as the Secretary may prescribe) each participant and beneficiary under the plan of such transfer. Such notice shall include information with respect to the amount of excess pension assets, the portion to be transferred, the amount of health benefits liabilities or applicable life insurance benefit liabilities expected to be provided with the assets transferred, and the amount of pension benefits of the participant which will be nonforfeitable immediately after the transfer.

(2) Notice to Secretaries, administrator, and employee organizations

(A) In general

Not later than 60 days before the date of any qualified transfer by an employee pension benefit plan of excess pension assets to a health benefits account or applicable life insurance account, the employer maintaining the plan from which the transfer is made shall provide the Secretary, the Secretary of the Treasury, the administrator, and each employee organization representing participants in the plan a written notice of such transfer. A copy of any such notice shall be available for inspection in the principal office of the administrator.

(B) Information relating to transfer

Such notice shall identify the plan from which the transfer is made, the amount of the transfer, a detailed accounting of assets projected to be held by the plan immediately before and immediately after the transfer, and the current liabilities under the plan at the time of the transfer.

(C) Authority for additional reporting requirements

The Secretary may prescribe such additional reporting requirements as may be necessary to carry out the purposes of this section.

(3) Definitions

For purposes of paragraph (1), any term used in such paragraph which is also used in section 420 of title 26 [26 U.S.C. § 420] (as in effect on December 29, 2022) shall have the same meaning as when used in such section.

(f) Defined benefit plan funding notices

(1) In general

The administrator of a defined benefit plan to which subchapter III applies shall for each plan year provide a plan funding notice to the Pension Benefit Guaranty Corporation, to each plan participant and beneficiary, to each labor organization representing such participants or beneficiaries, and, in the case of a multiemployer plan, to each employer that has an obligation to contribute to the plan.

(2) Information contained in notices

(A) Identifying information

Each notice required under paragraph (1) shall contain identifying information, including the name of the plan, the address and phone number of the plan administrator and the plan's principal administrative officer, each plan sponsor's employer identification number, and the plan number of the plan.

(B) Specific information

A plan funding notice under paragraph (1) shall include—

(i)(I) in the case of a single-employer plan, a statement as to whether the plan's funding target attainment percentage (as defined in section 1083(d)(2) of this title [29 U.S.C. § 1083(d)(2)]) for the plan year to which the notice relates, and for the 2 preceding plan years, is at least 100 percent (and, if not, the actual percentages), or

(II) in the case of a multiemployer plan, a statement as to whether the plan's funded percentage (as defined in section 1085(i) of this title [29 U.S.C. § 1085(j)]) for the plan year to which the notice relates, and for the 2 preceding plan years, is at least 100 percent (and, if not, the actual percentages),

(ii)(I) in the case of a single-employer plan, a statement of—

(aa) the total assets (separately stating the prefunding balance and the funding standard carryover balance) and liabilities of the plan, determined in the same manner as under section 1083 of this title [29 U.S.C. § 1083], for the plan year to which the notice relates and for the 2 preceding plan years, as reported in the annual report for each such plan year, and

(bb) the value of the plan's assets and liabilities for the plan year to which the notice relates as of the last day of the plan year to which the notice relates determined using the asset valuation under subclause (II) of section 1306(a)(3)(E)(iii) of this title [29 U.S.C. § 1306(a)(E)(iii)] and the interest rate under section 1306(a)(3)(E)(iv) of this title [29 U.S.C. § 1306(a)(3)(E)(iv)], and

(II) in the case of a multiemployer plan, a statement, for the plan year to which the notice relates and the preceding 2 plan years, of the value of the plan assets (determined both in the same manner as under section 1084 of this title [29 U.S.C. § 1084] and under the rules of subclause (I)(bb)) and the value of the plan liabilities (determined in the same manner as under section 1084 of this title [29 U.S.C. § 1084] except that the method specified in section 1085(i)(8) of this title [29 U.S.C. § 1085(j)] shall be used),

(iii) a statement of the number of participants who are—

(I) retired or separated from service and are receiving benefits,

(II) retired or separated participants entitled to future benefits, and

(III) active participants under the plan,

(iv) a statement setting forth the funding policy of the plan and the asset allocation of investments under the plan (expressed as percentages of total assets) as of the end of the plan year to which the notice relates,

(v) in the case of a multiemployer plan, whether the plan was in critical or endangered status under section 1085 of this title [29 U.S.C. § 1085] for such plan year and, if so—

(I) a statement describing how a person may obtain a copy of the plan's funding improvement or rehabilitation plan, as appropriate, adopted under section 1085 of this title [29 U.S.C. § 1085] and the actuarial and financial data that demonstrate any action taken by the plan toward fiscal improvement, and

(II) a summary of any funding improvement plan, rehabilitation plan, or modification thereof adopted under section 1085 of this title [29 U.S.C. § 1085] during the plan year to which the notice relates,

(vi) in the case of a multiemployer plan, whether the plan was in critical and declining status under section 1085 of this title [29 U.S.C. § 1085] for such plan year and, if so—

(I) the projected date of insolvency;

(II) a clear statement that such insolvency may result in benefit reductions; and

(III) a statement describing whether the plan sponsor has taken legally permitted actions to prevent insolvency.

(vii) in the case of any plan amendment, scheduled benefit increase or reduction, or other known event taking effect in the current plan year and having a material effect on plan liabilities or assets for the year (as defined in regulations by the Secretary), an explanation of the amendment, schedule increase or reduction, or event, and a projection to the end of such plan year of the effect of the amendment, scheduled increase or reduction, or event on plan liabilities,

(viii)(I) in the case of a single-employer plan, a summary of the rules governing termination of single-employer plans under subtitle C of subchapter III [29 U.S.C. §§ 1341–1350], or

(II) in the case of a multiemployer plan, a summary of the rules governing reorganization or insolvency, including the limitations on benefit payments,

(ix) a general description of the benefits under the plan which are eligible to be guaranteed by the Pension Benefit Guaranty Corporation, along with an explanation of the limitations on the guarantee and the circumstances under which such limitations apply,

(x) a statement that a person may obtain a copy of the annual report of the plan filed under section 1024(a) of this title [29 U.S.C. § 1024(a)] upon request, through the Internet website of the Department of Labor, or through an Intranet website maintained by the applicable plan sponsor (or plan administrator on behalf of the plan sponsor), and

(xi) if applicable, a statement that each contributing sponsor, and each member of the contributing sponsor's controlled group, of the single-employer plan was required to provide the information under section 1310 of this title [29 U.S.C. § 1310] for the plan year to which the notice relates.

(C) Other information

Each notice under paragraph (1) shall include—

(i) in the case of a multiemployer plan, a statement that the plan administrator shall provide, upon written request, to any labor organization representing plan participants and beneficiaries and any employer that has an obligation to contribute to the plan, a copy of the annual report filed with the Secretary under section 1024(a) of this title [29 U.S.C. § 1024(a)], and

(ii) any additional information which the plan administrator elects to include to the extent not inconsistent with regulations prescribed by the Secretary.

(D) Effect of segment rate stabilization on plan funding

(i) In general

In the case of a single-employer plan for an applicable plan year, each notice under paragraph (1) shall include—

(I) a statement that the MAP-21 [23 U.S.C. §§ 101 et seq.], the Highway and Transportation Funding Act of 2014 [23 U.S.C. §§ 101 et seq.], the Bipartisan Budget Act of 2015 [26 U.S.C. §§ 1 et seq.], the American Rescue Plan Act of 2021 [15 U.S.C. §§ 9001 et seq.], and the Infrastructure Investment and Jobs Act [23 U.S.C. §§ 101 et seq.] modified the method for determining the interest rates used to determine the actuarial value of benefits earned under the plan, providing for a 25-year average of interest rates to be taken into account in addition to a 2-year average,

(II) a statement that, as a result of the MAP-21 [23 U.S.C. §§ 101 et seq.], the Highway and Transportation Funding Act of 2014 [23 U.S.C. §§ 101 et seq.], the Bipartisan Budget Act of 2015 [26 U.S.C. §§ 1 et seq.], the American Rescue Plan Act of 2021 [15 U.S.C. §§ 9001 et seq.], and the Infrastructure Investment and Jobs Act [23 U.S.C. §§ 101 et seq.], the plan sponsor may contribute less money to the plan when interest rates are at historical lows, and

(III) a table which shows (determined both with and without regard to section 1083(h)(2)(C)(iv) of this title [29 U.S.C. § 1083(h)(2)(C)(iv)]) the funding target attainment percentage (as defined in section 1083(d)(2) of this title [29 U.S.C. § 1083(d)(2)]), the funding shortfall (as defined in section 1083(c)(4) of this title [29 U.S.C. § 1083(c)(4)]), and the minimum required contribution (as determined under section 1083 of this title [29 U.S.C. § 1083]), for the applicable plan year and each of the 2 preceding plan years.

(ii) Applicable plan year

For purposes of this subparagraph, the term "applicable plan year" means any plan year beginning after December 31, 2011, and before January 1, 2034, for which—

(I) the funding target (as defined in section 1083(d)(2) of this title [29 U.S.C. § 1083(d)(2)]) is less than 95 percent of such funding target determined without regard to section 1083(h)(2)(C)(iv) of this title [29 U.S.C. § 1083(h)(2)(C)(iv)],

(II) the plan has a funding shortfall (as defined in section 1083(c)(4) of this title [29 U.S.C. § 1083(c)(4)] and determined without regard to section 1083(h)(2)(C)(iv) of this title [29 U.S.C. § 1083(h)(2)(C)(iv)]) greater than $500,000, and

(III) the plan had 50 or more participants on any day during the preceding plan year.

For purposes of any determination under subclause (III), the aggregation rule under the last sentence of section 1083(g)(2)(B) of this title [29 U.S.C. § 1083(g)(2)(B)] shall apply.

(iii) Special rule for plan years beginning before 2012

In the case of a preceding plan year referred to in clause (i)(III) which begins before January 1, 2012, the information described in such clause shall be provided only without regard to section 1083(h)(2)(C)(iv) of this title [29 U.S.C. § 1083(h)(2)(C)(iv)].

(E) Effect of CSEC plan rules on plan funding

In the case of a CSEC plan, each notice under paragraph (1) shall include—

(i) a statement that different rules apply to CSEC plans than apply to single-employer plans,

(ii) for the first 2 plan years beginning after December 31, 2013, a statement that, as a result of changes in the law made by the Cooperative and Small Employer Charity Pension Flexibility Act [29 U.S.C. § 1001 et seq.], the contributions to the plan may have changed, and

(iii) in the case of a CSEC plan that is in funding restoration status for the plan year, a statement that the plan is in funding restoration status for such plan year.

A copy of the statement required under clause (iii) shall be provided to the Secretary, the Secretary of the Treasury, and the Director of the Pension Benefit Guaranty Corporation.

(3) Time for providing notice

(A) In general

Any notice under paragraph (1) shall be provided not later than 120 days after the end of the plan year to which the notice relates.

(B) Exception for small plans

In the case of a small plan (as such term is used under section 1083(g)(2)(B) of this title [29 U.S.C. § 1083(g)(2)(B)]) any notice under paragraph (1) shall be provided upon filing of the annual report under section 1024(a) of this title [29 U.S.C. § 1024(a)].

(4) Form and manner

Any notice under paragraph (1)—

(A) shall be provided in a form and manner prescribed in regulations of the Secretary,

(B) shall be written in a manner so as to be understood by the average plan participant, and

(C) may be provided in written, electronic, or other appropriate form to the extent such form is reasonably accessible to persons to whom the notice is required to be provided.

(g) Reporting by certain arrangements

The Secretary shall, by regulation, require multiple employer welfare arrangements providing benefits consisting of medical care (within the meaning of section 1191b(a)(2) of this title [29 U.S.C. § 1191b(a)(2)]) which are not group health plans to register with the Secretary prior to operating in a State and may, by regulation, require such multiple employer welfare arrangements to report, not more frequently than annually, in such form and such manner as the Secretary may require for the purpose of determining the extent to which the requirements of part 7 are being carried out in connection with such benefits.

(h) Simple retirement accounts

(1) No employer reports

Except as provided in this subsection, no report shall be required under this section by an employer maintaining a qualified salary reduction arrangement under section 408(p) of title 26 [26 U.S.C. § 408(p)].

(2) Summary description

The trustee of any simple retirement account established pursuant to a qualified salary reduction arrangement under section 408(p) of title 26 [26 U.S.C. § 408(p)] shall provide to the employer maintaining the arrangement each year a description containing the following information:

(A) The name and address of the employer and the trustee.

(B) The requirements for eligibility for participation.

(C) The benefits provided with respect to the arrangement.

(D) The time and method of making elections with respect to the arrangement.

(E) The procedures for, and effects of, withdrawals (including rollovers) from the arrangement.

(3) Employee notification

The employer shall notify each employee immediately before the period for which an election described in section 408(p)(5)(C) of title 26 [26 U.S.C. § 408(p)(5)(C)] may be made of the employee's opportunity to make such election. Such notice shall include a copy of the description described in paragraph (2).

(i) Notice of blackout periods to participant or beneficiary under individual account plan

(1) Duties of plan administrator

In advance of the commencement of any blackout period with respect to an individual account plan, the plan administrator shall notify the plan participants and beneficiaries who are affected by such action in accordance with this subsection.

(2) Notice requirements

(A) In general

The notices described in paragraph (1) shall be written in a manner calculated to be understood by the average plan participant and shall include—

(i) the reasons for the blackout period,

(ii) an identification of the investments and other rights affected,

(iii) the expected beginning date and length of the blackout period,

(iv) in the case of investments affected, a statement that the participant or beneficiary should evaluate the appropriateness of their current investment decisions in light of their inability to direct or diversify assets credited to their accounts during the blackout period, and

(v) such other matters as the Secretary may require by regulation.

(B) Notice to participants and beneficiaries

Except as otherwise provided in this subsection, notices described in paragraph (1) shall be furnished to all participants and beneficiaries under the plan to whom the blackout period applies at least 30 days in advance of the blackout period.

(C) Exception to 30-day notice requirement

In any case in which—

(i) a deferral of the blackout period would violate the requirements of subparagraph (A) or (B) of section 1104(a)(1) of this title [29 U.S.C. § 1104(a)(1)], and a fiduciary of the plan reasonably so determines in writing, or

(ii) the inability to provide the 30-day advance notice is due to events that were unforeseeable or circumstances beyond the reasonable control of the plan administrator, and a fiduciary of the plan reasonably so determines in writing, subparagraph (B) shall not apply, and the notice shall be furnished to all participants and beneficiaries under the plan to whom the blackout period applies as soon as reasonably possible under the circumstances unless such a notice in advance of the termination of the blackout period is impracticable.

(D) Written notice

The notice required to be provided under this subsection shall be in writing, except that such notice may be in electronic or other form to the extent that such form is reasonably accessible to the recipient.

(E) Notice to issuers of employer securities subject to blackout period

In the case of any blackout period in connection with an individual account plan, the plan administrator shall provide timely notice of such blackout period to the issuer of any employer securities subject to such blackout period.

(3) Exception for blackout periods with limited applicability

In any case in which the blackout period applies only to 1 or more participants or beneficiaries in connection with a merger, acquisition, divestiture, or similar transaction involving the plan or plan sponsor and occurs solely in connection with becoming or ceasing to be a participant or beneficiary under the plan by reason of such merger, acquisition, divestiture, or transaction, the requirement of this subsection that the notice be provided to all participants and beneficiaries shall be treated as met if the notice required under paragraph (1) is provided to such participants or beneficiaries to whom the blackout period applies as soon as reasonably practicable.

(4) Changes in length of blackout period

If, following the furnishing of the notice pursuant to this subsection, there is a change in the beginning date or length of the blackout period (specified in such notice pursuant to paragraph (2)(A)(iii)), the administrator shall provide affected participants and beneficiaries notice of the change as soon as reasonably practicable. In relation to the extended blackout period, such notice shall meet the requirements of paragraph (2)(D) and shall specify any material change in the matters referred to in clauses (i) through (v) of paragraph (2)(A).

(5) Regulatory exceptions

The Secretary may provide by regulation for additional exceptions to the requirements of this subsection which the Secretary determines are in the interests of participants and beneficiaries.

(6) Guidance and model notices

The Secretary shall issue guidance and model notices which meet the requirements of this subsection.

(7) Blackout period

For purposes of this subsection—

(A) In general

The term "blackout period" means, in connection with an individual account plan, any period for which any ability of participants or beneficiaries under the plan, which is otherwise available under the terms of such plan, to direct or diversify assets credited to their accounts, to obtain loans from the plan, or to obtain distributions from the plan is temporarily suspended, limited, or restricted, if such suspension, limitation, or restriction is for any period of more than 3 consecutive business days.

(B) Exclusions

The term "blackout period" does not include a suspension, limitation, or restriction—

(i) which occurs by reason of the application of the securities laws (as defined in section 78c(a)(47) of title 15 [15 U.S.C. § 78c(a)(47)]),

(ii) which is a change to the plan which provides for a regularly scheduled suspension, limitation, or restriction which is disclosed to participants or beneficiaries through any summary of material modifications, any materials describing specific investment alternatives under the plan, or any changes thereto, or

(iii) which applies only to 1 or more individuals, each of whom is the participant, an alternate payee (as defined in section 1056(d)(3)(K) of this title [29 U.S.C. § 1056(d)(3)(K)]), or any other beneficiary pursuant to a qualified domestic relations order (as defined in section 1056(d)(3)(B)(i) of this title [29 U.S.C. § 1056(d)(3)(B)(i)]).

(8) Individual account plan

(A) In general

For purposes of this subsection, the term "individual account plan" shall have the meaning provided such term in section 1002(34) of this title [29 U.S.C. § 1002(34)], except that such term shall not include a one-participant retirement plan.

(B) One-participant retirement plan

For purposes of subparagraph (A), the term "one-participant retirement plan" means a retirement plan that on the first day of the plan year—

(i) covered only one individual (or the individual and the individual's spouse) and the individual (or the individual and the individual's spouse) owned 100 percent of the plan sponsor (whether or not incorporated), or

(ii) covered only one or more partners (or partners and their spouses) in the plan sponsor.

(j) Notice of funding-based limitation on certain forms of distribution

The plan administrator of a single-employer plan shall provide a written notice to plan participants and beneficiaries within 30 days—

(1) after the plan has become subject to a restriction described in paragraph (1) or (3) of section 1056(g) of this title [29 U.S.C. § 1056(g)],

(2) in the case of a plan to which section 1056(g)(4) of this title [29 U.S.C. § 1056(g)(4)] applies, after the valuation date for the plan year described in section 1056(g)(4)(A) of this title [29 U.S.C. § 1056(g)(4)(A)] for which the plan's adjusted funding target attainment percentage for the plan year is less than 60 percent (or, if earlier, the date such percentage is deemed to be less than 60 percent under section 1056(g)(7) of this title [29 U.S.C. § 1056(g)(7)]), and

(3) at such other time as may be determined by the Secretary of the Treasury.

The notice required to be provided under this subsection shall be in writing, except that such notice may be in electronic or other form to the extent that such form is reasonably accessible to the recipient. The Secretary of the Treasury, in consultation with the Secretary, shall have the authority to prescribe rules applicable to the notices required under this subsection.

(k) Multiemployer plan information made available on request

(1) In general

Each administrator of a defined benefit plan that is a multiemployer plan shall, upon written request, furnish to any plan participant or beneficiary, employee representative, or any employer that has an obligation to contribute to the plan a copy of—

(A) the current plan document (including any amendments thereto),

(B) the latest summary plan description of the plan,

(C) the current trust agreement (including any amendments thereto), or any other instrument or agreement under which the plan is established or operated,

(D) in the case of a request by an employer, any participation agreement with respect to the plan for such employer that relates to the employer's plan participation during the current or any of the 5 immediately preceding plan years,

(E) the annual report filed under section 1024 of this title [29 U.S.C. § 1024] for any plan year,

(F) the plan funding notice provided under subsection (f) for any plan year,

(G) any periodic actuarial report (including any sensitivity testing) received by the plan for any plan year which has been in the plan's possession for at least 30 days,

(H) any quarterly, semi-annual, or annual financial report prepared for the plan by any plan investment manager or advisor or other fiduciary which has been in the plan's possession for at least 30 days,

(I) audited financial statements of the plan for any plan year,

(J) any application filed with the Secretary of the Treasury requesting an extension under section 1084(d) of this title [29 U.S.C. § 1084(d)] or section 431(d) of title 26 [26 U.S.C. § 431(d)] and the determination of such Secretary pursuant to such application, and

(K) in the case of a plan which was in critical or endangered status under section 1085 of this title [29 U.S.C. § 1085] for a plan year, the latest funding improvement or rehabilitation plan, and the contribution schedules applicable with respect to such funding improvement or rehabilitation plan (other than a contribution schedule applicable to a specific employer).

(2) Compliance

Information required to be provided under paragraph (1)—

(A) shall be provided to the requesting participant, beneficiary, or employer within 30 days after the request in a form and manner prescribed in regulations of the Secretary,

(B) may be provided in written, electronic, or other appropriate form to the extent such form is reasonably accessible to persons to whom the information is required to be provided, and

(C) shall not—

(i) include any individually identifiable information regarding any plan participant, beneficiary, employee, fiduciary, or contributing employer, or

(ii) reveal any proprietary information regarding the plan, any contributing employer, or entity providing services to the plan.

Subparagraph (C)(i) shall not apply to individually identifiable information with respect to any plan investment manager or adviser, or with respect to any other person (other than an employee of the plan) preparing a financial report required to be included under paragraph (1)(B).*

(3) Limitations

In no case shall a participant, beneficiary, employee representative, or employer be entitled under this subsection to receive more than one copy of any document described in paragraph (1) during any one 12-month period, or, in the case of any document described in subparagraph (E), (F), (G), (H) or (I) of paragraph (1), a copy of any such document that as of the date on which the request is received by the administrator, has been in the administrator's possession for 6 years or more. If the administrator provides a copy of a document described in paragraph (1) to any person upon request, the administrator shall be considered as having met any obligation the administrator may have under any other provision of this subchapter to furnish a copy of the same document to such person upon request. The administrator may make a reasonable charge to cover copying, mailing, and other costs of furnishing copies of information pursuant to paragraph (1). The Secretary may by regulations prescribe the maximum amount which will constitute a reasonable charge under the preceding sentence.

(*l*) Notice of potential withdrawal liability

(1) In general

The plan sponsor or administrator of a multiemployer plan shall, upon written request, furnish to any employer who has an obligation to contribute to the plan a notice of—

(A) the estimated amount which would be the amount of such employer's withdrawal liability under part 1 of subtitle E of subchapter III [29 U.S.C. §§ 1381–1405] if such employer

* The content of paragraph (1)(B) of subsec. (k) (relating to financial reports) was moved to subsec. (k)(1)(H) as a result of the general amendment of subsec. (k)(1) by Pub. L. 113–235, § 111(a).

withdrew on the last day of the plan year preceding the date of the request, and

(B) an explanation of how such estimated liability amount was determined, including the actuarial assumptions and methods used to determine the value of the plan liabilities and assets, the data regarding employer contributions, unfunded vested benefits, annual changes in the plan's unfunded vested benefits, and the application of any relevant limitations on the estimated withdrawal liability.

For purposes of subparagraph (B), the term "employer contribution" means, in connection with a participant, a contribution made by an employer as an employer of such participant.

(2) Compliance

Any notice required to be provided under paragraph (1)—

(A) shall be provided in a form and manner prescribed in regulations of the Secretary to the requesting employer within—

(i) 180 days after the request, or

(ii) subject to regulations of the Secretary, such longer time as may be necessary in the case of a plan that determines withdrawal liability based on any method described under paragraph (4) or (5) of section 1391(c) of this title [29 U.S.C. § 1391(c)]; and

(B) may be provided in written, electronic, or other appropriate form to the extent such form is reasonably accessible to employers to whom the information is required to be provided.

(3) Limitations

In no case shall an employer be entitled under this subsection to receive more than one notice described in paragraph (1) during any one 12-month period. The person required to provide such notice may make a reasonable charge to cover copying, mailing, and other costs of furnishing such notice pursuant to paragraph (1). The Secretary may by regulations prescribe the maximum amount which will constitute a reasonable charge under the preceding sentence.

(m) Notice of right to divest

Not later than 30 days before the first date on which an applicable individual of an applicable individual account plan is eligible to exercise the right under section 1054(j) of this title [29 U.S.C. § 1054(j)] to direct the proceeds from the divestment of employer securities with respect to any type of contribution, the administrator shall provide to such individual a notice—

(1) setting forth such right under such section, and

(2) describing the importance of diversifying the investment of retirement account assets.

The notice required by this subsection shall be written in a manner calculated to be understood by the average plan participant and may be delivered in written, electronic, or other appropriate form to the extent that such form is reasonably accessible to the recipient.

(n) Cross reference

For regulations relating to coordination of reports to the Secretaries of Labor and the Treasury, see section 1204 of this title [29 U.S.C. § 1204].

§ 1022. Summary plan description

(a) A summary plan description of any employee benefit plan shall be furnished to participants and beneficiaries as provided in section 1024(b) of this title [29 U.S.C. § 1024(b)]. The summary plan description shall include the information described in subsection (b), shall be written in a manner calculated to be understood by the average plan participant, and shall be sufficiently accurate and comprehensive to reasonably apprise such participants and beneficiaries of their rights and obligations under the plan. A summary of any material modification in the terms of the plan and any change in the information required under subsection (b) shall be written in a manner calculated to be understood by the average plan participant and shall be furnished in accordance with section 1024(b)(1) of this title [29 U.S.C. § 1024(b)(1)].

(b) The summary plan description shall contain the following information: The name and type of administration of the plan; in the case of a group health plan (as defined in section 1191b(a)(1) of this title [29 U.S.C. § 1191b(a)(1)]), whether a health insurance issuer (as defined in section 1191b(b)(2) of this title [29 U.S.C. § 1191b(b)(2)]) is responsible for the financing or administration (including payment of claims) of the plan and (if so) the name and address of such issuer; the name and address of the person designated as agent for the service of legal process, if such person is not the administrator; the name and address of the administrator; names, titles, and addresses of any trustee or trustees (if they are persons different from the administrator); a description of the relevant provisions of any applicable collective bargaining agreement; the plan's requirements respecting eligibility for participation and benefits; a description of the provisions providing for nonforfeitable pension benefits; circumstances which may result in disqualification, ineligibility, or denial or loss of benefits; the source of financing of the plan and the identity of any organization through which benefits are provided; the date of the end of the plan year and whether the records of the plan are kept on a calendar, policy, or fiscal year basis; the procedures to be followed in presenting claims for benefits under the plan including the office at the Department of Labor through which participants and beneficiaries may seek assistance or information regarding their rights under this chapter and the Health Insurance Portability and Accountability Act of 1996 [42 U.S.C. §§ 201 et seq.] with respect to health benefits that are offered through a group health plan (as defined in section 1191b(a)(1) of this title [29 U.S.C. § 1191b(a)(1)]), the remedies available under the plan for the redress of claims which are denied in whole or in part (including procedures required under section 1133 of this title [29 U.S.C. § 1133]), and if the employer so elects for purposes of complying with section 1181(f)(3)(B)(i) of this title [29 U.S.C. § 1181(f)(3)(B)(i)], the model notice applicable to the State in which the participants and beneficiaries reside.

§ 1023. Annual reports

(a) Publication and filing

(1)(A) An annual report shall be published with respect to every employee benefit plan to which this part applies. Such report shall be filed with the Secretary in accordance with section 1024(a) of this title [29 U.S.C. § 1024(a)], and shall be made available and furnished to participants in accordance with section 1024(b) of this title [29 U.S.C. § 1024(b)].

(B) The annual report shall include the information described in subsections (b) and (c) and where applicable subsections (d), (e), (f), and (g) and shall also include-

(i) a financial statement and opinion, as required by paragraph (3) of this subsection, and

(ii) an actuarial statement and opinion, as required by paragraph (4) of this subsection.

(2) If some or all of the information necessary to enable the administrator to comply with the requirements of this subchapter is maintained by-

(A) an insurance carrier or other organization which provides some or all of the benefits under the plan, or holds assets of the plan in a separate account,

(B) a bank or similar institution which holds some or all of the assets of the plan in a common or collective trust or a separate trust, or custodial account, or

(C) a plan sponsor as defined in section 1002(16)(B) of this title [29 U.S.C. § 1002(16)(B),

such carrier, organization, bank, institution, or plan sponsor shall transmit and certify the accuracy of such information to the administrator within 120 days after the end of the plan year (or such other date as may be prescribed under regulations of the Secretary).

(3)(A) Except as provided in subparagraph (C), the administrator of an employee benefit plan shall engage, on behalf of all plan participants, an independent qualified public accountant, who shall conduct such an examination of any financial statements of the plan, and of other books and records of the plan, as the accountant may deem necessary to enable the accountant to form an opinion as to whether the financial statements and schedules required to be included in the annual report by subsection (b) of this section are presented fairly in conformity with generally accepted accounting principles applied on a basis consistent with that of the preceding year. Such examination shall be conducted in accordance with generally accepted auditing standards, and shall involve such tests of the books and records of the plan as are considered necessary by the independent qualified public accountant. The independent qualified public accountant shall also offer his opinion as to whether the separate schedules specified in subsection (b)(3) of this section and the summary material required under section 1024(b)(3) of this title [29 U.S.C. § 1024(b)(3)] present fairly, and in all material respects the information contained therein when considered in conjunction with the financial statements taken as a whole. The opinion by the independent qualified public accountant shall be made a part of the annual report. In a case where a plan is not required to file an annual report, the requirements of this paragraph shall not apply. In a case where by reason of section 1024(a)(2) of this title [29 U.S.C. § 1024(a)(2)] a plan is required only to file a simplified annual report, the Secretary may waive the requirements of this paragraph.

(B) In offering his opinion under this section the accountant may rely on the correctness of any actuarial matter certified to by an enrolled actuary, if he so states his reliance.

(C) The opinion required by subparagraph (A) need not be expressed as to any statements required by subsection (b)(3)(G) prepared by a bank or similar institution or insurance carrier regulated and supervised and subject to periodic examination by a State or Federal agency if such statements are certified by the bank, similar institution, or insurance carrier as accurate and are made a part of the annual report.

(D) For purposes of this subchapter, the term "qualified public accountant" means-

(i) a person who is a certified public accountant, certified by a regulatory authority of a State;

(ii) a person who is a licensed public accountant, licensed by a regulatory authority of a State; or

(iii) a person certified by the Secretary as a qualified public accountant in accordance with regulations published by him for a person who practices in States where there is no certification or licensing procedure for accountants.

(4)(A) The administrator of an employee pension benefit plan subject to the reporting requirement of subsection (d) of this section shall engage, on behalf of all plan participants, an enrolled actuary who shall be responsible for the preparation of the materials comprising the actuarial statement required under subsection (d) of this section. In a case where a plan is not required to file an annual report, the requirement of this paragraph shall not apply, and, in a case where by reason of section 1024(a)(2) of this title [29 U.S.C. § 1024(a)(2)], a plan is required only to file a simplified report, the Secretary may waive the requirement of this paragraph.

(B) The enrolled actuary shall utilize such assumptions and techniques as are necessary to enable him to form an opinion as to whether the contents of the matters reported under subsection (d) of this section-

(i) are in the aggregate reasonably related to the experience of the plan and to reasonable expectations; and

(ii) represent his best estimate of anticipated experience under the plan.

The opinion by the enrolled actuary shall be made with respect to, and shall be made a part of, each annual report.

(C) For purposes of this subchapter, the term "enrolled actuary" means an actuary enrolled under subtitle C of subchapter II of this chapter [29 U.S.C. §§ 1241, 1242].

(D) In making a certification under this section the enrolled actuary may rely on the correctness of any accounting matter under subsection (b) to which any qualified public accountant has expressed an opinion, if he so states his reliance.

(b) Financial statement

An annual report under this section shall include a financial statement containing the following information:

(1) With respect to an employee welfare benefit plan: a statement of assets and liabilities; a statement of changes in fund balance; and a statement of changes in financial position. In the notes to financial statements, disclosures concerning the following items shall be considered by the accountant: a description of the plan including any

significant changes in the plan made during the period and the impact of such changes on benefits; a description of material lease commitments, other commitments, and contingent liabilities; a description of agreements and transactions with persons known to be parties in interest; a general description of priorities upon termination of the plan; information concerning whether or not a tax ruling or determination letter has been obtained; and any other matters necessary to fully and fairly present the financial statements of the plan.

(2) With respect to an employee pension benefit plan: a statement of assets and liabilities, and a statement of changes in net assets available for plan benefits which shall include details of revenues and expenses and other changes aggregated by general source and application. In the notes to financial statements, disclosures concerning the following items shall be considered by the accountant: a description of the plan including any significant changes in the plan made during the period and the impact of such changes on benefits; the funding policy (including policy with respect to prior service cost), and any changes in such policies during the year; a description of any significant changes in plan benefits made during the period; a description of material lease commitments, other commitments, and contingent liabilities; a description of agreements and transactions with persons known to be parties in interest; a general description of priorities upon termination of the plan; information concerning whether or not a tax ruling or determination letter has been obtained; and any other matters necessary to fully and fairly present the financial statements of such pension plan.

(3) With respect to all employee benefit plans, the statement required under paragraph (1) or (2) shall have attached the following information in separate schedules:

(A) a statement of the assets and liabilities of the plan aggregated by categories and valued at their current value, and the same data displayed in comparative form for the end of the previous fiscal year of the plan;

(B) a statement of receipts and disbursements during the preceding twelve-month period aggregated by general sources and applications;

(C) a schedule of all assets held for investment purposes aggregated and identified by issuer, borrower, or lessor, or similar party to the transaction (including a notation as to whether such party is known to be a party in interest), maturity date, rate of interest, collateral, par or maturity value, cost, and current value;

(D) a schedule of each transaction involving a person known to be party in interest, the identity of such party in interest and his relationship or that of any other party in interest to the plan, a description of each asset to which the transaction relates; the purchase or selling price in case of a sale or purchase, the rental in case of a lease, or the interest rate and maturity date in case of a loan; expense incurred in connection with the transaction; the cost of the asset, the current value of the asset, and the net gain (or loss) on each transaction;

(E) a schedule of all loans or fixed income obligations which were in default as of the close of the plan's fiscal year or were classified during the year as uncollectable and the following information with respect to each loan on such schedule (including a notation as to whether parties involved are known to be parties in interest): the original principal amount of the loan, the amount of principal and interest received during the reporting year, the unpaid balance, the identity and address of the obligor, a detailed description of the loan (including date of making and maturity, interest rate, the type and value of collateral, and other material terms), the amount of principal and interest overdue (if any) and an explanation thereof;

(F) a list of all leases which were in default or were classified during the year as uncollectable; and the following information with respect to each lease on such schedule (including a notation as to whether parties involved are known to be parties in interest): the type of property leased (and, in the case of fixed assets such as land, buildings, leasehold, and so forth, the location of the property), the identity of the lessor or lessee from or to whom the plan is leasing, the relationship of such lessors and lessees, if any, to the plan, the employer, employee organization, or any other party in interest, the terms of the lease regarding rent, taxes, insurance, repairs, expenses, and renewal options; the date the leased property was purchased and its cost, the date the property was leased and its approximate value at such date, the gross rental receipts during the reporting period, expenses paid for the leased property during the reporting period, the net receipts from the lease, the amounts in arrears, and a statement as to what steps have been taken to collect amounts due or otherwise remedy the default;

(G) if some or all of the assets of a plan or plans are held in a common or collective trust maintained by a bank or similar institution or in a separate account maintained by an insurance carrier or a separate trust maintained by a bank as trustee, the report shall include the most recent annual statement of assets and liabilities of such common or collective trust, and in the case of a separate account or a separate trust, such other information as is required by the administrator in order to comply with this subsection; and

(H) a schedule of each reportable transaction, the name of each party to the transaction (except that, in the case of an acquisition or sale of a security on the market, the report need not identify the person from whom the security was acquired or to whom it was sold) and a description of each asset to which the transaction applies; the purchase or selling price in case of a sale or purchase, the rental in case of a lease, or the interest rate and maturity date in case of a loan; expenses incurred in connection with the transaction; the cost of the asset, the current value of the asset, and the net gain (or loss) on each transaction. For purposes of the preceding sentence, the term "reportable transaction" means a transaction to which the plan is a party if such transaction is-

(i) a transaction involving an amount in excess of 3 percent of the current value of the assets of the plan;

(ii) any transaction (other than a transaction respecting a security) which is part of a series of transactions with or in conjunction with a person in a plan year, if the aggregate amount of such transactions exceeds 3 percent of the current value of the assets of the plan;

(iii) a transaction which is part of a series of transactions respecting one or more securities of the same issuer, if the aggregate amount of such transactions in the plan year exceeds 3 percent of the current value of the assets of the plan; or

(iv) a transaction with or in conjunction with a person respecting a security, if any other transaction with or in conjunction with such person in the plan year respecting a security is required to be reported by reason of clause (i).

(4) The Secretary may, by regulation, relieve any plan from filing a copy of a statement of assets and liabilities (or other information) described in paragraph (3)(G) if such statement and other information is filed with the Secretary by the bank or insurance carrier which maintains the common or collective trust or separate account.

(c) Information to be furnished by administrator

The administrator shall furnish as a part of a report under this section the following information:

(1) The number of employees covered by the plan.

(2) The name and address of each fiduciary.

(3) Except in the case of a person whose compensation is minimal (determined under regulations of the Secretary) and who performs solely ministerial duties (determined under such regulations), the name of each person (including but not limited to, any consultant, broker, trustee, accountant, insurance carrier, actuary, administrator, investment manager, or custodian who rendered services to the plan or who had transactions with the plan) who received directly or indirectly compensation from the plan during the preceding year for services rendered to the plan or its participants, the amount of such compensation, the nature of his services to the plan or its participants, his relationship to the employer of the employees covered by the plan, or the employee organization, and any other office, position, or employment he holds with any party in interest.

(4) An explanation of the reason for any change in appointment of trustee, accountant, insurance carrier, enrolled actuary, administrator, investment manager, or custodian.

(5) Such financial and actuarial information including but not limited to the material described in subsections (b) and (d) of this section as the Secretary may find necessary or appropriate.

(d) Actuarial statement

With respect to an employee pension benefit plan (other than (A) a profit sharing, savings, or other plan, which is an individual account plan, (B) a plan described in section 1081(b) of this title [29 U.S.C. § 1081(b)], or (C) a plan described both in section 1321(b) of this title [29 U.S.C. § 1321(b)]and in paragraph (1), (2), (3), (4), (5), (6), or (7) of section 1081(a) of this title [29 U.S.C. § 1081(a)]) an annual report under this section for a plan year shall include a complete actuarial statement applicable to the plan year which shall include the following:

(1) The date of the plan year, and the date of the actuarial valuation applicable to the plan year for which the report is filed.

(2) The date and amount of the contribution (or contributions) received by the plan for the plan year for which the report is filed and contributions for prior plan years not previously reported.

(3) The following information applicable to the plan year for which the report is filed: the normal costs or target normal costs, the accrued liabilities or funding target, an identification of benefits not included in the calculation; a statement of the other facts and actuarial assumptions and methods used to determine costs, and a justification for any change in actuarial assumptions or cost methods; and the

minimum contribution required under section 1082 of this title [29 U.S.C. § 1082].

(4) The number of participants and beneficiaries, both retired and nonretired, covered by the plan.

(5) The current value of the assets accumulated in the plan, and the present value of the assets of the plan used by the actuary in any computation of the amount of contributions to the plan required under section 1082 of this title [29 U.S.C. § 1082] and a statement explaining the basis of such valuation of present value of assets.

(6) Information required in regulations of the Pension Benefit Guaranty Corporation with respect to:

(A) the current value of the assets of the plan,

(B) the present value of all nonforfeitable benefits for participants and beneficiaries receiving payments under the plan,

(C) the present value of all nonforfeitable benefits for all other participants and beneficiaries,

(D) the present value of all accrued benefits which are not nonforfeitable (including a separate accounting of such benefits which are benefit commitments, as defined in section 1301(a)(16) of this title [29 U.S.C. § 1301(a)(16)]), and

(E) the actuarial assumptions and techniques used in determining the values described in subparagraphs (A) through (D).

(7) A certification of the contribution necessary to reduce the minimum required contribution determined under section 1083 of this title [29 U.S.C. § 1083], or the accumulated funding deficiency determined under section 1084 of this title [29 U.S.C. § 1084], to zero.

(8) A statement by the enrolled actuary-

(A) that to the best of his knowledge the report is complete and accurate, and

(B) the applicable requirements of sections 1083(h), 1084(c)(3), and 1085a(c)(3) of this title [29 U.S.C. §§ 1083(h), 1084(c)(3), 1085a(c)(3)] (relating to reasonable actuarial assumptions and methods) have been complied with.

(9) A copy of the opinion required by subsection (a)(4).

(10) A statement by the actuary which discloses-

(A) any event which the actuary has not taken into account, and

(B) any trend which, for purposes of the actuarial assumptions used, was not assumed to continue in the future,

but only if, to the best of the actuary's knowledge, such event or trend may require a material increase in plan costs or required contribution rates.

(11) If the current value of the assets of the plan is less than 70 percent of-

(A) in the case of a single-employer plan, the funding target (as defined in section 1083(d)(1) of this title [29 U.S.C. § 1083(d)(1)]) of the plan, or

(B) in the case of a multiemployer plan, the current liability (as defined in section 1084(c)(6)(D) of this title [29 U.S.C. § 1084(c)(6)(D)]) under the plan,

the percentage which such value is of the amount described in subparagraph (A) or (B).

(12) A statement explaining the actuarial assumptions and methods used in projecting future retirements and forms of benefit distributions under the plan.

(13) Such other information regarding the plan as the Secretary may by regulation require.

(14) Such other information as may be necessary to fully and fairly disclose the actuarial position of the plan.

Such actuary shall make an actuarial valuation of the plan for every third plan year, unless he determines that a more frequent valuation is necessary to support his opinion under subsection (a)(4) of this section.

(e) Statement from insurance company, insurance service, or other similar organizations which sell or guarantee plan benefits

If some or all of the benefits under the plan are purchased from and guaranteed by an insurance company, insurance service, or other similar organization, a report under this section shall include a statement from such insurance company, service, or other similar organization covering the plan year and enumerating-

(1) the premium rate or subscription charge and the total premium or subscription charges paid to each such carrier, insurance service, or other similar organization and the approximate number of persons covered by each class of such benefits; and

(2) the total amount of premiums received, the approximate number of persons covered by each class of benefits, and the total claims paid by such company, service, or other organization; dividends

or retroactive rate adjustments, commissions, and administrative service or other fees or other specific acquisition costs paid by such company, service, or other organization; any amounts held to provide benefits after retirement; the remainder of such premiums; and the names and addresses of the brokers, agents, or other persons to whom commissions or fees were paid, the amount paid to each, and for what purpose. If any such company, service, or other organization does not maintain separate experience records covering the specific groups it serves, the report shall include in lieu of the information required by the foregoing provisions of this paragraph (A) a statement as to the basis of its premium rate or subscription charge, the total amount of premiums or subscription charges received from the plan, and a copy of the financial report of the company, service, or other organization and (B) if such company, service, or organization incurs specific costs in connection with the acquisition or retention of any particular plan or plans, a detailed statement of such costs.

(f) Additional information with respect to defined benefit plans

(1) Liabilities under 2 or more plans

(A) In general

In any case in which any liabilities to participants or their beneficiaries under a defined benefit plan as of the end of a plan year consist (in whole or in part) of liabilities to such participants and beneficiaries under 2 or more pension plans as of immediately before such plan year, an annual report under this section for such plan year shall include the funded percentage of each of such 2 or more pension plans as of the last day of such plan year and the funded percentage of the plan with respect to which the annual report is filed as of the last day of such plan year.

(B) Funded percentage

For purposes of this paragraph, the term "funded percentage"-

(i) in the case of a single-employer plan, means the funding target attainment percentage, as defined in section 1083(d)(2) of this title [29 U.S.C. § 1083(d)(2)], and

(ii) in the case of a multiemployer plan, has the meaning given such term in section 1085(i)(2) of this title [29 U.S.C. § 1085(i)(2)].

(2) Additional information for multiemployer plans

With respect to any defined benefit plan which is a multiemployer plan, an annual report under this section for a plan year shall include, in addition to the information required under paragraph (1), the following, as of the end of the plan year to which the report relates:

(A) The number of employers obligated to contribute to the plan.

(B) A list of the employers that contributed more than 5 percent of the total contributions to the plan during such plan year.

(C) The number of participants under the plan on whose behalf no contributions were made by an employer as an employer of the participant for such plan year and for each of the 2 preceding plan years.

(D) The ratios of-

(i) the number of participants under the plan on whose behalf no employer had an obligation to make an employer contribution during the plan year, to

(ii) the number of participants under the plan on whose behalf no employer had an obligation to make an employer contribution during each of the 2 preceding plan years.

(E) Whether the plan received an amortization extension under section 1084(d) of this title [29 U.S.C. § 1084(d)] or section 431(d) of title 26 [26 U.S.C. § 431(d)] for such plan year and, if so, the amount of the difference between the minimum required contribution for the year and the minimum required contribution which would have been required without regard to the extension, and the period of such extension.

(F) Whether the plan used the shortfall funding method (as such term is used in section 1085 of this title [29 U.S.C. § 1085]) for such plan year and, if so, the amount of the difference between the minimum required contribution for the year and the minimum required contribution which would have been required without regard to the use of such method, and the period of use of such method.

(G) Whether the plan was in critical or endangered status under section 1085 of this title [29 U.S.C. § 1085] for such plan year, and if so, a summary of any funding improvement or rehabilitation plan (or modification thereto) adopted during the plan year, and the funded percentage of the plan.

(H) The number of employers that withdrew from the plan during the preceding plan year and the aggregate amount of withdrawal liability assessed, or estimated to be assessed, against such withdrawn employers.

(I) In the case of a multiemployer plan that has merged with another plan or to which assets and liabilities have been transferred, the actuarial valuation of the assets and liabilities of each affected plan during the year preceding the effective date of the merger or transfer, based upon the most recent data available as of the day before the first day of the plan year, or other valuation method performed under standards and procedures as the Secretary may prescribe by regulation.

(g) Additional information with respect to pooled employer and multiple employer plans

An annual report under this section for a plan year shall include-

(1) with respect to any plan to which section 1060(a) of this title applies [29 U.S.C. § 1060(a)] (including a pooled employer plan), a list of employers in the plan and a good faith estimate of the percentage of total contributions made by such employers during the plan year and the aggregate account balances attributable to each employer in the plan (determined as the sum of the account balances of the employees of such employer (and the beneficiaries of such employees)); and

(2) with respect to a pooled employer plan, the identifying information for the person designated under the terms of the plan as the pooled plan provider.

§ 1024. Filing with Secretary and furnishing of information to participants and certain employers

(a) Filing of annual report with Secretary

(1) The administrator of any employee benefit plan subject to this part shall file with the Secretary the annual report for a plan year within 210 days after the close of such year (or within such time as may be required by regulations promulgated by the Secretary in order to reduce duplicative filing). The Secretary shall make copies of such annual reports available for inspection in the public document room of the Department of Labor.

(2)(A) With respect to annual reports required to be filed with the Secretary under this part, the Secretary may by regulation prescribe simplified annual reports for any pension plan that-

(i) covers fewer than 100 participants; or

(ii) is a plan described in section 1060(a) of this title [29 U.S.C. § 1060(a)] that covers fewer than 1,000 participants, but only if no single employer in the plan has 100 or more participants covered by the plan.

(B) Nothing contained in this paragraph shall preclude the Secretary from requiring any information or data from any such plan to which this part applies where he finds such data or information is necessary to carry out the purposes of this subchapter nor shall the Secretary be precluded from revoking provisions for simplified reports for any such plan if he finds it necessary to do so in order to carry out the objectives of this subchapter.

(3) The Secretary may by regulation exempt any welfare benefit plan from all or part of the reporting and disclosure requirements of this subchapter, or may provide for simplified reporting and disclosure if he finds that such requirements are inappropriate as applied to welfare benefit plans.

(4) The Secretary may reject any filing under this section-

(A) if he determines that such filing is incomplete for purposes of this part; or

(B) if he determines that there is any material qualification by an accountant or actuary contained in an opinion submitted pursuant to section 1023(a)(3)(A) or section 1023(a)(4)(B) of this title [29 U.S.C. § 1023(a)(3)(A), 1023(a)(4)(B)].

(5) If the Secretary rejects a filing of a report under paragraph (4) and if a revised filing satisfactory to the Secretary is not submitted within 45 days after the Secretary makes his determination under paragraph (4) to reject the filing, and if the Secretary deems it in the best interest of the participants, he may take any one or more of the following actions-

(A) retain an independent qualified public accountant (as defined in section 1023(a)(3)(D) of this title [29 U.S.C. § 1023(a)(3)(D)]) on behalf of the participants to perform an audit,

(B) retain an enrolled actuary (as defined in section 1023(a)(4)(C) of this title [29 U.S.C. § 1023(a)(4)(C)]) on behalf of the plan participants, to prepare an actuarial statement,

(C) bring a civil action for such legal or equitable relief as may be appropriate to enforce the provisions of this part, or

(D) take any other action authorized by this subchapter.

The administrator shall permit such accountant or actuary to inspect whatever books and records of the plan are necessary for such audit. The plan shall be liable to the Secretary for the expenses for such audit or report, and the Secretary may bring an action against the plan in any court of competent jurisdiction to recover such expenses.

(6) The administrator of any employee benefit plan subject to this part shall furnish to the Secretary, upon request, any documents relating to the employee benefit plan, including but not limited to, the latest summary plan description (including any summaries of plan changes not contained in the summary plan description), and the bargaining agreement, trust agreement, contract, or other instrument under which the plan is established or operated.

(b) Publication of summary plan description and annual report to participants and beneficiaries of plan

Publication of the summary plan descriptions and annual reports shall be made to participants and beneficiaries of the particular plan as follows:

(1) The administrator shall furnish to each participant, and each beneficiary receiving benefits under the plan, a copy of the summary plan description, and all modifications and changes referred to in section 1022(a) of this title [29 U.S.C. § 1022(a)]-

(A) within 90 days after he becomes a participant, or (in the case of a beneficiary) within 90 days after he first receives benefits, or

(B) if later, within 120 days after the plan becomes subject to this part.

The administrator shall furnish to each participant, and each beneficiary receiving benefits under the plan, every fifth year after the plan becomes subject to this part an updated summary plan description described in section 1022 of this title [29 U.S.C. § 1022] which integrates all plan amendments made within such five-year period, except that in a case where no amendments have been made to a plan during such five-year period this sentence shall not apply. Notwithstanding the foregoing, the administrator shall furnish to each participant, and to each beneficiary receiving benefits under the plan, the summary plan description described in section 1022 of this title [29 U.S.C. § 1022] every tenth year after the plan becomes subject to this part. If there is a modification or change described in section 1022(a) of this title [29 U.S.C. § 1022(a)] (other than a material reduction in covered services or benefits provided in the case of a group health plan (as defined in section 1191b(a)(1) of this title [29 U.S.C. § 1191b(a)(1)])), a summary description of such modification or change shall be furnished not later than 210 days after the end of the plan year in which the change is adopted to each participant, and to each beneficiary who is receiving benefits under the plan. If there is a modification or change described in section 1022(a) of this title [29 U.S.C. § 1022(a)] that is a material reduction in covered services or benefits provided under a group health plan (as defined in section 1191b(a)(1) of this title [29 U.S.C. § 1191b(a)(1)]), a summary description of such modification or change shall be furnished to participants and beneficiaries not later than 60 days after the date of the adoption of the modification or change. In the alternative, the plan sponsors may provide such description at regular intervals of not more than 90 days. The Secretary shall issue regulations within 180 days after August 21, 1996, providing alternative mechanisms to delivery by mail through which group health plans (as so defined) may notify participants and beneficiaries of material reductions in covered services or benefits.

(2) The administrator shall make copies of the latest updated summary plan description and the latest annual report and the bargaining agreement, trust agreement, contract, or other instruments under which the plan was established or is operated available for examination by any plan participant or beneficiary in the principal office of the administrator and in such other places as may be necessary to make available all pertinent information to all participants (including such places as the Secretary may prescribe by regulations).

(3) Within 210 days after the close of the fiscal year of the plan, the administrator (other than an administrator of a defined benefit plan to which the requirements of section 1021(f) of this title [29 U.S.C. § 1021(f)] applies) shall furnish to each participant, and to each beneficiary receiving benefits under the plan, a copy of the statements and schedules, for such fiscal year, described in subparagraphs (A) and (B) of section 1023(b)(3) of this title [29 U.S.C. § 1023(b)(3)] and such other material (including the percentage determined under section 1023(d)(11) of this title [29 U.S.C. § 1023(d)(11)]) as is necessary to fairly summarize the latest annual report.

(4) The administrator shall, upon written request of any participant or beneficiary, furnish a copy of the latest updated summary, plan description, and the latest annual report, any terminal report, the bargaining agreement, trust agreement, contract, or other instruments under which the plan is established or operated. The administrator may make a reasonable charge to cover the cost of furnishing such complete copies. The Secretary may by regulation prescribe the maximum amount which will constitute a reasonable charge under the preceding sentence.

(5) Identification and basic plan information and actuarial information included in the annual report for any plan year shall be filed with the Secretary in an electronic format which accommodates display on the Internet, in accordance with regulations which shall be

prescribed by the Secretary. The Secretary shall provide for display of such information included in the annual report, within 90 days after the date of the filing of the annual report, on an Internet website maintained by the Secretary and other appropriate media. Such information shall also be displayed on any Intranet website maintained by the plan sponsor (or by the plan administrator on behalf of the plan sponsor) for the purpose of communicating with employees and not the public, in accordance with regulations which shall be prescribed by the Secretary.

(c) Statement of rights

The Secretary may by regulation require that the administrator of any employee benefit plan furnish to each participant and to each beneficiary receiving benefits under the plan a statement of the rights of participants and beneficiaries under this subchapter.

(d) Furnishing summary plan information to employers and employee representatives of multiemployer plans

(1) In general

With respect to a multiemployer plan subject to this section, within 30 days after the due date under subsection (a)(1) for the filing of the annual report for the fiscal year of the plan, the administrators shall furnish to each employee organization and to each employer with an obligation to contribute to the plan a report that contains-

(A) a description of the contribution schedules and benefit formulas under the plan, and any modification to such schedules and formulas, during such plan year;

(B) the number of employers obligated to contribute to the plan;

(C) a list of the employers that contributed more than 5 percent of the total contributions to the plan during such plan year;

(D) the number of participants under the plan on whose behalf no contributions were made by an employer as an employer of the participant for such plan year and for each of the 2 preceding plan years;

(E) whether the plan was in critical or endangered status under section 1085 of this title [29 U.S.C. § 1085] for such plan year and, if so, include-

(i) a list of the actions taken by the plan to improve its funding status; and

(ii) a statement describing how a person may obtain a copy of the plan's funding improvement or rehabilitation plan, as applicable, adopted under section 1085 of this title [29 U.S.C. § 1085] and the actuarial and financial data that demonstrate any action taken by the plan toward fiscal improvement;

(F) the number of employers that withdrew from the plan during the preceding plan year and the aggregate amount of withdrawal liability assessed, or estimated to be assessed, against such withdrawn employers, as reported on the annual report for the plan year to which the report under this subsection relates;

(G) in the case of a multiemployer plan that has merged with another plan or to which assets and liabilities have been transferred, the actuarial valuation of the assets and liabilities of each affected plan during the year preceding the effective date of the merger or transfer, based upon the most recent data available as of the day before the first day of the plan year, or other valuation method performed under standards and procedures as the Secretary may prescribe by regulation;

(H) a description as to whether the plan-

(i) sought or received an amortization extension under section 1084(d) of this title [29 U.S.C. § 1084(d)] or section 431(d) of title 26 [26 U.S.C. § 431(d)] for such plan year; or

(ii) used the shortfall funding method (as such term is used in section 1085 of this title [29 U.S.C. § 1085]) for such plan year; and

(I) notification of the right under this section of the recipient to a copy of the annual report filed with the Secretary under subsection (a), summary plan description, summary of any material modification of the plan, upon written request, but that-

(i) in no case shall a recipient be entitled to receive more than one copy of any such document described during any one 12-month period; and

(ii) the administrator may make a reasonable charge to cover copying, mailing, and other costs of furnishing copies of information pursuant to this subparagraph.

(2) Effect of subsection

Nothing in this subsection waives any other provision under this subchapter requiring plan administrators to provide, upon request, information to employers that have an obligation to contribute under the plan.

(e) Cross reference

For regulations respecting coordination of reports to the Secretaries of Labor and the Treasury, see section 1204 of this title [29 U.S.C. § 1204].

§ 1025. Reporting of participant's benefit rights

(a) Requirements to provide pension benefit statements

(1) Requirements

(A) Individual account plan

The administrator of an individual account plan (other than a one-participant retirement plan described in section 1021(i)(8)(B) of this title [29 U.S.C. § 1021(i)(8)(B)]) shall furnish a pension benefit statement-

(i) at least once each calendar quarter to a participant or beneficiary who has the right to direct the investment of assets in his or her account under the plan,

(ii) at least once each calendar year to a participant or beneficiary who has his or her own account under the plan but does not have the right to direct the investment of assets in that account, and

(iii) upon written request to a plan beneficiary not described in clause (i) or (ii).

(B) Defined benefit plan

The administrator of a defined benefit plan (other than a one-participant retirement plan described in section 1021(i)(8)(B) of this title [29 U.S.C. § 1021(i)(8)(B)]) shall furnish a pension benefit statement-

(i) at least once every 3 years to each participant with a nonforfeitable accrued benefit and who is employed by the employer maintaining the plan at the time the statement is to be furnished, and

(ii) to a participant or beneficiary of the plan upon written request.

Information furnished under clause (i) to a participant may be based on reasonable estimates determined under regulations prescribed by the Secretary, in consultation with the Pension Benefit Guaranty Corporation.

(2) Statements

(A) In general

A pension benefit statement under paragraph (1)-

(i) shall indicate, on the basis of the latest available information-

(I) the total benefits accrued, and

(II) the nonforfeitable pension benefits, if any, which have accrued, or the earliest date on which benefits will become nonforfeitable,

(ii) shall include an explanation of any permitted disparity under section 401(*l*) of title 26 [26 U.S.C. § 401(*l*)] or any floor-offset arrangement that may be applied in determining any accrued benefits described in clause (i),

(iii) shall be written in a manner calculated to be understood by the average plan participant, and

(iv) may be delivered in written, electronic, or other appropriate form to the extent such form is reasonably accessible to the participant or beneficiary.

(B) Additional information

In the case of an individual account plan, any pension benefit statement under clause (i) or (ii) of paragraph (1)(A) shall include-

(i) the value of each investment to which assets in the individual account have been allocated, determined as of the most recent valuation date under the plan, including the value of any assets held in the form of employer securities, without regard to whether such securities were contributed by the plan sponsor or acquired at the direction of the plan or of the participant or beneficiary,

(ii) in the case of a pension benefit statement under paragraph (1)(A)(i)-

(I) an explanation of any limitations or restrictions on any right of the participant or beneficiary under the plan to direct an investment,

(II) an explanation, written in a manner calculated to be understood by the average plan participant, of the importance, for the long-term retirement security of participants and beneficiaries, of a well-balanced and diversified investment portfolio, including a statement of the risk that holding more than 20 percent of a portfolio in the security of one entity (such as employer securities) may not be adequately diversified, and

(III) a notice directing the participant or beneficiary to the Internet website of the Department of Labor for sources of information on individual investing and diversification, and

(iii) the lifetime income disclosure described in subparagraph (D)(i).

In the case of pension benefit statements described in clause (i) of paragraph (1)(A), a lifetime income disclosure under clause (iii) of this subparagraph shall be required to be included in only one pension benefit statement during any one 12-month period.

(C) Alternative notice

The requirements of subparagraph (A)(i)(II) are met if, at least annually and in accordance with requirements of the Secretary, the plan-

(i) updates the information described in such paragraph which is provided in the pension benefit statement, or

(ii) provides in a separate statement such information as is necessary to enable a participant or beneficiary to determine their nonforfeitable vested benefits.

(D) Lifetime income disclosure

(i) In general

(I) Disclosure

A lifetime income disclosure shall set forth the lifetime income stream equivalent of the total benefits accrued with respect to the participant or beneficiary.

(II) Lifetime income stream equivalent of the total benefits accrued

For purposes of this subparagraph, the term "lifetime income stream equivalent of the total benefits accrued" means the amount of monthly payments the participant or beneficiary would receive if the total accrued benefits of such participant or beneficiary were used to provide lifetime income streams described in subclause (III), based on assumptions specified in rules prescribed by the Secretary.

(III) Lifetime income streams

The lifetime income streams described in this subclause are a qualified joint and survivor annuity (as defined in section 1055(d) of this title [29 U.S.C. § 1055(d)]), based on assumptions specified in rules prescribed by the Secretary, including the assumption that the participant or beneficiary has a spouse of equal age, and a single life annuity. Such lifetime income streams may have a term certain or other features to the extent permitted under rules prescribed by the Secretary.

(ii) Model disclosure

Not later than 1 year after December 20, 2019, the Secretary shall issue a model lifetime income disclosure, written in a manner so as to be understood by the average plan participant, which-

(I) explains that the lifetime income stream equivalent is only provided as an illustration;

(II) explains that the actual payments under the lifetime income stream described in clause (i)(III) which may be purchased with the total benefits accrued will depend on numerous factors and may vary substantially from the lifetime income stream equivalent in the disclosures;

(III) explains the assumptions upon which the lifetime income stream equivalent was determined; and

(IV) provides such other similar explanations as the Secretary considers appropriate.

(iii) Assumptions and rules

Not later than 1 year after December 20, 2019, the Secretary shall-

(I) prescribe assumptions which administrators of individual account plans may use in converting total accrued benefits into lifetime income stream equivalents for purposes of this subparagraph; and

(II) issue interim final rules under clause (i).

In prescribing assumptions under subclause (I), the Secretary may prescribe a single set of specific assumptions (in which case the Secretary may issue tables or factors which facilitate such conversions), or ranges of permissible assumptions. To the extent that an accrued benefit is or may be invested in a lifetime income stream described in clause (i)(III), the assumptions prescribed under subclause (I) shall, to the extent appropriate, permit administrators of individual account plans to use the amounts payable under such lifetime income stream as a lifetime income stream equivalent.

(iv) Limitation on liability

No plan fiduciary, plan sponsor, or other person shall have any liability under this subchapter solely by reason of the provision of lifetime income stream equivalents which are derived in accordance with the assumptions and rules described in clause (iii) and which include the explanations contained in the model lifetime income disclosure described in clause (ii). This clause shall apply without regard to whether the provision of such lifetime income stream equivalent is required by subparagraph (B)(iii).

(v) Effective date

The requirement in subparagraph (B)(iii) shall apply to pension benefit statements furnished more than 12 months after the latest of the issuance by the Secretary of-

(I) interim final rules under clause (i);

(II) the model disclosure under clause (ii); or

(III) the assumptions under clause (iii).

(3) Defined benefit plans

(A) Alternative notice

In the case of a defined benefit plan, the requirements of paragraph (1)(B)(i) shall be treated as met with respect to a participant if at least once each year the administrator provides to the participant notice of the availability of the pension benefit statement and the ways in which the participant may obtain such statement. Such notice may be delivered in written, electronic, or other appropriate form to the extent such form is reasonably accessible to the participant.

(B) Years in which no benefits accrue

The Secretary may provide that years in which no employee or former employee benefits (within the meaning of section 410(b) of title 26 [26 U.S.C. § 410(b)]) under the plan need not be taken into account in determining the 3-year period under paragraph (1)(B)(i).

(b) Limitation on number of statements

In no case shall a participant or beneficiary of a plan be entitled to more than 1 statement described in subparagraph (A)(iii) or (B)(ii) of subsection (a)(1), whichever is applicable, in any 12-month period.

(c) Individual statement furnished by administrator to participants setting forth information in administrator's Internal Revenue registration statement and notification of forfeitable benefits

Each administrator required to register under section 6057 of title 26 [26 U.S.C. § 6057] shall, before the expiration of the time prescribed for such registration, furnish to each participant described in subsection (a)(2)(C) of such section, an individual statement setting forth the information with respect to such participant required to be contained in the registration statement required by section 6057(a)(2) of title 26 [26 U.S.C. § 6057(a)(2)]. Such statement shall also include a notice to the participant of any benefits which are forfeitable if the participant dies before a certain date.

(d) Repealed. Pub.L. 109–280, Title V, § 508(a)(2)(A), Aug. 17, 2006, 120 Stat. 951

(§ 1026 through § 1051. Omitted)

§ 1052. Minimum participation standards

(a)(1)(A) No pension plan may require, as a condition of participation in the plan, that an employee complete a period of service with the employer or employers maintaining the plan extending beyond the later of the following dates-

(i) the date on which the employee attains the age of 21; or

(ii) the date on which he completes 1 year of service.

(B)(i) In the case of any plan which provides that after not more than 2 years of service each participant has a right to 100 percent of his accrued benefit under the plan which is nonforfeitable at the time such benefit accrues, clause (ii) of subparagraph (A) shall be applied by substituting "2 years of service" for "1 year of service".

(ii) In the case of any plan maintained exclusively for employees of an educational organization (as defined in section 170(b)(1)(A)(ii) of title 26 [26 U.S.C. § 170(b)(1)(A)(ii)]) by an employer which is exempt from tax under section 501(a) of title 26 [26 U.S.C. § 501(a)], which provides that each participant having at least 1 year of service has a right to 100 percent of his accrued benefit under the plan which is nonforfeitable at the time such benefit accrues, clause (i) of subparagraph (A) shall be applied by substituting "26" for "21". This clause shall not apply to any plan to which clause (i) applies.

(2) No pension plan may exclude from participation (on the basis of age) employees who have attained a specified age.

(3)(A) For purposes of this section, the term "year of service" means a 12-month period during which the employee has not less than 1,000 hours of service. For purposes of this paragraph, computation of any 12-month period shall be made with reference to the date on which the employee's employment commenced, except that, in accordance with regulations prescribed by the Secretary, such computation may be made by reference to the first day of a plan year in the case of an employee who does not complete 1,000 hours of service during the 12-month period beginning on the date his employment commenced.

(B) In the case of any seasonal industry where the customary period of employment is less than 1,000 hours during a calendar year, the term "year of service" shall be such period as may be determined under regulations prescribed by the Secretary.

(C) For purposes of this section, the term "hour of service" means a time of service determined under regulations prescribed by the Secretary.

(D) For purposes of this section, in the case of any maritime industry, 125 days of service shall be treated as 1,000 hours of service. The Secretary may prescribe regulations to carry out the purposes of this subparagraph.

(4) A plan shall be treated as not meeting the requirements of paragraph (1) unless it provides that any employee who has satisfied the minimum age and service requirements specified in such paragraph, and who is otherwise entitled to participate in the plan, commences participation in the plan no later than the earlier of-

(A) the first day of the first plan year beginning after the date on which such employee satisfied such requirements, or

(B) the date 6 months after the date on which he satisfied such requirements,

unless such employee was separated from the service before the date referred to in subparagraph (A) or (B), whichever is applicable.

(b)(1) Except as otherwise provided in paragraphs (2), (3), and (4), all years of service with the employer or employers maintaining the plan shall be taken into account in computing the period of service for purposes of subsection (a)(1).

(2) In the case of any employee who has any 1-year break in service (as defined in section 1053(b)(3)(A) of this title [29 U.S.C. § 1053(b)(3)(A)]) under a plan to which the service requirements of clause (i) of subsection (a)(1)(B) apply, if such employee has not satisfied such requirements, service before such break shall not be required to be taken into account.

(3) In computing an employee's period of service for purposes of subsection (a)(1) in the case of any participant who has any 1-year break in service (as defined in section 1053(b)(3)(A) of this title [29 U.S.C. § 1053(b)(3)(A)]), service before such break shall not be required

to be taken into account under the plan until he has completed a year of service (as defined in subsection (a)(3)) after his return.

(4)(A) For purposes of paragraph (1), in the case of a nonvested participant, years of service with the employer or employers maintaining the plan before any period of consecutive 1-year breaks in service shall not be required to be taken into account in computing the period of service if the number of consecutive 1-year breaks in service within such period equals or exceeds the greater of-

(i) 5, or

(ii) the aggregate number of years of service before such period.

(B) If any years of service are not required to be taken into account by reason of a period of breaks in service to which subparagraph (A) applies, such years of service shall not be taken into account in applying subparagraph (A) to a subsequent period of breaks in service.

(C) For purposes of subparagraph (A), the term "nonvested participant" means a participant who does not have any nonforfeitable right under the plan to an accrued benefit derived from employer contributions.

(5)(A) In the case of each individual who is absent from work for any period-

(i) by reason of the pregnancy of the individual,

(ii) by reason of the birth of a child of the individual,

(iii) by reason of the placement of a child with the individual in connection with the adoption of such child by such individual, or

(iv) for purposes of caring for such child for a period beginning immediately following such birth or placement,

the plan shall treat as hours of service, solely for purposes of determining under this subsection whether a 1-year break in service (as defined in section 1053(b)(3)(A) of this title [29 U.S.C. § 1053(b)(3)(A)]) has occurred, the hours described in subparagraph (B).

(B) The hours described in this subparagraph are-

(i) the hours of service which otherwise would normally have been credited to such individual but for such absence, or

(ii) in any case in which the plan is unable to determine the hours described in clause (i), 8 hours of service per day of such absence,

except that the total number of hours treated as hours of service under this subparagraph by reason of any such pregnancy or placement shall not exceed 501 hours.

(C) The hours described in subparagraph (B) shall be treated as hours of service as provided in this paragraph-

(i) only in the year in which the absence from work begins, if a participant would be prevented from incurring a 1-year break in service in such year solely because the period of absence is treated as hours of service as provided in subparagraph (A); or

(ii) in any other case, in the immediately following year.

(D) For purposes of this paragraph, the term "year" means the period used in computations pursuant to subsection (a)(3)(A).

(E) A plan may provide that no credit will be given pursuant to this paragraph unless the individual furnishes to the plan administrator such timely information as the plan may reasonably require to establish-

(i) that the absence from work is for reasons referred to in subparagraph (A), and

(ii) the number of days for which there was such an absence.

§ 1053. Minimum vesting standards

(a) Nonforfeitability requirements

Each pension plan shall provide that an employee's right to his normal retirement benefit is nonforfeitable upon the attainment of normal retirement age and in addition shall satisfy the requirements of paragraphs (1) and (2) of this subsection.

(1) A plan satisfies the requirements of this paragraph if an employee's rights in his accrued benefit derived from his own contributions are nonforfeitable.

(2)(A)(i) In the case of a defined benefit plan, a plan satisfies the requirements of this paragraph if it satisfies the requirements of clause (ii) or (iii).

(ii) A plan satisfies the requirements of this clause if an employee who has completed at least 5 years of service has a nonforfeitable right to 100 percent of the employee's accrued benefit derived from employer contributions.

(iii) A plan satisfies the requirements of this clause if an employee has a nonforfeitable right to a percentage of the employee's accrued benefit derived from employer contributions determined under the following table:

Years of service:	The nonforfeitable percentage is:
3	20
4	40
5	60
6	80
7 or more	100.

(B)(i) In the case of an individual account plan, a plan satisfies the requirements of this paragraph if it satisfies the requirements of clause (ii) or (iii).

(ii) A plan satisfies the requirements of this clause if an employee who has completed at least 3 years of service has a nonforfeitable right to 100 percent of the employee's accrued benefit derived from employer contributions.

(iii) A plan satisfies the requirements of this clause if an employee has a nonforfeitable right to a percentage of the employee's accrued benefit derived from employer contributions determined under the following table:

Years of service:	The nonforfeitable percentage is:
2	20
3	40
4	60
5	80
6 or more	100.

(3)(A) A right to an accrued benefit derived from employer contributions shall not be treated as forfeitable solely because the plan provides that it is not payable if the participant dies (except in the case of a survivor annuity which is payable as provided in section 1055 of this title [29 U.S.C. § 1055]).

(B) A right to an accrued benefit derived from employer contributions shall not be treated as forfeitable solely because the plan provides that the payment of benefits is suspended for such period as the employee is employed, subsequent to the commencement of payment of such benefits-

(i) in the case of a plan other than a multiemployer plan, by an employer who maintains the plan under which such benefits were being paid; and

(ii) in the case of a multiemployer plan, in the same industry, in the same trade or craft, and the same geographic area covered by the plan, as when such benefits commenced.

The Secretary shall prescribe such regulations as may be necessary to carry out the purposes of this subparagraph, including regulations with respect to the meaning of the term "employed".

(C) A right to an accrued benefit derived from employer contributions shall not be treated as forfeitable solely because plan amendments may be given retroactive application as provided in section 1082(d)(2) of this title [29 U.S.C. § 1082(d)(2)].

(D)(i) A right to an accrued benefit derived from employer contributions shall not be treated as forfeitable solely because the plan provides that, in the case of a participant who does not have a nonforfeitable right to at least 50 percent of his accrued benefit derived from employer contributions, such accrued benefit may be forfeited on account of the withdrawal by the participant of any amount attributable to the benefit derived from mandatory contributions (as defined in the last sentence of section 1054(c)(2)(C) of this title [29 U.S.C. § 1054(c)(2)(C)]) made by such participant.

(ii) Clause (i) shall not apply to a plan unless the plan provides that any accrued benefit forfeited under a plan provision described in such clause shall be restored upon repayment by the participant of the full amount of the withdrawal described in such clause plus, in the case of a defined benefit plan, interest. Such interest shall be computed on such amount at the rate determined for purposes of section 1054(c)(2)(C) of this title [29 U.S.C. § 1054(c)(2)(C)](if such subsection applies) on the date of such repayment (computed annually from the date of such withdrawal). The plan provision required under this clause may provide that such repayment must be made (I) in the case of a withdrawal on account of separation from service, before the earlier of 5 years after the first date on which the participant is subsequently re-employed by the employer, or the close of the first period of 5 consecutive 1-year breaks in service commencing after the withdrawal; or (II) in the case of any other withdrawal, 5 years after the date of the withdrawal.

(iii) In the case of accrued benefits derived from employer contributions which accrued before September 2, 1974, a right to such accrued benefit derived from employer contributions shall not be treated as forfeitable solely because the plan provides that an amount of such accrued benefit may be forfeited on account of the withdrawal by the participant of an amount attributable to the benefit derived from mandatory contributions, made by such participant before September 2, 1974, if such amount forfeited is proportional to such amount withdrawn. This clause shall not apply to any plan to which any mandatory contribution is made after September 2, 1974. The Secretary of the Treasury shall prescribe such regulations as may be necessary to carry out the purposes of this clause.

(iv) For purposes of this subparagraph, in the case of any class-year plan, a withdrawal of employee contributions shall be treated as a withdrawal of such contributions on a plan year by plan year basis in succeeding order of time.

(v) Cross reference.

For nonforfeitability where the employee has a nonforfeitable right to at least 50 percent of his accrued benefit, see section 1056(c) of this title [29 U.S.C. § 1056(c)].

(E)(i) A right to an accrued benefit derived from employer contributions under a multiemployer plan shall not be treated as forfeitable solely because the plan provides that benefits accrued as a result of service with the participant's employer before the employer had an obligation to contribute under the plan may not be payable if the employer ceases contributions to the multiemployer plan.

(ii) A participant's right to an accrued benefit derived from employer contributions under a multiemployer plan shall not be treated as forfeitable solely because-

(I) the plan is amended to reduce benefits under section 1425* or 1441 of this title [29 U.S.C. §§ 1425, 1441], or

* Section 1425 of this title . . . was repealed by Pub. L. 113–235, div. O, title I, § 108(a)(1), Dec. 16, 2014, 128 Stat. 2786.

(II) benefit payments under the plan may be suspended under section 1426 or 1441 of this title [29 U.S.C. §§ 1426, 1441].

(F) A matching contribution (within the meaning of section 401(m) of title 26 [26 U.S.C. § 401(m)]) shall not be treated as forfeitable merely because such contribution is forfeitable if the contribution to which the matching contribution relates is treated as an excess contribution under section 401(k)(8)(B) of title 26 [26 U.S.C. § 401(k)(8)(B)], an excess deferral under section 402(g)(2)(A) of title 26 [26 U.S.C. § 402(g)(2)(A)], an erroneous automatic contribution under section 414(w) of title 26 [26 U.S.C. § 414(w)], or an excess aggregate contribution under section 401(m)(6)(B) of title 26 [26 U.S.C. § 401(m)(6)(B)].

(4) Repealed. Pub.L. 109–280, Title IX, § 904(b)(2), Aug. 17, 2006, 120 Stat. 1050

(b) Computation of period of service

(1) In computing the period of service under the plan for purposes of determining the nonforfeitable percentage under subsection (a)(2), all of an employee's years of service with the employer or employers maintaining the plan shall be taken into account, except that the following may be disregarded:

(A) years of service before age 18,

(B) years of service during a period for which the employee declined to contribute to a plan requiring employee contributions,

(C) years of service with an employer during any period for which the employer did not maintain the plan or a predecessor plan, defined by the Secretary of the Treasury;

(D) service not required to be taken into account under paragraph (3);

(E) years of service before January 1, 1971, unless the employee has had at least 3 years of service after December 31, 1970;

(F) years of service before this part first applies to the plan if such service would have been disregarded under the rules of the plan with regard to breaks in service, as in effect on the applicable date; and

(G) in the case of a multiemployer plan, years of service-

(i) with an employer after-

(I) a complete withdrawal of such employer from the plan (within the meaning of section 1383 of this title [29 U.S.C. § 1383]), or

(II) to the extent permitted by regulations prescribed by the Secretary of the Treasury, a partial withdrawal described in section 1385(b)(2)(A)(i) of this title [29 U.S.C. § 1385(b)(2)(A)(i)] in connection with the decertification of the collective bargaining representative; and

(ii) with any employer under the plan after the termination date of the plan under section 1348 of this title [29 U.S.C. § 1348].

(2)(A) For purposes of this section, except as provided in subparagraph (C), the term "year of service" means a calendar year, plan year, or other 12-consecutive month period designated by the plan (and not prohibited under regulations prescribed by the Secretary) during which the participant has completed 1,000 hours of service.

(B) For purposes of this section, the term "hour of service" has the meaning provided by section 1052(a)(3)(C) of this title [29 U.S.C. § 1052(a)(3)(C)].

(C) In the case of any seasonal industry where the customary period of employment is less than 1,000 hours during a calendar year, the term "year of service" shall be such period as determined under regulations of the Secretary.

(D) For purposes of this section, in the case of any maritime industry, 125 days of service shall be treated as 1,000 hours of service. The Secretary may prescribe regulations to carry out the purposes of this subparagraph.

(3)(A) For purposes of this paragraph, the term "1-year break in service" means a calendar year, plan year, or other 12-consecutive-month period designated by the plan (and not prohibited under regulations prescribed by the Secretary) during which the participant has not completed more than 500 hours of service.

(B) For purposes of paragraph (1), in the case of any employee who has any 1-year break in service, years of service before such break shall not be required to be taken into account until he has completed a year of service after his return.

(C) For purposes of paragraph (1), in the case of any participant in an individual account plan or an insured defined benefit plan which satisfies the requirements of subsection 1054(b)(1)(F) of this title [29 U.S.C. § 1054(b)(1)(F)] who has 5 consecutive 1-year breaks in service, years of service after such 5-year period shall not be required to be taken into account for purposes of determining the nonforfeitable percentage of his accrued benefit derived from employer contributions which accrued before such 5-year period.

(D)(i) For purposes of paragraph (1), in the case of a nonvested participant, years of service with the employer or employers maintaining the plan before any period of consecutive 1-year breaks in service shall not be required to be taken into account if the number of consecutive 1-year breaks in service within such period equals or exceeds the greater of-

(I) 5, or

(II) the aggregate number of years of service before such period.

(ii) If any years of service are not required to be taken into account by reason of a period of breaks in service to which clause (i) applies, such years of service shall not be taken into account in applying clause (i) to a subsequent period of breaks in service.

(iii) For purposes of clause (i), the term "nonvested participant" means a participant who does not have any nonforfeitable right under the plan to an accrued benefit derived from employer contributions.

(E)(i) In the case of each individual who is absent from work for any period-

(I) by reason of the pregnancy of the individual,

(II) by reason of the birth of a child of the individual,

(III) by reason of the placement of a child with the individual in connection with the adoption of such child by such individual, or

(IV) for purposes of caring for such child for a period beginning immediately following such birth or placement,

the plan shall treat as hours of service, solely for purposes of determining under this paragraph whether a 1-year break in service has occurred, the hours described in clause (ii).

(ii) The hours described in this clause are-

(I) the hours of service which otherwise would normally have been credited to such individual but for such absence, or

(II) in any case in which the plan is unable to determine the hours described in subclause (I), 8 hours of service per day of absence,

except that the total number of hours treated as hours of service under this clause by reason of such pregnancy or placement shall not exceed 501 hours.

(iii) The hours described in clause (ii) shall be treated as hours of service as provided in this subparagraph-

(I) only in the year in which the absence from work begins, if a participant would be prevented from incurring a 1-year break in service in such year solely because the period of absence is treated as hours of service as provided in clause (i); or

(II) in any other case, in the immediately following year.

(iv) For purposes of this subparagraph, the term "year" means the period used in computations pursuant to paragraph (2).

(v) A plan may provide that no credit will be given pursuant to this subparagraph unless the individual furnishes to the plan administrator such timely information as the plan may reasonably require to establish-

(I) that the absence from work is for reasons referred to in clause (i), and

(II) the number of days for which there was such an absence.

(4) Cross references

(A) For definitions of "accrued benefit" and "normal retirement age", see sections 1002(23) and (24) of this title [29 U.S.C. §§ 1002(23), 1002(24)].

(B) For effect of certain cash out distributions, see section 1054(d)(1) of this title [29 U.S.C. § 1054(d)(1)].

(c) Plan amendments altering vesting schedule

(1)(A) A plan amendment changing any vesting schedule under the plan shall be treated as not satisfying the requirements of subsection (a)(2) of this section if the nonforfeitable percentage of the accrued benefit derived from employer contributions (determined as of the later of the date such amendment is adopted, or the date such amendment becomes effective) of any employee who is a participant in the plan is less than such nonforfeitable percentage computed under the plan without regard to such amendment.

(B) A plan amendment changing any vesting schedule under the plan shall be treated as not satisfying the requirements of subsection (a)(2) unless each participant having not less than 3 years of service is permitted to elect, within a reasonable period after adoption of such amendment, to have his nonforfeitable percentage computed under the plan without regard to such amendment.

(2) Subsection (a) shall not apply to benefits which may not be provided for designated employees in the event of early termination of the plan under provisions of the plan adopted pursuant to regulations prescribed by the Secretary of the Treasury to preclude the discrimination prohibited by section 401(a)(4) of title 26 [26 U.S.C. § 401(a)(4)].

(d) Nonforfeitable benefits after lesser period and in greater amounts than required

A pension plan may allow for nonforfeitable benefits after a lesser period and in greater amounts than are required by this part.

(e) Consent for distribution; present value; covered distributions

(1) If the present value of any nonforfeitable benefit with respect to a participant in a plan exceeds $5,000, the plan shall provide that such benefit may not be immediately distributed without the consent of the participant.

(2) For purposes of paragraph (1), the present value shall be calculated in accordance with section 1055(g)(3) of this title [29 U.S.C. § 1055(g)(3)].

(3) This subsection shall not apply to any distribution of dividends to which section 404(k) of title 26 [26 U.S.C. § 404(k)] applies.

(4) A plan shall not fail to meet the requirements of this subsection if, under the terms of the plan, the present value of the nonforfeitable accrued benefit is determined without regard to that portion of such benefit which is attributable to rollover contributions (and earnings allocable thereto). For purposes of this subparagraph, the term "rollover contributions" means any rollover contribution under sections 402(c), 403(a)(4), 403(b)(8), 408(d)(3)(A)(ii), and 457(e)(16) of title 26 [26 U.S.C. §§ 402(c), 403(a)(4), 403(b)(8), 408(d)(3)(A)(ii), and 457(e)(16)].

(f) Special rules for plans computing accrued benefits by reference to hypothetical account balance or equivalent amounts

(1) In general

An applicable defined benefit plan shall not be treated as failing to meet-

(A) subject to paragraph (2), the requirements of subsection (a)(2), or

(B) the requirements of section 1054(c) or 1055(g) of this title [29 U.S.C. §§ 1054(c), 1055(g)], or the requirements of subsection (e), with respect to accrued benefits derived from employer contributions,

solely because the present value of the accrued benefit (or any portion thereof) of any participant is, under the terms of the plan, equal to the amount expressed as the balance in the hypothetical account described in paragraph (3) or as an accumulated percentage of the participant's final average compensation.

(2) 3-year vesting

In the case of an applicable defined benefit plan, such plan shall be treated as meeting the requirements of subsection (a)(2) only if an employee who has completed at least 3 years of service has a nonforfeitable right to 100 percent of the employee's accrued benefit derived from employer contributions.

(3) Applicable defined benefit plan and related rules

For purposes of this subsection-

(A) In general

The term "applicable defined benefit plan" means a defined benefit plan under which the accrued benefit (or any portion thereof) is calculated as the balance of a hypothetical account maintained for the participant or as an accumulated percentage of the participant's final average compensation.

(B) Regulations to include similar plans

The Secretary of the Treasury shall issue regulations which include in the definition of an applicable defined benefit plan any defined benefit plan (or any portion of such a plan) which has an effect similar to an applicable defined benefit plan.

§ 1054. Benefit accrual requirements

(a) Satisfaction of requirements by pension plans

Each pension plan shall satisfy the requirements of subsection (b)(3), and-

(1) in the case of a defined benefit plan, shall satisfy the requirements of subsection (b)(1); and

(2) in the case of a defined contribution plan, shall satisfy the requirements of subsection (b)(2).

(b) Enumeration of plan requirements

(1)(A) A defined benefit plan satisfies the requirements of this paragraph if the accrued benefit to which each participant is entitled upon his separation from the service is not less than-

(i) 3 percent of the normal retirement benefit to which he would be entitled at the normal retirement age if he commenced participation at the earliest possible entry age under the plan and served continuously until the earlier of age 65 or the normal retirement age specified under the plan, multiplied by

(ii) the number of years (not in excess of 33 1/3) of his participation in the plan.

In the case of a plan providing retirement benefits based on compensation during any period, the normal retirement benefit to which a participant would be entitled shall be determined as if he continued to earn annually the average rate of compensation which he earned during consecutive years of service, not in excess of 10, for which his compensation was the highest. For purposes of this subparagraph, social security benefits and all other relevant factors used to compute benefits shall be treated as remaining constant as of the current year for all years after such current year.

(B) A defined benefit plan satisfies the requirements of this paragraph of a particular plan year if under the plan the accrued benefit payable at the normal retirement age is equal to the normal retirement benefit and the annual rate at which any individual who is or could be a participant can accrue the retirement benefits payable at normal retirement age under the plan for any later plan year is not more than 133 1/3 percent of the annual rate at which he can accrue benefits for any plan year beginning on or after such particular plan year and before such later plan year. For purposes of this subparagraph-

(i) any amendment to the plan which is in effect for the current year shall be treated as in effect for all other plan years;

(ii) any change in an accrual rate which does not apply to any individual who is or could be a participant in the current year shall be disregarded;

(iii) the fact that benefits under the plan may be payable to certain employees before normal retirement age shall be disregarded; and

(iv) social security benefits and all other relevant factors used to compute benefits shall be treated as remaining constant as of the current year for all years after the current year.

(C) A defined benefit plan satisfies the requirements of this paragraph if the accrued benefit to which any participant is entitled upon his separation from the service is not less than a fraction of the annual benefit commencing at normal retirement age to which he would be entitled under the plan as in effect on the date of his separation if he continued to earn annually until normal retirement age the same rate of compensation upon which his normal retirement benefit would be computed under the plan, determined as if he had attained normal retirement age on the date any such determination is made (but taking into account no more than the 10 years of service immediately preceding his separation from service). Such fraction shall be a fraction, not exceeding 1, the numerator of which is the total number of his years of participation in the plan (as of the date of his separation from the service) and the denominator of which is the total number of years he would have participated in the plan if he separated from the service at the normal retirement age. For purposes of this subparagraph, social security benefits and all other relevant factors used to compute benefits shall be treated as remaining constant as of the current year for all years after such current year.

(D) Subparagraphs (A), (B), and (C) shall not apply with respect to years of participation before the first plan year to which this section applies but a defined benefit plan satisfies the requirements of this subparagraph with respect to such years of participation only if the accrued benefit of any participant with respect to such years of participation is not less than the greater of-

(i) his accrued benefit determined under the plan, as in effect from time to time prior to September 2, 1974, or

(ii) an accrued benefit which is not less than one-half of the accrued benefit to which such participant would have been entitled if subparagraph (A), (B), or (C) applied with respect to such years of participation.

(E) Notwithstanding subparagraphs (A), (B), and (C) of this paragraph, a plan shall not be treated as not satisfying the requirements of this paragraph solely because the accrual of benefits under the plan does not become effective until the employee has two continuous years of service. For purposes of this subparagraph, the term "year of service" has the meaning provided by section 1052(a)(3)(A) of this title [29 U.S.C. § 1052(a)(3)(A).

(F) Notwithstanding subparagraphs (A), (B), and (C), a defined benefit plan satisfies the requirements of this paragraph if such plan-

(i) is funded exclusively by the purchase of insurance contracts, and

(ii) satisfies the requirements of paragraphs (2) and (3) of section 1081(b) of this title [29 U.S.C. § 1081(b)](relating to certain insurance contract plans),

but only if an employee's accrued benefit as of any applicable date is not less than the cash surrender value his insurance contracts would have on such applicable date if the requirements of paragraphs (4), (5), and (6) of section 1081(b) of this title [29 U.S.C. § 1081(b)] were satisfied.

(G) Notwithstanding the preceding subparagraphs, a defined benefit plan shall be treated as not satisfying the requirements of this paragraph if the participant's accrued benefit is reduced on account of any increase in his age or service. The preceding sentence shall not apply to benefits under the plan commencing before benefits payable under title II of the Social Security Act [42 U.S.C. § 401 et seq.] which benefits under the plan-

(i) do not exceed social security benefits, and

(ii) terminate when such social security benefits commence.

(H)(i) Notwithstanding the preceding subparagraphs, a defined benefit plan shall be treated as not satisfying the requirements of this paragraph if, under the plan, an employee's benefit accrual is ceased, or the rate of an employee's benefit accrual is reduced, because of the attainment of any age.

(ii) A plan shall not be treated as failing to meet the requirements of this subparagraph solely because the plan imposes (without regard to age) a limitation on the amount of benefits that the plan provides or a limitation on the number of years of service or years of participation which are taken into account for purposes of determining benefit accrual under the plan.

(iii) In the case of any employee who, as of the end of any plan year under a defined benefit plan, has attained normal retirement age under such plan-

(I) if distribution of benefits under such plan with respect to such employee has commenced as of the end of such plan year, then any requirement of this subparagraph for continued accrual of benefits under such plan with respect to such employee during such plan year shall be treated as satisfied to the extent of the actuarial equivalent of in-service distribution of benefits, and

(II) if distribution of benefits under such plan with respect to such employee has not commenced as of the end of such year in accordance with section 1056(a)(3) of this title [29 U.S.C. § 1056(a)(3)], and the payment of benefits under such plan with respect to such employee is not suspended during such plan year pursuant to section 1053(a)(3)(B) of this title [29 U.S.C. § 1053(a)(3)(B)], then any requirement of this subparagraph for continued accrual of benefits under such plan with respect to such employee during such plan year shall be treated as satisfied to the extent of any adjustment in the benefit payable under the plan during such plan year attributable to the delay in the distribution of benefits after the attainment of normal retirement age.

The preceding provisions of this clause shall apply in accordance with regulations of the Secretary of the Treasury. Such regulations may provide for the application of the preceding provisions of this clause, in the case of any such employee, with respect to any period of time within a plan year.

(iv) Clause (i) shall not apply with respect to any employee who is a highly compensated employee (within the meaning of section 414(q) of title 26 [26 U.S.C. § 414(q)]) to the extent provided in regulations prescribed by the

Secretary of the Treasury for purposes of precluding discrimination in favor of highly compensated employees within the meaning of subchapter D of chapter 1 of title 26 [26 U.S.C. §§ 401 et seq.].

(v) A plan shall not be treated as failing to meet the requirements of clause (i) solely because the subsidized portion of any early retirement benefit is disregarded in determining benefit accruals.

(vi) Any regulations prescribed by the Secretary of the Treasury pursuant to clause (v) of section 411(b)(1)(H) of title 26 [26 U.S.C. § 411(b)(1)(H)] shall apply with respect to the requirements of this subparagraph in the same manner and to the same extent as such regulations apply with respect to the requirements of such section 411(b)(1)(H).

(2)(A) A defined contribution plan satisfies the requirements of this paragraph if, under the plan, allocations to the employee's account are not ceased, and the rate at which amounts are allocated to the employee's account is not reduced, because of the attainment of any age.

(B) A plan shall not be treated as failing to meet the requirements of subparagraph (A) solely because the subsidized portion of any early retirement benefit is disregarded in determining benefit accruals.

(C) Any regulations prescribed by the Secretary of the Treasury pursuant to subparagraphs (B) and (C) of section 411(b)(2) of title 26 [26 U.S.C. § 411(b)(2)] shall apply with respect to the requirements of this paragraph in the same manner and to the same extent as such regulations apply with respect to the requirements of such section 411(b)(2).

(3) A plan satisfies the requirements of this paragraph if-

(A) in the case of a defined benefit plan, the plan requires separate accounting for the portion of each employee's accrued benefit derived from any voluntary employee contributions permitted under the plan; and

(B) in the case of any plan which is not a defined benefit plan, the plan requires separate accounting for each employee's accrued benefit.

(4)(A) For purposes of determining an employee's accrued benefit, the term "year of participation" means a period of service (beginning at the earliest date on which the employee is a participant in the plan and which is included in a period of service required to be taken into account under section 1052(b) of this title [29 U.S.C. § 1052(b)], determined without regard to section 1052(b)(5) of this title [29 U.S.C. § 1052(b)(5)]) as determined under regulations prescribed by the Secretary which provide for the calculation of such period on any reasonable and consistent basis.

(B) For purposes of this paragraph, except as provided in subparagraph (C), in the case of any employee whose customary employment is less than full time, the calculation of such employee's service on any basis which provides less than a ratable portion of the accrued benefit to which he would be entitled under the plan if his customary employment were full time shall not be treated as made on a reasonable and consistent basis.

(C) For purposes of this paragraph, in the case of any employee whose service is less than 1,000 hours during any calendar year, plan year or other 12-consecutive-month period designated by the plan (and not prohibited under regulations prescribed by the Secretary) the calculation of his period of service shall not be treated as not made on a reasonable and consistent basis merely because such service is not taken into account.

(D) In the case of any seasonal industry where the customary period of employment is less than 1,000 hours during a calendar year, the term "year of participation" shall be such period as determined under regulations prescribed by the Secretary.

(E) For purposes of this subsection in the case of any maritime industry, 125 days of service shall be treated as a year of participation. The Secretary may prescribe regulations to carry out the purposes of this subparagraph.

(Subsections (b)(5) and (b)(6) omitted.)

(c) Employee's accrued benefits derived from employer and employee contributions

(1) For purposes of this section and section 1053 of this title [29 U.S.C. § 1053] an employee's accrued benefit derived from employer contributions as of any applicable date is the excess (if any) of the accrued benefit for such employee as of such applicable date over the accrued benefit derived from contributions made by such employee as of such date.

(2)(A) In the case of a plan other than a defined benefit plan, the accrued benefit derived from contributions made by an employee as of any applicable date is-

(i) except as provided in clause (ii), the balance of the employee's separate account consisting only of his contributions and the income, expenses, gains, and losses attributable thereto, or

(ii) if a separate account is not maintained with respect to an employee's contributions under such a plan, the amount which bears the same ratio to his total accrued benefit as the total amount of the employee's contributions (less withdrawals) bears to the sum of such contributions and the contributions made on his behalf by the employer (less withdrawals).

(B) Defined benefit plans.

In the case of a defined benefit plan, the accrued benefit derived from contributions made by an employee as of any applicable date is the amount equal to the employee's accumulated contributions expressed as an annual benefit commencing at normal retirement age, using an interest rate which would be used under the plan under section 1055(g)(3) of this title [29 U.S.C. § 1055(g)(3)] (as of the determination date).

(C) For purposes of this subsection, the term "accumulated contributions" means the total of-

(i) all mandatory contributions made by the employee,

(ii) interest (if any) under the plan to the end of the last plan year to which section 1053(a)(2) of this title [29 U.S.C. § 1053(a)(2)] does not apply (by reason of the applicable effective date), and

(iii) interest on the sum of the amounts determined under clauses (i) and (ii) compounded annually-

(I) at the rate of 120 percent of the Federal midterm rate (as in effect under section 1274 of title 26 [26 U.S.C. § 1274] for the 1st month of a plan year for the period beginning with the 1st plan year to which subsection (a)(2) of this section applies by reason of the applicable effective date) and ending with the date on which the determination is being made, and

(II) at the interest rate which would be used under the plan under section 1055(g)(3) of this title [29 U.S.C. § 1055(g)(3)](as of the determination date) for the period beginning with the determination date and ending on the date on which the employee attains normal retirement age.

For purposes of this subparagraph, the term "mandatory contributions" means amounts contributed to the plan by the employee which are required as a condition of employment, as a condition of participation in such plan, or as a condition of obtaining benefits under the plan attributable to employer contributions.

(D) The Secretary of the Treasury is authorized to adjust by regulation the conversion factor described in subparagraph (B) from time to time as he may deem necessary. No such adjustment shall be effective for a plan year beginning before the expiration of 1 year after such adjustment is determined and published.

(3) For purposes of this section, in the case of any defined benefit plan, if an employee's accrued benefit is to be determined as an amount other than an annual benefit commencing at normal retirement age, or if the accrued benefit derived from contributions made by an employee is to be determined with respect to a benefit other than an annual benefit in the form of a single life annuity (without ancillary benefits) commencing at normal retirement age, the employee's accrued benefit, or the accrued benefits derived from contributions made by an employee, as the case may be, shall be the actuarial equivalent of such benefit or amount determined under paragraph (1) or (2).

(4) In the case of a defined benefit plan which permits voluntary employee contributions, the portion of an employee's accrued benefit derived from such contributions shall be treated as an accrued benefit derived from employee contributions under a plan other than a defined benefit plan.

(d) Employee service which may be disregarded in determining employee's accrued benefits under plan

Notwithstanding section 1053(b)(1) of this title [29 U.S.C. § 1053(b)(1)], for purposes of determining the employee's accrued benefit under the plan, the plan may disregard service performed by the employee with respect to which he has received-

(1) a distribution of the present value of his entire nonforfeitable benefit if such distribution was in an amount (not more than the dollar limit under section 1053(e)(1) of this title [29 U.S.C. § 1053(e)(1)]) permitted under regulations prescribed by the Secretary of the Treasury, or

(2) a distribution of the present value of his nonforfeitable benefit attributable to such service which he elected to receive.

Paragraph (1) shall apply only if such distribution was made on termination of the employee's participation in the plan. Paragraph (2) shall apply only if such distribution was made on termination of the employee's participation in the plan or under such other circumstances as may be provided under regulations prescribed by the Secretary of the Treasury.

(e) Opportunity to repay full amount of distributions which have been reduced through disregarded employee service

For purposes of determining the employee's accrued benefit, the plan shall not disregard service as provided in subsection (d) unless the plan provides an opportunity for the participant to repay the full amount of a distribution described in subsection (d) with, in the case of a defined benefit plan, interest at the rate determined for purposes of subsection (c)(2)(C) and provides that upon such repayment the employee's accrued benefit shall be recomputed by taking into account service so disregarded. This subsection shall apply only in the case of a participant who-

(1) received such a distribution in any plan year to which this section applies which distribution was less than the present value of his accrued benefit,

(2) resumes employment covered under the plan, and

(3) repays the full amount of such distribution with, in the case of a defined benefit plan, interest at the rate determined for purposes of subsection (c)(2)(C).

The plan provision required under this subsection may provide that such repayment must be made (A) in the case of a withdrawal on account of separation from service, before the earlier of 5 years after the first date on which the participant is subsequently re-employed by the employer, or the close of the first period of 5 consecutive 1-year breaks in service commencing after the withdrawal; or (B) in the case of any other withdrawal, 5 years after the date of the withdrawal.

(f) Employer treated as maintaining a plan

For the purposes of this part, an employer shall be treated as maintaining a plan if any employee of such employer accrues benefits under such plan by reason of service with such employer.

(g) Decrease of accrued benefits through amendment of plan

(1) The accrued benefit of a participant under a plan may not be decreased by an amendment of the plan, other than an amendment described in section 1082(d)(2) or 1441 of this title [29 U.S.C. §§ 1082(d)(2), 1441].

(2) For purposes of paragraph (1), a plan amendment which has the effect of-

(A) eliminating or reducing an early retirement benefit or a retirement-type subsidy (as defined in regulations), or

(B) eliminating an optional form of benefit,

with respect to benefits attributable to service before the amendment shall be treated as reducing accrued benefits. In the case of a retirement-type subsidy, the preceding sentence shall apply only with respect to a participant who satisfies (either before or after the amendment) the preamendment conditions for the subsidy. The Secretary of the Treasury shall by regulations provide that this paragraph shall not apply to any plan amendment which reduces or eliminates benefits or subsidies which create significant burdens or complexities for the plan and plan participants, unless such amendment adversely affects the rights of any participant in a more than de minimis manner. The Secretary of the Treasury may by regulations provide that this subparagraph shall not apply to a plan amendment described in subparagraph (B) (other than a plan amendment having an effect described in subparagraph (A)).

(3) For purposes of this subsection, any-

(A) tax credit employee stock ownership plan (as defined in section 409(a) of title 26 [26 U.S.C. § 409(a)]), or

(B) employee stock ownership plan (as defined in section 4975(e)(7) of title 26 [26 U.S.C. § 4975(e)(7)]),

shall not be treated as failing to meet the requirements of this subsection merely because it modifies distribution options in a nondiscriminatory manner.

(4)(A) A defined contribution plan (in this subparagraph referred to as the "transferee plan") shall not be treated as failing to meet the requirements of this subsection merely because the transferee plan does not provide some or all of the forms of distribution previously available under another defined contribution plan (in this subparagraph referred to as the "transferor plan") to the extent that-

(i) the forms of distribution previously available under the transferor plan applied to the account of a participant or beneficiary under the transferor plan that was transferred from the transferor plan to the transferee plan pursuant to a direct transfer rather than pursuant to a distribution from the transferor plan;

(ii) the terms of both the transferor plan and the transferee plan authorize the transfer described in clause (i);

(iii) the transfer described in clause (i) was made pursuant to a voluntary election by the participant or beneficiary whose account was transferred to the transferee plan;

(iv) the election described in clause (iii) was made after the participant or beneficiary received a notice describing the consequences of making the election; and

(v) the transferee plan allows the participant or beneficiary described in clause (iii) to receive any distribution to which the participant or beneficiary is entitled under the transferee plan in the form of a single sum distribution.

(B) Subparagraph (A) shall apply to plan mergers and other transactions having the effect of a direct transfer, including consolidations of benefits attributable to different employers within a multiple employer plan.

(5) Except to the extent provided in regulations promulgated by the Secretary of the Treasury, a defined contribution plan shall not be treated as failing to meet the requirements of this subsection merely because of the elimination of a form of distribution previously available thereunder. This paragraph shall not apply to the elimination of a form of distribution with respect to any participant unless-

(A) a single sum payment is available to such participant at the same time or times as the form of distribution being eliminated; and

(B) such single sum payment is based on the same or greater portion of the participant's account as the form of distribution being eliminated.

(h) Notice of significant reduction in benefit accruals

(1) An applicable pension plan may not be amended so as to provide for a significant reduction in the rate of future benefit accrual unless the plan administrator provides the notice described in paragraph (2) to each applicable individual (and to each employee organization representing applicable individuals) and to each employer who has an obligation to contribute to the plan.

(2) The notice required by paragraph (1) shall be written in a manner calculated to be understood by the average plan participant and shall provide sufficient information (as determined in accordance with regulations prescribed by the Secretary of the Treasury) to allow applicable individuals to understand the effect of the plan amendment. The Secretary of the Treasury may provide a simplified form of notice for, or exempt from any notice requirement, a plan-

(A) which has fewer than 100 participants who have accrued a benefit under the plan, or

(B) which offers participants the option to choose between the new benefit formula and the old benefit formula.

(3) Except as provided in regulations prescribed by the Secretary of the Treasury, the notice required by paragraph (1) shall be provided within a reasonable time before the effective date of the plan amendment.

(4) Any notice under paragraph (1) may be provided to a person designated, in writing, by the person to which it would otherwise be provided.

(5) A plan shall not be treated as failing to meet the requirements of paragraph (1) merely because notice is provided before the adoption of the plan amendment if no material modification of the amendment occurs before the amendment is adopted.

(6)(A) In the case of any egregious failure to meet any requirement of this subsection with respect to any plan amendment, the provisions of the applicable pension plan shall be applied as if such plan amendment entitled all applicable individuals to the greater of-

(i) the benefits to which they would have been entitled without regard to such amendment, or

(ii) the benefits under the plan with regard to such amendment.

(B) For purposes of subparagraph (A), there is an egregious failure to meet the requirements of this subsection if such failure is within the control of the plan sponsor and is-

(i) an intentional failure (including any failure to promptly provide the required notice or information after the plan administrator discovers an unintentional failure to meet the requirements of this subsection),

(ii) a failure to provide most of the individuals with most of the information they are entitled to receive under this subsection, or

(iii) a failure which is determined to be egregious under regulations prescribed by the Secretary of the Treasury.

(7) The Secretary of the Treasury may by regulations allow any notice under this subsection to be provided by using new technologies.

(8) For purposes of this subsection-

(A) The term "applicable individual" means, with respect to any plan amendment-

(i) each participant in the plan; and

(ii) any beneficiary who is an alternate payee (within the meaning of section 1056(d)(3)(K) of this title [29 U.S.C. § 1056(d)(3)(K)]) under an applicable qualified domestic relations order (within the meaning of section 1056(d)(3)(B)(i) of this title [29 U.S.C. § 1056(d)(3)(B)(i)]),

whose rate of future benefit accrual under the plan may reasonably be expected to be significantly reduced by such plan amendment.

(B) The term "applicable pension plan" means-

(i) any defined benefit plan; or

(ii) an individual account plan which is subject to the funding standards of section 412 of title 26 [26 U.S.C. § 412].

(9) For purposes of this subsection, a plan amendment which eliminates or reduces any early retirement benefit or retirement-type subsidy (within the meaning of subsection (g)(2)(A)) shall be treated as having the effect of reducing the rate of future benefit accrual.

(Subsections (i) and (j) omitted.)

(§ 1055 through § 1085 omitted.)

§ 1101. Coverage

(a) Scope of coverage

This part shall apply to any employee benefit plan described in section 1003(a) of this title [29 U.S.C. § 1003(a)] (and not exempted under section 1003(b) of this title [29 U.S.C. § 1003(b)]), other than-

(1) a plan which is unfunded and is maintained by an employer primarily for the purpose of providing deferred compensation for a select group of management or highly compensated employees; or

(2) any agreement described in section 736 of title 26 [26 U.S.C. § 736], which provides payments to a retired partner or deceased partner or a deceased partner's successor in interest.

(b) Securities or policies deemed to be included in plan assets

For purposes of this part:

(1) In the case of a plan which invests in any security issued by an investment company registered under the Investment Company Act of 1940 [15 U.S.C. § 80a–1 et seq.], the assets of such plan shall be deemed to include such security but shall not, solely by reason of such investment, be deemed to include any assets of such investment company.

(2) In the case of a plan to which a guaranteed benefit policy is issued by an insurer, the assets of such plan shall be deemed to include such policy, but shall not, solely by reason of the issuance of such policy, be deemed to include any assets of such insurer. For purposes of this paragraph:

(A) The term "insurer" means an insurance company, insurance service, or insurance organization, qualified to do business in a State.

(B) The term "guaranteed benefit policy" means an insurance policy or contract to the extent that such policy or contract provides for benefits the amount of which is guaranteed by the insurer. Such term includes any surplus in a separate account, but excludes any other portion of a separate account.

(c) Clarification of application of ERISA to insurance company general accounts * * *

§ 1102. Establishment of plan

(a) Named fiduciaries

(1) Every employee benefit plan shall be established and maintained pursuant to a written instrument. Such instrument shall provide for one or more named fiduciaries who jointly or severally shall have authority to control and manage the operation and administration of the plan.

(2) For purposes of this subchapter, the term "named fiduciary" means a fiduciary who is named in the plan instrument, or who, pursuant to a procedure specified in the plan, is identified as a fiduciary (A) by a person who is an employer or employee organization with respect to the plan or (B) by such an employer and such an employee organization acting jointly.

(b) Requisite features of plan

Every employee benefit plan shall-

(1) provide a procedure for establishing and carrying out a funding policy and method consistent with the objectives of the plan and the requirements of this subchapter,

(2) describe any procedure under the plan for the allocation of responsibilities for the operation and administration of the plan (including any procedure described in section 1105(c)(1) of this title [29 U.S.C. § 1105(c)(1)]),

(3) provide a procedure for amending such plan, and for identifying the persons who have authority to amend the plan, and

(4) specify the basis on which payments are made to and from the plan.

(c) Optional features of plan

Any employee benefit plan may provide-

(1) that any person or group of persons may serve in more than one fiduciary capacity with respect to the plan (including service both as trustee and administrator);

(2) that a named fiduciary, or a fiduciary designated by a named fiduciary pursuant to a plan procedure described in section 1105(c)(1) of this title [29 U.S.C. § 1105(c)(1)], may employ one or more persons to render advice with regard to any responsibility such fiduciary has under the plan; or

(3) that a person who is a named fiduciary with respect to control or management of the assets of the plan may appoint an investment manager or managers to manage (including the power to acquire and dispose of) any assets of a plan.

§ 1103. Establishment of trust

(a) Benefit plan assets to be held in trust; authority of trustees

Except as provided in subsection (b), all assets of an employee benefit plan shall be held in trust by one or more trustees. Such trustee or trustees shall be either named in the trust instrument or in the plan instrument described in section 1102(a) of this title [29 U.S.C. § 1102(a)] or appointed by a person who is a named fiduciary, and upon acceptance of being named or appointed, the trustee or trustees shall have exclusive authority and discretion to manage and control the assets of the plan, except to the extent that-

(1) the plan expressly provides that the trustee or trustees are subject to the direction of a named fiduciary who is not a trustee, in which case the trustees shall be subject to proper directions of such fiduciary which are made in accordance with the terms of the plan and which are not contrary to this chapter, or

(2) authority to manage, acquire, or dispose of assets of the plan is delegated to one or more investment managers pursuant to section 1102(c)(3) of this title [29 U.S.C. § 1102(c)(3)].

(b) Exceptions

The requirements of subsection (a) of this section shall not apply-

(1) to any assets of a plan which consist of insurance contracts or policies issued by an insurance company qualified to do business in a State;

(2) to any assets of such an insurance company or any assets of a plan which are held by such an insurance company;

(3) to a plan-

(A) some or all of the participants of which are employees described in section 401(c)(1) of title 26 [26 U.S.C. § 401(c)(1)]; or

(B) which consists of one or more individual retirement accounts described in section 408 of title 26 [26 U.S.C. § 408];

to the extent that such plan's assets are held in one or more custodial accounts which qualify under section 401(f) or 408(h) of title 26 [26 U.S.C. §§ 401(f), 408(h)], whichever is applicable.

(4) to a plan which the Secretary exempts from the requirement of subsection (a) and which is not subject to any of the following provisions of this chapter-

(A) part 2 of this subtitle [29 U.S.C. §§ 1051–1061],

(B) part 3 of this subtitle [29 USCS §§ 1081–1085a], or

(C) subchapter III of this chapter [29 U.S.C. §§ 1301–1453]; or

(5) to a contract established and maintained under section 403(b) of title 26 [26 U.S.C. § 403(b)] to the extent that the assets of the contract are held in one or more custodial accounts pursuant to section 403(b)(7) of title 26 [26 U.S.C. § 403(b)(7)].

(6) Any plan, fund or program under which an employer, all of whose stock is directly or indirectly owned by employees, former employees or their beneficiaries, proposes through an unfunded arrangement to compensate retired employees for benefits which were forfeited by such employees under a pension plan maintained by a former employer prior to the date such pension plan became subject to this chapter.

(c) Assets of plan not to inure to benefit of employer; allowable purposes of holding plan assets

(1) Except as provided in paragraph (2), (3), or (4)* or subsection (d), or under sections 1342 and 1344 of this title [29 U.S.C. §§ 1342, 1344] (relating to termination of insured plans), or under section 420 of title 26 [26 U.S.C. § 420](as in effect on December 29, 2022), the assets of a plan shall never inure to the benefit of any employer and shall be held for the exclusive purposes of providing benefits to

* The official version's "references in text" notation states that the original paragraph (3) here referenced was struck and the original paragraph (4) was redesignated as paragraph (3) by Pub. L. 101–239, title VII, § 7881(k), Dec. 19, 1989, 103 Stat. 2443. As such, the reference here to "paragraph (2), (3), or (4)" should only be "paragraph (2) or (3)."

participants in the plan and their beneficiaries and defraying reasonable expenses of administering the plan.

(2)(A) In the case of a contribution, or a payment of withdrawal liability under part 1 of subtitle E of subchapter III [29 U.S.C. §§ 1381–1405]-

(i) if such contribution or payment is made by an employer to a plan (other than a multiemployer plan) by a mistake of fact, paragraph (1) shall not prohibit the return of such contribution to the employer within one year after the payment of the contribution, and

(ii) if such contribution or payment is made by an employer to a multiemployer plan by a mistake of fact or law (other than a mistake relating to whether the plan is described in section 401(a) of title 26 [26 U.S.C. § 401(a)] or the trust which is part of such plan is exempt from taxation under section 501(a) of title 26 [26 U.S.C. § 501(a)]), paragraph (1) shall not prohibit the return of such contribution or payment to the employer within 6 months after the plan administrator determines that the contribution was made by such a mistake.

(B) If a contribution is conditioned on initial qualification of the plan under section 401 or 403(a) of title 26 [26 U.S.C. §§ 401, 403(a)], and if the plan receives an adverse determination with respect to its initial qualification, then paragraph (1) shall not prohibit the return of such contribution to the employer within one year after such determination, but only if the application for the determination is made by the time prescribed by law for filing the employer's return for the taxable year in which such plan was adopted, or such later date as the Secretary of the Treasury may prescribe.

(C) If a contribution is conditioned upon the deductibility of the contribution under section 404 of title 26 [26 U.S.C. § 404], then, to the extent the deduction is disallowed, paragraph (1) shall not prohibit the return to the employer of such contribution (to the extent disallowed) within one year after the disallowance of the deduction.

(3) In the case of a withdrawal liability payment which has been determined to be an overpayment, paragraph (1) shall not prohibit the return of such payment to the employer within 6 months after the date of such determination.

(d) Termination of plan

(1) Upon termination of a pension plan to which section 1321 of this title [29 U.S.C. § 1321] does not apply at the time of termination and to which this part applies (other than a plan to which no employer contributions have been made) the assets of the plan shall be allocated in accordance with the provisions of section 1344 of this title [29 U.S.C. § 1344], except as otherwise provided in regulations of the Secretary.

(2) The assets of a welfare plan which terminates shall be distributed in accordance with the terms of the plan, except as otherwise provided in regulations of the Secretary.

§ 1104. Fiduciary duties

(a) Prudent man standard of care

(1) Subject to sections 1103(c) and (d), 1342, and 1344 of this title [29 U.S.C. §§ 1103(c), 1103(d), 1342, 1344], a fiduciary shall discharge his duties with respect to a plan solely in the interest of the participants and beneficiaries and-

(A) for the exclusive purpose of:

(i) providing benefits to participants and their beneficiaries; and

(ii) defraying reasonable expenses of administering the plan;

(B) with the care, skill, prudence, and diligence under the circumstances then prevailing that a prudent man acting in a like capacity and familiar with such matters would use in the conduct of an enterprise of a like character and with like aims;

(C) by diversifying the investments of the plan so as to minimize the risk of large losses, unless under the circumstances it is clearly prudent not to do so; and

(D) in accordance with the documents and instruments governing the plan insofar as such documents and instruments are consistent with the provisions of this subchapter [29 U.S.C. §§ 1001–1193c] and subchapter III [29 U.S.C. §§ 1301–1461].

(2) In the case of an eligible individual account plan (as defined in section 1107(d)(3) of this title [29 U.S.C. § 1107(d)(3)]), the diversification requirement of paragraph (1)(C) and the prudence requirement (only to the extent that it requires diversification) of paragraph (1)(B) is not violated by acquisition or holding of qualifying employer real property or qualifying employer securities (as defined in section 1107(d)(4) and (5) of this title [29 U.S.C. § 1107(d)(4), (5)]).

(b) Indicia of ownership of assets outside jurisdiction of district courts

Except as authorized by the Secretary by regulations, no fiduciary may maintain the indicia of ownership of any assets of a plan outside the jurisdiction of the district courts of the United States.

(c) Control over assets by participant or beneficiary

(1)(A) In the case of a pension plan which provides for individual accounts and permits a participant or beneficiary to exercise control over the assets in his account, if a participant or beneficiary exercises control over the assets in his account (as determined under regulations of the Secretary)-

(i) such participant or beneficiary shall not be deemed to be a fiduciary by reason of such exercise, and

(ii) no person who is otherwise a fiduciary shall be liable under this part for any loss, or by reason of any breach, which results from such participant's or beneficiary's exercise of control except that this clause shall not apply in connection with such participant or beneficiary for any blackout period during which the ability of such participant or beneficiary to direct the investment of the assets in his or her account is suspended by a plan sponsor or fiduciary.

(B) If a person referred to in subparagraph (A)(ii) meets the requirements of this subchapter in connection with authorizing and implementing the blackout period, any person who is otherwise a fiduciary shall not be liable under this subchapter for any loss occurring during such period

(C) For purposes of this paragraph, the term "blackout period" has the meaning given such term by section 1021(i)(7) of this title [29 U.S.C. § 1021(i)(7)].

(2) In the case of a simple retirement account established pursuant to a qualified salary reduction arrangement under section 408(p) of title 26 [26 U.S.C. § 408(p)], a participant or beneficiary shall, for purposes of paragraph (1), be treated as exercising control over the assets in the account upon the earliest of-

(A) an affirmative election among investment options with respect to the initial investment of any contribution,

(B) a rollover to any other simple retirement account or individual retirement plan, or

(C) one year after the simple retirement account is established.

No reports, other than those required under section 1021(g) of this title [29 U.S.C. § 1021(g)], shall be required with respect to a simple retirement account established pursuant to such a qualified salary reduction arrangement.

(3) In the case of a pension plan which makes a transfer to an individual retirement account or annuity of a designated trustee or issuer under section 401(a)(31)(B) of title 26 [26 U.S.C. § 401(a)(31)(B)], the participant or beneficiary shall, for purposes of paragraph (1), be treated as exercising control over the assets in the account or annuity upon-

(A) the earlier of-

(i) a rollover of all or a portion of the amount to another individual retirement account or annuity; or

(ii) one year after the transfer is made; or

(B) a transfer that is made in a manner consistent with guidance provided by the Secretary.

(4)(A) In any case in which a qualified change in investment options occurs in connection with an individual account plan, a participant or beneficiary shall not be treated for purposes of paragraph (1) as not exercising control over the assets in his account in connection with such change if the requirements of subparagraph (C) are met in connection with such change.

(B) For purposes of subparagraph (A), the term "qualified change in investment options" means, in connection with an individual account plan, a change in the investment options offered to the participant or beneficiary under the terms of the plan, under which-

(i) the account of the participant or beneficiary is reallocated among one or more remaining or new investment options which are offered in lieu of one or more investment options offered immediately prior to the effective date of the change, and

(ii) the stated characteristics of the remaining or new investment options provided under clause (i), including characteristics relating to risk and rate of return, are, as of immediately after the change, reasonably similar to those of the existing investment options as of immediately before the change.

(C) The requirements of this subparagraph are met in connection with a qualified change in investment options if-

(i) at least 30 days and no more than 60 days prior to the effective date of the change, the plan administrator furnishes written notice of the change to the participants and beneficiaries, including information comparing the existing and new investment options and an explanation that, in the absence of affirmative investment instructions from the participant or beneficiary to the contrary, the account of the participant or beneficiary will be invested in the manner described in subparagraph (B),

(ii) the participant or beneficiary has not provided to the plan administrator, in advance of the effective date of the change, affirmative investment instructions contrary to the change, and

(iii) the investments under the plan of the participant or beneficiary as in effect immediately prior to the effective date of the change were the product of the exercise by such participant or beneficiary of control over the assets of the account within the meaning of paragraph (1).

(5) Default investment arrangements.

(A) In general.

For purposes of paragraph (1), a participant or beneficiary in an individual account plan meeting the notice requirements of subparagraph (B) shall be treated as exercising control over the assets in the account with respect to the amount of contributions and earnings which, in the absence of an investment election by the participant or beneficiary, are invested by the plan in accordance with regulations prescribed by the Secretary. The regulations under this subparagraph shall provide guidance on the appropriateness of designating default investments that include a mix of asset classes consistent with capital preservation or long-term capital appreciation, or a blend of both.

(B) Notice requirements.

(i) In general.

The requirements of this subparagraph are met if each participant or beneficiary-

(I) receives, within a reasonable period of time before each plan year, a notice explaining the employee's right under the plan to designate how contributions and earnings will be invested and explaining how, in the absence of any investment election by the participant or beneficiary, such contributions and earnings will be invested, and

(II) has a reasonable period of time after receipt of such notice and before the beginning of the plan year to make such designation.

(ii) Form of notice.

The requirements of clauses (i) and (ii) of section 401(k)(12)(D) of title 26 [26 U.S.C. § 401(k)(12)(D)] shall apply with respect to the notices described in this subparagraph.

(6) Default investment arrangements for a pension-linked emergency savings account.

For purposes of paragraph (1), a participant in a pension-linked emergency savings account shall be treated as exercising control over the assets in the account with respect to the amount of contributions and earnings which are invested in accordance with section 1193(c)(1)(A)(iii) of this title [29 U.S.C. § 1193(c)(1)(A)(iii)].

(d) Plan terminations

(1) If, in connection with the termination of a pension plan which is a single-employer plan, there is an election to establish or maintain a qualified replacement plan, or to increase benefits, as provided under section 4980(d) of title 26 [26 U.S.C. § 4980(d)], a fiduciary shall discharge the fiduciary's duties under this subchapter [29 U.S.C. §§ 1001–1193c] and subchapter III of this chapter [29 U.S.C. §§ 1301–1461] in accordance with the following requirements:

(A) In the case of a fiduciary of the terminated plan, any requirement-

(i) under section 4980(d)(2)(B) of title 26 [26 U.S.C. § 4980(d)(2)(B)] with respect to the transfer of assets from the terminated plan to a qualified replacement plan, and

(ii) under section 4980(d)(2)(B)(ii) or 4980(d)(3) of title 26 [26 U.S.C. §§ 4980(d)(2)(B)(ii), 4980(d)(3)] with respect to any increase in benefits under the terminated plan.

(B) In the case of a fiduciary of a qualified replacement plan, any requirement-

(i) under section 4980(d)(2)(A) of title 26 [26 U.S.C. § 4980(d)(2)(A)] with respect to participation in the qualified replacement plan of active participants in the terminated plan,

(ii) under section 4980(d)(2)(B) of title 26 [26 U.S.C. § 4980(d)(2)(B)] with respect to the receipt of assets from the terminated plan, and

(iii) under section 4980(d)(2)(C) of title 26 [26 U.S.C. § 4980(d)(2)(C)] with respect to the allocation of assets to participants of the qualified replacement plan.

(2) For purposes of this subsection-

(A) any term used in this subsection which is also used in section 4980(d) of title 26 [26 U.S.C. § 4980(d)] shall have the same meaning as when used in such section, and

(B) any reference in this subsection to title 26 shall be a reference to title 26 as in effect immediately after the enactment of the Omnibus Budget Reconciliation Act of 1990 [Pub. L. 101–508, Nov. 5, 1990,104 Stat. 1388].

(e) Safe harbor for annuity selection

(1) In general

With respect to the selection of an insurer for a guaranteed retirement income contract, the requirements of subsection (a)(1)(B) will be deemed to be satisfied if a fiduciary-

(A) engages in an objective, thorough, and analytical search for the purpose of identifying insurers from which to purchase such contracts;

(B) with respect to each insurer identified under subparagraph (A)-

(i) considers the financial capability of such insurer to satisfy its obligations under the guaranteed retirement income contract; and

(ii) considers the cost (including fees and commissions) of the guaranteed retirement income contract offered by the insurer in relation to the benefits and product features of the contract and administrative services to be provided under such contract; and

(C) on the basis of such consideration, concludes that-

(i) at the time of the selection, the insurer is financially capable of satisfying its obligations under the guaranteed retirement income contract; and

(ii) the relative cost of the selected guaranteed retirement income contract as described in subparagraph (B)(ii) is reasonable.

(2) Financial capability of the insurer

A fiduciary will be deemed to satisfy the requirements of paragraphs (1)(B)(i) and (1)(C)(i) if-

(A) the fiduciary obtains written representations from the insurer that-

(i) the insurer is licensed to offer guaranteed retirement income contracts;

(ii) the insurer, at the time of selection and for each of the immediately preceding 7 plan years-

(I) operates under a certificate of authority from the insurance commissioner of its domiciliary State which has not been revoked or suspended;

(II) has filed audited financial statements in accordance with the laws of its domiciliary State under applicable statutory accounting principles;

(III) maintains (and has maintained) reserves which satisfies all the statutory requirements of all States where the insurer does business; and

(IV) is not operating under an order of supervision, rehabilitation, or liquidation;

(iii) the insurer undergoes, at least every 5 years, a financial examination (within the meaning of the law of its domiciliary State) by the insurance commissioner of the domiciliary State (or representative, designee, or other party approved by such commissioner); and

(iv) the insurer will notify the fiduciary of any change in circumstances occurring after the provision of the representations in clauses (i), (ii), and (iii) which would preclude the insurer from making such representations at the time of issuance of the guaranteed retirement income contract; and

(B) after receiving such representations and as of the time of selection, the fiduciary has not received any notice described in subparagraph (A)(iv) and is in possession of no other information which would cause the fiduciary to question the representations provided.

(3) No requirement to select lowest cost

Nothing in this subsection shall be construed to require a fiduciary to select the lowest cost contract. A fiduciary may consider the value of a contract, including features and benefits of the contract and attributes of the insurer (including, without limitation, the insurer's financial strength) in conjunction with the cost of the contract.

(4) Time of selection

(A) In general

For purposes of this subsection, the time of selection is-

(i) the time that the insurer and the contract are selected for distribution of benefits to a specific participant or beneficiary; or

(ii) if the fiduciary periodically reviews the continuing appropriateness of the conclusion described in paragraph (1)(C) with respect to a selected insurer, taking into account the considerations described in such paragraph, the time that the insurer and the contract are selected to provide benefits at future dates to participants or beneficiaries under the plan.

Nothing in the preceding sentence shall be construed to require the fiduciary to review the appropriateness of a selection after the purchase of a contract for a participant or beneficiary.

(B) Periodic review

A fiduciary will be deemed to have conducted the periodic review described in subparagraph (A)(ii) if the fiduciary obtains the written representations described in clauses (i), (ii), and (iii) of paragraph (2)(A) from the insurer on an annual basis, unless the fiduciary receives any notice described in paragraph (2)(A)(iv) or otherwise becomes aware of facts that would cause the fiduciary to question such representations.

(5) Limited liability

A fiduciary which satisfies the requirements of this subsection shall not be liable following the distribution of any benefit, or the investment by or on behalf of a participant or beneficiary pursuant to the selected guaranteed retirement income contract, for any losses that may result to the participant or beneficiary due to an insurer's inability to satisfy its financial obligations under the terms of such contract.

(6) Definitions

For purposes of this subsection-

(A) Insurer

The term "insurer" means an insurance company, insurance service, or insurance organization, including affiliates of such companies.

(B) Guaranteed retirement income contract

The term "guaranteed retirement income contract" means an annuity contract for a fixed term or a contract (or provision or feature thereof) which provides guaranteed benefits annually (or more frequently) for at least the remainder of the life of the participant or the joint lives of the participant and the participant's designated beneficiary as part of an individual account plan.

§ 1105. Liability for breach of co-fiduciary

(a) Circumstances giving rise to liability

In addition to any liability which he may have under any other provision of this part, a fiduciary with respect to a plan shall be liable for a breach of fiduciary responsibility of another fiduciary with respect to the same plan in the following circumstances:

(1) if he participates knowingly in, or knowingly undertakes to conceal, an act or omission of such other fiduciary, knowing such act or omission is a breach;

(2) if, by his failure to comply with section 1104(a)(1) of this title [29 U.S.C. § 1104(a)(1)] in the administration of his specific responsibilities which give rise to his status as a fiduciary, he has enabled such other fiduciary to commit a breach; or

(3) if he has knowledge of a breach by such other fiduciary, unless he makes reasonable efforts under the circumstances to remedy the breach.

(b) Assets held by two or more trustees

(1) Except as otherwise provided in subsection (d) and in section 1103(a)(1) and (2) of this title [29 U.S.C. § 1103(a)(1), (a)(2)], if the assets of a plan are held by two or more trustees-

(A) each shall use reasonable care to prevent a co-trustee from committing a breach; and

(B) they shall jointly manage and control the assets of the plan, except that nothing in this subparagraph (B) shall preclude any agreement, authorized by the trust instrument, allocating specific responsibilities, obligations, or duties among trustees, in which event a trustee to whom certain responsibilities, obligations, or duties have not been allocated shall not be liable by reason of this subparagraph (B) either individually or as a trustee for any loss resulting to the plan arising from the acts or omissions on the part of another trustee to whom such responsibilities, obligations, or duties have been allocated.

(2) Nothing in this subsection shall limit any liability that a fiduciary may have under subsection (a) or any other provision of this part.

(3)(A) In the case of a plan the assets of which are held in more than one trust, a trustee shall not be liable under paragraph (1) except with respect to an act or omission of a trustee of a trust of which he is a trustee.

(B) No trustee shall be liable under this subsection for following instructions referred to in section 1103(a)(1) of this title [29 U.S.C. § 1103(a)(1)].

(c) Allocation of fiduciary responsibility; designated persons to carry out fiduciary responsibilities

(1) The instrument under which a plan is maintained may expressly provide for procedures (A) for allocating fiduciary responsibilities (other than trustee responsibilities) among named fiduciaries, and (B) for named fiduciaries to designate persons other than named fiduciaries to carry out fiduciary responsibilities (other than trustee responsibilities) under the plan.

(2) If a plan expressly provides for a procedure described in paragraph (1), and pursuant to such procedure any fiduciary responsibility of a named fiduciary is allocated to any person, or a person is designated to carry out any such responsibility, then such named fiduciary shall not be liable for an act or omission of such person in carrying out such responsibility except to the extent that-

(A) the named fiduciary violated section 1104(a)(1) of this title [29 U.S.C. § 1104(a)(1)]-

(i) with respect to such allocation or designation,

(ii) with respect to the establishment or implementation of the procedure under paragraph (1), or

(iii) in continuing the allocation or designation; or

(B) the named fiduciary would otherwise be liable in accordance with subsection (a).

(3) For purposes of this subsection, the term "trustee responsibility" means any responsibility provided in the plan's trust instrument (if any) to manage or control the assets of the plan, other than a power under the trust instrument of a named fiduciary to appoint an investment manager in accordance with section 1102(c)(3) of this title [29 U.S.C. § 1102(c)(3)].

(d) Investment managers

(1) If an investment manager or managers have been appointed under section 1102(c)(3) of this title [29 U.S.C. § 1102(c)(3)], then, notwithstanding subsections (a)(2) and (3) and subsection (b), no trustee shall be liable for the acts or omissions of such investment manager or managers, or be under an obligation to invest or otherwise manage any asset of the plan which is subject to the management of such investment manager.

(2) Nothing in this subsection shall relieve any trustee of any liability under this part for any act of such trustee.

§ 1106. Prohibited transactions

(a) Transactions between plan and party in interest

Except as provided in section 1108 of this title [29 U.S.C. § 1108]:

(1) A fiduciary with respect to a plan shall not cause the plan to engage in a transaction, if he knows or should know that such transaction constitutes a direct or indirect-

(A) sale or exchange, or leasing, of any property between the plan and a party in interest;

(B) lending of money or other extension of credit between the plan and a party in interest;

(C) furnishing of goods, services, or facilities between the plan and a party in interest;

(D) transfer to, or use by or for the benefit of a party in interest, of any assets of the plan; or

(E) acquisition, on behalf of the plan, of any employer security or employer real property in violation of section 1107(a) of this title [29 U.S.C. § 1107(a)].

(2) No fiduciary who has authority or discretion to control or manage the assets of a plan shall permit the plan to hold any employer security or employer real property if he knows or should know that holding such security or real property violates section 1107(a) of this title [29 U.S.C. § 1107(a)].

(b) Transactions between plan and fiduciary

A fiduciary with respect to a plan shall not-

(1) deal with the assets of the plan in his own interest or for his own account,

(2) in his individual or in any other capacity act in any transaction involving the plan on behalf of a party (or represent a party) whose interests are adverse to the interests of the plan or the interests of its participants or beneficiaries, or

(3) receive any consideration for his own personal account from any party dealing with such plan in connection with a transaction involving the assets of the plan.

(c) Transfer of real or personal property to plan by party in interest

A transfer of real or personal property by a party in interest to a plan shall be treated as a sale or exchange if the property is subject to a mortgage or similar lien which the plan assumes or if it is subject to a mortgage or similar lien which a party-in-interest placed on the property within the 10-year period ending on the date of the transfer.

§ 1107. Limitation with respect to acquisition and holding of employer securities and employer real property by certain plans

(a) Percentage limitation

Except as otherwise provided in this section and section 1114 of this title [29 U.S.C. § 1114]:

(1) A plan may not acquire or hold-

(A) any employer security which is not a qualifying employer security, or

(B) any employer real property which is not qualifying employer real property.

(2) A plan may not acquire any qualifying employer security or qualifying employer real property, if immediately after such acquisition the aggregate fair market value of employer securities and employer real property held by the plan exceeds 10 percent of the fair market value of the assets of the plan.

(3)(A) After December 31, 1984, a plan may not hold any qualifying employer securities or qualifying employer real property (or both) to the extent that the aggregate fair market value of such securities and property determined on December 31, 1984, exceeds 10 percent of the greater of-

(i) the fair market value of the assets of the plan, determined on December 31, 1984, or

(ii) the fair market value of the assets of the plan determined on January 1, 1975.

(B) Subparagraph (A) of this paragraph shall not apply to any plan which on any date after December 31, 1974; and before January 1, 1985, did not hold employer securities or employer real property (or both) the aggregate fair market value of which determined on such date exceeded 10 percent of the greater of

(i) the fair market value of the assets of the plan, determined on such date, or

(ii) the fair market value of the assets of the plan determined on January 1, 1975.

(4)(A) After December 31, 1979, a plan may not hold any employer securities or employer real property in excess of the amount specified in regulations under subparagraph (B). This subparagraph shall not apply to a plan after the earliest date after December 31, 1974, on which it complies with such regulations.

(B) Not later than December 31, 1976, the Secretary shall prescribe regulations which shall have the effect of requiring that a plan divest itself of 50 percent of the holdings of employer securities and employer real property which the plan would be required to divest before January 1, 1985, under paragraph (2) or subsection (c) of this section (whichever is applicable).

(b) Exception

(1) Subsection (a) of this section shall not apply to any acquisition or holding of qualifying employer securities or qualifying employer real property by an eligible individual account plan.

(2)(A) If this paragraph applies to an eligible individual account plan, the portion of such plan which consists of applicable elective deferrals (and earnings allocable thereto) shall be treated as a separate plan-

(i) which is not an eligible individual account plan, and

(ii) to which the requirements of this section apply.

(B)(i) This paragraph shall apply to any eligible individual account plan if any portion of the plan's applicable elective deferrals (or earnings allocable thereto) are required to be invested in qualifying employer securities or qualifying employer real property or both-

(I) pursuant to the terms of the plan, or

(II) at the direction of a person other than the participant on whose behalf such elective deferrals are made to the plan (or a beneficiary).

(ii) This paragraph shall not apply to an individual account plan for a plan year if, on the last day of the preceding plan year, the fair market value of the assets of all individual account plans maintained by the employer equals not more than 10 percent of the fair market value of the assets of all pension plans (other than multiemployer plans) maintained by the employer.

(iii) This paragraph shall not apply to an individual account plan that is an employee stock ownership plan as defined in section 4975(e)(7) of title 26 [26 U.S.C. § 4975(e)(7)].

(iv) This paragraph shall not apply to an individual account plan if, pursuant to the terms of the plan, the portion of any employee's applicable elective deferrals which is required to be invested in qualifying employer securities and qualifying employer real property for any year may not exceed 1 percent of the employee's compensation which is taken into account under the plan in determining the maximum amount of the employee's applicable elective deferrals for such year.

(C) For purposes of this paragraph, the term "applicable elective deferral" means any elective deferral (as defined in section 402(g)(3)(A) of title 26 [26 U.S.C. § 402(g)(3)(A)]) which is made pursuant to a qualified cash or deferred arrangement as defined in section 401(k) of title 26 [26 U.S.C. § 401(k)].

(3) Cross references * * *

(c) Election * * *

(d) Definitions

For purposes of this section-

(1) The term "employer security" means a security issued by an employer of employees covered by the plan, or by an affiliate of such employer. A contract to which section 1108(b)(5) of this title [29 U.S.C. § 1108(b)(5)] applies shall not be treated as a security for purposes of this section.

(2) The term "employer real property" means real property (and related personal property) which is leased to an employer of employees covered by the plan, or to an affiliate of such employer. For purposes of determining the time at which a plan acquires employer real property for purposes of this section, such property shall be deemed to be acquired by the plan on the date on which the plan acquires the property or on the date on which the lease to the employer (or affiliate) is entered into, whichever is later.

(3)(A) The term "eligible individual account plan" means an individual account plan which is (i) a profit-sharing, stock bonus, thrift, or savings plan; (ii) an employee stock ownership plan; or (iii) a money purchase plan which was in existence on September 2, 1974, and which on such date invested primarily in qualifying employer securities. Such term excludes an individual retirement account or annuity described in section 408 of title 26 [26 U.S.C. § 408].

(B) Notwithstanding subparagraph (A), a plan shall be treated as an eligible individual account plan with respect to the acquisition or holding of qualifying employer real property or qualifying employer securities only if such plan explicitly provides for acquisition and holding of qualifying employer securities or qualifying employer real property (as the case may be). * * *

(C) The term "eligible individual account plan" does not include any individual account plan the benefits of which are taken into account in determining the benefits payable to a participant under any defined benefit plan.

(4) The term "qualifying employer real property" means parcels of employer real property-

(A) if a substantial number of the parcels are dispersed geographically;

(B) if each parcel of real property and the improvements thereon are suitable (or adaptable without excessive cost) for more than one use;

(C) even if all of such real property is leased to one lessee (which may be an employer, or an affiliate of an employer); and

(D) if the acquisition and retention of such property comply with the provisions of this part (other than section 1104(a)(1)(B) of this title [29 U.S.C. § 1104(a)(1)(B)] to the extent it requires diversification, and sections 1104(a)(1)(C), 1106 of this title [29 U.S.C. §§ 1104(a)(1)(C), 1106], and subsection (a) of this section).

(5) The term "qualifying employer security" means an employer security which is-

(A) stock,

(B) a marketable obligation (as defined in subsection (e)), or

(C) an interest in a publicly traded partnership (as defined in section 7704(b) of title 26 [26 U.S.C. § 7704(b)]), but only if such partnership is an existing partnership as defined in section 10211(c)(2)(A) of the Revenue Act of 1987 (Public Law 100–203).

After December 17, 1987, in the case of a plan other than an eligible individual account plan, an employer security described in subparagraph (A) or (C) shall be considered a qualifying employer security only if such employer security satisfies the requirements of subsection (f)(1).

(6) The term "employee stock ownership plan" means an individual account plan-

(A) which is a stock bonus plan which is qualified, or a stock bonus plan and money purchase plan both of which are qualified, under section 401 of title 26 [26 U.S.C. § 401], and which is designed to invest primarily in qualifying employer securities, and

(B) which meets such other requirements as the Secretary of the Treasury may prescribe by regulation.

(7) A corporation is an affiliate of an employer if it is a member of any controlled group of corporations (as defined in section 1563(a) of title 26 [26 U.S.C. § 1563(a)], except that "applicable percentage" shall be substituted for "80 percent" wherever the latter percentage appears in such section) of which the employer who maintains the plan is a member. For purposes of the preceding sentence, the term "applicable percentage" means 50 percent, or such lower percentage as the Secretary may prescribe by regulation. A person other than a corporation shall be treated as an affiliate of an employer to the extent provided in regulations of the Secretary. An employer which is a person other than a corporation shall be treated as affiliated with another person to the extent provided by regulations of the Secretary. Regulations under this paragraph shall be prescribed only after consultation and coordination with the Secretary of the Treasury.

(8) The Secretary may prescribe regulations specifying the extent to which conversions, splits, the exercise of rights, and similar transactions are not treated as acquisitions.

(9) For purposes of this section, an arrangement which consists of a defined benefit plan and an individual account plan shall be treated as 1 plan if the benefits of such individual account plan are taken into account in determining the benefits payable under such defined benefit plan.

(e) Marketable obligations

For purposes of subsection (d)(5), the term "marketable obligation" means a bond, debenture, note, or certificate, or other evidence of indebtedness (hereinafter in this subsection referred to as "obligation") if-

(1) such obligation is acquired-

(A) on the market, * * *

(B) from an underwriter, at a price (i) not in excess of the public offering price for the obligation * * * and (ii) at which a substantial portion of the same issue is acquired by persons independent of the issuer; or

(C) directly from the issuer, at a price not less favorable to the plan than the price paid currently for a substantial portion of the same issue by persons independent of the issuer;

(2) immediately following acquisition of such obligation-

(A) not more than 25 percent of the aggregate amount of obligations issued in such issue and outstanding at the time of acquisition is held by the plan, and

(B) at least 50 percent of the aggregate amount referred to in subparagraph (A) is held by persons independent of the issuer; and

(3) immediately following acquisition of the obligation, not more than 25 percent of the assets of the plan is invested in obligations of the employer or an affiliate of the employer.

(f) Maximum percentage of stock held by plan; time of holding or acquisition; necessity of legally binding contract

(1) Stock satisfies the requirements of this paragraph if, immediately following the acquisition of such stock-

(A) no more than 25 percent of the aggregate amount of stock of the same class issued and outstanding at the time of acquisition is held by the plan, and

(B) at least 50 percent of the aggregate amount referred to in subparagraph (A) is held by persons independent of the issuer.

(2) Until January 1, 1993, a plan shall not be treated as violating subsection (a) solely by holding stock which fails to satisfy the requirements of paragraph (1) if such stock-

(A) has been so held since December 17, 1987, or

(B) was acquired after December 17, 1987, pursuant to a legally binding contract in effect on December 17, 1987, and has been so held at all times after the acquisition.

(§ 1108. Exemptions from prohibited transactions, omitted.)

§ 1109. Liability for breach of fiduciary duty

(a) Any person who is a fiduciary with respect to a plan who breaches any of the responsibilities, obligations, or duties imposed upon fiduciaries by this subchapter shall be personally liable to make good to such plan any losses to the plan resulting from each such breach, and to restore to such plan any profits of such fiduciary which have been made through use of assets of the plan by the fiduciary, and shall be subject to such other equitable or remedial relief as the court may deem appropriate, including removal of such fiduciary. A fiduciary may also be removed for a violation of section 1111 of this title [29 U.S.C. § 1111].

(b) No fiduciary shall be liable with respect to a breach of fiduciary duty under this subchapter if such breach was committed before he became a fiduciary or after he ceased to be a fiduciary.

(§ 1110 through § 1114 omitted.)

§ 1131. Criminal penalties

(a) Any person who willfully violates any provision of part 1 of this subtitle, or any regulation or order issued under any such provision, shall upon conviction be fined not more than $100,000 or imprisoned not more than 10 years, or both; except that in the case of such violation by a person not an individual, the fine imposed upon such person shall be a fine not exceeding $500,000.

(b) Any person that violates section 1149 of this title [29 U.S.C. § 1149] shall upon conviction be imprisoned not more than 10 years or fined under title 18, or both.

§ 1132. Civil enforcement

(a) Persons empowered to bring a civil action

A civil action may be brought-

(1) by a participant or beneficiary-

(A) for the relief provided for in subsection (c) of this section, or

(B) to recover benefits due to him under the terms of his plan, to enforce his rights under the terms of the plan, or to clarify his rights to future benefits under the terms of the plan;

(2) by the Secretary, or by a participant, beneficiary or fiduciary for appropriate relief under section 1109 of this title [29 U.S.C. § 1109];

(3) by a participant, beneficiary, or fiduciary (A) to enjoin any act or practice which violates any provision of this subchapter or the terms of the plan, or (B) to obtain other appropriate equitable relief (i) to redress such violations or (ii) to enforce any provisions of this subchapter or the terms of the plan;

(4) by the Secretary, or by a participant, or beneficiary for appropriate relief in the case of a violation of 1025(c) or 1032(a) of this title [29 U.S.C. §§ 1025(c), 1032(a)];

(5) except as otherwise provided in subsection (b), by the Secretary (A) to enjoin any act or practice which violates any provision of this

subchapter, or (B) to obtain other appropriate equitable relief (i) to redress such violation or (ii) to enforce any provision of this subchapter;

(6) by the Secretary to collect any civil penalty under paragraph (2), (4), (5), (6), (7), (8), or (9) of subsection (c) or under subsection (i) or (*l*);

(7) by a State to enforce compliance with a qualified medical child support order (as defined in section 1169(a)(2)(A) of this title [29 U.S.C. § 1169(a)(2)(A)]);

(8) by the Secretary, or by an employer or other person referred to in section 1021(f)(1) of this title [29 U.S.C. § 1021(f)(1)], (A) to enjoin any act or practice which violates subsection (f) of section 1021 of this title [29 U.S.C. § 1021(f)], or (B) to obtain appropriate equitable relief (i) to redress such violation or (ii) to enforce such subsection;

(9) in the event that the purchase of an insurance contract or insurance annuity in connection with termination of an individual's status as a participant covered under a pension plan with respect to all or any portion of the participant's pension benefit under such plan constitutes a violation of part 4 of this title or the terms of the plan, by the Secretary, by any individual who was a participant or beneficiary at the time of the alleged violation, or by a fiduciary, to obtain appropriate relief, including the posting of security if necessary, to assure receipt by the participant or beneficiary of the amounts provided or to be provided by such insurance contract or annuity, plus reasonable prejudgment interest on such amounts.

(10) in the case of a multiemployer plan that has been certified by the actuary to be in endangered or critical status under section 1085 of this title [29 U.S.C. § 1085], if the plan sponsor-

(A) has not adopted a funding improvement or rehabilitation plan under that section by the deadline established in such section, or

(B) fails to update or comply with the terms of the funding improvement or rehabilitation plan in accordance with the requirements of such section,

by an employer that has an obligation to contribute with respect to the multiemployer plan or an employee organization that represents active participants in the multiemployer plan, for an order compelling the plan sponsor to adopt a funding improvement or rehabilitation plan or to update or comply with the terms of the funding improvement or rehabilitation plan in accordance with the requirements of such section and the funding improvement or rehabilitation plan; or

(11) in the case of a multiemployer plan, by an employee representative, or any employer that has an obligation to contribute to the plan, (A) to enjoin any act or practice which violates subsection (k) of section 1021 of this title [29 U.S.C. § 1021](or, in the case of an employer, subsection (*l*) of such section), or (B) to obtain appropriate equitable relief (i) to redress such violation or (ii) to enforce such subsection.

(b) Plans qualified under Internal Revenue Code; maintenance of actions involving delinquent contributions

(1) In the case of a plan which is qualified under section 401(a), 403(a), or 405(a)* of title 26 [26 U.S.C. §§ 401(a), 403(a), 405(a)](or with respect to which an application to so qualify has been filed and has not been finally determined) the Secretary may exercise his authority under subsection (a)(5) with respect to a violation of, or the enforcement of, parts 2 and 3 of this subtitle (relating to participation, vesting, and funding), only if-

(A) requested by the Secretary of the Treasury, or

(B) one or more participants, beneficiaries, or fiduciaries, of such plan request in writing (in such manner as the Secretary shall prescribe by regulation) that he exercise such authority on their behalf. * * *

(2) The Secretary shall not initiate an action to enforce section 1145 of this title [29 U.S.C. § 1145].

(3) Except as provided in subsections (c)(9) and (a)(6) (with respect to collecting civil penalties under subsection (c)(9)), the Secretary is not authorized to enforce under this part any requirement of part 7 against a health insurance issuer offering health insurance coverage in connection with a group health plan (as defined in section 1191b(a)(1) of this title [29 U.S.C. § 1191b(a)(1)]). Nothing in this paragraph shall affect the authority of the Secretary to issue regulations to carry out such part.

(c) Administrator's refusal to supply requested information; penalty for failure to provide annual report in complete form

(1) Any administrator (A) who fails to meet the requirements of paragraph (1) or (4) of section 1166† of this title, section 1021(e)(1) of this title, section 1021(f) of this title, section 1025(a) of this title, or section 1032(a) of this title [29 U.S.C. §§ 1021(e)(1), 1021(f), 1025(a), 1032(a), 1166] with respect to a participant or beneficiary, or (B) who

---

* 16 U.S.C. § 405(a) was repealed by Pub. L. 98–369, div. A, title IV, § 491(a), July 18, 1984, 98 Stat. 848.

† Paragraphs (1) and (4) of § 1166 were redesignated as pars. (1) and (4) of § 1166(a) of this title by Pub. L. 101–239, title VII, § 7891(d)(1)(A)(ii)(I), Dec. 19, 1989, 103 Stat. 2445.

fails or refuses to comply with a request for any information which such administrator is required by this subchapter to furnish to a participant or beneficiary (unless such failure or refusal results from matters reasonably beyond the control of the administrator) by mailing the material requested to the last known address of the requesting participant or beneficiary within 30 days after such request may in the court's discretion be personally liable to such participant or beneficiary in the amount of up to $100 a day from the date of such failure or refusal, and the court may in its discretion order such other relief as it deems proper. For purposes of this paragraph, each violation described in subparagraph (A) with respect to any single participant, and each violation described in subparagraph (B) with respect to any single participant or beneficiary, shall be treated as a separate violation.

(2) The Secretary may assess a civil penalty against any plan administrator of up to $1,000 a day from the date of such plan administrator's failure or refusal to file the annual report required to be filed with the Secretary under section 1021(b)(1) of this title [29 U.S.C. § 1021(b)(1)]. For purposes of this paragraph, an annual report that has been rejected under section 1024(a)(4) of this title [29 U.S.C. § 1024(a)(4)] for failure to provide material information shall not be treated as having been filed with the Secretary.

(3) Any employer maintaining a plan who fails to meet the notice requirement of section 1021(d) of this title [29 U.S.C. § 1021(d)] with respect to any participant or beneficiary or who fails to meet the requirements of section 1021(e)(2) of this title [29 U.S.C. § 1021(e)(2)] with respect to any person or who fails to meet the requirements of section 1082(d)(12)(E) of this title [29 U.S.C. § 1082] with respect to any person may in the court's discretion be liable to such participant or beneficiary or to such person in the amount of up to $100 a day from the date of such failure, and the court may in its discretion order such other relief as it deems proper.

(4) The Secretary may assess a civil penalty of not more than $1,000 a day for each violation by any person of subsection (j), (k), or (*l*) of section 1021 of this title or section 1144(e)(3) of this title [29 U.S.C. §§ 1021, 1144(e)(3)].

(5) The Secretary may assess a civil penalty against any person of up to $1,000 a day from the date of the person's failure or refusal to file the information required to be filed by such person with the Secretary under regulations prescribed pursuant to section 1021(g) of this title [29 U.S.C. § 1021(g)].

(6) If, within 30 days of a request by the Secretary to a plan administrator for documents under section 1024(a)(6) of this title [29

U.S.C. § 1024(a)(6)], the plan administrator fails to furnish the material requested to the Secretary, the Secretary may assess a civil penalty against the plan administrator of up to $100 a day from the date of such failure (but in no event in excess of $1,000 per request). No penalty shall be imposed under this paragraph for any failure resulting from matters reasonably beyond the control of the plan administrator.

(7) * * *

(d) Status of employee benefit plan as entity

(1) An employee benefit plan may sue or be sued under this subchapter as an entity. Service of summons, subpoena, or other legal process of a court upon a trustee or an administrator of an employee benefit plan in his capacity as such shall constitute service upon the employee benefit plan. In a case where a plan has not designated in the summary plan description of the plan an individual as agent for the service of legal process, service upon the Secretary shall constitute such service. The Secretary, not later than 15 days after receipt of service under the preceding sentence, shall notify the administrator or any trustee of the plan of receipt of such service.

(2) * * *

(e) Jurisdiction

(1) Except for actions under subsection (a)(1)(B) of this section, the district courts of the United States shall have exclusive jurisdiction of civil actions under this subchapter brought by the Secretary or by a participant, beneficiary, fiduciary, or any person referred to in section 1021(f)(1) of this title [29 U.S.C. § 1021(f)(1)]. State courts of competent jurisdiction and district courts of the United States shall have concurrent jurisdiction of actions under paragraphs (1)(B) and (7) of subsection (a) of this section.

(2) Where an action under this subchapter is brought in a district court of the United States, it may be brought in the district where the plan is administered, where the breach took place, or where a defendant resides or may be found, and process may be served in any other district where a defendant resides or may be found.

(f) Amount in controversy; citizenship of parties

The district courts of the United States shall have jurisdiction, without respect to the amount in controversy or the citizenship of the parties, to grant the relief provided for in subsection (a) of this section in any action.

(g) Attorney's fees and costs; awards in actions involving delinquent contributions

(1) In any action under this subchapter (other than an action described in paragraph (2)) by a participant, beneficiary, or fiduciary, the court in its discretion may allow a reasonable attorney's fee and costs of action to either party.

(2) In any action under this subchapter by a fiduciary for or on behalf of a plan to enforce section 1145 of this title [29 U.S.C. § 1145] in which a judgment in favor of the plan is awarded, the court shall award the plan-

(A) the unpaid contributions,

(B) interest on the unpaid contributions,

(C) an amount equal to the greater of-

(i) interest on the unpaid contributions, or

(ii) liquidated damages provided for under the plan in an amount not in excess of 20 percent (or such higher percentage as may be permitted under Federal or State law) of the amount determined by the court under subparagraph (A),

(D) reasonable attorney's fees and costs of the action, to be paid by the defendant, and

(E) such other legal or equitable relief as the court deems appropriate.

For purposes of this paragraph, interest on unpaid contributions shall be determined by using the rate provided under the plan, or, if none, the rate prescribed under section 6621 of title 26 [26 U.S.C. § 6621].

(h) Service upon Secretary of Labor and Secretary of the Treasury

A copy of the complaint in any action under this subchapter by a participant, beneficiary, or fiduciary (other than an action brought by one or more participants or beneficiaries under subsection (a)(1)(B) which is solely for the purpose of recovering benefits due such participants under the terms of the plan) shall be served upon the Secretary and the Secretary of the Treasury by certified mail. Either Secretary shall have the right in his discretion to intervene in any action, except that the Secretary of the Treasury may not intervene in any action under part 4 of this subtitle. If the Secretary brings an action under subsection (a) of this section on behalf of a participant or beneficiary, he shall notify the Secretary of the Treasury.

(i) Administrative assessment of civil penalty

In the case of a transaction prohibited by section 1106 of this title [29 U.S.C. § 1106] by a party in interest with respect to a plan to which this part applies, the Secretary may assess a civil penalty against such party in interest. The amount of such penalty may not exceed 5 percent of the amount involved in each such transaction (as defined in section 4975(f)(4) of title 26 [26 U.S.C. § 4975(f)(4)]) for each year or part thereof during which the prohibited transaction continues, except that, if the transaction is not corrected (in such manner as the Secretary shall prescribe in regulations which shall be consistent with section 4975(f)(5) of title 26 [26 U.S.C. § 4975(f)(5)]) within 90 days after notice from the Secretary (or such longer period as the Secretary may permit), such penalty may be in an amount not more than 100 percent of the amount involved. This subsection shall not apply to a transaction with respect to a plan described in section 4975(e)(1) of title 26 [26 U.S.C. § 4975(e)(1)].

(j) Direction and control of litigation by Attorney General

* * *

(k) Jurisdiction of actions against the Secretary of Labor

Suits by an administrator, fiduciary, participant, or beneficiary of an employee benefit plan to review a final order of the Secretary, to restrain the Secretary from taking any action contrary to the provisions of this chapter, or to compel him to take action required under this subchapter, may be brought in the district court of the United States for the district where the plan has its principal office, or in the United States District Court for the District of Columbia.

(*l*) Civil penalties on violations by fiduciaries

(1) In the case of-

(A) any breach of fiduciary responsibility under (or other violation of) part 4 of this subtitle by a fiduciary, or

(B) any knowing participation in such a breach or violation by any other person,

the Secretary shall assess a civil penalty against such fiduciary or other person in an amount equal to 20 percent of the applicable recovery amount.

(2) For purposes of paragraph (1), the term "applicable recovery amount" means any amount which is recovered from a fiduciary or other person with respect to a breach or violation described in paragraph (1)-

(A) pursuant to any settlement agreement with the Secretary, or

(B) ordered by a court to be paid by such fiduciary or other person to a plan or its participants and beneficiaries in a judicial proceeding instituted by the Secretary under subsection (a)(2) or (a)(5).

(3) The Secretary may, in the Secretary's sole discretion, waive or reduce the penalty under paragraph (1) if the Secretary determines in writing that-

(A) the fiduciary or other person acted reasonably and in good faith, or

(B) it is reasonable to expect that the fiduciary or other person will not be able to restore all losses to the plan (or to provide the relief ordered pursuant to subsection (a)(9)) without severe financial hardship unless such waiver or reduction is granted.

(4) The penalty imposed on a fiduciary or other person under this subsection with respect to any transaction shall be reduced by the amount of any penalty or tax imposed on such fiduciary or other person with respect to such transaction under subsection (i) of this section and section 4975 of title 26 [26 U.S.C. § 4975].

(m) Penalty for improper distribution

In the case of a distribution to a pension plan participant or beneficiary in violation of section 1056(e) of this title [29 U.S.C. § 1056(e)] by a plan fiduciary, the Secretary shall assess a penalty against such fiduciary in an amount equal to the value of the distribution. Such penalty shall not exceed $10,000 for each such distribution.

(§§ 1133–1139 omitted.)

§ 1140. Interference with protected rights

It shall be unlawful for any person to discharge, fine, suspend, expel, discipline, or discriminate against a participant or beneficiary for exercising any right to which he is entitled under the provisions of an employee benefit plan, this subchapter, section 1201 of this title [29 U.S.C. § 1201], or the Welfare and Pension Plans Disclosure Act [29 U.S.C. § 301 et seq.], or for the purpose of interfering with the attainment of any right to which such participant may become entitled under the plan, this subchapter, or the Welfare and Pension Plans Disclosure Act. It shall be unlawful for any person to discharge, fine, suspend, expel, or discriminate against any person because he has given information or has testified or is about to testify in any inquiry or proceeding relating to this chapter or the Welfare and Pension Plans Disclosure Act. In the case of a multiemployer plan, it shall be unlawful for the plan sponsor or any other person to discriminate against any contributing employer for exercising rights under this chapter or for giving information or testifying in any inquiry or proceeding relating to this chapter before Congress. The provisions of section 1132 of this title [29 U.S.C. § 1201] shall be applicable in the enforcement of this section.

(§§ 1141–1193c, 1201–1242, 1301–1323 omitted.)

§ 1341. Termination of single-employer plans

(a) General rules governing single-employer plan terminations

(1) Exclusive means of plan termination

Except in the case of a termination for which proceedings are otherwise instituted by the corporation as provided in section 1342 of this title [29 U.S.C. § 1342], a single-employer plan may be terminated only in a standard termination under subsection (b) or a distress termination under subsection (c).

(2) 60-day notice of intent to terminate

Not less than 60 days before the proposed termination date of a standard termination under subsection (b) or a distress termination under subsection (c), the plan administrator shall provide to each affected party (other than the corporation in the case of a standard termination) a written notice of intent to terminate stating that such termination is intended and the proposed termination date. The written notice shall include any related additional information required in regulations of the corporation.

(3) Adherence to collective bargaining agreements

The corporation shall not proceed with a termination of a plan under this section if the termination would violate the terms and conditions of an existing collective bargaining agreement. Nothing in the preceding sentence shall be construed as limiting the authority of the corporation to institute proceedings to involuntarily terminate a plan under section 1342 of this title [29 U.S.C. § 1342].

(b) Standard termination of single-employer plans

(1) General requirements

A single-employer plan may terminate under a standard termination only if-

(A) the plan administrator provides the 60-day advance notice of intent to terminate to affected parties required under subsection (a)(2),

(B) the requirements of subparagraphs (A) and (B) of paragraph (2) are met,

(C) the corporation does not issue a notice of noncompliance under subparagraph (C) of paragraph (2), and

(D) when the final distribution of assets occurs, the plan is sufficient for benefit liabilities (determined as of the termination date).

(2) Termination procedure

(A) Notice to the corporation

As soon as practicable after the date on which the notice of intent to terminate is provided pursuant to subsection (a)(2), the plan administrator shall send a notice to the corporation setting forth-

(i) certification by an enrolled actuary-

(I) of the projected amount of the assets of the plan (as of a proposed date of final distribution of assets),

(II) of the actuarial present value (as of such date) of the benefit liabilities (determined as of the proposed termination date) under the plan, and

(III) that the plan is projected to be sufficient (as of such proposed date of final distribution) for such benefit liabilities,

(ii) such information as the corporation may prescribe in regulations as necessary to enable the corporation to make determinations under subparagraph (C), and

(iii) certification by the plan administrator that-

(I) the information on which the enrolled actuary based the certification under clause (i) is accurate and complete, and

(II) the information provided to the corporation under clause (ii) is accurate and complete.

Clause (i) and clause (iii)(I) shall not apply to a plan described in section 412(i) of title 26 [26 U.S.C. § 412].

(B) Notice to participants and beneficiaries of benefit commitments*

No later than the date on which a notice is sent by the plan administrator under subparagraph (A), the plan administrator shall send a notice to each person who is a participant or beneficiary under the plan-

(i) specifying the amount of the benefit liabilities (if any) attributable to such person as of the proposed termination date and the benefit form on the basis of which such amount is determined, and

(ii) including the following information used in determining such benefit liabilities:

(I) the length of service,

(II) the age of the participant or beneficiary,

(III) wages,

* Official comment: "So in original. Probably should be 'benefit liabilities'."

(IV) the assumptions, including the interest rate, and

(V) such other information as the corporation may require.

Such notice shall be written in such manner as is likely to be understood by the participant or beneficiary and as may be prescribed in regulations of the corporation.

(C) Notice from the corporation of noncompliance

(i) In general

Within 60 days after receipt of the notice under subparagraph (A), the corporation shall issue a notice of noncompliance to the plan administrator if-

(I) it determines, based on the notice sent under paragraph (2)(A) of subsection (b), that there is reason to believe that the plan is not sufficient for benefit liabilities,

(II) it otherwise determines, on the basis of information provided by affected parties or otherwise obtained by the corporation, that there is reason to believe that the plan is not sufficient for benefit liabilities, or

(III) it determines that any other requirement of subparagraph (A) or (B) of this paragraph or of subsection (a)(2) has not been met, unless it further determines that the issuance of such notice would be inconsistent with the interests of participants and beneficiaries.

(ii) Extension

The corporation and the plan administrator may agree to extend the 60-day period referred to in clause (i) by a written agreement signed by the corporation and the plan administrator before the expiration of the 60-day period. The 60-day period shall be extended as provided in the agreement and may be further extended by subsequent written agreements signed by the corporation and the plan administrator made before the expiration of a previously agreed upon extension of the 60-day period. Any extension may be made upon such terms and conditions (including the payment of benefits) as are agreed upon by the corporation and the plan administrator.

(D) Final distribution of assets in absence of notice of noncompliance

The plan administrator shall commence the final distribution of assets pursuant to the standard termination of the plan as soon as practicable after the expiration of the 60-day (or extended) period referred to in subparagraph (C), but such final distribution may occur only if-

(i) the plan administrator has not received during such period a notice of noncompliance from the corporation under subparagraph (C), and

(ii) when such final distribution occurs, the plan is sufficient for benefit liabilities (determined as of the termination date).

(3) Methods of final distribution of assets

(A) In general

In connection with any final distribution of assets pursuant to the standard termination of the plan under this subsection, the plan administrator shall distribute the assets in accordance with section 1344 of this title [29 U.S.C. § 1344]. In distributing such assets, the plan administrator shall-

(i) purchase irrevocable commitments from an insurer to provide all benefit liabilities under the plan, or

(ii) in accordance with the provisions of the plan and any applicable regulations, otherwise fully provide all benefit liabilities under the plan. A transfer of assets to the corporation in accordance with section 1350 of this title [29 U.S.C. § 1350] on behalf of a missing participant shall satisfy this subparagraph with respect to such participant.

(B) Certification to the corporation of final distribution of assets

Within 30 days after the final distribution of assets is completed pursuant to the standard termination of the plan under this subsection, the plan administrator shall send a notice to the corporation certifying that the assets of the plan have been distributed in accordance with the provisions of subparagraph (A) so as to pay all benefit liabilities under the plan.

(4) Continuing authority

Nothing in this section shall be construed to preclude the continued exercise by the corporation, after the termination date of a plan terminated in a standard termination under this subsection, of its authority under section 1303 of this title [29 U.S.C. § 1303] with respect to matters relating to the termination. A certification under paragraph (3)(B) shall not affect the corporation's obligations under section 1322 of this title [29 U.S.C. § 1322].

(5) Special rule for certain plans where cessation or change in membership of a controlled group

(A) In general

Except as provided in subparagraphs (B) and (D), if-

(i) there is* transaction or series of transactions which result in a person ceasing to be a member of a controlled group, and

(ii) such person immediately before the transaction or series of transactions maintained a single-employer plan which is a defined benefit plan which is fully funded,

then the interest rate used in determining whether the plan is sufficient for benefit liabilities or to otherwise assess plan liabilities for purposes of this subsection or section 1342(a)(4) of this title [29 U.S.C. § 1342(a)(4)] shall be not less than the interest rate used in determining whether the plan is fully funded.

(B) Limitations

Subparagraph (A) shall not apply to any transaction or series of transactions unless-

(i) any employer maintaining the plan immediately before or after such transaction or series of transactions-

(I) has an outstanding senior unsecured debt instrument which is rated investment grade by each of the nationally recognized statistical rating organizations for corporate bonds that has issued a credit rating for such instrument, or

(II) if no such debt instrument of such employer has been rated by such an organization but 1 or more of such organizations has made an issuer credit rating for such employer, all such organizations which have so rated the employer have rated such employer investment grade, and

(ii) the employer maintaining the plan after the transaction or series of transactions employs at least 20 percent of the employees located in the United States who were employed by such employer immediately before the transaction or series of transactions.

(C) Fully funded

For purposes of subparagraph (A), a plan shall be treated as fully funded with respect to any transaction or series of transactions if-

(i) in the case of a transaction or series of transactions which occur in a plan year beginning before January 1, 2008, the funded current liability percentage determined under section 1082(d) of this title [29 U.S.C. § 1082(d)] for the plan year is at least 100 percent, and

* Official footnote: "So in original. The word 'a' probably should appear."

(ii) in the case of a transaction or series of transactions which occur in a plan year beginning on or after such date, the funding target attainment percentage determined under section 1083 of this title [29 U.S.C. § 1083] is, as of the valuation date for such plan year, at least 100 percent.

(D) 2 year limitation

Subparagraph (A) shall not apply to any transaction or series of transactions if the plan referred to in subparagraph (A)(ii) is terminated under subsection (c) or section 1342 of this title [29 U.S.C. § 1342] after the close of the 2-year period beginning on the date on which the first such transaction occurs.

(c) Distress termination of single-employer plans

(1) In general

A single-employer plan may terminate under a distress termination only if-

(A) the plan administrator provides the 60-day advance notice of intent to terminate to affected parties required under subsection (a)(2),

(B) the requirements of subparagraph (A) of paragraph (2) are met, and

(C) the corporation determines that the requirements of subparagraphs (B) and (D) of paragraph (2) are met.

(2) Termination requirements

(A) Information submitted to the corporation

As soon as practicable after the date on which the notice of intent to terminate is provided pursuant to subsection (a)(2), the plan administrator shall provide the corporation, in such form as may be prescribed by the corporation in regulations, the following information:

(i) such information as the corporation may prescribe by regulation as necessary to make determinations under subparagraph (B) and paragraph (3);

(ii) unless the corporation determines the information is not necessary for purposes of paragraph (3)(A) or section 1362 of this title [29 U.S.C. § 1362], certification by an enrolled actuary of-

(I) the amount (as of the proposed termination date and, if applicable, the proposed distribution date) of the current value of the assets of the plan,

(II) the actuarial present value (as of such dates) of the benefit liabilities under the plan,

(III) whether the plan is sufficient for benefit liabilities as of such dates,

(IV) the actuarial present value (as of such dates) of benefits under the plan guaranteed under section 1322 of this title [29 U.S.C. § 1322], and

(V) whether the plan is sufficient for guaranteed benefits as of such dates;

(iii) in any case in which the plan is not sufficient for benefit liabilities as of such date-

(I) the name and address of each participant and beneficiary under the plan as of such date, and

(II) such other information as shall be prescribed by the corporation by regulation as necessary to enable the corporation to be able to make payments to participants and beneficiaries as required under section 1322(c) of this title [29 U.S.C. § 1322(c)]; and

(iv) certification by the plan administrator that-

(I) the information on which the enrolled actuary based the certifications under clause (ii) is accurate and complete, and

(II) the information provided to the corporation under clauses (i) and (iii) is accurate and complete.

Clause (ii) and clause (iv)(I) shall not apply to a plan described in section 412(i) of title 26 [26 U.S.C. § 412].

(B) Determination by the corporation of necessary distress criteria

Upon receipt of the notice of intent to terminate required under subsection (a)(2) and the information required under subparagraph (A), the corporation shall determine whether the requirements of this subparagraph are met as provided in clause (i), (ii), or (iii). The requirements of this subparagraph are met if each person who is (as of the proposed termination date) a contributing sponsor of such plan or a member of such sponsor's controlled group meets the requirements of any of the following clauses:

(i) Liquidation in bankruptcy or insolvency proceedings

The requirements of this clause are met by a person if-

(I) such person has filed or has had filed against such person, as of the proposed termination date, a petition seeking liquidation in a case under title 11 or under any similar Federal law or law of a State or political subdivision of a State (or a case described in clause (ii) filed by or against such person has been converted, as of such date, to a case in which liquidation is sought), and

(II) such case has not, as of the proposed termination date, been dismissed.

(ii) Reorganization in bankruptcy or insolvency proceedings

The requirements of this clause are met by a person if-

(I) such person has filed, or has had filed against such person, as of the proposed termination date, a petition seeking reorganization in a case under title 11 or under any similar law of a State or political subdivision of a State (or a case described in clause (i) filed by or against such person has been converted, as of such date, to such a case in which reorganization is sought),

(II) such case has not, as of the proposed termination date, been dismissed,

(III) such person timely submits to the corporation any request for the approval of the bankruptcy court (or other appropriate court in a case under such similar law of a State or political subdivision) of the plan termination, and

(IV) the bankruptcy court (or such other appropriate court) determines that, unless the plan is terminated, such person will be unable to pay all its debts pursuant to a plan of reorganization and will be unable to continue in business outside the chapter 11 [11 U.S.C. §§ 1101–1195] reorganization process and approves the termination.

(iii) Termination required to enable payment of debts while staying in business or to avoid unreasonably burdensome pension costs caused by declining workforce

The requirements of this clause are met by a person if such person demonstrates to the satisfaction of the corporation that-

(I) unless a distress termination occurs, such person will be unable to pay such person's debts when due and will be unable to continue in business, or

(II) the costs of providing pension coverage have become unreasonably burdensome to such person, solely as a result of a decline of such person's workforce covered as participants under all single-employer plans of which such person is a contributing sponsor.

(C) Notification of determinations by the corporation

The corporation shall notify the plan administrator as soon as practicable of its determinations made pursuant to subparagraph (B).

(D) Disclosure of termination information

(i) In general

A plan administrator that has filed a notice of intent to terminate under subsection (a)(2) shall provide to an affected party any information provided to the corporation under subparagraph (A) or the regulations under subsection (a)(2) not later than 15 days after-

(I) receipt of a request from the affected party for the information; or

(II) the provision of new information to the corporation relating to a previous request.

(ii) Confidentiality

(I) In general

The plan administrator shall not provide information under clause (i) in a form that includes any information that may directly or indirectly be associated with, or otherwise identify, an individual participant or beneficiary.

(II) Limitation

A court may limit disclosure under this subparagraph of confidential information described in section 552(b) of title 5 [5 U.S.C. § 552(b)] to any authorized representative of the participants or beneficiaries that agrees to ensure the confidentiality of such information.

(iii) Form and manner of information; charges

(I) Form and manner

The corporation may prescribe the form and manner of the provision of information under this subparagraph, which shall include delivery in written, electronic, or other appropriate form to the extent that such form is reasonably accessible to individuals to whom the information is required to be provided.

(II) Reasonable charges

A plan administrator may charge a reasonable fee for any information provided under this subparagraph in other than electronic form.

(iv) Authorized representative

For purposes of this subparagraph, the term "authorized representative" means any employee organization representing participants in the pension plan.

(3) Termination procedure

(A) Determinations by the corporation relating to plan sufficiency for guaranteed benefits and for benefit liabilities

If the corporation determines that the requirements for a distress termination set forth in paragraphs (1) and (2) are met, the corporation shall-

(i) determine that the plan is sufficient for guaranteed benefits (as of the termination date) or that the corporation is unable to make such determination on the basis of information made available to the corporation,

(ii) determine that the plan is sufficient for benefit liabilities (as of the termination date) or that the corporation is unable to make such determination on the basis of information made available to the corporation, and

(iii) notify the plan administrator of the determinations made pursuant to this subparagraph as soon as practicable.

(B) Implementation of termination

After the corporation notifies the plan administrator of its determinations under subparagraph (A), the termination of the plan shall be carried out as soon as practicable, as provided in clause (i), (ii), or (iii).

(i) Cases of sufficiency for benefit liabilities

In any case in which the corporation determines that the plan is sufficient for benefit liabilities, the plan administrator shall proceed to distribute the plan's assets, and make certification to the corporation with respect to such distribution, in the manner described in subsection (b)(3), and shall take such other actions as may be appropriate to carry out the termination of the plan.

(ii) Cases of sufficiency for guaranteed benefits without a finding of sufficiency for benefit liabilities

In any case in which the corporation determines that the plan is sufficient for guaranteed benefits, but further determines that it is unable to determine that the plan is sufficient for benefit liabilities on the basis of the information made available to it, the plan administrator shall proceed to distribute the plan's assets in the manner described in subsection (b)(3), make certification to the corporation that the distribution has occurred, and take such actions as may be appropriate to carry out the termination of the plan.

(iii) Cases without any finding of sufficiency

In any case in which the corporation determines that it is unable to determine that the plan is sufficient for guaranteed benefits on the basis of the information made available to it, the corporation shall commence proceedings in accordance with section 1342 of this title [29 U.S.C. § 1342].

(C) Finding after authorized commencement of termination that plan is unable to pay benefits

(i) Finding with respect to benefit liabilities which are not guaranteed benefits

If, after the plan administrator has begun to terminate the plan as authorized under subparagraph (B)(i), the plan administrator finds that the plan is unable, or will be unable, to pay benefit liabilities which are not benefits guaranteed by the corporation under section 1322 of this title [29 U.S.C. § 1322], the plan administrator shall notify the corporation of such finding as soon as practicable thereafter.

(ii) Finding with respect to guaranteed benefits

If, after the plan administrator has begun to terminate the plan as authorized by subparagraph (B)(i) or (ii), the plan administrator finds that the plan is unable, or will be unable, to pay all benefits under the plan which are guaranteed by the corporation under section 1322 of this title [29 U.S.C. § 1322], the plan administrator shall notify the corporation of such finding as soon as practicable thereafter. If the corporation concurs in the finding of the plan administrator (or the corporation itself makes such a finding), the corporation shall institute appropriate proceedings under section 1342 of this title [29 U.S.C. § 1342].

(D) Administration of the plan during interim period

(i) In general

The plan administrator shall-

(I) meet the requirements of clause (ii) for the period commencing on the date on which the plan administrator provides a notice of distress termination to the corporation under subsection (a)(2) and ending on the date on which the plan administrator receives notification from the corporation of its determinations under subparagraph (A), and

(II) meet the requirements of clause (ii) commencing on the date on which the plan administrator or the corporation makes a finding under subparagraph (C)(ii).

(ii) Requirements

The requirements of this clause are met by the plan administrator if the plan administrator-

(I) refrains from distributing assets or taking any other actions to carry out the proposed termination under this subsection,

(II) pays benefits attributable to employer contributions, other than death benefits, only in the form of an annuity,

(III) does not use plan assets to purchase irrevocable commitments to provide benefits from an insurer, and

(IV) continues to pay all benefit liabilities under the plan, but, commencing on the proposed termination date, limits the payment of benefits under the plan to those benefits which are guaranteed by the corporation under section 1322 of this title [29 U.S.C. § 1322] or to which assets are required to be allocated under section 1344 of this title [29 U.S.C. § 1342].

In the event the plan administrator is later determined not to have met the requirements for distress termination, any benefits which are not paid solely by reason of compliance with subclause (IV) shall be due and payable immediately (together with interest, at a reasonable rate, in accordance with regulations of the corporation).

(d) Sufficiency

For purposes of this section-

(1) Sufficiency for benefit liabilities

A single-employer plan is sufficient for benefit liabilities if there is no amount of unfunded benefit liabilities under the plan.

(2) Sufficiency for guaranteed benefits

A single-employer plan is sufficient for guaranteed benefits if there is no amount of unfunded guaranteed benefits under the plan.

(e) Limitation on the conversion of a defined benefit plan to a defined contribution plan

The adoption of an amendment to a plan which causes the plan to become a plan described in section 1321(b)(1) of this title [29 U.S.C. § 1321(b)(1)] constitutes a termination of the plan. Such an amendment may take effect only after the plan satisfies the requirements for standard termination under subsection (b) or distress termination under subsection (c).